Contents

Introduction	**4**
Discover	6
Top 20	**10**
Itineraries	**20**
Copenhagen Today	**28**
Eating & Drinking	**36**
Shopping	**46**
Explore	54
Getting Started	**56**
South Central Copenhagen	**64**
North Central Copenhagen	**98**
Christianshavn, Holmen & Refshaleøen	**118**
Vesterbro & Frederiksberg	**134**
Nørrebro & Østerbro	**150**
Day Trips	**166**
Experience	180
Events	**182**
Film & TV	**188**
Nightlife	**194**
Performing Arts	**202**
Understand	210
History	**212**
Design & Architecture	**222**
Plan	230
Accommodation	**232**
Getting Around	**238**
Resources A-Z	**241**
Vocabulary	**248**
Further Reference	**249**
Index	**251**

Introduction

The hipster capital of Northern Europe, Copenhagen is small but mighty. Cobbled streets and half-timbered houses characterise its historic zones, while modern developments in former warehouses include art galleries, Michelin-starred restaurants and shiny palaces to interior design. Fashionistas love its designers, foodies revere its groundbreaking chefs, and modern architecture fans are dazzled by its liveable edifices.

This fairy-tale city might be small enough to cycle around in a day, but there's always something new to discover, hidden behind graffitied doors and in concealed courtyards. Set on the water with everything that brings – boats, kayaks, hot tubs, swimming pools and more – Copenhagen has a cosy, easy-going charm, a friendly population and an environmentally friendly focus: it aims to be carbon neutral by 2025. Visit to experience what it's like to live in a forward-thinking capital city that still acts like a small town, where *hygge* is the order of the day, and where there are more bikes than people.

View from Vor Frelsers Kirke p123

ABOUT THE GUIDE

This is one of a series of Time Out guidebooks to cities across the globe. Written by local experts, our guides are thoroughly researched and meticulously updated. They aim to be inspiring, irreverent, well-informed and trustworthy.

Time Out Copenhagen is divided into five sections: Discover, Explore, Experience, Understand and Plan.

Discover introduces the city and provides inspiration for your visit.

Explore is the main sightseeing section of the guide and includes detailed listings and reviews for sights and museums, restaurants ⑩, cafés & bars ⑩, and shops & services ⑩, all organised by area with a corresponding street map. To help navigation, each area of Copenhagen has been assigned its own colour.

Experience covers the cultural life of the city in depth, including festivals, film, LGBT, music, nightlife, theatre and more.

Understand provides in-depth background information that places Copenhagen in its historical and cultural context.

Plan offers practical visitor information, including accommodation options and details of public transport.

Hearts

We use hearts ❤ to pick out venues, sights and experiences in the city that we particularly recommend. The very best of these are featured in the Top 20 (*see p10*) and receive extended coverage in the guide.

Maps

A detachable fold-out map can be found on the inside back cover. There's also an overview map (*see p8*) and individual streets maps for each area of the city. The venues featured in the guide have been given a grid reference so that you can find them easily on the maps and on the ground.

Prices

All our **restaurant listings** are marked with a krone symbol category from budget ♛ to blow-out ♛♛♛♛, indicating the price you should expect to pay for an average main course: ♛ = under 300kr; ♛♛ = 300kr -600kr; ♛♛♛ = 600kr-1,000kr; ♛♛♛♛ = over 1,000kr.

A similar system is used in our **Accommodation** chapter based on the hotel's standard prices for one night in a double room: **Budget** = up to 1,000kr; **Moderate** = 1,000kr-2,000kr; **Expensive** = 2,000kr-3,000kr; **Luxury** = over 3,000kr.

Discover

Nyhavn *p108*

Top 20	10
Itineraries	20
Copenhagen Today	28
Eating & Drinking	36
Shopping	46

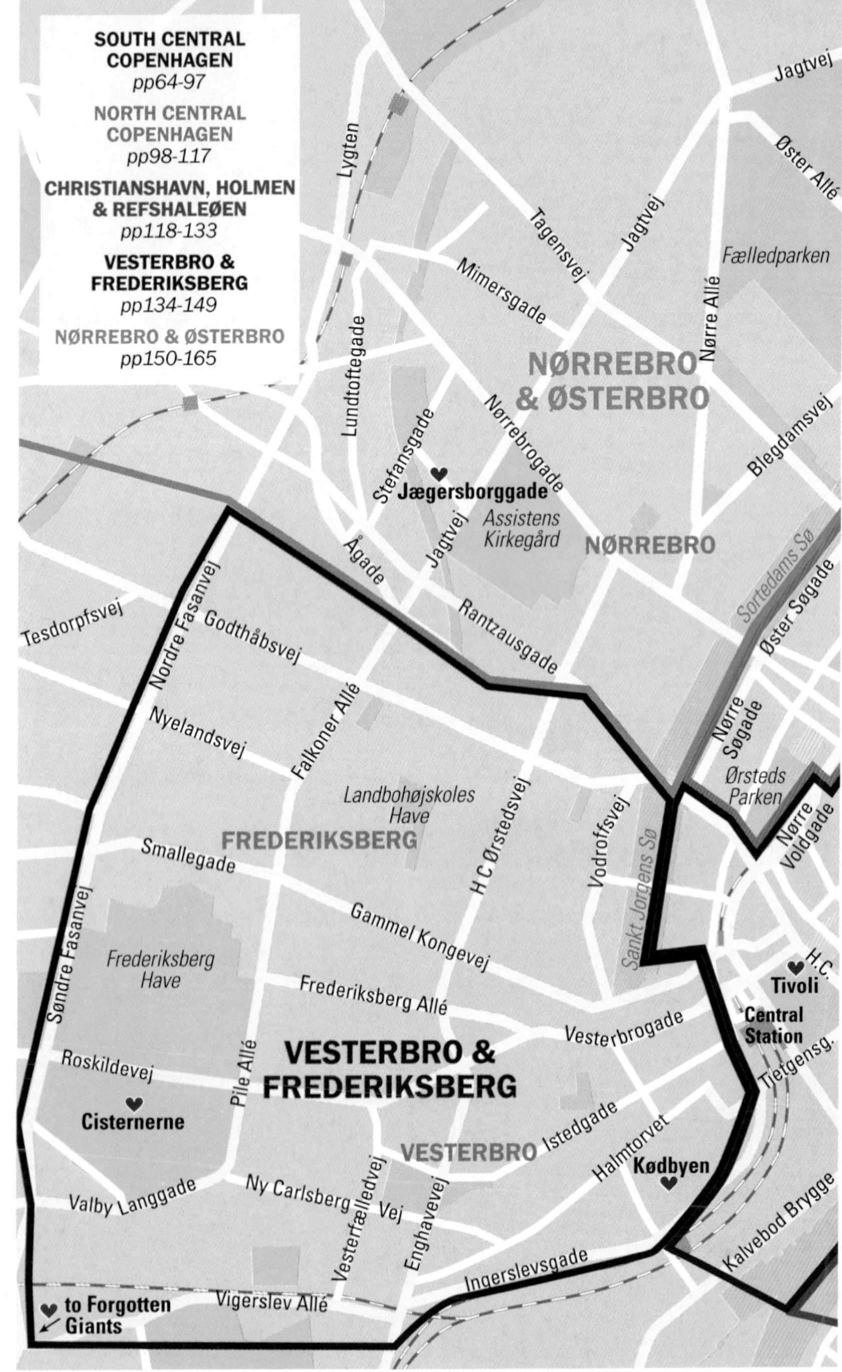
SOUTH CENTRAL COPENHAGEN
pp64-97
NORTH CENTRAL COPENHAGEN
pp98-117
CHRISTIANSHAVN, HOLMEN & REFSHALEØEN
pp118-133
VESTERBRO & FREDERIKSBERG
pp134-149
NØRREBRO & ØSTERBRO
pp150-165
NØRREBRO & ØSTERBRO
NØRREBRO
FREDERIKSBERG
VESTERBRO & FREDERIKSBERG
VESTERBRO
Jægersborggade
Cisternerne
Tivoli
Central Station
Kødbyen
to Forgotten Giants
Assistens Kirkegård
Fælledparken
Landbohøjskoles Have
Frederiksberg Have
Ørsteds Parken
Sortedams Sø
Sankt Jørgens Sø
Jagtvej
Øster Allé
Tagensvej
Lygten
Mimersgade
Nørre Allé
Lundtoftegade
Nørrebrogade
Stefansgade
Blegdamsvej
Ågade
Rantzausgade
Øster Søgade
Tesdorpfsvej
Nordre Fasanvej
Godthåbsvej
Falkoner Allé
Nyelandsvej
Nørre Søgade
H C Ørstedsvej
Vodroffsvej
Nørre Voldgade
Smallegade
Gammel Kongevej
Søndre Fasanvej
Frederiksberg Allé
H.C.
Vesterbrogade
Tietgensg.
Roskildevej
Pile Allé
Istedgade
Halmtorvet
Valby Langgade
Ny Carlsberg Vej
Vesterfælledvej
Enghavevej
Kalvebod Brygge
Ingerslevsgade
Vigerslev Allé

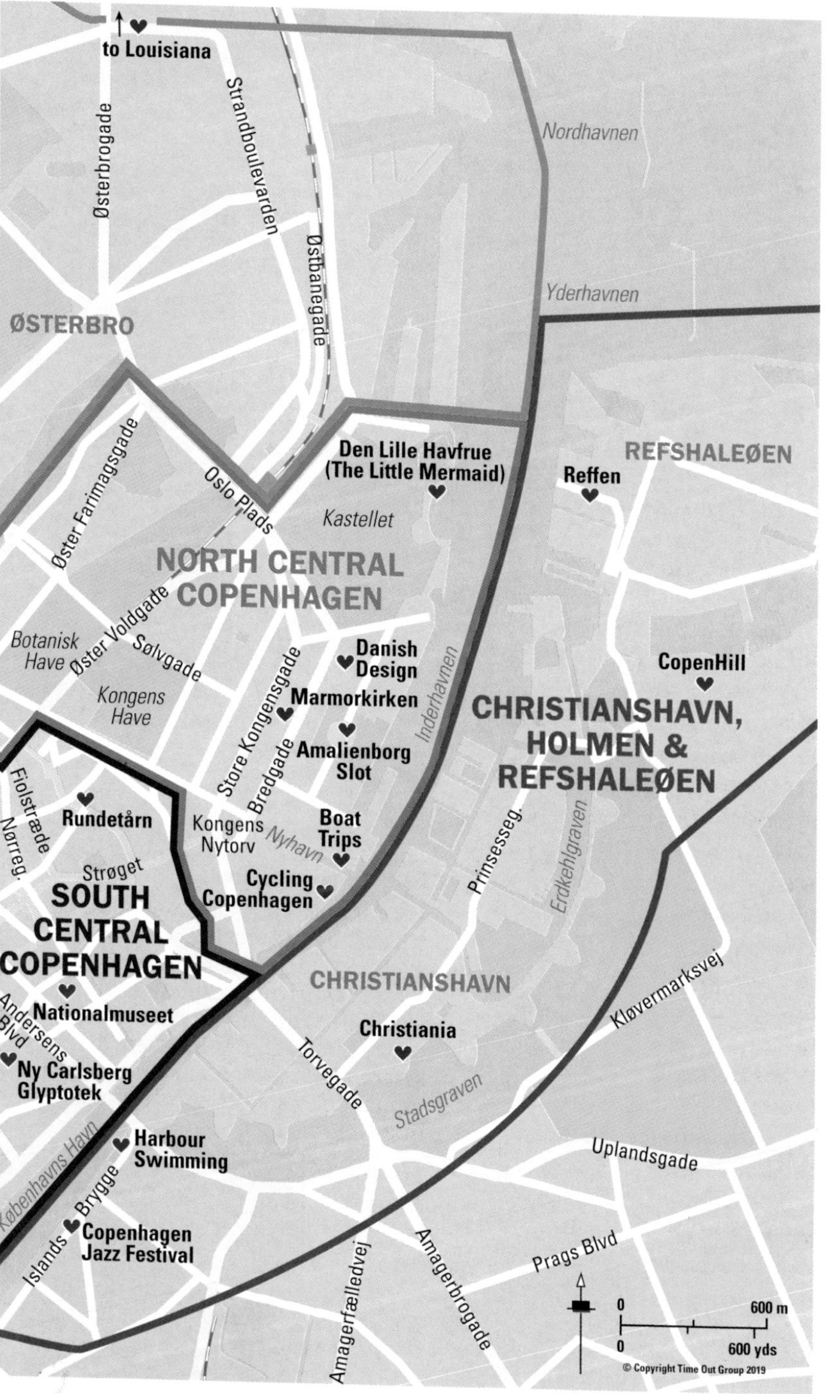
to Louisiana
Østerbrogade
Strandboulevarden
Østbanegade
Nordhavnen
Yderhavnen
ØSTERBRO
Øster Farimagsgade
Oslo Plads
Den Lille Havfrue
(The Little Mermaid)
Kastellet
REFSHALEØEN
Reffen
NORTH CENTRAL
COPENHAGEN
Botanisk
Have
Øster Voldgade
Sølvgade
Kongens
Have
Store Kongensgade
Danish
Design
Marmorkirken
Bredgade
Amalienborg
Slot
Inderhavnen
CopenHill
CHRISTIANSHAVN,
HOLMEN &
REFSHALEØEN
Fiolstræde
Nørreg.
Rundetårn
Kongens
Nytorv
Nyhavn
Boat
Trips
Strøget
SOUTH
CENTRAL
COPENHAGEN
Cycling
Copenhagen
Prinsesseg.
Erdkehlgraven
CHRISTIANSHAVN
Nationalmuseet
Andersens
Blvd
Ny Carlsberg
Glyptotek
Christiania
Torvegade
Kløvermarksvej
Stadsgraven
Københavns Havn
Harbour
Swimming
Uplandsgade
Islands Brygge
Copenhagen
Jazz Festival
Prags Blvd
Amagerfælledvej
Amagerbrogade
0
600 m
0
600 yds
© Copyright Time Out Group 2019

Top 20

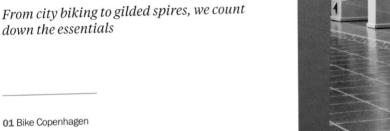

From city biking to gilded spires, we count down the essentials

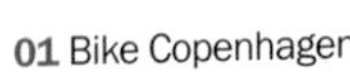

01 Bike Copenhagen
02 Ny Carlsberg Glyptotek
03 Harbour swimming
04 CopenHill
05 Louisiana Museum of Modern Art
06 Nationalmuseet
07 Boat trips
08 Cisternerne
09 Rundetårn
10 Christiania
11 Marmorkirken
12 Tivoli
13 Jaegersborggade
14 Reffen
15 From Nyhavn to *The Little Mermaid*
16 Danish design
17 Copenhagen Jazz Festival
18 Kødbyen
19 Forgotten Giants
20 Amalienborg Slot

01

Bike Copenhagen *p60*

It's not until you get on your own two wheels that you realise what a joy it is to cycle in Copenhagen, one of the world's most bike-friendly capitals. Wide lanes, with kerbs to separate riders from other road users, make cycling here much safer than in most other cities, and the number of bikes never ceases to amaze first-time visitors.

02

Ny Carlsberg Glyptotek *p75*

With a breathtaking line-up of ancient sculptures and an exceptional array of more recent Danish and French paintings and sculpture – including an impressive collection of French Impressionist works – the Ny Carlsberg Glyptotek is a world-class museum. Its Winter Garden palm house and café is an inspiring place for a coffee break.

03

Harbour swimming *p124*

This seafaring nation loves the water. Whether you dive into the Bjarke Ingels-designed Islands Brygge Harbour Baths, head for the floating pools at Copencabana and Koralbadet or follow the Harbour Circle cycle route to one of the new harbours, it's hard not to be tempted. For the hardcore, a dip in the ocean followed by a sauna (then repeat) is a winter must-do.

04

CopenHill *p133*

Possibly Copenhagen's quirkiest attraction is a ski slope atop a tall waste-recycling plant. Designed by starchitect Bjarke Ingels, the artificial ski slope plus inner-city hiking area is the ultimate in offbeat ways to experience the city. If you don't fancy adventure sports, you can walk up and stop for views of the Øresund as you go.

05

Louisiana Museum of Modern Art *p170*

Louisiana is as much about its blissful setting as the modern artworks it houses. Located in Humlebæk, a 45-minute train ride from Copenhagen, the sculpture-filled grounds cascade down to the shore. As well as its diverse permanent collection – with works by Alexander Calder, Asger Jorn and Francis Bacon – it also houses dynamic temporary exhibitions.

06

Nationalmuseet *p93*

Located in the Prince's Palace, the National Museum is *the* place to go for Viking swords, gleaming gold rings and ancient rune stones, as well as the rest of Denmark's history from Stone Age to modern day. A specialist kids' section provides somewhere to play and interact with lifestyles from the past.

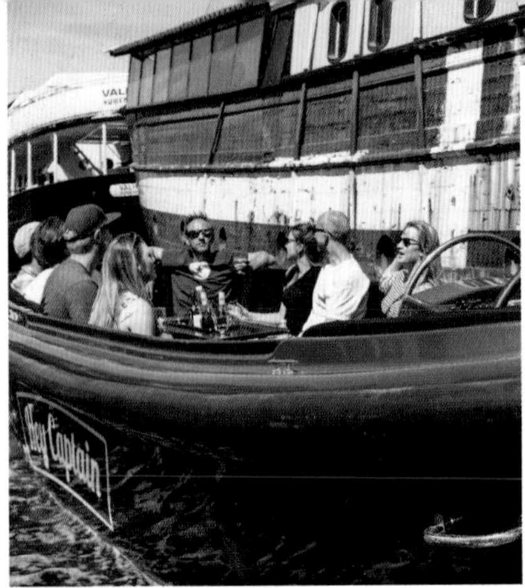

07

Boat trips *p162*

The traditional tourist boats offer a guided tour of Copenhagen's waterways. But that's not the only way to do it. You can hire small motor boats by the hour or, for the ultimate in-water experience, take a tour in a hot tub. For a more retro trip, rent a swan boat and pedal around the Peblinge Sø in Østerbro.

08

Cisternerne *p147*

It looks like nothing from the outside, but walk down the steps to this art space hidden under Søndermarken park in Frederiksberg's former underground water reservoir and prepare to be taken on a fairy-tale journey by candlelight through echoing chambers and dark corners. Exhibitions change regularly and the possibilities are endless.

09

Rundetårn *p81*

Copenhagen's 17th-century Round Tower is unique for its cobbled spiral walkway that winds seven and a half times round its core. Peter the Great supposedly rode to the top in 1716, followed in a carriage by the Tsarina. The tower houses Europe's oldest functioning astronomical observatory and offers superb views of the city.

10

Christiania *p128*

The Freetown of Christiania is one of Denmark's biggest tourist sells, off-beat though it is. Home to around 1,000 people, the hippie commune was set up in the 1970s and is still dominated by an alternative cultural ideology. The most interesting thing about Christiania, however, is the extraordinary hand-built houses lining the water.

11

Marmorkirken *p115*

The breathtaking 'Marble Church' was designed by Nicolai Eigtved in the 1740s as the focal point of the new quarter of Frederiksstaden, although the building wasn't completed until the late 1800s. Its impressive dome, inspired by St Peter's in Rome, remains one of the largest of its kind in Europe, and offers far-reaching views from the top.

12

Tivoli *p70*

The amusement park in the heart of Copenhagen is a blend of escapist, fairy-tale gaiety and defiant traditionalism, home to a variety of rides (including a 100-year-old rollercoaster), funfair activities, music venues and high-profile restaurants. As Denmark's No.1 tourist attraction, it draws the crowds; but it's much more than an ordinary theme park. In many ways, it's the definitive Danish experience.

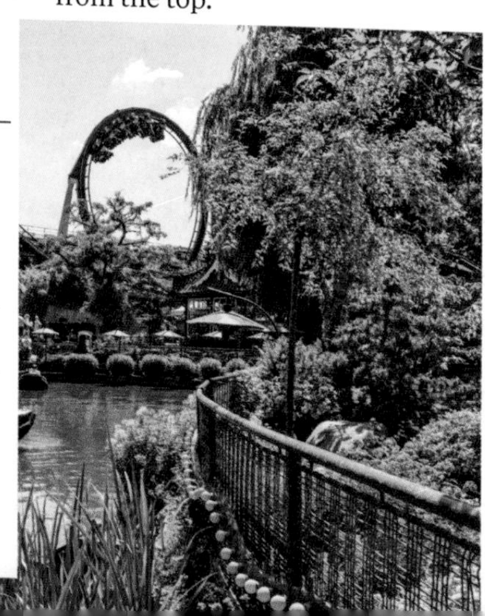

13

Jægersborggade p157

Nørrebro's most beloved hipster street is lined with boutiques, cafés and independent shops you won't find elsewhere in the city. With a dark and checkered past, it's an emblem of how Copenhagen is changing, embracing new ideas and developing. Get your organic liquid nitrogen ice-creams here, along with a pocketful of specialist caramels to take home with you.

14

14

Reffen p43

Copenhagen's latest food extravaganza on the island of Refshaleøen is best reached by harbour bus. Once you're there, you have the run of the place, with a Hawaiian shave ice stall sitting alongside vintage fashion boutiques, a plastic recycling workshop, sushi, burgers and drinks stands. On long summer nights, the party starts here.

15

From Nyhavn to The Little Mermaid p109

Nyhavn's colourful quayside is Copenhagen's most photographed spot. Hans Christian Andersen lived at three different addresses on Nyhavn, at a time when it was full of bars, knocking shops and tattoo parlours. These days, you can wander from here up to his diminutive mermaid and know you've ticked off the classic sights of the city.

16

Danish design *p159*

Wherever you go in the city, you can't escape the influence of modern Danish design. Lighting by Poul Henningsen and Louis Poulsen, tables by Arne Jacobsen and chairs by Finn Juhl are just the beginning. Check out Designmuseum Danmark and the luxurious interior design shop, Illums Bolighus. If you're on a budget, try one of the flea markets – you might get lucky.

17

Copenhagen Jazz Festival *p185*

The Danes love their jazz, and, thankfully, that passion isn't limited to the Dixieland tourist-fodder you'll hear on Nyhavn of a summer's afternoon. The Copenhagen Jazz Festival is delightfully ad hoc, with impromptu gigs, jam sessions, improvisations, free outdoor concerts and street parades happening all over the city. Its success has spawned a winter jazz event, Vinterjazz, in February.

18

Kødbyen *p141*

Copenhagen's hottest casual drinking and dining area is great fun. Located in Vesterbrø, the former Meatpacking District is now home to cocktail bars, shared workspaces, a specialist sausage shop, Italian restaurant Mother and the super-hip Hija de Sanchez, a Danish taco stand. It's easy to have a good time in this mixed-up, messy and dynamic spot.

19

Forgotten Giants *p177*

This enchanting treasure hunt on the outskirts of the city is a fantastic alternative to a traditional tourist trail. Artist Thomas Dambo's six giant sculptures are built from recycled scrap wood and hide under bridges, behind trees and in a variety of natural settings.

20

Amalienborg Slot *p112*

Copenhagen's grand Frederiksstaden quarter has been home to the Amalienborg Palace, the residence of the Danish royal family, since 1794. Composed of four rococo buildings, the palace provides a major photo-op for tourists with its daily changing of the guards ceremony. Head inside to discover a charming and warm take on being a royal in this most egalitarian of cities.

Itineraries

Make the most of every Copenhagen minute with our tailored travel plans

ESSENTIAL WEEKEND

Budget 2,200kr (less with a Copenhagen Card, *see p239*)
Getting around Walk, bike, harbour bus

DAY 1

Morning

Copenhagen is small by city standards, and eminently walkable or cyclable, so it's not difficult to pack several key sights into one day. Start the morning with a coffee and a pastry at **Picnic** (*see p74*), Glyptoteket's café set amid palm trees and marble sculptures, before heading over to neighbouring Slotsholmen, the 'island' where the city was founded. This is where you will find **Christiansborg Slot** (*see p92*), **Thorvaldsens Museum** (*see p96*), and the **Nationalmuseet** (*see p93*); the Danish Architecture Center is also nearby at **BLOX** (*see p91*), so take your pick. Have a wander around the historic streets between Slotsholmen and pedestrianised Strædet. The colourful cobbled streets are Copenhagen at its most quaint; Magstraede is especially iconic. Then head down Strædet itself (like parallel Strøget, this street is actually made up of several streets – Kompagnistræde and Læderstræde form the central part) to browse some unique-to-Copenhagen shops, before heading to the cafés of Amagertorv, including **Café Europa** (*see p78*), for lunch.

Picnic, Ny Carlsberg Glyptotek

► *Budgets include food, drink, transport and admission prices, but not accommodation or shopping.*

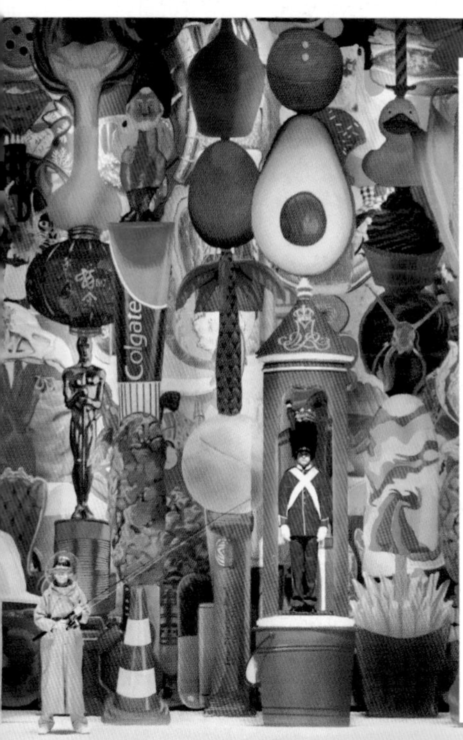

Halfdans Hokus Pokus, Det Kongelige Teater

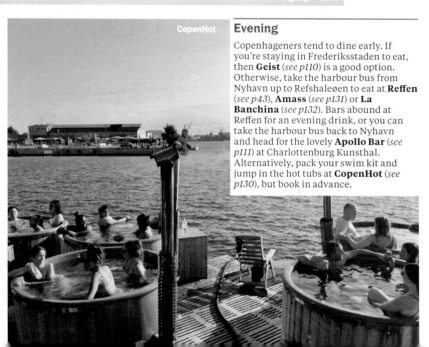

Afternoon

Once you've been fed and watered, take the ten-minute stroll up pedestrianised Købmagergade to the **Rundetårn** (*see p81*), the city's 17th-century observatory tower. From the viewpoint at the top you can gaze down at the lovely old streets of the **Latin Quarter** (*see p80*) and beyond. Walk through the Grønnegade quarter to get to Kongens Nytorv square, home to the grand **Kongelige Teater** (*see p209*), the Royal Danish Theatre, and then along to **Nyhavn** (*see p108*). This stretch of colourful canalside buildings should be instantly recognisable – they are practically the symbol of the city.

This is a popular, though expensive, spot for a beer if you're tired from the day's activities. If you still have sightseeing energy left, however, you could either stroll north along the canal to see **The Little Mermaid** (*see p109*), or else walk down salubrious Bredgade to reach the beautiful **Marmorkirken**, the Marble Church (*see p115*). Fans of Danish furniture design might prioritise **Designmuseum Danmark** (*see p114*), a few steps further along the street.

CopenHot

Evening

Copenhageners tend to dine early. If you're staying in Frederiksstaden to eat, then **Geist** (*see p110*) is a good option. Otherwise, take the harbour bus from Nyhavn up to Refshaleøen to eat at **Reffen** (*see p43*), **Amass** (*see p131*) or **La Banchina** (*see p132*). Bars abound at Reffen for an evening drink, or you can take the harbour bus back to Nyhavn and head for the lovely **Apollo Bar** (*see p111*) at Charlottenburg Kunsthal. Alternatively, pack your swim kit and jump in the hot tubs at **CopenHot** (*see p130*), but book in advance.

DAY 2

Morning

Your second day focuses on the vibrant neighbourhoods of Nørrebro and Vesterbro. Copenhagen's most interesting independent shops and cafés are located in these residential districts, and each has its own distinct character. Start the day in Nørrebro at café-bakery **Mirabelle** (*see p160*), where you can pick up excellent Danish pastries and quality coffee. From here it's a 15-minute walk to **Assistens Kirkegård** (*see p155*), the city's cemetery and a popular place for a leisurely amble or bike ride – as well as being the final resting place of Hans Christian Andersen.

Exit Assistens Kirkegård at the Jagtvej gate, cross the road, and head up **Jægersborggade** (*see p157*). This cobbled street is among the city's most hipster-focused and is lined with a range of independent stores.

Assistens Kirkegård

Superkilen

Afternoon

If you're ready for lunch, you'll find a host of good options on Jægersborggade; we recommend **Grød** (*see p158*), or, if you want to splash out, make for **Manfreds & Vin** (*see p156*), owned by Michelin-starred restaurant Relæ, opposite. Nørrebro's not just about laid-back cafés and cool shops, however. For an insight into the area's multiculturalism, head north-west up Nørrebrogade (a 25-minute walk, or a five-minute cycle) to **Superkilen** (*see p155*). This urban park and playground celebrates the area's ethnic diversity with landscaping objects brought from around the world, including swings from Iraq and benches from Brazil. Make your way back down Nørrebrogade and explore the area around Elmegade, Sankt Hans Torv and Ravnsborggade, with more independent shops. Cross the lakes at Dronning Louises Bro and head over to **Torvehallerne** (*p104*), the city's covered food market, where you can pick yourself up with an afternoon treat.

Torvehallerne

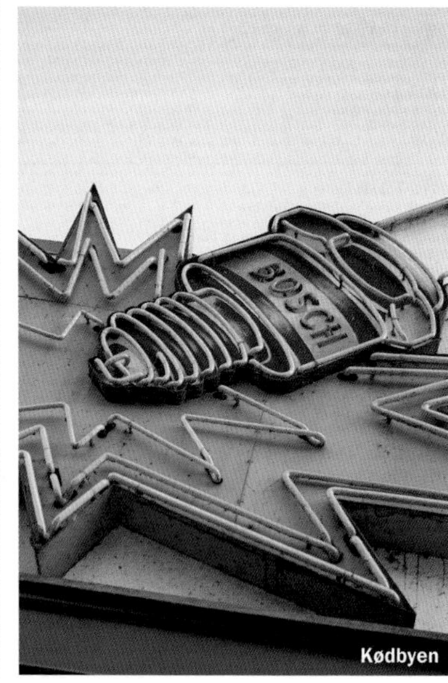

Kødbyen

Mother

Evening

The south-western neighbourhood of Vesterbro is Copenhagen's other hotspot. It's been transformed over the past 15 years from red-light district to the city's most-popular 'hood for artists and media types. Its Meatpacking District, **Kødbyen** (*see p139*), is home to cutting-edge restaurants and lively bars and is a great place to spend an evening. Sourdough pizza parlour **Mother** (*see p142*) is one of the many great options for food, along with street food stall **Hija de Sanchez** (*see p140*). For a post-meal tipple, head west along Sønder Boulevard to **Dyrehavn** (*see p144*). A short stroll away, where Vesterbrogade meets Enghavevej, you'll find **Vega** (*see p199*), the city's best live music venue for pop, rock and electro.

BUDGET BREAK

Budget 1,100kr
Getting around Walk, bike

Morning

If you are lucky enough to be staying in a hotel or apartment with free bikes, make use of them. If not, hire some! Start your morning with a walk along the waterfront. Head north for the lovely **Amaliehaven waterfront gardens** (*see p109*), **Kastellet** (*see p116*), **The Little Mermaid** (*see p109*) and wide-open views. Stop into **Lagkagehuset** (*see p38*), one of the city's big bakery chains for a *pølsehorn* (Danish-style sausage roll) and chocolate milk for elevenses. Alternatively, you could detour to the **Marmorkirken**, Marble Church (*see p115*), for city views from its beautiful dome, or walk through the old town and stop at **Rundetårn** (*see p81*), where you can also see the city from above and get a slice of culture for a handful of coins. **DØP** (*see p78*), for organic Danish hotdogs, is just next door.

Amaliehaven

Nyhavn

Absalon

Afternoon

Cycle down to **Nyhavn** (*see p109*) and across the bridge to discover **Christianshavn** (*see p122*), a canalside neighbourhood of historic houses, and **Christiania** (*see p128*) beyond it. Though the commune – which was established on a former military barracks in the 1970s – has now been 'normalised' by the city authorities, it still offers an interesting counter-cultural experience, especially through its fascinating alternative architecture down by the lake. It's a lovely place for a walk; if you're hungry, you'll find good-value food, especially vegetarian, at, for example, **Morgenstedet** or **Spiseloppen** (*see p127*).

Evening

Don't leave dining too late; head to **Absalon** (*see p140*) at 5pm (no later!) to get a seat at this excellent-value communal dining experience. Lively and with a no-choice menu shared with the table, you're likely to make friends and meet some interesting people. Stay for drinks and participate in one of the many random themed nights, or wander down the road to have a drink in **Kødbyen** (*see p139*) or one of Vesterbro's many **bodegas** (*see p200*), where you'll find the cheapest beer in town.

If it's a lovely evening, you could take a picnic to the **Islands Brygge Harbour Baths** (*see p124*), go for a dip and lounge on the grass nearby, or take a boat to **Refshaleøen** and have an evening swim and sauna at **La Banchina** (*see p132*). If you skipped supper, dine on tapas at **The Corner 108** (*see p123*) for a flavour of the New Nordic scene without the huge price tag.

Torvehallerne

FAMILY DAY OUT

Budget 1,800kr for two adults, two children
Getting around Walk, bike, bus, harbour bus, metro

Morning

Start the day at **Torvehallerne** (*see p103*), the food hall where picky eaters can choose from pastries at **Laura's Bakery** or porridge at **Grød** (*see p158*). There's plenty to look at and you'll be starting your day in the heart of the action. From here, you're a short walk from both **Kongens Have** (*see p105*), where younger kids can play in the dragon-themed playground, and the **Peblinge Sø**, where you can go for a spin on a swan boat (*see p162*). On a rainy day, **SMK** (*see p106*) is a good place to hide out and create your own art.

Copenhagen Zoo

Afternoon

Head to Nyhavn and take a yellow harbour bus to Refshaleøen for lunch at **Reffen** (*see p43*), where the kids can choose from an array of street food stalls. Choose your activity for the afternoon: skiing on **CopenHill**'s slopes (*see p133*), or even hiking to the top can be great fun on a nice day; or return to Nyhavn and take a **boat tour** of the waterways (*see p162*).

Evening

As night falls, plan for a trip to **Tivoli** (*see p70*), where twinkling lights and outdoor concerts add to the thrills and spills. Food is not cheap – you might like to take a snack dinner from a local bakery or grab hot dogs and eat them on the lawn.

► *Once you've explored the city, you could easily spend a whole day at the zoo (see p146), at the local beach, Amager Strandpark (see p174), or discovering the Forgotten Giants (see p177) dotted around the countryside.*

Forgotten Giants

When to Visit

Copenhagen by season

The experience you have in Copenhagen will depend on the time of year you visit. There are four clear seasons in this Nordic city – some would say five, including the hypnotic *sensommer*, a lingering Indian summer that sometimes precedes the autumn – and events, prices and atmosphere are different in all of them. The best time to visit is the summer, but travelling in May or September offers a chance of sunny days and cheaper prices as the shoulder season kicks in.

Bispebjerg Cemetery

Spring

Copenhagen in spring is delightful – as long as the weather is on your side. April can be sunny but on the cold side; it can also be windy, icy and snowy. The last weekend of the month marks the start of **Sakura season** when Bispebjerg Cemetery, among other green spaces, is full of people walking and talking under the pink cherry blossom.

Prices tend to be lower in spring than summer; but note that, as in winter, not everything will be open during the week and, if there is a particular museum or attraction you want to see, you should check opening times before your visit.

Rosenborg Slot

Summer

Summer is a joyous time in Copenhagen: long sunny days stretch from 6am until nearly midnight; people swim, cycle, smile and relax in the parks, and everything is open. Prices do peak at this time of year, although you'll also find the highest concentration of the city's free festivals and events, including **Distortion** (*see p184*). It can also be very busy. Note that as high summer approaches, many of the city's administrative offices close; the typical holiday month is July, when people take two or three weeks off. Schools are on vacation during June and July and return for the new academic year in the first week of August. In the height of summer, you can expect temperatures of around 20-25°C.

Tivoli

Kastrup Søbad

Kulturnatten

Autumn

The weather is still warm at the start of autumn, and it can be a lovely time to visit, with fewer tourists than in the peak summer season but still plenty of things to see and do. Prices are lower, and a visit in October timed with **Kulturnatten** (*see p186*) or **Tivoli's Halloween Season** (*see p187*) can be great fun. But all the same, don't forget your waterproofs. As autumn turns to winter, the days shorten and the warmth disappears.

Tivoli's Halloween Season

Winter

Pre-Christmas winter in Copenhagen is wonderful: windows are decorated with white fairy lights and branches of fir, Christmas markets are around from November, and there is a definite feeling of *hygge* in the air. It can be very cold and windy, however, and, with a little less daylight than in the summer, wandering the streets and sightseeing is not quite such fun. Temperatures can drop to -15°C so be prepared with gloves, hats and wool sweaters. On the other side of Christmas, January to March can be brutal: winds are icy and many attractions are closed. Pick your dates carefully if you plan to visit at the start of the year and make sure the places you want to visit are open (weekends are your best bet). Most restaurants and bars are still operational, as are the city's shops (with sales in January) but the streets are nowhere near as lively as during the summer.

Christmas market

Copenhagen Today

Designed for life

There is a mystery hanging over the city of Copenhagen. How has this bijou place, seven times smaller than London, made such a big mark on the world? As the home of minimalist design trends, wind energy, New Nordic food, Nordic noir TV dramas and *hygge*, Copenhagen's influence has overreached its small confines and influenced 21st-century living on a much wider scale. Perhaps it has something to do with the city's attitude towards life itself.

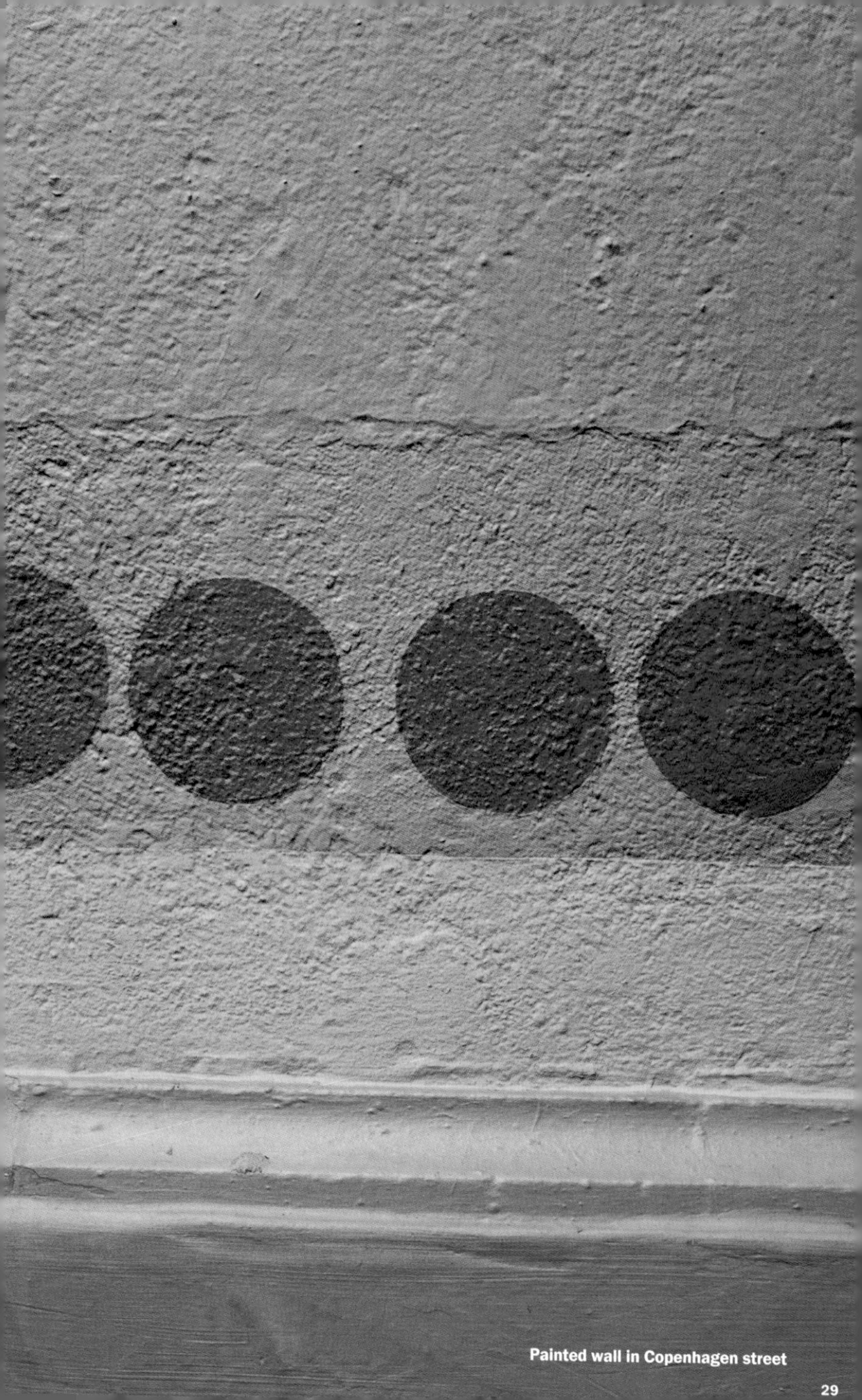

Painted wall in Copenhagen street

Copenhagen's multiple waterfronts mean a quiet spot can always be found

World's happiest city

Copenhagen regularly features at or near the top of lists of the world's happiest cities. What's the secret? It's not just about candles and sheepskins – although *hygge* does have something to do with it. Taxes are high, but, in the main, people don't mind paying for good-quality public institutions, clean streets, decent childcare and a state that looks after its citizens. With this backdrop of security in daily life, it's easier to take risks – try a new creative project, open a pop-up, change careers, or have children while you're in your twenties – and that confidence breeds happiness as a result.

There's also a high level of social cohesion in Denmark – as a rule, everyone is paid a decent living wage, resulting in a narrower gap between rich and poor. This encourages greater acceptance and equality in behaviour and attitudes. The fact that many Danish people are still in touch with their childhood friends – moving around the country for work does not happen as much as it does in the UK, for example – and the feeling that everyone knows or has a family connection with everyone else, breeds a sense of trust and collective responsibility. With a smaller population, the distance between power and the people is much reduced; politicians' decisions will have a direct affect on people they know personally, and their policies tend to be more 'human' as a result.

People don't mind paying for good-quality public institutions, clean streets, decent childcare and a state that looks after its citizens

In the know
Nordic or Scandinavian

Scandinavian as an adjective refers exclusively to the kingdoms of Denmark, Norway and Sweden. Nordic means Denmark, Norway, Sweden, Iceland and Finland. Greenland and the Faroe Island are autonomous countries administered politically as part of Denmark.

Designing a good life

Design also plays a major role in Danish contentedness. Minimalist Scandinavian interior design began in the 1930s with ideas about clean lines and simplistic ways of living. Its formal design principles stress the importance of living in harmony with the environment; items should be made to last, and home living style should be comfortable and unencumbered. Developed almost 90 years ago, these ideas couldn't be more contemporary, and they relate to many aspects of living in Copenhagen today.

Copenhagen life continues as normal whatever the weather

Being in harmony with your surroundings means more than decorating your apartment in neutral colours. By cycling to work, as at least 62 per cent of the city does, Copenhageners are in touch with their environment every day, whether that's wind, snow and ice on the lakes in the winter months, or sunlight, blossom and pavement cafés as it warms up. Being in touch with the world around you is conducive to happiness, as is regular daily exercise, along with the vitamin D absorbed by your skin as you ride.

The rejection of throwaway culture in favour of one in which things are built to last has always been a key tenet of Danish living. Price shock – £5 for a cup of coffee! – is something experienced by all newcomers to the city, but by recalibrating their perception of value, visitors will discover that the Danish attitude to shopping is rather different – less acquisitive. In Copenhagen, buying stuff isn't a pastime; purchases are carefully considered: that beautiful new Louis Poulsen lighting is an investment to be enjoyed forever. This longer-term pleasure far outweighs the instant dopamine hit from so-called 'retail therapy'.

Dating from the 1920s, the interior of Grundtvigs Kirke combines Gothic features with a minimalist modern aesthetic

The concept of design for practicality and ease of living filters out beyond the open-plan apartments and free-flowing kitchen-diners. The whole city is an open living space, where you can walk just about everywhere; where new bike-only

bridges are built so that cyclists can get around with ease; and where people are at the heart of new developments. The famed 'five-finger plan' developed for the city's transport infrastructure melded through-routes, residential units and green space; today's mixed-use spaces operate on similar lines. There's an understanding that life is multifaceted and the most direct way to a happy life is to design for it.

Offshore wind turbines in the Øresund Strait

A unique take on sustainability

Denmark was a world leader in the development of wind energy in the 1970s and continues to make sustainable development part of its future. While turbines spin on windy days in the Øresund Strait, in the city itself, Amager Bakke, a waste management plant, is on a mission to make waste desirable. Well, not the waste itself, but the leisure opportunities you can derive with a huge multi-use building that has an urban ski-slope up top and recycling down below. Time will tell whether this is just one of Bjarke Ingels' overly outlandish ideas, but it has certainly become the talk of architecture communities around the world and has put a fun, 'hedonistic' and less worthy spin on sustainability and the city's interest in green living.

Dedicated high-speed cycle routes, super-safe bike lanes and electric buses make it easy to get around the city

On the Waterfront

Architecture, top-class restaurants and cultural gems

Wherever you are in Copenhagen, you're never far from a stretch of water, whether that's the harbourside, where new apartment buildings, art institutions and restaurants are growing and flourishing; the lakes, where Copenhageners run, walk their dogs and relax in pavement cafés; or at the many beaches nearby, where you can gaze out across the limpid pale blue Øresund Strait to Sweden.

The 1999 Black Diamond extension to the National Library, by architects Schmidt Hammer Lassen, kickstarted an enormous development programme along the harbour. These days you can walk along the waterfront and admire architecture, old and new, along with museums and other cultural institutions. Guided architecture tours from the newest harbourside building, BLOX, have plenty to talk about right on their doorstep.

Newer still, the former warehouses at Nordhavn have spawned super-stylish residential units, start-up spaces and 3XN's Norway ferry terminal, while in Sydhavn, a new canalside neighbourhood with modern apartments has taken over two islands that used to house dilapidated warehouses and industrial buildings. Little fishing villages at both ends hang on for dear life as modern apartments, speedboats and yachts occupy the waterfront.

To the northeast, the island of Refshaleøen is at the forefront of food, housing both Amass and Noma, and is also a frontier in terms of development. Low rents and a less-developed transport network, plus the city's architecture school, have long made the neighbourhood edgier and more creative than other well-heeled areas, but now it is starting to take off and the gentrification process is well under way.

The coastline is bookended by two great art institutions, The Louisiana to the north and Arken to the south, with pretty villages strung between them facing the calm sea. The beach at Amager Strandpark is within easy reach of the city and is very popular with cyclists, in-line skaters, dog walkers and families. To live in Copenhagen, whether you're in chi-chi Hellerup to the north or in the charming heart of Islands Brygge, is to be connected to the sea at every turn.

Copenhagen is still growing and changing along its coastline. Plans to create a series of nine man-made islands to the south of the city were made public in 2019. Powered by green energy, these are to accommodate international tech businesses, close to the airport and less than an hour from the city. There has also been talk of adding another artificial island near the harbour with a primarily residential focus.

The development of the Øresund Region, also known as Greater Copenhagen, means that the borders of the metropolitan area reach across the bridge to the Swedish province of Skåne and include Malmö.

Still a small city by international standards, and that certainly is part of its charm, Copenhagen is making waves with every waterside development, keen to future-proof itself and stay relevant as the world moves forward.

Copenhagen finds ways to incorporate sustainability into daily life: dedicated high-speed cycle routes, super-safe bike lanes and electric buses make it easy to get around the city, which is on a mission to be carbon neutral by 2025. It is an international model for healthy and sustainable urban design, and it's so well integrated that, a lot of the time, you don't even notice.

The future of food

This innovative spirit affects every part of life in Copenhagen. New Nordic food emerged from the city in 2004, led by Danish chef Claus Meyer and, 15 years later, it has reached its pinnacle at Noma 2.0, which René Redzepi opened in the city in 2018. The experimental dining style is not the only thing the city's food scene has going for it – its strong roots in breadmaking and bakeries are accessible to all-comers, whether you look for a classic corner bakery or seek out one of the more forward-thinking chef-influenced boutique bakeries. The fusion of traditional roots and local ingredients with modern food technology innovations have been a hit around the world.

Eating healthily is part of the Danish way (pastries are more of a weekend treat than a daily snack); those classic vitamin-D infused pickled herrings are perhaps another reason why the city's inhabitants are so happy.

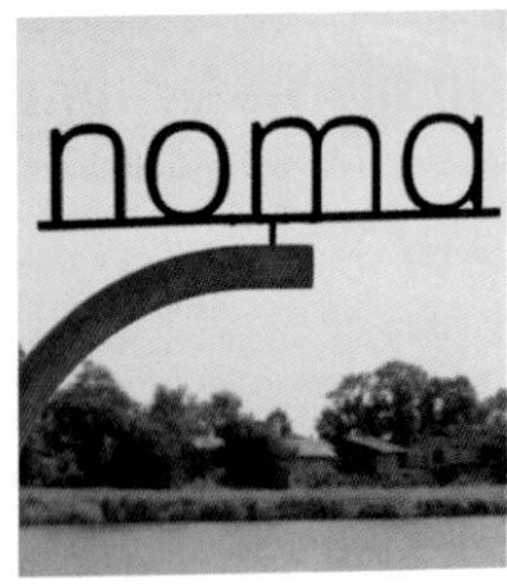

Noma 2.0 opened in 2018

Copenhagen's strong roots in breadmaking and bakeries are accessible to all-comers

A hole in the dream

But this small city is no paradise, and not everybody is happy.

At present, the anti-immigrant Danske Folkeparti adds an undercurrent that makes it feel that you're entitled to a good life here only if you are Danish through and through. It's a great and welcoming place to be, but there is a sense that the welcome does not extend to everybody to the same degree.

Immigration, which affects Denmark just as it does the rest of Europe, is one of the biggest issues currently facing Copenhagen. The Danish position has been relatively hard line and, in recent years, the country has accepted fewer asylum seekers per capita than any of its neighbours and comparable European countries, with only the UK receiving fewer.

Those vitamin D-infused pickled herrings are perhaps another reason why the city's inhabitants are so happy

Controversial approaches to integration include the 'ghetto neighbourhood programme' to regulate life in the city's few low-income and predominantly Muslim areas, where parents are obliged to enrol their children in Danish kindergartens for a minimum of 25 hours a week from the age of one, or potentially have their welfare payments stopped. This punitive and paternalistic approach feels at odds with an open, progressive society, and is not universally popular.

Other concerns include income inequality, which is on the rise in the city, and the gentrification of Copenhagen's more traditionally low-rent areas, with all its associated problems. Shiny apartment blocks keep appearing in the city centre while some on the outskirts stay empty; key workers find it increasingly hard to afford to live in the inner city, and a housing crash is being whispered about.

The hope is that with collaborative government and an engaged population, consultations will achieve innovative solutions typical of Copenhagen, but these are big issues that need sustained, nuanced work and will not go away quietly.

Adopt Danish design principles during your stay, by appreciating the local environment, rejecting a throwaway culture and embracing the *hygge*

Changes afoot

The arrival of the long-awaited metro ring after many years of development means it will be possible to get around the city faster than ever before, and visitors will have easier access to the city's most diverse areas, beyond the centre. It's going to be a great time to explore.

New hotels, from Carlsberg Byen to Sydhavn, are opening up all across the city centre. New rooms in new places increase the opportunities to get away from the main tourist trail and experience a more colourful and authentic way of living. It's also hoped that the hotel room boom will lead to lower per night prices, which can only be a good thing for visitors.

Adopt Scandinavian design principles during your stay in Copenhagen, by appreciating the local environment, rejecting a throwaway culture and embracing the *hygge*. And, if all else fails, reach for Denmark's newest international buzzword: *pyt*. It means 'never mind, move on' – to be used if something goes wrong, but you aren't going to beat yourself up about it.

Eating & Drinking

From New Nordic cuisine to Scandinavian street food

Copenhagen's dining scene attracts visitors from all over the world. Spearheaded of course by super-hot Noma 2.0, the city has a haul of 22 Michelin stars across 17 restaurants; pretty impressive given its diminutive size. But it's not all about super-pricey food, and if you don't like this style of New Nordic or high-end dining, there are still plenty of other options. A trickle-down effect means that you can find experimental bakeries headed by ex-Noma pastry chefs, not to mention great Mexican taco stalls, organic hot dog stands and supermarkets where fresh local food is the norm.

Lagkagehuset *p38*

Danish food

There is a lot of local love for *smørrebrød*, the Danish open sandwich that is eaten for breakfast, lunch and even dinner in some cases. It is a slice of dark ryebread with a range of traditional toppings – fried fish and remoulade, chicken salad, or egg and mayonnaise. Eat it with a knife and fork; most people order two at a time. For a simpler sandwich add *leverpostej*, a kind of liver pâte. There are plenty of traditional restaurants where you can try *smørrebrød*; **Aamanns** (*see p107*) is one of the very best. A simple *bolle med ost* – bread roll with cheese – makes a good alternative snack. Danish Blue may be known around the world, but one of Denmark's best-kept secrets is its range of incredible cheeses, including extremely strong and stinky types, such as Lille Ø and Viking Blue. Try them at the **Unik** market stall (*see p104*) at Torvehallerne.

Nearly as popular is *flæskesteg* (roast pork), which is eaten either on the street in a bun from a *pølsevøgn* (sausage wagon; *see p42*) or as part of a traditional dinner in a restaurant. Other local favourites include *fiskefrikadeller* (fishcakes) and *frikadeller* (meatballs), the latter eaten in a brown gravy and served with mashed potato and a little lingonberry jam for tartness. *Pølser* (frankfurter sausages) are also very popular as a snack at any time of day. And there's *sild* (herring), available in a range of sauces, and traditionally served as a starter for celebratory meals.

Danish bread and pastries are rightly prized. Everyone in Copenhagen has a favourite bakery; just some to look out for include two chains, **Lagkagehuset** (lagkagehuset.dk) and **Meyers** (www.meyersmad.dk), as well as **Lille Bakery & Eatery** (*see p132*) **Hart Bageri** (*see p149*) and **Brød** (*see p142*). Bakeries produce a variety of fabulous confections, from *drømmekage* (dreamcake), a sponge-style

❤ Only in Copenhagen

Bæst *p156*
Some of the best buffalo mozzarella you'll ever eat.

Gro Spiseri *p164*
Sustainable food in the city's chicest neighbourhood.

Lidkoeb *p197*
Three floors of cocktails in a hidden courtyard.

Noma 2.0 *p131*
World-beating food and architecture.

Relae *p158*
New Nordic with a twist.

Noma 2.0

In the know
Price categories

All our restaurant listings are marked with a krone symbol category, indicating the price you should expect to pay for a meal, excluding drinks. The final bill will of course depend on the number of courses and drinks consumed.

♛ = under 300kr

♛♛ = 300kr-600kr

♛♛♛ = 600kr-1,000kr

♛♛♛♛ = over 1,000kr

cake topped with caramelised coconut), to *flødeboller*, gourmet chocolate 'tea cakes' with gooey marshmallow and a wafer inside. What we might call 'Danish pastries' are known as *wienerbrød* – 'Viennese bread' – and come in varieties not limited to *kanelsnegl* (cinnamon buns), croissants and *spandauer* (pastry with custard and jam). Festive days, including Christmas and Fastelavn (*see p187*), are celebrated with special cream-filled buns, and every bakery has its own style. For kids, the approach of Christmas means *æbleskiver*, a sort of small doughnut eaten with icing sugar and jam. But sweet things can be found year-round, and ice-cream is a big deal in the summer. Hansen's make the best ice-cream you can buy, but there are independent sellers all over the city. **Istid** (Jægersborggade 13, 61 31 18 34, www.istid.dk) on Jægersborggade is a modern take on it all, with ice-creams made with liquid nitrogen (including vegan and sorbet options). Many streets also have a pick'n'mix *slik* (sweet) shop on the corner where kids can go for a Friday treat.

Preparing sustainable food at Gro Spiseri

The New Nordic Revolution

You are forgiven if you think that 'New Nordic' cuisine is all about Noma-style experimental food foraged from shorelines and wild countryside, prepared using cutting-edge treatments by a breed of hyper-obsessed chefs and presented in the most unlikely ways. It is unusual to hear the phrase talked about in any other way. But its real history has more humble beginnings and less elite aims.

In 2004, Danish food entrepreneur Claus Meyer got together with Noma's René Redzepi and 12 other stellar chefs from Sweden, Finland, Norway, Iceland and the Faroe Islands to discuss how best to develop Nordic food culture. The result was the 'New Nordic Kitchen Manifesto', a set of ten guiding principles to determine the future of food in the region. Local, seasonal and

In the know
Dine with the Danes

For a chance to meet the locals and try some proper home cooking, sign up with www.meetthedanes.com.

Gemyse

sustainable food is at the heart of it all, and the resulting movement is widely considered the region's strongest and most important culinary revolution ever. Chefs, integrating knowledge about health and well-being with good-tasting food, looked to traditional cooking as well as the future to develop new ideas.

Noma's huge success as a restaurant serving this style of produce put it firmly in the spotlight, but you can find New Nordic restaurants serving local and sustainable food without a waiting list and such a high price tag. Even the fresh organic meat, fruit and vegetables sold at **Torvehallerne** (*see p104*) demonstrate a New Nordic influence, as does eating an on-street hot dog at **DØP** (*see p78*). Find out more at newnordicfood.org.

High-end and experimental

When it comes to experiencing the very best food that Copenhagen has to offer, look no further than the Michelin list, but plan ahead and have a credit card to hand. There are multiple restaurants to choose from across the city: **Geranium** (*see p164*) was awarded

❤ Best vegetarian and vegan

42° Raw *p83*
Everything is raw and vegan-friendly.

Gemyse *p69*
A greenhouse vegetarian restaurant set within a theme park.

Morgensted *p127*
Vegetarian with a bohemian atmosphere and great prices.

simpleRAW *p83*
Stylish and super-Instagrammable vegan food.

Souls *p165*
Charming service, vegan food and a *hyggelig* space.

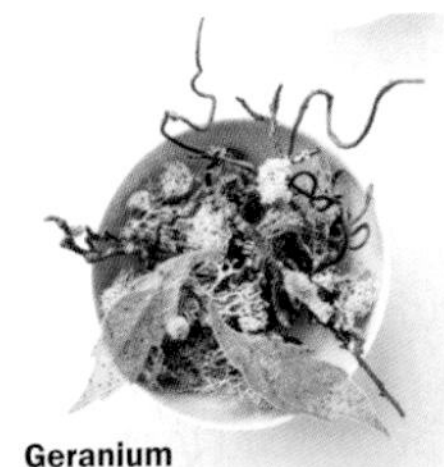
Geranium

three Michelin stars in 2019 and is the very best of the best; **Noma 2.0** (*see p131*) is, of course, the most talked about, housed in a beautiful BIG-designed building, while **Relæ** (*see p158*), **Amass** (*see p131*) and **Kiin Kiin** (*see p156*) are among the other outstanding places to eat.

Beyond the Michelin stars, plenty of delicious fare is available from some exceptional chefs. The couple behind Relæ also run **Manfreds & Vin** (*see p156*) as well as the bakery/café/bistro **Mirabelle** (*see p160*) and the fabulous Italian restaurant **Bæst** (*see p156*) next door to it. Ex-Noma chef, Rosio Sanchez, runs relaxed Mexican restaurant **Sanchez** (*see p142*), a great bet for brunch, along with fantastic taco stalls in Torvehallerne and Kødbyen. The drinks – margaritas at the stalls and *horchata*, among other things, in the restaurant – are a particular high point. Another hot tip is **The Corner 108**, next door and linked to the Michelin-starred **108** (*see p123*), where you can eat small plates, breakfast and lunch with a New Nordic flavour but more traditional prices.

Bakeries are not immune to the Noma effect: **Lille Bakery & Eatery** (*see p132*), was opened in Refshaleøen in 2018 by yet another former Noma chef, Jesper Gøtz, who hosts occasional dinners and events. **Leckerbær** (Ryesgade 118, 28 40 48 64, leckerbaer.dk) in Nørrebro, is run by ex-AOC and Alberto K Michelin-starred chefs Jakob Mogensen and Gabi Bär Mogensen, and bakes experimental and gourmet cookies. In Frederiksberg, the superb **Meyers Deli** (*see p149*) on Gammel Kongevej is Claus Meyer's most approachable and wallet-friendly place to eat. Nearly next door, **Hart Bageri** (*see p149*), opened in 2018 by Richard Hart in partnership with Noma, focuses on exquisite sourdough bread.

Manfreds & Vin

❤ Best cafés

La Banchina *p132*
Perfect for a coffee after a swim and sauna.

Café Atelier September *p107*
Great style, lovely location.

Coffee Collective *p45*
Copenhagen chain with great coffee, all over the city.

Picnic *p74*
The city's newest museum café is French-inspired and fabulous.

SMK *p106*
Everything here is a work of art.

Sonny *p84*
Stylish and with a cute garden.

Lille Bakery & Eatery

Sausage Wagons

The traditional Danish street food

Until relatively recently, street food meant one thing in Copenhagen: frankfurter sausages. The city's ubiquitous *pølsevogne* are a Danish institution. Cute, caravan-like mobile or stationary stalls, with their fold-out windows and counters, have dotted Copenhagen since the 1920s, and their bright red *pølser* (sausages), served in a hot dog bun, are still a popular snack for locals. Eat them, Danish-style, with remoulade, mustard, ketchup, pickled cucumbers, and fried and raw onions.

One of the city's most famous and traditional hot dog stands is **Harry's Place** (Nordre Fasanvej 269, 35 81 26 69), on the outskirts of Nørrebro. The seriously hungry should opt for Harry's famously huge 'Børge' sausage.

If you prefer local fast food without the excess cholesterol, the popular **DØP** (Den Økologiske Pølsemand, or Organic Sausage Man) wagon can be found beside the Round Tower and near the Church of the Holy Spirit on Strøget. On offer are top-quality *pølser* in sourdough buns topped with rye and linseed.

Today, international-style street food is making its presence felt in Copenhagen. There are multiple kebab shops in Nørrebro and Vesterbro, handy after a night out, while a range of street food markets introduce experimental tastes from around the world.

Mid-range and affordable

DØP organic hot dog stand

Dining out is notoriously expensive, but recent times have seen a growth in mid-range eateries across the city – food halls such as the one at Tivoli, where you can eat sushi, burgers and more without the need to book or dress up, are a good example. Chain restaurants such as **Gorms** (pizza; www.gormspizza.dk), **Sticks'n'Sushi** (sushi; sticksnsushi.com/da), **Cock's & Cows** (burgers; www.cocksandcows.dk) and **Grød** (stew; groed.com) are popular and easy to find. More unusual and distinctive restaurants are also opening up around the city, with bakeries hosting dining events and spin-off pop-ups enriching the mid-range dining scene. The good news is that, with careful planning, two people can eat out for 500kr including drinks. The Kødbyen area is a good place to look, with the likes of **Magasasa** (Flæsketorvet 54-56, magasasa.dk) serving up affordable dim sum in a fun environment. Typically, you will need to book a table in advance. Nearby, on Sønder Boulevard, **Absalon** (*see p140*) is a former church-turned-communal dining hall where you can eat for around 50kr per head on long shared tables and buy drinks at the bar. It's a unique Copenhagen experience and is highly recommended. There is no choice on the menu, but you won't go hungry.

❤ Reffen

Refshalevej 167A (33 93 07 60, reffen.dk). Bus 40, 991, 992. Bring a bike with you on the harbour bus and speed up your journey here substantially. ***Open*** *noon-8pm Fri-Sun, with extended opening hours in summer, closed in winter. Pay by card if you can; if you only have cash, you can go to the Ref Bar to exchange it for a prepaid credit card.* ***Map*** *p120 X7.*

Part of the fun of Reffen, Copenhagen's newest food market, is getting there. The best route is to take the harbour bus from its stop at the end of Nyhavn canal to its conclusion at Refshaleøen, then walk with most of the passengers along the post-industrial route, beside converted warehouses and occasional piles of pallets, to the rusted-up car and festival signs that announce you have arrived.

Reffen grew out of the hugely successful Papirøen street food market that stood on the island facing Nyhavn until December 2017. Ramshackle, edgy, energetic and international in focus, it couldn't have been more different from the city's well-mannered, precision-focused dining scene. Sitting outside in the sun, with music in the background and a mélange of outsiders, locals and visitors cutting loose was an extremely enjoyable way to spend an afternoon.

Regeneration came calling, of course, and the hippie feeling soon evaporated as Papirøen was demolished and a new super-sleek architectural leisure facility, including a Japanese-designed spa, was planned in the same space (opening in 2021). With the huge success of Papirøen, it was only a matter of time before a new location for a street food market in the same vein would be found.

Reffen is perched on a windy spot on Refshaleøen, close to BIG's **CopenHill** *(see p133)* and with foodie-focused neighbours **Amass** *(see p131)*, **La Banchina** *(see p132)* and **Lille Bakery & Eatery** *(see p132)* to keep it company. Expect to find a festival-style atmosphere at any time of year.

Its 54 start-ups include food stalls, bars and creative workshops. There are Japanese, Mexican and Icelandic food stalls standing side by side with bars, a Hawaiian shave ice stall and vintage clothes boutiques, all with a focus on sustainable packaging and ethos. On long summer nights, the party starts here – people rest up in hammocks and deck chairs, drink and dive into the water, and take the party boat to and from Nyhavn to continue the feeling.

In the know
Postprandial fun

Once you've eaten your fill, there's a little skateboard park and a van offering skateboard hire next door, or else there's CopenHot (see *p130*; book in advance), where you can enjoy a hot tub or spa boat tour of the canals.

Brunch is a beloved institution in the city, with many bottomless buffets that can be especially affordable for families. Two particularly good options are **Mother** (*see p142*) in Kødbyen and **Café Sonja** (no.86, cafesonja.dk) on Saxogade. A left-field choice is to eat out at one of the city's many museum cafés: **SMK** (*see p106*), **BLOX** (*see p91*), the **National Museum** (*see p93*) or **Glyptoteket** (*see p75*).

What to drink

Danes love to drink; Carlsberg and Tuborg, of course, with or without a *snaps* chaser. The presence of one of the world's largest breweries in the city is surely just coincidence, but the city's beer scene is a great attraction and microbreweries are popping up all over the place: fashionable **Mikkeler's** many offerings, **Brus** (*see p160*) in Nørrebro and a new development from **Amass** (*see p131*) in Refshaleøen. Danish beer tends to be more flavoursome, thicker and more like an IPA than most UK lagers.

Less developed is the wine culture, but if you don't want to drink beer, you certainly have options. Natural and orange wines are appearing in wine bars across Nørrebro, Kødbyen and Vesterbro, and specialist bars offer tastings and wines from around the world.

The cocktail scene provides late-night fun in the city too. Stellar bars such as **Ruby** (*see p88*) and **Lidkoeb** (*see p197*) have led the way for years, with stylish interior design and great atmosphere, adding music and occasional dance floors and sitting somewhere between a bar and a club. Cocktail bars of note are included in the nightlife section (*see p196*): unassuming from the outside, many of them bring together super-chic design, unique Nordic flavours, great music and a certain type of hipster local; shake them around and create a night out to remember.

❤ Best cheap eats

Absalon *p140*
Community dining at its finest.

DØP *p78*
Fast food and nearly healthy too.

Grød *p158*
Porridge, risotto, rice-based dishes and more.

Lille Bakery & Eatery *p132*
Friday night dinners reimagined.

Mother *p142*
Bottomless brunch is a bargain.

Grød

Mother

What if you don't drink alcohol? Coffee is more popular than tea. Look out in particular for the popular chains **Joe and the Juice** (www.joejuice.com) and **Coffee Collective** (coffeecollective.dk). Local soft drinks include *hyldeblomst*, elderflower soda, or Faxe Kondi, a local lemonade. Kids love *kakao*, chocolate milk, or *varm kakao*, hot chocolate, which you can order in every café and bakery.

Practical information

To find out what's going on in the foodie world, check the lifestyle blog Scandinaviastandard.com, which showcases up-and-coming food events, or the Danish-only website www.berlingske.dk/aok (use Google Translate). Or visit Mad About Copenhagen (www.madaboutcopenhagen.dk) and request a personal guide to your kind of food in the city. The group, whose name is a pun (*mad* means food in Danish), has its finger on the pulse of everything foodie.

Booking in advance is essential if you plan to visit any of the city's Michelin-starred eateries. The best way to get a seat at Noma, for example, is to sign up to their website (noma.dk) and set yourself an alert for when the next season's seats are made available. Book as early as you can on the day they are released – they sell out fast. Other restaurants use a more typical booking procedure, with booking online the norm. Advance bookings for Friday and Saturday night dining are usual for all restaurants across the city.

❤ Best bars

Bip Bip *p158*
For when you want computer games as well as drinks.

Duck and Cover *p197*
Vesterbro's super cosy cocktail hideaway.

Halvandet *p132*
The closest thing to a beach bar in the city.

Nørrebro Bryghus *p158*
One of the city's most highly esteemed microbreweries.

Ved Stranden *p88*
Expertly chosen wine by the waiter.

Lidkoeb

Mikkeler

Shopping

Designer boutiques, specialist shops and flea markets with harbour views

Copenhagen has a distinctive attitude to shopping. Despite being filled with designer boutiques, high-end fashion and interior design that wows the rest of the world, it gives a little shrug when it comes to making shopping a hobby. As reflected in shop opening hours – stores close early on Saturdays and sometimes don't open at all on a Sunday – by and large, local people are too busy cycling, running, catching up with friends and family and enjoying *hygge* to spend their weekends shopping.

Prices are probably the first thing you will notice as a visitor to the city. It is not cheap. Even the vintage boutiques are not cheap (though you might discover some bargains in a summer *loppemarked* or flea market). But look twice and you'll find that it is all down to a different shopping philosophy: quality over quantity; investment pieces over fast fashion. There is a clear preference for selecting the perfect item rather than buying a lot of mediocre stuff. If you're coming to Copenhagen to shop for design items and fashion, bring twice the money you think you need, and half the suitcase space.

The Louisiana Butik *p170*

What to buy

Copenhagen is known for its minimalist mens- and womenswear, and its interior design and homewares. Prices vary – though they are usually on the high side. The good news is that the city has plenty of well-stocked and carefully chosen vintage and pre-loved fashion boutiques where you can pick up classic Danish designs for a little less. Try **I Blame Lulu** (iblamelulu.com), **Time's Up Vintage** (timesupshop.com), **Tú a Tú** (*see p161*), **Bye Bye Love** (byebyelove.dk) and **Second Society** (secondsociety.dk), just to start. Hot tip: follow these boutiques on Instagram and send a message if you want them to hold anything for you to try.

A handful of the city's designers to look out for include **Silas Adler**, menswear designer behind the street-style label **Soulland** (*see p149*; soulland.eu), who has a flagship shop on Gammel Kongevej; **Stine Goya** (stinegoya.com), a womenswear designer who loves colour, with stores on Gothersgade, Ravnsborggade and Østerbrogade; **Henrik Vibskov** (henrikvibskov.com), a graduate of London's Central Saint Martins art college who sells streetwear-inspired clothes; and **Mads Nørgaard** (madsnorgaard.dk), without whose stripes a true Danish wardrobe is not complete. **Ganni** (ganni.dk), a regular feature in *Vogue*, is the opposite of Danish minimalism, all bright colours, frills and flounces.

You can't miss the Scandinavian-style interior design influence – it's everywhere you go. Modern design shops across the city – including the likes of **Stilleben No.22** (*see p104*) and **Dansk Made For Rooms** (*see p144*) – sell the look beautifully, with decorative items such as vases, coffee cups and bedding that can easily fit in your carry-on bag.

A spin-off of this love of beautiful interiors is a profusion of florists and specialist plant

❤ Copenhagen originals

HAY House *p85*
Worth a visit for the views of Amagertorv from the top at least.

Illums Bolighus *p78*
A multi-floored gallery showing the best Danish interior design.

Loppemarked på Brygge *p123*
The definitive Copenhagen flea market held once a month in spring and twice in summer.

Naked *p86*
Sneakers just for women.

Den Sidste Dråbe *p161*
Sells some of the most beautifully designed liquor bottles in town.

Torvehallerne *p104*
For excellent-quality food from all over the world.

Naked

HAY House

shops. You may not be able to fit these into your luggage but it is a charming experience to browse the florists on Istedgade (*see p139*), the concept cactus and succulents boutique **Plant København** (www. plantkbh.dk) on Jægersborggade, and the subterranean, sculptural and creative plant store **Stalks and Roots** (www.stalksandroots.com) on Vendersgade, behind Torvehallerne, along with its spin-off cut-flower stall in the centre of Torvehallerne. If you're invited to dinner at a Danish person's house, a bunch of their designer blooms makes a perfect gift for the host.

Shopping by area

Indre By, the inner city, is by far the most charming place to start a shopping tour. Gothersgade is a good street to start on – here and on the neighbouring streets, you'll find interior design showrooms such as **Beau Marché** (*see p107*), boutiques including **Isabel Marant** (www.isabelmarant.com), **Won Hundred** (wonhundred.com) and **Stine Goya** (stinegoya.com), and cafés such as **Café Atelier September** (*see p107*). You can walk all the way up the street to the Botanical Gardens and on to the Nørreport area and finally Nørrebro itself.

If you don't head north, Strøget (*see p76*), the city's best-known shopping street, is where you'll find the LEGO Store as well as any number of international fashion brands from H&M to **Arket** (www.arket.com), **& Other Stories** (www. stories.com) and **Weekday** (www.weekday. com). It is easily reached from the old and chi-chi area around Café Atelier September; head southwest through a maze of half-timbered buildings and short cobbled streets and you'll find it. This end of Strøget is the best for high-end fashion and puts you close to **Illums** (*see p78*), **HAY House** (*see p85*) and **Magasin** (*see p111*), three of the biggest stores. Strædet, parallel, has more unusual shops, and it is also

❤ Best hipster streets

Blågårdsgade *p155*
Especially for cosy cafés and internationally influenced independent shops.

Elmegade *p155*
Close to the centre and great for fashion and pop-up shops.

Gammel Kongevej *p145*
A street full of fashion boutiques, hip bakeries and independents.

Istedgade *p139*
Vintage shops, great restaurants and a rebellious vibe.

Jægersborggade *p157*
Unique one-off shops line this cobbled Nørrebro street.

Saxogade *p51*
Just off Istedgade, this little street epitomises shopping with a conscience.

Strøget *p76*

In the know
English insight

Scandinavia Standard (www.scandinaviastandard.com) is a great English-language resource for finding out about the latest fashion and lifestyle brands, and you can usually buy online via its links.

worth stopping at Nikolai Plads, where there is a specialist cookware shop, **H. Skalm P.** (www.hskalmp.dk) and a lovely toy shop for little children, **Astas** (astas.dk).

Nørrebro is the hipster borough of choice, where kebab shops sit alongside pop-up shops, boutiques hosting endless closing down sales, and wine bars selling natural wine. Just over the bridge around Nørreport station, **Torvehallerne** (*see p104*) is a good place to start, before hitting Ravnsborggade, a mixture of art shops, boutiques (including Stine Goya), wine bars, and basement bric-a-brac and antiques shops; **Bungalow** (bungalow.dk) sells pretty cushions and interior design. **Elmegade** (*see p155*) is great for mens- and womenswear, with regular pop-ups and plenty of independent boutiques, while nearby **Blågårdsgade** (*see p155*) has a handful of independent art shops, street grocers and boutiques. The epitome of hipster shopping, however, is **Jægersborggade** (*see p157*), a little stroll away, which is lined with one-offs, including a Noma-linked delicatessen, Michelin-starred restaurant **Relæ** (*see p158*) and interior and fashion shops.

Upmarket Østerbro offers high-end boutiques all the way along Østerbrogade, and cafés to rest your tired feet at the Triangle and down quiet cobbled side streets (we'd especially recommend bakery **Leckerbær**, leckerbaer.dk, at the Østerbro end of Ryesgade). **Ganni**'s (*see p165*) flagship showroom is on Østerbrogade, along with the gorgeous kids' boutique **Søstjernen** (*see p165*), furniture maker **Normann Copenhagen** (*see p165*), and fashion boutique **Moshi Moshi Mind** (*see p165*).

The main shopping hub for Vesterbro is the independent-spirited Istedgade, where you'll find shops selling everything from Red Cross charity goods to pre-loved fashion, handmade bikes and custom-made neon signs (sygns.dk); **Dansk Made for Rooms** (*see p144*) is

Stilleben No.22

In the know
Opening hours

Shops are typically open until 6pm or 7pm during the week, offering the many workers who clock off at 4pm a chance to buy what they need after they leave the office. If you're looking for a quiet time to hit the shops, weekdays before 4pm are your best bet. Shops are closed on public holidays (*see p245*). Most supermarkets are closed too, although Irma often keeps irregular hours on public holidays.

If you are staying in a self-catering apartment during the Easter, Christmas or New Year holidays, ask if your host can offer a pre-arrival shop so you arrive to a stocked fridge as most supermarkets will be closed.

Dansk Made For Rooms

also on this street, as well as some lovely plant shops. Saxogade runs off Istedgade to the south and has a cluster of shops focused on sustainability, including **Løs Market** (loes-market.dk), a packaging-free supermarket, and **Naturli** (naturli-foods.dk/saxogade), a vegan supermarket. On the corner, **Heidi and Bjarne** (heidiogbjarne.dk) sells lovely toys and childrenswear.

Away from Istedgade, there are a lot of tourist-focused souvenir shops around Tivoli that are not really worth mentioning bar the small **Illums Bolighus** offshoot (*see p78*) opposite the main station, which has a good selection of design goods. Head up side street Bagerstræde to find **Akustikken** (akustikken.dk), one of the city's best guitar shops. Further up Vesterbrogade, Værnedamsvej is locally nicknamed 'The French Street' for its pavement cafés, bakeries, cheese shop, chocolate shop, florists and fashion: **Summerbird** (*see p86*) and **Helges Ost** (helgesost.dk) are particular highlights.

Gammel Kongevej is truly one of the best streets to roam. Alongside flagship boutiques from all the major designers, you'll find

❤ Best for interior design

Beau Marché *p107*
French- and vintage-inspired furniture.

BLOX shop *p91*
Architecture books just right for your coffee table, plus a few other museum shop-style treats.

DanskMadeForRooms *p144*
Ceramics and neutral, minimalist furniture.

The Louisiana Butik *p170*
A dazzling showroom of design, fashion and kids' toys.

Royal Copenhagen *p79*
Classic blue and white design tableware.

Stilleben No.22 *p104*
Handmade ceramics, well-chosen bedding and art prints.

Soulland *p149*

independent shops, Chinese importers, a Noma-led bakery and some of the best pre-loved fashion stores. **Nué** (nuecph.com), **Soulland** and **I Blame Lulu** are just a handful of the fashion stores; for kids, **Prik** (prik.info) sells great toys at good prices, and **Mini Me** (minimecph.com) is a specialist sneaker store just for kids.

Torvehallerne *p104*

Shopping centres and department stores

Convenience shopping isn't really a thing in Copenhagen, and can't compare to wandering cobbled streets in search of one-off treasures. But, if you're short of time, you'll find most of what you're looking for under one roof at the city's small shopping centres and department stores.

Frederiksberg Centret (frbc-shopping.dk) has 90 shops in a two-floor modern shopping centre in the heart of Frederiksberg, mainly selling fashion and homewares, and including a Føtex supermarket that sells everything and is open daily from 8am to 9pm. **Fisketorvet** (fisketorvet.dk), to the south of Vesterbro near Kødbyen, is larger still, with three floors of shops, a food hall, a cinema and a large Føtex. There is also a shopping centre in Valby called

In the know
Payment

Copenhagen is largely cash free: the most common form of payment for everything in the city, even a cup of coffee, is a credit or debit card. Visa is accepted everywhere. Flea markets most often accept MobilPay, a Danish phone payment app, and cash, but some stall holders will take cards.

The standard VAT rate in Copenhagen is 25%. Shopping is tax-free for non-EU residents (*see p245*). Tax-free shopping is available in most major department stores including Magasin – just bring your passport with you. You normally have up to 90 days after purchase to claim the refund.

Spinderiet (spinderiet.dk), while further to the south and accessible by metro, **Field's** (fields-en.steenstrom.dk) is a mall in the American style with a dizzying range of shops, a huge cinema complex, food hall and large Sainsbury's-style supermarket Bilka.

Two department stores rule the Kongens Nytorv area of the city, with beautiful window displays and a wide choice of carefully selected Danish and international fashion, interiors, food and beauty brands to choose from. **Magasin** (*see p111*) is the most accessible and least expensive, while **Illums** (*see p78*) is more upmarket and carries top designer names, with a rooftop foodhall and great city views from the top balconies.

Flea markets and fairs

Copenhagen's flea markets – *loppemarked* – are legendary. Generally running at weekends from late spring to late September, they are full of old crockery, second-hand fashion and plenty of designer light fittings. If you love nothing more than rummaging around in Danish design and recreating a kitschy, 1970s-era look at home, you'll be in heaven. Kids can pick up toys and books for a handful of coins, and you might also find vintage jewellery and antiques.

Regular markets take place at Frederiksberg Town Hall every Saturday, 10am-3pm (Frederiksberg.dk/loppetorv) and along the water at **Islands Brygge Kulturhus** (*see p123*) on a Sunday, once a month in spring and twice a month in summer. For more information go to www.loppemarked.nu and www.fleamarketinsiders.com.

Design fairs such as **Finders Keepers** (finderskeepers.dk) take place seasonally through the year in major exhibition halls including Frederiksberg Centret and Øksnehallen at Kødbyen.

In the know
Sales and bargains

Sales generally take place in January and in September, as the seasons end. Black Friday has recently become a selling opportunity, although some brands choose to resist the international pressure to participate. You can buy discontinued and factory seconds at the **Royal Copenhagen Outlet** (Søndre Fasanvej 9, 38 34 10 04, www.royalcopenhagen.com) all year round.

Flea market

In the know
Buying food

Prices are not wildly different to those in the UK. The key supermarkets are Irma (similar to Waitrose), Netto (similar to Tesco), Rema 1000, Lidl and SuperBrugsen. Greengrocers abound on Istedgade, Blågardsgade and in most major residential neighbourhoods.

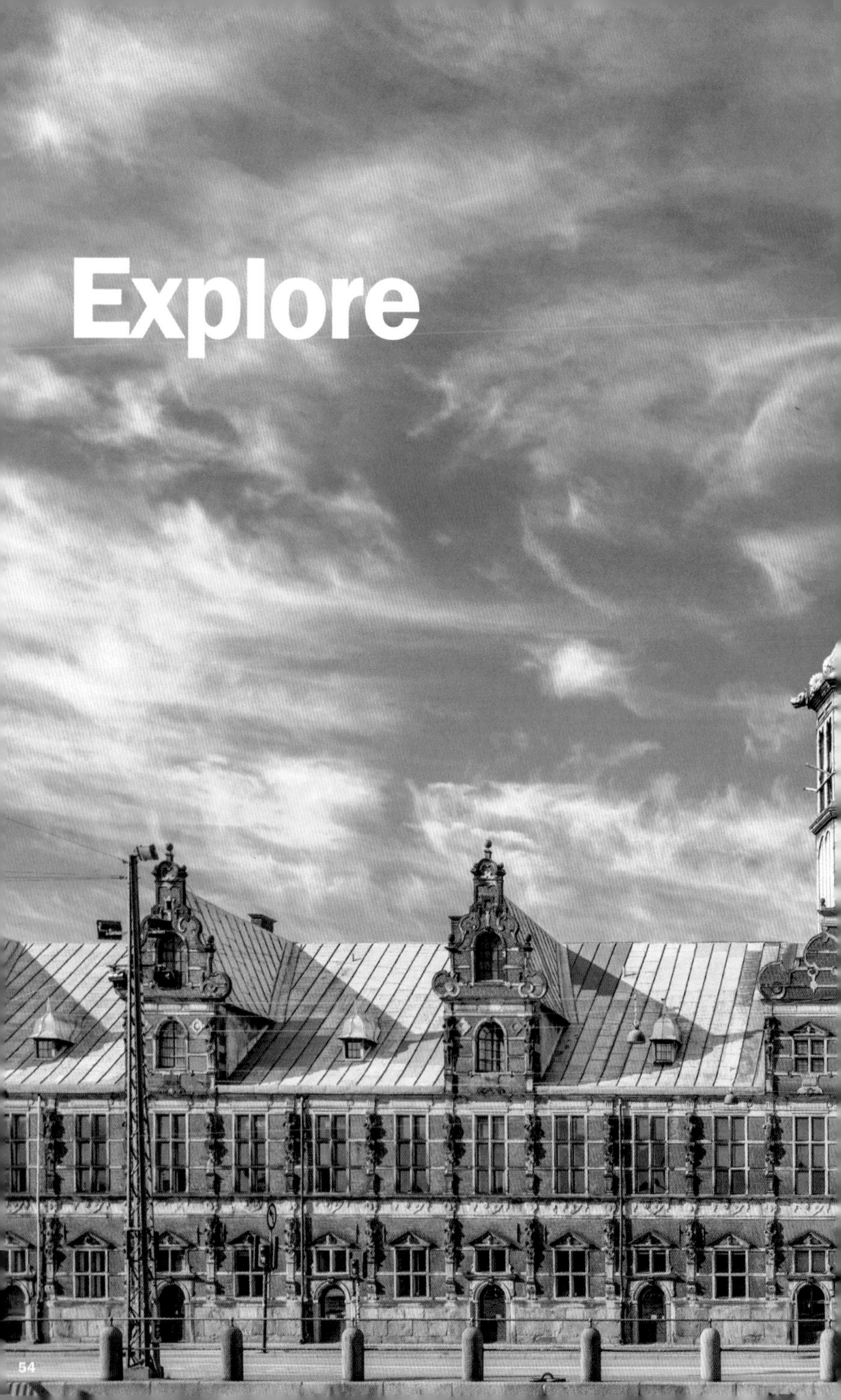

Explore

Getting Started	56
South Central Copenhagen	64
North Central Copenhagen	98
Christianshavn, Holmen & Refshaleøen	118
Vesterbro & Frederiksberg	134
Nørrebro & Østerbro	150
Day Trips	166

Børsen *p89*

Getting Started

Famously happy and bike-friendly, Copenhagen's metropolitan area covers 86.6 square kilometres (33.4 square miles), with most of the historic buildings and key sights clustered in the centre. When it comes to key sights, many people outside the country might be able to name Tivoli or *The Little Mermaid*, and may recognise Nyhavn's colourful canalside buildings, but maybe not much more. That's all to the good. Visiting this city isn't about ticking off sights on a list; it's about experiencing the warmth and good humour of Danish life, immersing yourself in its impressive design and dining cultures, and just plain enjoying yourself.

❤ Best views

Amaliehaven *p109*
A picture-perfect scene of gardens, a lavish fountain, the royal square and the glorious Marble Church.

CopenHill *p133*
Views of Copenhagen's rooftops and as far as the Øresund Strait on a good day.

Illum rooftop *p78*
Look down on all the shoppers on Strøget from this vantage point, with a cup of coffee in hand.

Marmorkirken *p115*
Drink in lovely views of the old city from the top of this beautiful and iconic church.

Rundetårn *p81*
Walk up wide, sloping floors designed for horses – really – and catch great views at the top.

Vor Frelsers Kirke *p123*
Spy the wind farms and Sweden from the top of this charming church.

View from Vor Frelsers Kirke

An overview of the city

Copenhagen is made up of a patchwork of small and characterful areas. In the very centre is the historic Copenhagen K or Indre By, the former walled city that ends at the city lakes on one side and at the harbour front on the other. Divided in this guide into **South Central** (*see p64*) and **North Central** (*see p98*), it is where you'll discover all the key city centre attractions, including Tivoli, the Ny Carlsberg Glyptotek, the Rundetårn (*see p81*), the Nationalmuseet, Nyhavn (*see p109*), Amalienborg Slot (*see p112*) and the Marmorkirken (*see p115*). Moving to the north-east, you'll find *The Little Mermaid* (*see p109*), where Copenhagen K meets Copenhagen Ø, **Østerbro** (*see p161*), an upmarket family-friendly area of the city with plenty of green spaces, wide pavements and great places to eat and shop. **Nørrebro** (*see p155*) borders Østerbro to the west and has its own personality: a gritty, urban, sometimes edgy, always colourful, and diverse area, with great nightlife, interesting street art and the fascinating Superkilen at the heart of it. The city's most desirable suburb, leafy **Frederiksberg** (*see p145*), is to the south-west of Nørrebro and has tree-lined streets, the city's zoo and yet more beautiful boutiques to browse. The former red-light district **Vesterbro** (*see p139*) links Frederiksberg and Copenhagen K, and accommodates everything from cocktail bars to pavement cafés.

Ny Carlsberg Glyptotek

Across the water from Copenhagen K, linked by bike and pedestrian-friendly bridges, the areas of **Christianshavn**, **Holmen** and **Refshaleøen** (*see p118*) sit on the water with a network of canals. Christianshavn and Holmen are a delight to visit by boat or on foot; you can discover historic cafés, painted houses, and marinas of desirable yachts. Museums and culture spaces line the waterways – from the Operaen to Nordatlantens Brygge, and you don't have to step into a museum to experience the work of artist Olafur Eliasson, who designed the beautiful Circle Bridge right on the harbourside. Controversial Christiania (*see p128*) adds an anarchic, creative spirit. Former shipyard Refshaleøen (*see p129*) is now full of foodie adventurers, with everything from Reffen (*see p43*), a food market with a festival atmosphere, to Amass and Noma, two of the most highly regarded places to eat in the city. Out in the far north-east, you'll also find Copenhagen Contemporary, along with CopenHill (*see p133*) and CopenHot.

The city is undergoing change at a rapid rate. Anywhere you look along the harbour front, on both sides of the water, luxury flats are being built. Completely new areas have been created at Nordhavn, next to Østerbro, and in Sluseholmen, south of

❤ Best art collections

Arken Museum for Moderne Kunst *p176*
Right on the beach and full of groundbreaking modern art.

Ny Carlsberg Glyptotek *p75*
Tea and scones in the café in the Winter Garden at the heart of the building is a highlight.

The Louisiana Museum of Modern Art *p170*
Look out over the Øresund to Sweden once you've enjoyed the truly outstanding collection.

Statens Museum for Kunst *p106*
Luminous Nordic painters plus a wonderful ancient-meets-modern building and a designer café for a Danish lunch.

❤ Best parks

Amager Strandpark *p174*
Walk along it all the way to the wonderful Kastrup Sea Baths.

Assistens Kirkegard *p155*
A graveyard-turned-public recreation space.

Botanisk Have *p105*
Especially for the rickety walk up to the top of the Palm House.

Fælledparken *p161*
The city's biggest green space – ideal for picnics, impromptu kick abouts and gentle Sunday strolls.

Kongens Have *p105*
Fairytale gardens with tumbling roses and a Renaissance-era castle.

Vesterbro; Valby and Amager in the west and south are the city's furthest borders, along with Hellerup in the north, and, as the city expands, they are more connected than ever. Some of these outer suburbs, plus manageable excursions from the city are covered in the **Day Trips** chapter (*see p166*).

Getting around

This bijou city is best navigated on foot or by bike. The local public transport system is great if you want to get out of the city or plan to travel to a different side of it, perhaps from Vesterbrø to Amager, but most of the key attractions are within walking distance of each other in the centre of the city; cyclists in the city should make sure they are confident and know the local laws of the road before they set off. The train is the ideal way to reach The Louisiana, Roskilde or Arken. Hire cars are not recommended in the city as parking is difficult. For more information on fares and public transport routes, *see p238*.

Sights and museums

Copenhagen's two most visited and most Instagrammed attractions are likely to disappoint well-travelled visitors. **The Little Mermaid** is indeed as diminutive as she sounds, found at the end of a windy and often grey waterfront walk, while **Nyhavn** (for both, *see p109*) on a good day is a bright backdrop of colourful houses, but on a bad day can feel like a tourist trap filled with a jostle of people. Fortunately, there are plenty of other things to see.

Copenhagen's best sight is the **waterfront**. Stroll along the pedestrianised harbour front, cruise along the canals in a GoBoat or take a harbour bus (for both, *see p162*): tour up and down it to see modern and classic architecture, people picnicking in quiet parks, cafés next to the water and the minutiae of daily life.

If you want to delve into Denmark's history, the **Nationalmuseet** (*see p93*), **Designmuseum Danmark** (*see p114*) and the **Danish Architecture Centre** (*see p91*) are three great places to start. For modern art, **The Louisiana** (*see p170*) is a day out to remember, and, likewise, **Arken** (*see p176*) is great fun. Within the city itself, visit **Copenhagen Contemporary** (*see p130*), the **Statens Museum for Kunst** (*see p106*) and **Ny Carlsberg Glyptotek** (*see p75*) to see a range of ultra-modern installations, 19th-century Nordic art and world-renowned sculpture.

Whatever your taste, try to put some *hygge* into your trip. Experience the city like a local by travelling on two wheels; take your time, enjoy your food and try to create special, enjoyable and meaningful moments during the trip. It could be as inconsequential as drinking a cocktail in a candlelit bar, or discovering a sunny swimming spot in the harbour and diving in. The little things are what matter in this cosy and friendly city.

In the know
Monday blues

Most museums in the city are closed on Mondays, with the exception of the Rundetårn. Roskilde's Vikingeskibsmuseet (Viking Ship Museum; see *p179*) is open every day of the week.

Arken Museum for Moderne Kunst

❤ Bike Copenhagen

Scandinavians are famous for using bicycles as everyday transport. And Danes cycle, on average, 1.6 kilometres (1 mile) per day. But Copenhageners take things a step further: almost everyone in the city, regardless of income or social status, cycles an average of 3 kilometres (2 miles) per person per day; there are five times more bikes than cars in the city, and cycling is not merely a means of transport but, rather, a way of life.

Copenhagen's bike lanes and bike culture have become a model for forward-thinking cities around the globe, to the point where a new verb, 'Copenhagenize', is used to describe urban planning that emulates the city. And despite, or because of, the international attention, Copenhagen hasn't rested on its laurels: ambitions for the future include increasing the number of bike commuters in the city to from 41 per cent to 50 per cent by 2025, and reducing commuting times by 15%. New cycle bridges have already started to make that a reality.

Urban cycling infrastructure

Although Copenhagen's bike lanes were created first along the Esplanaden in 1892 and later around the lakes in 1910, it wasn't until the 1980s that the city's present-day lanes – with their kerbs segregating cyclists from other road users – came into effect. As elsewhere, the 1960s witnessed a decline in cycling culture, with the increasing affordability of cars. But by the '70s, cycling experienced a revival in the city, in line with the growing green movement in Denmark. In the mid 1980s, local planners such as Jan Gehl began to develop the urban infrastructure for a bike- (and pedestrian-) friendly city, which now boasts some 390 kilometres (242 miles) of bike lanes. And from the early 1990s, cycling as a form of transportation has steadily risen year by year.

Of course, the comparatively small size of the capital and its flat terrain are particularly conducive to a strong cycling community. But the extensive and well-designed system of bike lanes and cycle paths, along with other measures to encourage cycling – such as being able to take your bike on the Metro and local trains – are what has really earned the city the tag of 'most bike-friendly city in the world'.

The busiest cycling street in Copenhagen is Nørrebrogade, and the bicycle rush hour on the connecting Dronning Louises Bro (bridge) is a sight to behold; join the throngs, and you'll feel a sense of community and belonging that just isn't possible in a car.

The city's 100 kilometres (62 miles) of new 'green routes' aim to provide especially safe routes in the city. Many have already been completed, including the Nørrebro green route, which runs from Lyngbyvej in the north to Valby in the south. And many city-to-suburb 'bicycle highways', which extend the city's cycling infrastructure to the suburbs and beyond, have been completed in the last few years.

Etiquette and practicalities

There are certain cast-iron rules that visitors should take note of when cycling around the city. For instance, passengers at bus stops (either embarking or disembarking) have right of way: all cyclists must stop and wait until the bus doors have closed. Left-hand turns on main roads are not permitted for cyclists: you must cross the road (with the green light, of course) as a pedestrian would. As a rule, you should ride on the right-hand side of the cycle path; if someone rings a bell behind you (never more than once, that is considered rude), it is to indicate that you should move over and let them pass on the left. When you want to stop, raise your right hand, in a sort of salute, to signal this to other cyclists.

Remember to lock your bike. Although Copenhageners are, on the whole, a trustworthy bunch, bicycle theft does still happen (though the thief is more likely to be a drunken chancer coming back from a bar than a member of an organised-crime

racket). Most bikes have locks built into the back wheel, meaning that locking up is quick and simple. You should also make sure that you use lights at night, or you'll get pulled over by local police.

It's possible to take bikes on the Metro and on S-trains, and on local, regional and InterCity trains outside rush hour (so not 7am-9am and 3.30-5.30pm). Some trains (not the S-train) require a special bike ticket, which can be purchased at the station. Most S-trains have a special area for bikes.

Copenhageners are a hardy bunch, and many cycle all year round – even during January blizzards. Local authorities keep bike lanes well gritted throughout the winter, ensuring that the bike is a viable form of transport even in the coldest months.

Bike hire

The city has an on-street bike hire facility called **Bycyklen** (www.bycyklen.dk), which launched in 2014. The chunky white electric bikes have GPS and navigation touchscreens with, for instance, train information, and can be booked online (from 30kr per hour, with various options for packages).

A better bet is to rent a bike from a bike shop (*see p240*) or to rent a bright orange Donkey bike from the street, for which you will need the **Donkey Republic Bike Rental** app ('Donkey Republic Bike Rental'). Typical cost is 110kr per day.

Bikes can often be hired from your hotel, but it can be cheaper to go direct to the rental place. **Baisikeli** (*see p240*) is especially recommended, being a well-priced, friendly and ethical bike-hire organisation set in a large space overlooking Dybbølsbro station.

► *For boutique bike shops in Copenhagen, see p86 and p129. For information on the city's iconic Christiania bikes, see p130 Cargo Collective.*

Bike tours

Guided bike tours lasting 2.5 hours are available in English from **Copenhagen Bicycles** (*see p240*) between April and September at 11am daily (100kr). Bike rental is not included in the price. Another option is **Bike Copenhagen with Mike** (26 39 56 88, www.bikecopenhagenwithmike.dk, check website for times). These sociable bike tours leave from the Latin Quarter in Indre By and take in all the sights and also get off the beaten track. Bike rental is included in the price (300kr) and personalised tours are also available.

In the know
The Harbour Circle

This 13-kilometre (eight-mile) cycle route takes you around the best of Copenhagen's waterfront areas, beside rickety houseboats and yuppie flats, along a quiet common and beside the city's busiest streets. It's highly recommended as a way to see the city, and can be broken into smaller sections of two, four and seven kilometres for shorter trips. Go to www.visitcopenhagen.com/harbourcircle to download a map and find out more.

In the know
Indre By

The words *Indre By* mean Inner City, and this term is used to indicate the central (and most historic) area of Copenhagen, bounded by the lakes and the harbour. In this guide we have divided *Indre By* into North Central and South Central Copenhagen.

Tourist information

Visit Copenhagen is run by the city council and provides great information on the city from its base opposite Tivoli in the heart of the city. There, you'll find friendly staff, free maps and information on all the city's attractions, plus the rules of the road for cyclists. You can also purchase a Copenhagen Card (*see p239*), use the internet or the toilets, and have a cup of coffee at the adjoining bakery, Lagkagehuset (one of the city's best bakery chains). The website www.visitcopenhagen.com is an excellent source of advice, inspiration and ideas. For more on tourist offices, *see p247*. Tourist offices do not make hotel bookings but can advise on vacancies.

▶ *Full information on what's on is in local papers and listings magazines (see p244). For useful websites, see p249.*

Tours

One really great way to see the city is to take a tour – it's also a fun way to get a local perspective on the culture and life of Copenhagen. In recent years, red tourist buses have become something of a plague on the city; but don't worry, there's more than one way to see the sights. Hop on a bike (*see p60*), hire a boat (*see p162*), join a walking tour or check out the following offbeat and themed options available to get a sense of Copenhagen's most characterful delights.

For details of personal guided tours, visit www.guides.dk. **Airbnb Experiences** (Airbnb.dk/experiences) is also a great way to find a quirky tour in the city, with a range of options including *hygge* and happiness tours, cooking, cargo bike tours and a variety of craft and photo-led options. **Copenhagen free walking tours** (Copenhagenfreewalkingtours.dk, free but tips are welcome) include the Grand Tour of Copenhagen, Classical Copenhagen and Christianshavn tour.

The longest-running food tour company in the city, **Copenhagen Food Tours** (Copenhagen.foodtours.eu, 50 12 36 45), take in the best of Copenhagen cuisine on foot, including *smørrebrød*, cheese, liquorice and beer. Guides are knowledgeable, and food allergies and preferences are catered for (just let them know in advance). Themed options, including Christmas food, are also available at certain times of year.

Starting from the new Danish Architecture Centre, **Danish Architecture Tours** (32 57 19 30, dac.dk, 110kr, includes free entrance to DAC's exhibitions) take in stories from architects and the mix of architectural styles in the areas surrounding BLOX, including Nyhavn itself.

With its old architecture and romantic atmosphere, Copenhagen is ideal for a **Ghost Tour** (51 92 55 51, www.ghosttour.dk, 2,500kr for up to 20 people). These walks (available in English if arranged in advance) will take you to some of the city's spookier sites.

With **Urban Explorer CPH Tours** (28 87 75 51, urbexplorer.dk) you will experience the more offbeat and unusual sides of the city. Expect to discover street art, quiet canals and urban design, all led by an experienced city planner with an eye for detail.

Statens Museum for Kunst *p106*

South Central Copenhagen

Two of Copenhagen's most-visited areas – Tivoli Gardens and shopping street Strøget – are located in this part of the city. Close to Central Station and several of the city's best museums, a visit to Tivoli is in many ways the definitive Danish experience. There are thrilling rides, but none is too extreme (apart from the Demon rollercoaster, perhaps); and there are hot dogs, candy floss and beer, as well as all kinds of family entertainment.

A short stroll away, you'll find a breathtaking line-up of ancient sculptures at Ny Carlsberg Glyptotek; Viking history at the Nationalmuseet; and the Rådhuset (town hall) at the start of Strøget.

Strøget, the best-known street in Copenhagen, is actually made up of five streets running from Kongens Nytorv at its eastern end to Rådhuspladsen in the west. In this area you'll find all the main international shopping brands, along with a large LEGO store, and a selection of bars and restaurants. To the north-west, the Latin Quarter and vibrant Pisserenden have more independent shops and bars, while laid-back Strædet, to the south, also has more character. Further south still is the island of Slotsholmen, where Bishop Absalon built his fortress in the 12th century, and a city was born.

❤ Don't miss

1 A tour of Tivoli *p68*
A 100-year-old wooden rollercoaster, fabulous food and magical gardens.

2 Ny Carlsberg Glyptotek *p75*
Ancient sculptures and French Impressionist paintings.

3 Rundetårn *p81*
Great views of the city from this historic Round Tower.

4 Nationalmuseet *p93*
The place to swot up on Danish history.

5 BLOX *p91*
For serious architecture fans, and a fun guided walk for all.

Rundetårn p81

SOUTH CENTRAL

Restaurants

1. Bøf & Ost *p82*
2. Brdr. Price in Tivoli *p69*
3. Café GL Torv *p82*
4. Gemyse Tivoli *p69*
5. Nimb Brasserie *p69*
6. Peder Oxe *p82*
7. Restaurant L'Alsace *p83*
8. Rice Market *p83*
9. Riz Raz *p87*
10. simpleRaw *p83*
11. Slotskælderen Hos Gitte *p88*
12. Søren K *p97*
13. Trio *p73*

Cafés & bars

1. 42°Raw *p83*
2. Bastard *p88*
3. Bertels Salon *p88*
4. Bryggeriet Apollo *p72*
5. Café Europa *p78*
6. Café Norden *p78*
7. Café Victor *p83*
8. Cakenhagen *p72*
9. DAC Café *p97*
10. Din Nye Ven *p83*
11. DØP organic hot dog stand *p78*
12. Floss Bar *p84*
13. Flottenheimer *p84*
14. Fru Nimb *p72*
15. La Glace *p84*
16. Kayak Bar *p97*
17. Library Bar *p73*
18. Øieblikket *p97*
19. Palæ Bar *p84*
20. Picnic at Glyptoteket *p74*
21. Restaurant Smör *p97*
22. Ruby *p88*
23. Sonny *p84*
24. Studenterhuset *p84*
25. Tivoli Food Hall *p72*
26. Ved Stranden 10 *p88*
27. Zirup *p88*
28. Zoo Bar *p84*

Shops & services

1. A.C. Perchs Thehandel *p84*
2. Arnold Busck *p84*
3. Bang & Olufsen *p78*
4. By Malene Birger *p85*
5. Casa Shop *p85*
6. Le Fix *p85*
7. Ganni *p85*
8. Georg Jensen *p78*
9. HAY House *p85*
10. Henrik Vibskov *p86*
11. Illum *p78*
12. Illums Bolighus Tivoli *p72*
13. Illums Bolighus *p78*
14. Le Klint *p79*
15. LEGO Flagship *p79*
16. Mads Nørgaard *p79*
17. Munthe plus Simonsen *p86*
18. Naked *p86*
19. Nordisk Korthandel *p86*
20. Norse Store *p86*
21. Peter Beier *p86*
22. Royal Copenhagen *p79*
23. Sögreni of Copenhagen *p86*
24. Sømods Bolcher *p86*
25. Søstrene Grene *p79*
26. Summerbird *p86*
27. Time's Up Vintage *p86*
28. Tivoli's Christmas Market *p72*
29. Wood Wood *p87*

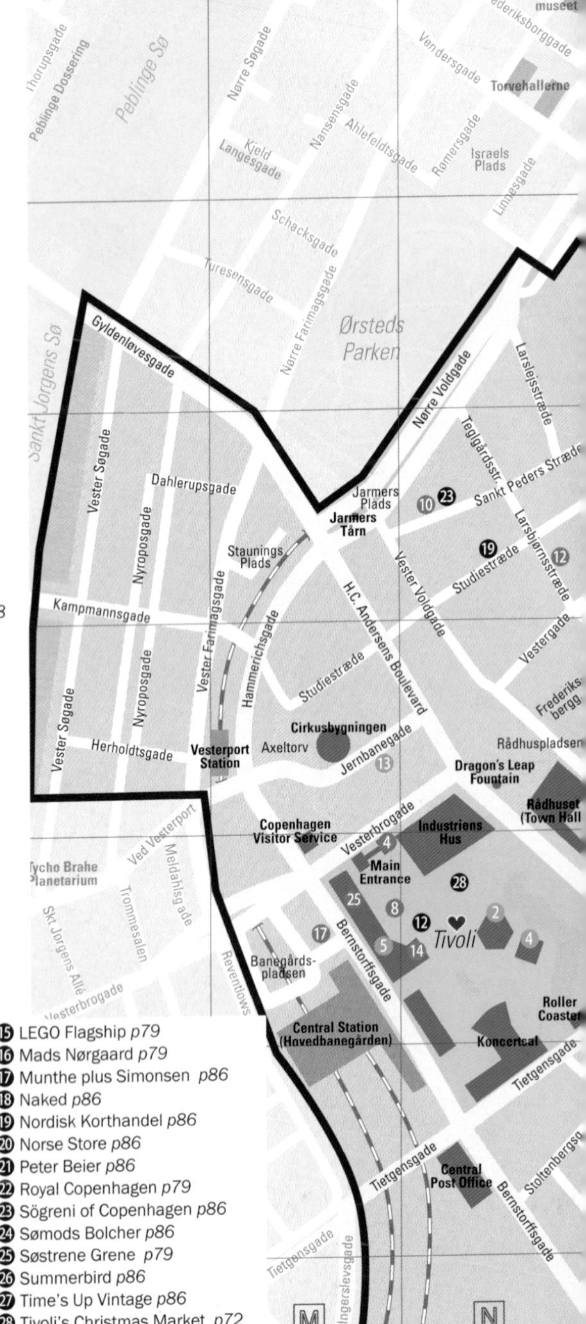

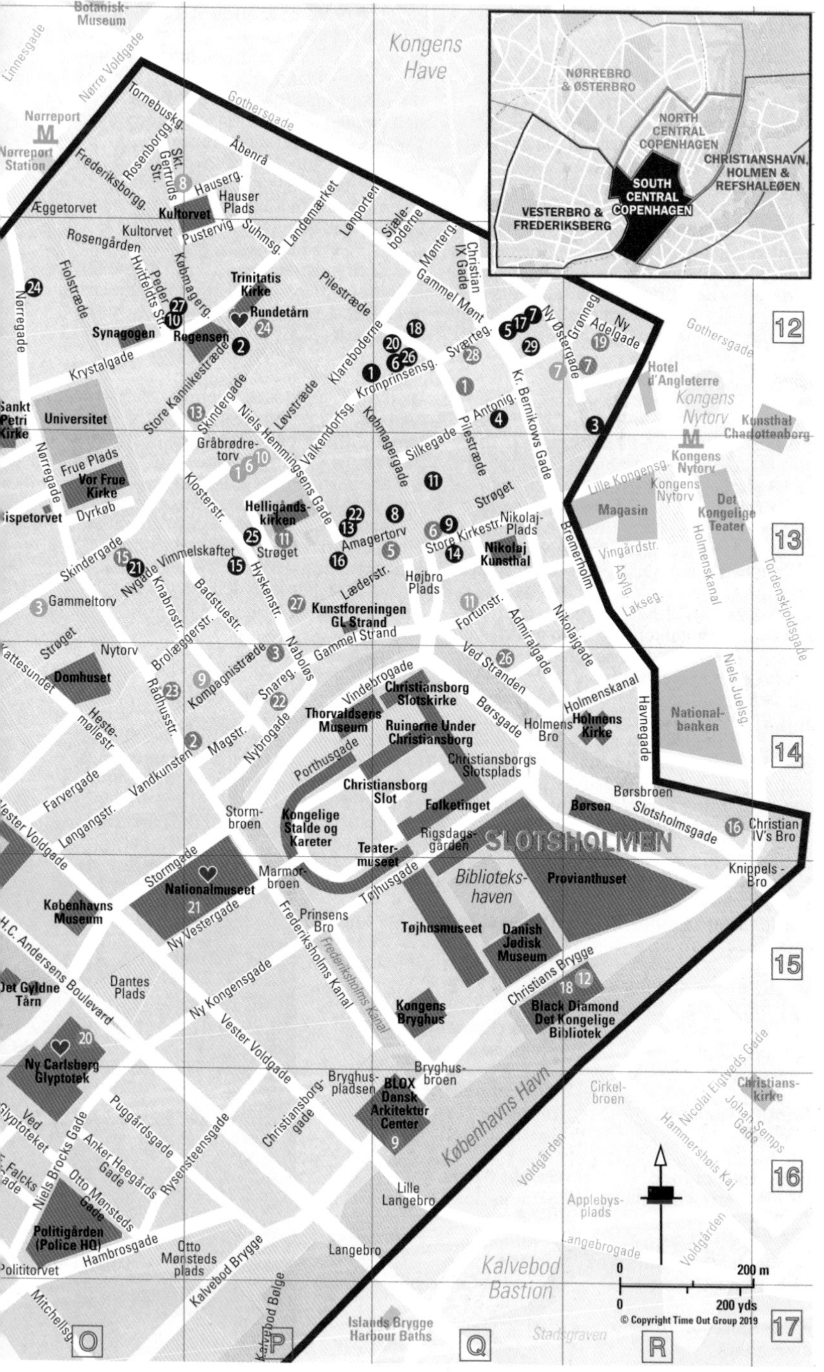
Botanisk-Museum
Kongens Have
NØRREBRO & ØSTERBRO
NORTH CENTRAL COPENHAGEN
CHRISTIANSHAVN, HOLMEN & REFSHALEØEN
SOUTH CENTRAL COPENHAGEN
VESTERBRO & FREDERIKSBERG
Nørreport
Nørreport Station
Linnésgade
Nørre Voldgade
Gothersgade
Tornebuskg.
Rosenborgg.
Skt. Gertruds Str.
Frederiksborgg.
Åbenrå
Hauserg.
Hauser Plads
Æggetorvet
Kultorvet
Pustervig
Suhmsg.
Landemærket
Løngangsten
Sjæleboderne
Møntergade
Christian IX Gade
Gammel Mønt
Rosengården
Fiolstræde
Peder Hvitfeldts Str.
Købmagerg.
Trinitatis Kirke
Rundetårn
Pilestræde
Nørregade
Synagogen
Regensen
Krystalgade
Store Kannikestræde
Klareboderne
Kronprinsensg.
Sværteg.
Ny Østergade
Grønneg.
Ny Adelgade
Hotel d'Angleterre
Kongens Nytorv
Kunsthal Charlottenborg
Sankt Petri Kirke
Universitet
Skindergade
Niels Hemmingsens Gade
Løvstræde
Valkendorfsg.
Købmagergade
Silkegade
Antonig.
Kr. Bernikows Gade
Gråbrødretorv
Frue Plads
Vor Frue Kirke
Dyrkøb
Bispetorvet
Klosterstr.
Helligåndskirken
Strøget
Amagertorv
Store Kirkestr.
Nikolaj Plads
Nikolaj Kunsthal
Bremerholm
Lille Kongensg.
Magasin
Det Kongelige Teater
Vingårdstr.
Asylg.
Lakseg.
Holmenskanal
Tordenskjoldsgade
Gammeltorv
Nygade
Vimmelskaftet
Knabrostr.
Badstuestr.
Hyskenstr.
Læderstr.
Højbro Plads
Kunstforeningen GL Strand
Gammel Strand
Fortunstr.
Admiralgade
Nikolajgade
Nytorv
Domhuset
Kattesundet
Brolæggerstr.
Rådhusstr.
Kompagnistræde
Naboløs
Snareg.
Vindebrogade
Christiansborg Slotskirke
Ved Stranden
Børsgade
Holmens Bro
Holmens Kirke
Havnegade
Niels Juelsg.
Nationalbanken
Hestemøllestr.
Magstr.
Nybrogade
Thorvaldsens Museum
Ruinerne Under Christiansborg
Christiansborgs Slotsplads
Porthusgade
Farvergade
Vandkunsten
Christiansborg Slot
Folketinget
Børsbroen
Børsen
Slotsholmsgade
Christian IV's Bro
Vester Voldgade
Løngangstr.
Stormbroen
Kongelige Stalde og Kareter
Rigsdagsgården
SLOTSHOLMEN
Teatermuseet
Stormgade
Nationalmuseet
Marmorbroen
Tøjhusgade
Bibliotekshaven
Provianthuset
Knippelsbro
Københavns Museum
Ny Vestergade
Prinsens Bro
Frederiksholms Kanal
Tøjhusmuseet
Danish Jødisk Museum
H.C. Andersens Boulevard
Det Gyldne Tårn
Dantes Plads
Ny Kongensgade
Christians Brygge
Black Diamond Det Kongelige Bibliotek
Kongens Bryghus
Ny Carlsberg Glyptotek
Vester Voldgade
Bryghusbroen
Bryghuspladsen
BLOX Dansk Arkitektur Center
Cirkelbroen
Christianskirke
Nicolai Eigtveds Gade
Johan Semps Gade
Hammershøis Kaj
Ved Glyptoteket
Puggårdsgade
Niels Brocks Gade
Anker Heegårds Gade
Christiansborggade
Københavns Havn
Voldgården
Otto Mønsteds Gade
Rysensteensgade
Lille Langebro
Applebys plads
Politigården (Police HQ)
Hambrosgade
Otto Mønsteds plads
Langebro
Langebrogade
Politiorvet
Kalvebod Brygge
Kalvebod Bastion
Mitchellsg.
Kalvebod Bølge
Islands Brygge Harbour Baths
Stadsgraven
0
200 m
200 yds
© Copyright Time Out Group 2019
12
13
14
15
16
17
O
P
Q
R

TIVOLI

Charming Tivoli has a special place in Danish culture. This central hub of the city, steps from Central Station, is full of places to play, from Monstrum playgrounds to rollercoasters, a boating lake, and gardens stalked by strutting peacocks. The inspiration for Walt Disney's Disneyland, it couldn't be further from the shameless commercialism of the American theme park today, with cute corners, little shops selling handmade items, specialist restaurants and a fairy-tale feeling. Note though, that there are plenty of snack stalls, candyfloss and some steepish entry fees (*see p70*), so it's not the perfect paradise...

Tivoli Gardens has been going strong since 1843 and was often visited by Hans Christian Andersen. The real charm of the place is that it has something for everyone – older people who love the gardens and sense of nostalgia as much as children who want to go on the gentle rides, and teens and adults who are seeking a thrill. Evenings are lit up with fairy lights; on select Fridays in summer, entry includes Friday Rock, a concert given by either a major Danish artist or an international touring band or singer. Michael Jackson tried (unsuccessfully) to buy the whole place after he played there in the early 1990s; more recent performers included Lauryn Hill and Jason Derulo. For more about music, ballet and drama at Tivoli, *see p205*.

As well as being an amusement park, Tivoli is quite the diner's haven. Lots of people will bring a picnic, which works well on a sunny day on the lawns; you can also buy a wide array of traditional fairground-style food – hot dogs, ice-cream, sweets, donuts and more – from the park's snack stalls, and then there are the restaurants (*see p69*). In 2018, a food hall opened on the Bernstoffsgade side of Tivoli, opposite Central Station, and rapidly became a popular place to eat, with a range of bakeries, burger bars, sushi stalls and international food. It's not exactly cheap, but sits somewhere between the snack stalls and the other attraction in Tivoli: fine dining. Inside the park itself, you'll find French bistros and a superb vegetarian restaurant, Asian food from the Michelin-starred chef Henrik Yde, and a specialist coffee, cake and champagne café.

Tivoli is a place of tradition, and it's customary for kids to celebrate their birthday here every year, just as their parents did before them; but recent years have brought some changes. Now open in winter, beyond the Christmas season, and at Halloween as well as in the summer, you can expect to see lavishly decorated settings with fake snow, a traditional Christmas scene or dancing pumpkins, as well as a backdrop to delight you on long summer nights.

History

Like most Copenhagen landmarks, Tivoli has royal roots. In 1841, King Christian VIII was vexed by the burgeoning civil unrest in his country and his increasingly untenable position as absolute monarch, and so he allowed the Danish architect Georg Carstensen to build the park as

❤ Time to eat & drink

Best for board games
Bastard *p88*

The city's best sun deck
The rooftop café at BLOX *p91*

A culture-filled brunch
Restaurant Smör *p97*

Inventive cocktails
Ruby *p88*

Organic street food
DØP organic hot dog stand *p78*

Tea, cakes and palm trees
Picnic at Glyptoteket *p74*

Vegetarian food to write home about
Gemyse Tivoli *p69*

❤ Time to shop

The best fairy lights and gløgg
Tivoli's Christmas Market *p72 and p187*

Danish chocolate treats
Summerbird *p86*

Gifts at pocket money prices
Søstrene Grene *p79*

Sweet treats
Sømods Bolcher *p86*

A temple to Scandinavian design
Illums Bolighus *p78*

Gemyse Tivoli

a distraction. 'When people amuse themselves they forget politics', the king is reputed to have said. Carstensen, a self-made publishing magnate and son of a diplomat, was born in Algiers in 1812. Tivoli grew out of a carnival he arranged for his readers in Kongens Nytorv. The park opened on 15 August 1843, and on its first day welcomed 16,000 visitors, Hans Christian Andersen among them.

Unlike many other amusement parks, Tivoli is now right in the centre of the city. But it wasn't always so. When it was built, the park stood in the countryside among fields dotted with cattle and crops, on land that was once part of Copenhagen's old fortifications, donated by the government. Today, Tivoli Lake is the model of picturesque charm – with flower borders, weeping willows and, at night, illuminated artificial dragonflies – but it used to be part of the city's defensive moat (the remains of which can be seen in the lakes of Botanisk Have Ørstedsparken and Østre Anlæg park).

In 1944, Tivoli's peace was shattered by the occupying forces of Nazi Germany, who were quick to recognise the significance of the park to the Danish people. They used it as a target for retaliatory attacks following the increased activity of the Danish Resistance. The main victim was the original Concert Hall; however, within a week the resilient Danes had erected a tent in the grounds to replace it. A permanent, new hall (still standing) was built in 1956.

Many of the buildings constructed in Tivoli in the post-war era were seen by Denmark's architects as an opportunity to let their creative hair down, and so the park is packed with boisterous structures.

Restaurants

Brdr. Price in Tivoli ♕♕

Tivoli, Vesterbrogade 3 (38 41 51 51, https://brdr-price.dk/tivoli). Train København H. ***Open*** *noon-3.30pm, 4.30-10pm daily during Tivoli seasons (see p70).* ***Map*** *p66 N15* ❷ Danish

This might be one of the most typical places to eat Danish food – *smørrebrød* topped with herring, liver pâté or salmon – that we've ever come across. Located in a beautiful glasshouse with a history stretching back to the very start of Tivoli, this restaurant, run by two brothers, is known for its classic lunches. It also has a kids' menu. Evening meals include the likes of chicken liver mousse followed by steak or the catch of the day, with pineapple soaked in rum and served with ice cream to finish. Not experimental, but sometimes classic is what you're looking for.

❤ Gemyse Tivoli ♕♕

Tivoli, Bernstorffsgade 5 (88 70 00 00, www.nimb.dk/gemyse). Train København H. ***Open*** *11am-10pm daily during Tivoli seasons (see p70).* ***Map*** *p66 N15* ❹ Vegetarian

This super-special vegetarian restaurant is run by Mette Dahlgaard and serves beautifully prepared dishes using organic vegetables, topped with herbs from its own kitchen garden. The menu includes a special of six green courses served 'family style' for the whole table to enjoy, along with individual dishes. While not a full 'New Nordic' experience, it certainly has a flavour of it, alongside dishes that add a taste of Asia and the Middle East. For non-vegetarians, fish and meat servings can be added. Dishes hover around the 110kr mark and include the likes of pickled beetroot, tortilla of butternut squash and nasturtium, and roasted pear with yuzu and parsley. A drinks-matched menu can also be ordered. As well as the dining option, you can drop in for coffee and snacks: the kitchen garden has bonfires where you can bake bread, roast marshmallows or make your own popcorn.

Nimb Brasserie ♕♕

Nimb Hotel, Bernstorffsgade 5 (88 70 00 10, www.nimb.dk). Train København H. ***Open*** *7am-10pm daily.* ***Map*** *p66 M15* ❺ Modern European

French with a Danish accent, this restaurant in the city's most exclusive boutique hotel is the setting for a long and luxurious lunch or dinner. Previously run by Thomas Herman, it is a relaxed Nordic-infused space serving European brasserie classics for breakfast, lunch and dinner. Main courses include grilled rib-eye steak with bordelaise

❤ A tour of Tivoli

Vesterbrogade 3 (33 15 10 01, www.tivoli.dk). Train København H. ***Winter season*** *1-24 Feb open daily.* ***Summer season*** *4 Apr-22 Sept open daily. Check website for general opening hours and for* ***Christmas*** *and* ***Halloween*** *dates and times, which vary.* ***Ticket centre*** *11am-8pm daily.* ***Admission*** *130-175kr (the more expensive price is charged for major concerts and on Fri after 7pm); 60kr 3-7 year-olds; free under-3s. Multi-ride tickets and packages are also available.* ***Map*** *p66 N15.*

Enter the gardens through the main gate on Vesterbrogade. This Renaissance-inspired confection dating from 1889 and decorated with Corinthian columns and a dome is by far the grandest of Tivoli's three entrances.

Tivoli is a riotous collage of architectural styles, from Moorish palaces to Chinese towers, and everything in between. The oldest building in the park is the 1874 Chinese-style **Peacock Theatre** (*see p205*), which you'll see on your right as you come in through the Nordic village area. Also on your right after the main gate is a statue to the garden's architect, Georg Carstensen.

Continue ahead to see the extraordinary Moorish façade of **Nimb Brasserie**, part of the super-chic Nimb Hotel, and a **Perspex fountain** (the Boblespringvandet) with bubbling tubes, like a gigantic lava lamp. It was designed by the Nobel Prize-winning Danish physicist Niels Bohr. In front of you is **Plænen** (the Lawn; *see p205*), the open-air concert venue with capacity for 8,500 people, and beyond that is the 1956 **Tivolis Koncertsal** (concert hall, *see p205*), a camp orgy of pastel colours. This area also includes all the traditional fun of the fair, with shooting alleys, electronic arcade games, a hall of mirrors, bumper cars, a test-your-strength machine, a chamber of horrors, the unintentionally creepy HC Andersen fairy-tale ride and Det Muntre Køkken (The Crazy Kitchen), where you can vent pent-up frustration by hurling tennis balls at crockery targets.

Talking of kitchens, there's plenty of food to choose from in this area, including hot dog stands, popcorn and the **Tivoli Food Hall** (*see p72*), which is accessed via the park to the west and has a wealth of fast-food options. If you have a ticket to Tivoli you will be checked in and out.

There are over 30 rides to choose from in Tivoli, from tame roundabouts decorated with winsome HC Andersen characters, to the newer **Star Flyer** carousel and the mad exhilaration of **Det Gyldne Tårn** (The Golden Tower), a vertical drop built in 1999, with views of Sweden from the top. The tower was likened by one sniffy critic to a high-tension pylon, but few rides unleash the butterflies with quite the force of this terrifying 63-metre (207-foot) vertical drop. Predictably, the structure – which, like

much of Tivoli, is designed in a faux-Arabian style – has prompted accusations of blatant Disneyfication from the older generation of Tivoleans. But if you only go on one ride, make it the **Rutschebanen**, the wooden rollercoaster which dates to 1914 and offers a chance to have your photo taken while you dive and swoop around the track.

Further on, in the far left-hand corner, an Oriental theme continues through the **Chinese Pagoda**, which overlooks a small boating lake – a legacy of Georg Carstensen's peripatetic childhood, which fuelled a love of exotic cultures.

The western side of the park is dominated by a lake, complete with fake pirate boat (fun to climb aboard as well as being a restaurant), a Monstrum-designed playground, rides for smaller children and gardens with light installations by Olafur Eliasson. Many visitors, particularly the elderly who flock here in their thousands, come simply to enjoy the flora. Within its perimeter fence Tivoli has 850 trees (including lime, chestnut, weeping willow and elm) and many more flowers. You're also likely to find peacocks strutting about the grounds.

As day turns to evening, there are some great places to eat. Look out in particular for **Gemyse Tivoli** (*see p69*), a superb vegetarian restaurant and **Brdr. Price** (*see p69*), for traditional and super-stylish Danish food. The theme park puts on shows most nights of the week, including traditional theatre and musicals in the **Glassalen** and open-air gigs in summer in **Plænen**. Many don't need pre-booking and can be attended if you just pay for entry to the park – check the precise times and ticketing requirements on the website before you go.

In the know
Practicalities

There are three entrances to Tivoli: the main gate is on Vesterbrogade (*see above*); another is located opposite the main entrance to Hovedbanegården (Central Station); and the third is across the road from the Ny Carlsberg Glyptotek.

There are luggage lockers at the park, making it easy if you're on the move with suitcases. If you are travelling with small children, you can also rent pushchairs at the entrance to save carrying them when their legs tire. There are baby-changing rooms throughout the park and a specialist area near the the Rasmus Klump playground allows you to heat baby food. Discounts are available on parking if you park at the APCOA car park nearby. The Tivoli app is easy to download and includes a map of the gardens plus an updated list of the day's events.

sauce, roast duck breast with beetroot, and roast lobster with lemon, salad and mayonnaise. The theatre menu is a two-hour meal starting at 5pm, fitting with Tivoli's entertainment schedule. An organic bakery serves up pastries for morning and mid-afternoon breaks.

Cafés & bars

Bryggeriet Apollo

Tivoli, Vesterbrogade 3 (33 12 33 13, www. bryggeriet.dk). Train København H. ***Open*** *Bar 11am-midnight daily. Kitchen 11am-10.30pm* ***Map*** *p66 M15* ❹

For a decent pint at Tivoli, head to the Bryggeriet Apollo, Copenhagen's first microbrewery, situated next to the main Tivoli entrance. The food is fairly standard tourist fodder.

Cakenhagen

Tivoli, Vesterbrogade 3 (88 70 00 10, www. nimb.dk/da/cakenhagen). Train København H. ***Open*** *11am-10pm Mon-Sat, 11am-9pm Sun.* ***Map*** *p66 M15* ❽

Cakenhagen serves up whimsical Danish cakes with a French overtone, accompanied by the finest champagne and a dollop of whipped cream. Typically, you have to pay to enter Tivoli to eat here; outside the main Tivoli opening times, you can access the café via Nimb Hotel. There are always at least 12 types of cake to choose from, with a couple of salty and savoury items on the menu too.

Fru Nimb

Tivoli, Vesterbrogade 3 (88 70 00 00, www. nimb.dk/da/frunimb). Train København H. ***Open*** *noon-4pm, 5-10pm daily.* ***Map*** *p66 N15* ⓮

Named after Mrs Louise Nimb, its founder in the 19th century, Fru Nimb is a *smørrebrød* restaurant/café, serving lunch and dinner plus a theatre menu. Expect classic open-faced sandwich combinations on rye bread including fried plaice with remoulade and lemon, roast beef with horseradish, and chicken salad with mushrooms and bacon, made to Mrs Nimb's own recipe.

Tivoli Food Hall

Tivoli, Vesterbrogade 3 (33 15 10 01, www. tivoligardens.com). Train København H. ***Open*** *11am-9pm Mon-Thur, Sun; 7am-11pm Fri-Sat; 9am-9pm Sun. Note that Brødflov sandwich shop as well as Hellernes Smørrebrød open slightly earlier than the rest of the stalls.* ***Map*** *p66 M15* ㉕

Across the road from Central Station, the hall is open to the public on the main street with entry to those with Tivoli tickets on the other side. You do not need to buy Tivoli tickets to dine here and it is open all year round. Choose from over 15 food stalls serving anything from burgers to Mexican food, *smørrebrød* and sushi. There are some fun bars and the place is always lively. Coffee shops serving a range of baked goods do well early in the morning, while in the afternoon/evening, the bars and burger joints – including Copenhagen staple **Cocks & Cows** and **Bobbabella**, fast food produced by the owners of Michelin-starred restaurant Kadeau – come into play.

Shops & services

Illums Bolighus Tivoli

Tivoli, Vesterbrogade 3 (33 91 18 45, www. illumsbolighus.com). Train København H. ***Open*** *11am-9pm Mon-Thu; 11am-11pm Fri-Sat, 11am-10pm Sun.* ***Map*** *p66 N15* ⓬ *Homewares*

Homeware and gifts from Danish and Scandinavian brands, such as Royal Copenhagen, Georg Jensen and Design House Stockholm. **Other location** *see p78.*

❤ Tivoli's Christmas Market

Tivoli, Vesterbrogade 3 (33 15 10 01, www. tivoligardens.com). Train København H. ***Open*** *late Nov-31 Dec.* ***Map*** *p66 N15* ㉘ *Christmas market*

The Christmas Market has been a fixture since 1994, with stalls selling *gløgg* (mulled wine), traditional Scandinavian decorations, candles, chocolates and festive foodstuffs, and craft-style gifts. Complete with moving snowmen, a Christmas train and fake snow everywhere, it's a fun place to shop, although you do have to pay entry to access it, unlike the city's other Christmas markets. *See also p187.*

AROUND VESTERPORT & CENTRAL STATION

Across the road from the Radisson Collection hotel you'll find the **Visit Copenhagen Tourist Information Bureau** (*see p247*). A little further down the street stands **Hovedbanegården** (Central Station), from where you can catch trains to the airport, the rest of the country and beyond. The station has two main entrances, one on Bernstoffsgade directly opposite Tivoli and Tivoli Food Hall, and the other on Vesterbrogade, where a fleet of taxis wait beside busy bike racks.

Immediately north of the main entrance to Tivoli is Copenhagen's cinema district. The most striking cinema to visit is the

Palads Teatret (*see p193*), a bright pink, orange, blue and yellow building dating from 1912 and built on the site of an old station. It has 17 screens and regularly shows international films with Danish subtitles. It's on Axeltorv, steps away from **Axel Towers**, five round towers that house shops, the Michelin-starred restaurant, **Trio** (*see p73*), and offices. These groundbreaking buildings opened in 2017 with a view to revitalise an area that is between the old and new parts of the city and in need of a focal point. With curvaceous shapes and interesting views along panels of zinc, architecturally interested photographers have had a field day. You can take a walk around or just have a coffee or beer in Trio's bar and enjoy the view.

Restaurants

Trio

Axel Towers, Jernebanegade 11 (44 22 74 74, www.restauranttrio.dk). Train København H. ***Open*** *Restaurant noon-2.30pm, 5.30-10pm Mon-Sat. Cocktail bar 3pm-midnight Mon-Thur; noon-2am Fri; 3pm-2am Sat.* ***Map*** *p66 M14* ⑬ *Modern Danish*

Contemporary Danish design melds with unique flavour combinations and exceptional views in this restaurant from the team behind Michelin-starred AOC and No.2. Run by renowned restaurateur Christian Aarø, it is on the 10th floor of Axel Towers and serves the likes of beef wellington with black mushrooms; lobster; sautéed beef with bordelaise sauce and marrow; with liquorice meringue and pickled blackberries for dessert. The restaurant is open for lunch (two courses for 300kr, three for 400kr and four for 500kr) and dinner (six courses for 695kr or à la carte from around 145-195kr per course).

Head down a level to discover the sweeping circular bar, with herringbone floors and exposed concrete walls. It's a great place for a cocktail or two. Some of the most talked about loos in the city, Trio's toilets also enjoy a spectacular view.

Cafés & bars

Library Bar

Copenhagen Plaza, Bernstorffsgade 4 (33 14 92 62, www.librarybar.dk). Train København H. ***Open*** *4pm-midnight Mon-Thur; 4pm-1am Fri-Sat.* ***Map*** *p66 M15* ⑰

Most visitors are taken by the characterful wood panelling, crystal chandeliers, book-lined walls and Chesterfield-style sofas of this faux-exclusive bar, voted one of the finest gentlemen's bars in the world by *Forbes Magazine*. Steak and cocktail nights take place on a Wednesday and Thursday, offering a 300g rib-eye plus triple-cooked fries and a cocktail for a bargain 299kr (normally 465kr). Book a table via dinnerbooking.com.

RÅDHUSPLADSEN & NY CARLSBERG GLYPTOTEK

Tivoli's neighbour to the east is **Rådhuspladsen** (Town Hall Square). Though the square is less architecturally appealing than Kongens Nytorv at the other end of Strøget, Denmark's answer to Times Square or Piccadilly Circus is friendlier to pedestrians, but only just (watch out for cyclists!). With a new metro station set to open in summer 2019, after nearly 10 years of building activity, the square will finally be fully open and operational for the public. Stretching out from the Rådhuset (Town Hall), the square is typically full of shoppers, sightseers, tour parties and *pølse* (hot dog) sellers (*see p42* Sausage Wagons) and, at weekends and on holidays, street performers, gatherings and protests. It is an important focal point, and in the Danish version of Monopoly, is the most expensive piece of real estate on the board.

Rådhuspladsen was originally a hay market located outside the medieval city walls; it is also where the last western city gate stood until the middle of the 19th century. All that remains of the medieval fortifications today is **Jarmers Tårn**, a small ruin located on a roundabout in Jarmers Plads (at the north end of Vester Voldgade). In 1888, the square hosted a million visitors at a huge exhibition of industry, agriculture and art. At the time, the 'square' was in fact a shell shape, like the famous piazza in Siena, but the pressures of the internal combustion engine soon saw its corners squared off.

There's a lot to see in and around this area. On **HC Andersens Boulevard** is a large statue of, guess who? In front of that stands the striking Dragon Fountain, by Joachim Skovgaard. Nearby is a small carved stone pillar that marks the centre or 'zero point' of Copenhagen. And high on the corner of the Unibank building on HC Andersens Boulevard and Vesterbrogade is one of the city's quirkiest talking points: a barometer erected in 1936 and designed by Danish artist E Utzon-Frank, featuring a girl on a bicycle (if it's fair) or under an umbrella (if it's not).

Towering over the opposite side of Rådhuspladsen is a pillar crowned by a bronze statue of two Vikings blowing *lurs* (S-shaped bronze horns). These are similar to the ones you can see in the **Nationalmuseet** (*see p93*). The statue, by

Siegfried Wagner, was erected in 1914. Next to the pillar is the elegant façade of the Anton Rosen-designed **Palace Hotel**.

Rådhuset, situated on the southern side of Rådhuspladsen, is the city's administrative and political heart, as well as a venue for exhibitions and concerts. Denmark's second-tallest tower (105.6 metres/346 feet; the tallest is part of Christiansborg Slot), located on its east side, is almost incidental to the decorative splendour of this, the sixth town hall in Copenhagen's history.

To the south-east of Tivoli and Rådhuspladsen is the **Ny Carlsberg Glyptotek** (*see opposite*), which houses a breathtaking line-up of ancient sculptures and the largest collection of Etruscan art outside Italy, as well as an exceptional array of more recent Danish and French paintings and sculpture. Follow this road to its conclusion and you'll find the inner harbour waterfront, bustling with people enjoying the water on a sunny day.

Sights & museums

Københavns Museum

Stormgade 18 (33 21 07 72, www.copenhagen.dk). Train København H, or bus 6A, 26. ***Open*** *8.30am-6pm Mon-Fri; 10am-5 pm Sat, Sun.* ***Admission*** *75kr; check the website for reductions.* ***Map*** *p66 O15.*

Reopened in 2019, this museum charts the history of Copenhagen from prehistory through its incarnation as a fishing village to today's cosmopolitan capital. Centrally located on the main tourist drag, it aims to showcase international exhibits to appeal to both locals and visitors. In addition to three floors of history, there's a great café and shop; its all set in an iconic and rather beautiful building full of 19th-century stained-glass windows and frescoes. In the kids' workshop, children get the chance to be an archaeologist, among other things.

Rådhuset

Rådhuset

Rådhuspladsen (33 66 25 85, www.kk.dk/artikel/rundvisninger-paa-raadhuset). Train København H. ***Open*** *9am-4pm Mon-Fri; 9.30am-1pm Sat. Guided tours in English 1pm Mon-Fri; 10am Sat. Rådhuset Tower tour 11am, 2pm Mon-Fri; noon Sat.* ***Admission*** *Guided tour 50kr. Rådhuset Tower tour 30kr. Jens Olsens Clock free.* ***Map*** *p66 N14.*

Completed in 1905, Rådhuset (Town Hall) has been the site of numerous elections; home to as many city administrations; has endured occupation by the Nazis in World War II; and has welcomed home returning football heroes.

At first glance, the building – inspired, like the square, by its counterpart in Siena – looks imposing, monolithic and a little bit dull, but at close quarters this National Romantic masterpiece by architect Martin Nyrop reveals its witty, sometimes gruesome, but invariably exuberant architectural detail. There's a balcony above the front door, and above that a golden statue of Bishop Absalon by HW Bissen. Higher up, lining the front of the roof, stand six watchmen, separated by the flagpole (watch for a swallow-tailed flag on special occasions, such as the Queen's birthday). This rises from the city's coat of arms, presented in 1661 by King Frederik III in thanks for the people's support during a siege. Across the façade are countless gargoyles, reliefs and individually crafted stone and iron figures.

Inside, Rådhuset's endless corridors, halls, council chambers and meeting rooms offer a decorative feast. Highlights include busts of HC Andersen, the physicist Niels Bohr, Professor Nyrop and the sculptor Bertel Thorvaldsen; the library; the banqueting hall; and Jens Olsen's World Clock. The last is a horological masterpiece that cost one million kroner to build (and took 27 years to make – it was first set in 1955). It's incredibly accurate, losing only milliseconds each century. The clock is in a room on the right by the main door.

Cafés & bars

The area around Rådhuspladsen lacks decent places to eat, with a few fast-food outlets, average sushi joints and *pølsevogne* (*see p42* Sausage Wagons), but not much else.

❤ Picnic at Glyptoteket

Dantes Plads 7 (33 41 81 28, www.glyptoteket.dk). Train København H. ***Open*** *11am-6pm Tue-Sun; 11am-10pm Thu, closed Mon.* ***Map*** *p66 O15* ⑳

❤ Ny Carlsberg Glyptotek

Dantes Plads 7 (33 41 81 41, www.glyptoteket.dk). Train København H. ***Open*** *11am-6pm Tue-Sun, Fri-Sun; 11am-10pm Thu.* ***Admission*** *115kr; 85kr under 27s and students; free under-18s. Free to all on Tue.* ***Map*** *p66 O15.*

If you're looking for somewhere to escape a rainy day, wintry weather or the busy city, there is nowhere better than this. With the Winter Garden at its heart, plus a fantastic café, inspiring sculpture collection, design-led shop and special exhibitions, it has plenty to recommend it.

The original *glyptotek* (sculpture collection) was donated to the city in 1888 by brewer/philanthropist Carl Jacobsen (son of Carlsberg brewery's founder) and his wife Ottilia. He intended the museum to have 'a beauty all its own, to which the people of the city would feel themselves irresistibly drawn.' His vision has been financed, run and expanded for more than a century by the Ny Carlsberg Foundation, and is housed in a building rich in architectural delights that was specially designed for the original collection by Vilhelm Dahlerup and Hack Kampmann. The highlight of the old building is the glass-domed Winter Garden – a steamy palm house bursting with subtropical plants and graced by Kai Nielsen's beautiful fountain piece, *Water Mother with Children*.

The Glyptotek's thousands of pieces can be roughly divided into two groups: ancient Mediterranean; and 18th- and 19th-century French and Danish. The first four rooms are dedicated to the oldest pieces, some dating back 5,000 years (the Egyptian hippopotamus is a crowd favourite). The exhibits proceed to trace the history of sculpture from the Sumerians, Assyrians, Persians and Phoenicians, through to a collection of ancient Greek pieces (one of the best in Europe) and some highly entertaining, privately commissioned Roman busts. Jacobsen's Etruscan collection – including bronzes, vases, and stone and terracotta sculptures – is another highlight.

The French painting collection is housed in Henning Larsen's intriguing extension. It includes 35 works by the post-Impressionist Paul Gauguin (*see p76*) and one of only three complete sets of Degas bronzes in the world. There are also paintings by the Impressionist movement's leading lights, including Manet, Renoir, Monet and Pissarro, and a remarkable self-portrait by Cézanne. The rest of the post-Impressionist movement is represented by Van Gogh, Toulouse-Lautrec and Bonnard.

Over 30 works by Auguste Rodin dominate the French sculpture rooms. Anyone who thought that Danish sculpture began and ended with Bertel Thorvaldsen will be surprised by the collection that includes works by other leading lights, such as Dahl, Købke and Eckersberg. However, the collection of sculpture from the Danish Golden Age (1815-50) is surpassed by those of Statens Museum for Kunst (*see p106*) and Den Hirschsprungske Samling (*see p105*).

In the know
Gauguin's Danish period

Paul Gauguin lived in Frederiksberg, at Gammel Kongevej 105 (long since demolished) for one winter. The impoverished artist had met a Danish woman, Mette Sofie Gad, in Paris in 1873; after marrying, they moved to his wife's home. Gauguin never got to grips with the weather, the coldness of the Danes or the suffocating ways of the bourgeoisie, though he did stay long enough to hold his first ever exhibition at the Kunstforeningen (Arts Society). Gauguin fathered five children with Mette during their nine-year marriage (the rest of which they spent in France), and has over 50 descendants living in Denmark. Several of his works are displayed in the Ny Carlsberg Glyptotek (*see p75*).

Set in the lovely Winter Garden, Picnic is a great example of Danish café style. The atmosphere is charming and food delicious, with plenty of local specialities from curried herring to *smørrebrød*, croissants and soups (85-150kr). The kids' menu includes a DIY pitta bread option with chicken meatballs. Just as nice is their afternoon tea menu, cakes and coffee. It's a classic place to meet friends for a coffee and a chat. The café is also open on Thursday evenings and it is possible to book a table; note that you have to pay for entry to the museum on every day but Tuesday.

STRØGET

Broadly speaking, Strøget becomes more upmarket as you head east, with the poshest shops, including Gucci and Prada, as well as global chains such as Urban Outfitters and Topshop, clustered towards Kongens Nytorv. The 'posh watershed' is Amagertorv, where you'll find the Royal Copenhagen stores. The middle of Strøget from Amagertorv to Gammeltorv and Nytorv is middlebrow, dotted with the likes of H&M and Zara, and with backpacker bars and a few strip clubs lowering the tone around Gammeltorv.

In truth, you'll find more interesting, independent and specialist shops off the main drag – on parallel streets, in Nørrebro's hipster lanes and along Istedgade; but with quirky side alleys, churches, beautiful façades and a heart-of-the-city location, there is always something new to see and interesting people to watch along this main street.

The first stretch of Strøget leads from the town hall square *(see p73)* to Nytorv (not to be confused with Kongens Nytorv, which is a little further on). A jumble of pizza stalls and cut-price clothing shops, it is not an inspiring start to your walk, but stick with it, it gets better.

In 1848, **Nytorv** served as the starting point for the relatively peaceful march by 10,000 Copenhageners on Christiansborg Slot, demanding the end of absolute monarchy. Frederik VII had conceded defeat before they even arrived. The philosopher

Strøget

Søren Kierkegaard lived for a while on Nytorv in a house on a site now occupied by Den Danske Bank. Look out, too, for the outline of Copenhagen's first town hall (before it moved to Rådhuspladsen) traced in the paving of Nytorv beneath the fruit and veg sellers who usually pitch here.

Of interest chiefly because of its grand neoclassical façade featuring six Ionic columns, Copenhagen's imposing and elegant **Domhuset** (Court House) on Nytorv was built in 1805-15 (work was suspended for a while in 1807 due to the bombardment by the British). The dusky pink building was designed by CF Hansen, who was also responsible for Vor Frue Kirke (*see p82*), just a short walk away up Nørregade. Domhuset was built on the site of the former town hall and, until 1905, served as both courthouse and town hall. Today, it houses court rooms, conference rooms and chambers. The nearby Slutterigade (Prison Street) annexe was built as a jail in 1816 and converted to court rooms and chambers in 1944. It's attached to Domhuset via two recently restored arches, one of which is known as the **Bridge of Sighs** (as are many such crossings around the world) – prisoners, bemoaning their fate, are led across it when going to and from the court rooms.

When visitors arrive in Gammeltorv, one of the first things they notice (apart from the neon lights of the neighbouring bars and stripclubs) is the **Caritas Springvandet** (Charity Fountain). Dating from 1608, this Renaissance masterpiece, made of copper, depicts a pregnant woman and two children with fishy gargoyles at their feet. On royal birthdays, golden apples dance on the water jets. During the 14th century, **Gammeltorv**, the oldest square in the city, was the hub of Copenhagen, a busy market, meeting place and (occasional) jousting site for the 5,000 residents of what was then the largest settlement in northern Europe.

The next major sight as you continue east along Strøget is **Helligåndskirken** (Church of the Holy Spirit), dating from 1400. It is a short stroll from here to **Amagertorv**, the central part of Strøget and a place to see and be seen. In the 17th century, a law was passed to the effect that all the produce grown on Amager island (where Copenhagen Airport is now located) had to be sold at the market here. This has since been one of Copenhagen's main markets and meeting places, and though the stalls have long gone, the fountain is still much used as a rendezvous. Amagertorv is also the site of **Royal Copenhagen**, the pride of the city's retail portfolio, formed from the amalgamation of three Strøget institutions in 1985. Adjoining Amagertorv, towards Slotsholmen, is another busy square, Højbro Plads. Its main feature is a 1902 equestrian statue of **Bishop Absalon**, the founder of Copenhagen, by HW Bissen; it has an inscription that reads: 'He was courageous, wise and far-sighted, a friend of scholarship, in the intensity of his striving a true son of Denmark.'

The eastern end of Strøget, near Kongens Nytorv, is home to lots of designer fashion stores. **Illum** (*see p78*), the city's premier department store, stretches to the corner of Købmagergade, while **Magasin du Nord** (*see p111*), the other grande dame of retail, sits just beyond it at Kongens Nytorv. Head south of Illum and you'll come to the historic Nikolaj Plads, with Sankt Nikolaj Kirke. The church dates from the 13th century, but the fire of 1795 destroyed all but the tower; it was rebuilt in 1917 and has been reborn today as a venue for innovative art and culture: **Nikolaj Kunsthal**.

In the know
Getting around

This area is best explored on foot. Avoid, if you can, taking your wheeled suitcase with you as you explore – many streets are cobbled. It is also easy to cycle around this area but beware of other tourists stepping into the bike lanes – it can be very busy, particularly around the shopping streets and key attractions. Know that you have to jump off and push your bike on Strøget, but the same does not go for the parallel streets. Wherever you are staying in the city, it is very easy to take a bus, train or metro into Central Station and explore on foot – nearly all routes and roads lead here.

Sights & museums

Nikolaj Kunsthal

Nikolaj Plads 10 (33 18 17 80, www.nikolajkunsthal.dk). Metro Kongens Nytorv. ***Open*** *noon-6pm Tue-Fri, 11am-5pm Sat-Sun.* ***Admission*** *70kr; 50kr students; 30kr children 2-17. Free on Wed.* ***Map*** *p66 Q13.*

Defiantly not a church, this former church is a centre for international contemporary art both inside and out. Expect to see anything from an immersive installation to Danish street art and graffiti. Each year sees between seven and nine Danish and international exhibitions, mainly on the theme of experimental and innovative art, with at least one catering for children, and one celebrating an older artist whose work has influenced contemporary art.

Cafés & bars

Café Europa

Amagertorv 1 (33 14 28 89, www.europa1989.dk). Metro Kongens Nytorv. ***Open*** *7.45am-10pm Mon-Thur; 7.45am-11pm Fri-Sat; 9am-10pm Sun.* ***Map*** *p66 Q13* ❺

With a location right in the heart of the shopping district on Amagertorv, Café Europa is one of the city's most popular meeting places. Prices can be high, but the food isn't bad and it's a nice place to stop off for a drink during an afternoon's shopping. Sandwiches are reasonable value. There's seating outside in summer with a view of buskers at the fountain.

Café Norden

Østergade 61 (33 11 77 91, www.cafenorden.dk). Metro Kongens Nytorv. ***Open*** *8.30am-11pm Sun-Thur; 8.30am-midnight Fri-Sat.* ***Map*** *p66 Q13* ❻

This large and grand café overlooks Amagertorv, with a two-storey, Parisian-style interior, complete with chandeliers and wood panelling. Pricey because of its location, and usually busy, it serves breakfasts, snacks, coffee and lunches, including soup and *smørrebrød* for shopping-fatigued city-goers.

❤ DØP organic hot dog stand

Outside Heligandskirken (30 20 40 25, www.doep.dk). Metro Kongens Nytorv. ***Open*** *11am-6.30pm Mon-Sat; 11.30am-5.30pm Sun.* ***Map*** *p66 P13* ⓫

A quick snack that's, well, nearly healthy. As an alternative refuel station for shoppers, DØP serves a variety of different types of sausage in whole grain, slowly risen bread. It's a gourmet take on the typical *pølser* stand, and recommended (try one with everything: onions, remoulade, ketchup, mustard and mashed potato). **Other location** At the foot of the Rundetaarn.

DØP organic hot dog stand

Shops & services

Bang & Olufsen

Østergade 18 (33 11 14 15, www.bang-olufsen.com). Metro Kongens Nytorv. ***Open*** *10am-6pm Mon-Thur; 10am-7pm Fri; 10am-4pm Sat.* ***Map*** *p66 R12* ❸ *Electronics*

Danes are proud of this smart brand of televisions and stereos, the minimalist modern tech masterpieces. This store has a large selection from their covetable range of electronics. **Other location** Falkoner Alle 7, Frederiksberg (71 99 98 88).

Georg Jensen

Amagertorv 4 (33 11 40 80, www.georgjensen.com). Metro Kongens Nytorv. ***Open*** *10am-6pm Mon-Sat.* ***Map*** *p66 Q13* ❽ *Accessories*

The undisputed daddy of Danish silver design, Jensen's showroom has elaborate flower arrangements artfully complementing the ornate jewellery on display. A museum at the back showcases the history of the company.

Illum

Østergade 52 (33 14 40 02, www.illum.dk). Metro Kongens Nytorv. ***Open*** *10am-8pm daily.* ***Map*** *p66 Q13* ⓫ *Department store*

Illum's interior design and magnificent glass dome, plus food hall on the rooftop, complete with city views gives it the edge over its competitor, Magasin. The ground floor has cosmetics and accessories, and a concession for Danish bike brand Velorbis. Womenswear and menswear by Scandinavian designers (including Acne, Bruuns Bazaar, Ganni, WhyRed and Filippa K) and international labels are on the first and second floors, while the basement houses a branch of supermarket Irma and a café.

❤ Illums Bolighus

Amagertorv 10 (33 14 19 41, www.illumsbolighus.com). Metro Kongens Nytorv. ***Open*** *10am-7pm Mon-Thur, Sat; 10am-8pm Fri; 11am-6pm Sun.* ***Map*** *p66 P13* ⓭ *Homewares*

The Liberty of Copenhagen, Illums Bolighus is a temple to interior design, housed in an inspiring space with plenty to look at. Browse candlesticks, chopping boards and homeware on the ground floor, then head upstairs to admire Danish-designed furniture and more heavyweight items. The homeware arm of department store Illum (*see p78*) features a selection of premium brands including Orrefors, Arabia and Alessi, while connecting doors lead into the Royal Copenhagen, Holmegaard and Georg Jensen shops. As a site for design inspiration, it does not get much better – it's

Scandinavia's premier centre for Danish and international design, celebrating the very best craftsmanship the country has produced over the years. **Other location** Illums Bolighus Tivoli, *see p72*.

Le Klint

Store Kirkestræde 1 (33 11 66 63, www.leklint.com). Metro Kongens Nytorv. ***Open*** *10am-6pm Tue-Fri; 10am-4pm Sat.* ***Map*** *p66 Q13* ⓮ *Homewares*

This is the main stockist for Kaare Klint's trademark concertina-style lampshades, including his perennially popular 'Model 1', folded by hand since 1943.

LEGO Flagship

Vimmelskaftet 37 (52 15 91 57, www.lego.dk). Metro Kongens Nytorv. ***Open*** *10am-6pm Mon-Thur; 10am-7pm Fri; 10am-6pm Sat; 11am-5pm Sun.* ***Map*** *p66 P13* ⓯ *Toys*

The LEGO flagship store consists of three main areas: a 'Pick-a-Brick' wall showcasing the famous colourful bricks; an interactive play area in the centre of the store; and the 'brand ribbon', which runs the circumference of the store and features displays and presentations of fun facts.

Mads Nørgaard

Amagertorv 13-15 (33 12 24 28, www.madsnorgaard.dk). Metro Kongens Nytorv. ***Open*** *10am-6pm Mon-Thur; 10am-7pm Fri; 10am-5pm Sat.* ***Map*** *p66 P13* ⓰ *Fashion*

A wide range of international labels sit alongside Mads Nørgaard's bold and bright own-brand clothing, not forgetting his distinctive striped T-shirts for both sexes and all ages.

Royal Copenhagen

Amagertorv 6 (38 14 96 05, www.royalcopenhagen.com). Metro Kongens Nytorv. ***Open*** *10am-7pm Mon-Fri; 10am-6pm Sat; 11am-4pm Sun.* ***Map*** *p66 P13* ㉒ *Homewares*

The Royal Copenhagen flagship, housed in a 16th-century building, is the place to head for the famous porcelain, whose designs span the traditional to the modern and include the world-famous 'Flora Danica' collection.

❤ Søstrene Grene

Amagertorv 24 (no phone, www.sostrenegrene.com). Metro Kongens Nytorv. ***Open*** *10am-7pm Mon-Fri; 10am-6pm Sat; 11am-5pm Sun.* ***Map*** *p66 P13* ㉕ *Gifts & homewares*

People either love Søstrene Grene's lucky-dip potential or loathe its often brazenly poor-quality stock, but there's no denying that there are gems aplenty lurking among its collection of crockery, toys, bedding, glassware and miscellaneous gifts.

Illums Bolighus

LEGO Flagship

Søstrene Grene

NORTH OF STRØGET

Pisserenden

West of Frue Plads, in an area bordered by Nørregade, Vester Voldgade and Vestergade, lies the liveliest area around Strøget, known as Pisserenden. 'Piss' means the same in Danish as it does in English, and this district was so-named due to its notoriety as a malodorous dwelling place for prostitutes and criminals, until it was purged by the first great fire of 1728. Today, Pisserenden's streets (which include Kattesundet, Vestergade, Larsbjørnsstræde and Teglgårdstræde) are blessed with great restaurants, cafés and bars, and make up Copenhagen's unofficial gay district.

Latin Quarter

North of the middle part of Strøget lies Copenhagen's 'Latin Quarter', all narrow alleyways, cobbled café squares and bustling student life, bordered at its northern end by **Kultorvet**, a large square at the end of Købmagergade.

At the heart of the Latin Quarter is **Gråbrødretorv**, a delightful restaurant square – like Nyhavn without the canal. It comes alive in summer as tables from its (good but costly) restaurants spill out on to the cobbles. The square was created in 1664 after Corfitz Ulfeldt, the secretary of war, had his mansion torn down as punishment for high treason. After a fire in 1728, many of the houses were rebuilt with triangular gable ends, typical of the period. Outdoor gigs are often held here during the Copenhagen Jazz Festival.

West, on Nørregade, is Copenhagen's modest cathedral, **Vor Frue Kirke** (Church of Our Lady), where Crown Prince Frederik married his Australian wife, Mary Donaldson in 2004.

Next to Vor Frue Kirke is a large cobbled square, **Frue Plads**. The rather grimy building opposite the church is part of the **University of Copenhagen**, founded by Christian I in 1479. The building stands on the same site as the original (itself built over the Bishop's Palace); it was designed by Peter Malling and inaugurated by Frederik VI in 1836. The ornate Great Hall is worth a look and, if you have time, pop into the University Library round the corner in Fiolstræde. Halfway up the stairs is a small glass cabinet containing some fragments of a cannon ball and the book in which they were found embedded after the British bombardment. The title of the book, by Marsilius of Padua, is *Defender of Peace*.

Købmagergade and around

Head north-west from Østergade to the area that surrounds Grønnegade, one of Copenhagen's best shopping districts – if you're not short on money and love design, that is. The streets situated between Grønnegade and pedestrianised Købmagergade – Pilestræde, Grønnegade, Ny Adelgade and Ny Østergade – are eminently wanderable, and home to lots of excellent independent fashion shops, with Scandinavian brands dominating. Kronprinsensgade has some particularly good shops and cafés, including Copenhagen's venerated tea emporium and café **A.C. Perchs Thehandel**.

Gråbrødretorv

❤ Rundetårn

Købmagergade 52A (33 73 03 73, www.rundetaarn.dk). Metro/train Nørreport. ***Tower*** *late May-late Sept 10am-8pm daily; late Sept-late May 10am-6pm Thur-Mon, 10am-9pm Tue-Wed.* ***Observatory*** *times vary; see website for details.* ***Admission*** *25kr; 5kr reductions; free under-5s.* ***Map*** *p66 P12.*

One of the few genuinely cheap tourist spots in the city, the Round Tower is unique in European architecture for its cobbled spiral walkway that winds seven and a half times round its core for 209 metres (686 feet), almost to the top of the tower, which is 35 metres (114 feet) above the city. It's a lovely winding walk over photogenic cobbles and under curvaceous white archways to the top, where you will find a kissing seat and a tight set of steep stairs to the open viewing platform. Walk around and see how many quirky spires you can spot, from Vor Frelsers Kirke, with a gold ball at the top, to the Børsen and its four twisted dragon tails. The view stretches as far as the steel ski slope at Amager Bakke. Peter the Great rode all the way to the top in 1716 (the Tsarina followed in a carriage), while a car is said to have driven up in 1902. These days, it's strictly a footpath, with no horses or cars allowed.

Halfway up, an exhibition space (formerly the university library hall) has a changing programme of artistic, scientific and historical displays. There is also an old drop privy that kids love exploring and giggling about, and a section in the centre of the tower with a perspex floor that allows you to stand and look down, down, down. The observatory at the top is sometimes open, with an astronomer on hand to explain what you can see through the telescope. The Rundetårn was deemed such a significant building that, in the 18th century, the Royal Danish Academy of Sciences used it as the main reference point for a survey of Denmark. It certainly has plenty of stories to tell, to go hand in hand with its fairy-tale appeal. One such story is that in the 1800s, the blind niches and bricked up openings around the centre of the tower – where for hundreds of years children have routinely jumped out and said boo to their parents – were decorated with ancient rune stones, a Roman tombstone and a cannon, to delight the enlightenment priest Jacob Nicolai Wilse, who had the idea of creating a kind of mini national museum in these unused spaces. The objects are now in the actual **Nationalmuseet** (*see p93*).

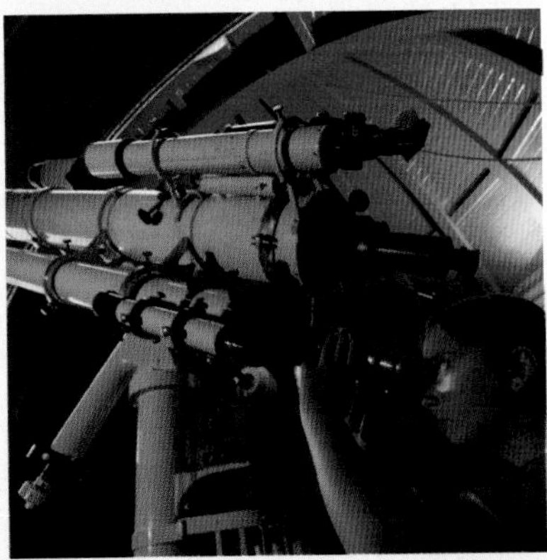

Vor Frue Kirke

A little further up is Købmagergade's main draw: the **Rundetårn** (*see p81*). Completed in 1642 at the behest of Christian IV (it was his last major building project), the red-brick Round Tower was originally intended as an observatory for the nearby university and it is still the oldest functioning observatory in Europe. A stroll up to the top of the tower on the wide cobbles, is pushchair-friendly with plenty of places to take a rest as you go. The view from the top is worth it.

Behind the tower stands **Trinitatiskirke** (Trinity Church). Opposite the Rundetårn you'll find Regensen, built in 1616 as a student hall of residence for the nearby university, and still in use as such today. Round the corner, on Krystalgade, is the city's **Synagoge** (synagogue), dating from 1833.

Sights & museums

Trinitatis Kirke

Pilestræde 67 (33 37 65 40, www.trinitatiskirke.dk). Metro/train Nørreport. ***Open*** *9.30am-4.30pm Mon-Sat; High Mass 10.30am Sun.* ***Admission*** *free.* ***Map*** *p66 P12.*

Trinity Church was erected in 1637, and features a Baroque altar by Friedrich Ehbisch, as well as a three-faced rococo clock from 1757.

Vor Frue Kirke

Nørregade 8 (33 15 10 78, www.koebenhavnsdomkirke.dk). Metro/train Nørreport. ***Open*** *8am-5pm daily.* ***Admission*** *free.* ***Map*** *p66 O13.*

Six churches have stood on this site since 1191, the first five suffering a variety of misfortunes. The destruction of Vor Frue Kirke's art treasures by the Lutherans during the Reformation in the 16th century stands as one of their more barbaric acts. The current structure, by CF Hansen, was consecrated in 1829 and replaced the church destroyed by the British bombardment of 1807. The whitewashed interior is relieved by several Bertel Thorvaldsen sculptures (*see opposite*), including his famous depiction of Christ. The church often hosts musical events.

Restaurants

Bøf & Ost ♛♛

Gråbrødretorv 13 (33 11 99 11, www.boef-ost.dk). Metro/train Nørreport, or Metro Kongens Nytorv. ***Open*** *3-10pm daily.* ***Map*** *p66 P13* ❶ Steakhouse

The restaurant is situated on the southern side of the square in the oldest of the so-called Fire Houses, built after the great fire of 1728 that razed Copenhagen. Chargrilled beef is the house speciality; you can also enjoy a lovely selection of cheeses, from Fourme d'Amerbert to Comté, for 30kr per piece.

Café GL Torv ♛

Gammeltorv 20 (33 12 87 86, www.cafegammeltorv.dk). Metro/train Nørreport, or bus 11A. ***Open*** *11.30am-5pm Mon-Sat; noon-4pm 1st Sun of the month.* ***Map*** *p66 O13* ❸ Traditional Danish

This old-style lunch restaurant is frequented by journalists, local businessmen and lawyers from the nearby courthouse. Offering traditional Danish *smørrebrød* in a small, spartan, cellar café with yellowed ceilings and wood-panelled walls, this is an authentic taste of basic Danish cuisine.

Peder Oxe ♛♛

Gråbrødretorv 11 (33 11 00 77, www.pederoxe.dk). Metro/train Nørreport, or Metro Kongens Nytorv. ***Open*** *11.30am-10.30pm Sun-Thur, 11am-11pm Fri-Sat.* ***Map*** *p66 P13* ❻ Danish

Peder Oxe is sleek, stylish and very popular. The wide-ranging menu covers all the bases, from steaks and burgers, to light lunches of *smørrebrød* and lobster soup, all of which are well presented and reasonably priced. There is also a wine bar in the vaulted cellars.

Denmark's Wandering Hero

Bertel Thorvaldsen, the nation's most famous (and prolific) sculptor

Denmark's greatest sculptor was born in Copenhagen on 19 November 1768. He studied at the Academy of Art, where he won the Gold Medal; then, in 1797, a scholarship sent him to Rome, where he lived for nearly 40 years developing a style that was heavily influenced by Greco-Roman mythology and creating works of a wonderfully majestic, classical beauty, frequently on an epic scale. Thorvaldsen's monument to Pope Pius VII is the only work by a non-Italian in Rome's St Peter's Basilica.

His breakthrough, which catapulted him into the highest echelons of the neoclassical sculpture fraternity, came with the piece *Jason and the Golden Fleece*. It was completed in 1803 and is now housed in the **Thorvaldsens Museum** (*see p96*). His figure of Christ, which can be seen in **Vor Frue Kirke** (*see opposite*), became the model for statues of Christ the world over and remains a religious icon to this day.

Thorvaldsen's return to Copenhagen towards the end of his life helped boost a general artistic revival and contributed to the emergence of a cultural and social essence that is still recognisably Danish today. In 1833, he was appointed Director of the Danish Academy of Fine Arts. Before his death in March 1844, Thorvaldsen bequeathed his works (plaster moulds, sketches, finished works in marble) and a collection of ancient Mediterranean art to the city and the Thorvaldsens Museum. He is buried in the museum's inner courtyard.

Restaurant L'Alsace 

*Ny Østergade 9 (33 14 57 43, www.alsace.dk). Metro Kongens Nytorv. **Open** 11.30am-midnight Mon-Sat. **Map** p66 Q12* 7 French

L'Alsace is authentically French, serving delicacies such as foie gras, goose and choucroute, along with excellent cheeses and wines. The restaurant manages to evoke the crucial *hyggelige* atmosphere so valued by the Danes, with summer seating in the garden terrace surrounded by the half-timbered building.

Rice Market 

*Hausergade 38 (35 35 75 30, www.ricemarket.dk). Metro/train Nørreport. **Open** noon-midnight (kitchen closes 10pm) daily. **Map** p66 O11* 8 Oriental

This cute little basement restaurant has become a firm fixture on the city's Asian dining scene, and is run by the team behind Michelin-starred **Kiin Kiin** (*see p156*). It is extremely popular. Food consists of crowd-pleasing classics such as Chinese steamed dumplings; Thai soups, salads and curries; satay, tempura and stir-fries. It's all good-quality fare, and served in a chic, atmospheric and colourful space. Book in advance for one of the dining beds to mark a special occasion.

Cafés & bars

42°Raw

*Pilestræde 32 (32 12 32 10, www.42raw.dk). Metro Kongens Nytorv. **Open** 8am-8pm Mon-Fri; 9am-6pm Sat-Sun. **Map** p66 Q12* 1

Devoted to raw cuisine (no food sold here is heated to more than 42°C – the temperature at which enzymes are destroyed), 42°Raw is a fast-food joint selling healthy eat-in and takeaway café grub, all gluten-free, lactose-free and 100% plant-based. Expect to find smoothies and beetroot lattes, matcha bowls, protein burgers and every type of avocado sandwich under the sun.

▶ *Another great option for vegans are the stylish dishes at nearby simpleRAW (Gråbrødretorv 9, 35 35 30 05, www.simpleraw.dk,* ♛♛, 10*).*

Café Victor

*Ny Østergade 8 (33 13 36 13, www.cafevictor.dk). Metro Kongens Nytorv. **Open** Café 8am-1am Mon-Wed; 8am-2am Thur-Sat; 11am-midnight Sun. Restaurant 11am-1am Mon-Thu; 11am-2am Fri-Sat; 11am-midnight Sun. **Map** p66 R12* 7

A Copenhagen institution, Café Victor serves ultra-classic French fare – lobster bisque, sole meunière – of a high standard. However, you don't come here just for the food, but to soak up the atmosphere, marvel at the art deco interior and do battle with the supercilious staff. If you don't fancy a full meal, half a dozen oysters at the bar, accompanied by a glass of champagne, will give you a taste of the Victor experience.

Din Nye Ven

*Sankt Peders Stræde 34A (dinnyeven.dk). Metro/train Nørreport. **Open** 8am-midnight Mon-Wed; 8am-1am Thur; 8am-2am Fri; 10am-2am Fri. **Map** p66 N13* 10

This cosy pub/café is great for a quick, traditional *smørrebrød* lunch while you're stalking the quirky streets around the Latin Quarter, and is lovely for a low-key breakfast too, serving fresh croissants and morning plates with eggs, cheese, avocado, bacon and ryebread. They also serve dinner from a very small menu that changes daily, plus snacks such as salsa and cheese to accompany beers, cider, *snaps* and anything else you might like to drink.

Floss Bar

Larbjørnsstræde 10 (33 11 67 45, no website). Metro/train Nørreport. ***Open*** *2pm-2am Mon-Sat, 2pm-midnight Sun.* ***Map*** *p66 N13* ⓬

Once a dive bar known for its punk rockers, Floss is still sweaty, dirty, small and anarchic, but serves very good-value beer, at least by this city's standards, along with absinthe and tequila. Happy hour is from 10-11pm. Smoking is allowed inside – it's that kind of a place.

Flottenheimer

Skindergade 20 (35 38 32 12, www.cafeflottenheimer.dk). Metro/train Nørreport. ***Open*** *10am-10.30pm Mon-Thur; 10am-2am Fri; 9.30am-2am Sat; 9.30am-10pm Sun.* ***Map*** *p66 P12* ⓭

Based just round the corner from the lovely Gråbrødretorv square, Flottenheimer is a feminine space (think fairy lights, vintage tables and a tango soundtrack), appealing to fashionable ladies who lunch and discerning tourists. The diverse menu offers a good range of sandwiches and small bites (nachos, soup, tzatziki and bread), as well as a full Danish brunch for 135kr.

La Glace

Skoubogade 3 (33 14 46 46, www.laglace.dk). Metro/train Nørreport, or bus 11A. ***Open*** *8.30am-6pm Mon-Fri; 9am-6pm Sat; 10am-6pm Sun.* ***Map*** *p66 O13* ⓯

One of Copenhagen's most venerable bakeries, La Glace was founded in 1870 and is famous for its speciality Sports Kage (Sport Cake), an over-the-top cream, caramel and nougat mousse confection.

Palæ Bar

Ny Adelgade 5 (33 12 54 71, www.palaebar.dk). Metro Kongens Nytorv. ***Open*** *11am-1am Mon; 11am-3am Tue-Sat; 4pm-1am Sun.* ***Map*** *p66 R12* ⓳

This esteemed boho bodega, just round the corner from the Hotel d'Angleterre (*see p233*), has an unrushed, understated mood and rich, old-fashioned Parisian-style boozer atmosphere. It's a place to come and listen to jazz, with a cultured, cosy feel.

Sonny

Rådhusstræde 5 (33 14 72 72, sonnycph.dk). Metro Rådhusplads or Central Station. ***Open*** *7.30am-4pm Mon; 7.30am-6pm Tue-Fri; 9am-6pm Sat; 9am-4pm Sun.* ***Map*** *p66 O14* ㉓

Full of French finesse and Copenhagen cool, this coffee shop is a small specialist spot for coffee lovers. Run by a pair of coffee experts, one of whom worked at Coutume in Paris, the café has a chic atmosphere and a backyard opened up in good weather for an even more relaxing morning brew.

Studenterhuset

University of Copenhagen, Købmagergade 52 (35 32 38 61, www.studenterhuset.com). Metro/train Nørreport. ***Open*** *9am-midnight Mon-Wed; 9am-1am Thur; 9am-3am Fri; 10am-2am Sat; 10am-10pm Sun.* ***Map*** *p66 P12* ㉔

This subsidised student drinking den and music venue is a few steps from the Rundetårn. There's usually something fun happening of an evening, from board game tournaments to swing-dance nights or live music, with incredible value clothes sales and flea markets at the weekend.

Zoo Bar

Sværtegade 6 (26 13 45 10, www.zoobar.dk). Metro Kongens Nytorv. ***Open*** *8pm-5am Thur-Sat.* ***Map*** *p66 Q12* ㉘

A favourite hangout for downtown darlings, this cosy bar has DJs at weekends and an excellent cocktail list.

Shops & services

A.C. Perchs Thehandel

Kronprinsensgade 5 (33 15 35 62, www.perchs.dk). Metro Kongens Nytorv. ***Open*** *Shop 9am-5.30pm Mon-Thur; 9am-7pm Fri; 9.30am-4pm Sat. Café 11.30am-5.30pm Mon-Fri; 11am-5pm Sat.* ***Map*** *p66 P12* ❶ *Food & drink*

Copenhagen's venerable tea emporium dates from 1834 and is currently in the hands of the sixth generation of the Perch family. The glorious, wood-panelled interior is lined with old-fashioned jars of tea leaves; you can treat yourself to a classic afternoon tea in a similar vintage style, in the tea rooms above.

Arnold Busck

Købmagergade 49 (33 73 35 00, www.arnoldbusck.dk). Metro/train Nørreport. ***Open*** *10am-6pm Mon-Thur; 10am-7pm Fri; 10am-5pm Sat; noon-6pm Sun.* ***Map*** *p66 P12* ❷ *Books*

Busck is one of Denmark's leading bookshops, and this three-storey branch – its biggest – has a large department dedicated to English-language paperbacks and guides. **Other locations** Torvehallerne; Skindergade 2 (children's); Guldbergsgade 29D, Nørrebro.

By Malene Birger

Galleri K, Antonigade 10 (35 43 22 33, www.bymalenebirger.dk). Metro Kongens Nytorv. ***Open*** *10am-6pm Mon-Thur; 10am-7pm Fri; 10am-5pm Sat; noon-4pm 1st and last Sun of the month.* ***Map*** *p66 Q13* ❹ *Fashion*

Luxurious ready-to-wear clothing is the remit of Malene Birger's elegant flagship store, with glamorous but highly wearable designs in beautiful fabrics.

Casa Shop

Store Regnegade 2 (33 32 70 41, www.casashop.dk). Metro Kongens Nytorv. ***Open*** *10am-5.30pm Mon-Thur; 10am-6pm Fri; 10am-4pm Sat.* ***Map*** *p66 Q12* ❺ *Homewares*

Casa is one of the country's premier retailers of contemporary furniture, and there are plenty of smaller, quirkier pieces too, such as David Rockwell magazine racks and George Nelson clocks.

Le Fix

Kronprinsensgade 9B (88 61 41 01, www.le-fix.com). Metro Kongens Nytorv. ***Open*** *11am-6pm Mon-Thur; 11am-7pm Fri; 10am-5pm Sat; noon-3pm 1st and last Sun of the month.* ***Map*** *p66 Q12* ❻ *Fashion*

Accessed via a passageway off Kronprinsensgade, Le Fix offers streetwear from heritage brands (Birkenstock, Dr Martens, Grenson) and sportswear labels (Adidas, Fred Perry, Puma). It also has graffiti prints for sale, and an on-site tattoo studio.

► *Another streetwear shop, Streetmachine (27 89 30 83, www.streetmachine.com), is nearby at Kronprinsensgade 3.*

Ganni

Store Regnegade 12 (20 88 53 11, www.ganni.com). Metro Kongens Nytorv. ***Open*** *10am-6pm Mon-Fri; 10am-5pm Sat.* ***Map*** *p66 Q12* ❼ *Fashion*

Founded by Frans Truelsen in 2000, Danish womenswear brand Ganni is a fashion-lover's must-have. The clothes, lingerie, shoes and accessories are often more feminine than your typical Danish fashion brand (with delicate patterns and pastel colours), but with the same emphasis on quality fabrics and on-trend cuts. **Other locations** Gammel Kongevej 82, Frederiksberg; Østerbrogade 50, Østerbro.

HAY House

Østergade 61 (42 82 08 20, www.hay.dk). Metro Kongens Nytorv. ***Open*** *10am-6pm Mon-Fri; 10am-5pm Sat.* ***Map*** *p66 Q13* ❾ *Homewares*

HAY is one of the modern icons in Danish design and homeware, and recently had a sell-out collaboration with IKEA. Simple, rounded forms and modular, felt-covered

HAY House

chairs in primary colours abound. There's another showroom upstairs and the website gives a good idea of what's in store: contemporary fabrics, muted colours and quirky accessories.

Henrik Vibskov

Krystalgade 6 (33 14 61 00, www. henrikvibskov.com). Metro/train Nørreport. ***Open*** *11am-7pm Mon-Sat; 11am-6pm Sun.* ***Map*** *p66 O12* ❿ *Fashion*

Henrik Vibskov's cutting-edge designs – for women and men – grace fashion pages around the world. This flagship store offers the complete Vibskov experience, with the full collection of his coveted, edgy creations on sale.

▶ *Garage boutique (sales, archives and samples): Bryggenes Plads 19, open Fri-Sun.*

Munthe plus Simonsen

Store Regnegade 2 (33 32 03 12, www. munthe.com). Metro Kongens Nytorv. ***Open*** *10am-6pm Mon-Fri; 10am-4pm Sat.* ***Map*** *p66 Q12* ⓱ *Fashion*

Luxurious muted colours abound at this women's clothing shop – reportedly a favourite of supermodel Helena Christensen and Crown Princess Mary.

Naked

Pilestræde 46 (33 15 83 80, www.nakedcph. com). Metro Kongens Nytorv. ***Open*** *11am-6pm Mon-Thur; 11am-7pm Fri; 11am-5pm Sat.* ***Map*** *p66 Q12* ⓲ *Accessories*

This specialist women-only sneaker shop is the number 1 place to buy kicks in the city. Shoes from New Balance, Wood Wood and Vans are in large supply. **Other location** Klosterstræde 10, Indre By (33 15 83 83).

Nordisk Korthandel

Studiestræde 30 (33 38 26 38, www.scanmaps. dk). Metro/train Nørreport. ***Open*** *10am-6pm Mon-Fri; 10am-4pm Sat.* ***Map*** *p66 N13* ⓳ *Books*

Nordisk Korthandel is Copenhagen's finest source of maps, travel books and globes, and is staffed by knowledgeable travel enthusiasts.

Norse Store

Pilestræde 41 (33 93 26 26, www.norsestore. com). Metro Kongens Nytorv. ***Open*** *10am-6pm Mon-Thur; 10am-7pm Fri; 11am-5pm Sat.* ***Map*** *p66 Q12* ⓴ *Fashion*

Established in 2004, Norse Store has become one of the most popular shops in town for style-savvy young men. This store has a women's version right next door. Clothes combine street fashion, classic workwear and contemporary designs, with a hand-picked selection from its own label Norse Projects and other brands, including Adidas Yeezy, Comme des Garçons, A.P.C., Levis, Anderson's and Converse.

Peter Beier

Skoubogade 1 (33 93 07 17, www. peterbeierchokolade.dk). Bus 11A, 14. ***Open*** *10am-6pm Mon-Thur; 10am-7pm Fri; 10am-5pm Sat.* ***Map*** *p66 O13* ㉑ *Food & drink*

The essence of chocolate chic, this modern shop, run by the charming Beier family, offers premium-quality chocolates, plus dessert and port wines to accompany more refined tasting sessions.

Sögreni of Copenhagen

Sankt Peders Stræde 30A (33 12 78 79, www. sogrenibikes.com). Metro/train Nørreport, or train Vesterport. ***Open*** *10am-6pm Mon-Sun.* ***Map*** *p100 N13* ㉓ *Bicycles*

This high-end bicycle maker produces a limited quantity of traditional-looking, yet ultra-modern bikes, several of which have been featured in *Wallpaper** magazine and sold at the Conran Shop in London. Bikes cost around €1,755.

❤ Sømods Bolcher

Nørregade 24 & 36B (33 12 60 46, soemods. com). Metro/train/bus Nørreport. ***Open*** *9.15am-5.30pm Mon-Thu; 9.15am-6pm Fri, 10am-3.30pm Sat; 11am-3pm Sun.* ***Map*** *p100 O12* ㉔ *Food & drink*

This little sweet shop tended to by the owner's family has been running for 125 years. Choose from experimental flavours (warning: like everyone in Denmark, they love their licorice!) and fill your shopping bags with 1950s-style hard candy, rock and lollipops. Watching the team shape the sweets in the small factory at the back is fun.

❤ Summerbird

Kronprinsensgade 11 (33 93 80 40, www. summerbird.dk). Metro Kongens Nytorv. ***Open*** *11am-5.30pm Mon-Thur; 10am-6pm Fri; 10am-4pm Sat.* ***Map*** *p66 Q12* ㉖ *Food & drink*

This chocolatier specialises in gourmet *flødeboller* –Danish treats consisting of marshmallow and a biscuit base covered in chocolate (a little bit like an extravagant version of a Tunnock's teacake). **Other locations** Torvehallerne market, Nørreport; Værnedamsvej 9, Vesterbro (33 25 25 50).

Time's Up Vintage

Krystalgade 4 (no phone, www.timesupshop. com). Metro/train Nørreport. ***Open*** *11am-6pm Mon-Thur; 11am-7pm Fri; 10am-5pm Sat.* ***Map*** *p66 O12* ㉗ *Fashion*

Summerbird

Time's Up has a well-edited selection of designer vintage clothing, including art deco pieces (with notably good jewellery), and couture from Chanel, Dior and Givenchy. The range of shoes is also strong.

Wood Wood

Grønnegade 1 (35 35 62 64, www.woodwood.dk). Metro Kongens Nytorv. ***Open*** *10am-6pm Mon-Fri; 10am-5pm Sat; noon-4pm Sun.* ***Map*** *p66 Q12* ㉙ *Fashion*

Wood Wood started life as a graphic T-shirt brand, moving on to become one of Copenhagen's most stylish streetwear-influenced labels. Expect their own brand plus the best of Adidas, The North Face, Nike, Vans and Mizuno; it stocks men's, women's and childrenswear.

SOUTH OF STRØGET

The parallel stretch of **Strædet** (literally 'strait') is, like Strøget, actually formed of several streets (Farvergade, Kompagnistræde, Læderstræde, Store Kirkestræde and Lille Kongensgade). These historic streets are lovely to walk around: more laid-back than Strøget, and with a greater number of independent shops and cafés.

South of Strædet, just above the island of Slotsholmen, is **Gammel Strand** (Old Beach), home to some pricey restaurants. In the time of Bishop Absalon (12th century), and for hundreds of years afterwards, Gammel Strand was where fish was sold (and it therefore served as the city's commercial centre). It was here that the Øresund herring were landed before they were transported throughout Catholic Europe – fish being vital for a population that often abstained from meat. Gammel Strand remained part of Copenhagen's seafront, which stretched from what is today Fortunstræde, along Gammel Strand to Snaregade, Magstræde and Løngangstræde, until well into the Middle Ages.

By the bridge from Højbro Plads to Slotsholmen is a stout stone statue (dating from 1940) of a foul-mouthed and quarrelsome fishwife grasping a huge flounder by the gills, in memory of a trade that lasted into the 20th century. You can still find some great fish in the area, mainly sushi. Cross to the other side of the bridge and look into the water and you'll see the bronze sculpture of the *Merman with his Sons* (it's illuminated at night), which commemorates the story of Agnete, who left her family on land to start a new life underwater with a merman. They had seven children together, but one day the calling of distant church bells reminded her of her old life, and she went back, never to return. Danish artist Suste Bonnén created the sculpture in 1992 and it is one of the city's most magical, haunting yet easily missed sights. In summer, you can take a canal tour or harbour trip to *The Little Mermaid* (*see p109*) from Gammel Strand.

Sights & museums

Kunstforeningen GL Strand

Gammel Strand 48 (33 36 02 60, www.glstrand.dk). Metro Kongens Nytorv; bus 1A, 2A, 6A, 15, 26, 29. ***Open*** *11am-5pm Tue-Sun; 11am-8pm Wed.* ***Admission*** *75kr; 65kr reductions; free under-16s.* ***Map*** *p66 P13.*

This bijou art gallery shows the more contemporary and outrageous (sometimes hitting the mark, sometimes not) in its beautiful building just steps from the canal. Even if you're not in the mood, a coffee or glass of wine in the intimate café is always a good idea.

Restaurants

Riz Raz ♛♛

Kompagnistræde 20 (33 15 05 75, www.rizraz.dk). Metro Kongens Nytorv, or bus 11A. ***Open*** *11.30am-midnight daily.* ***Map*** *p66 P14* ⑨ *Mediterranean*

The southern Mediterranean food at this convivial cellar restaurant is a favourite with tourists and Copenhageners, and consistently wins over reviewers from the Danish press. It always seems to be packed with an eclectic mix of diners in for a quick bite before heading somewhere groovier. **Other location** Store Kannikstraæde 19, Indre By (33 32 33 45).

Slotskælderen Hos Gitte 

Fortunstræde 4 (33 11 15 37, www. slotskaelderen.dk). Metro Kongens Nytorv. ***Open*** *10am-5pm Tue-Sat.* ***Map*** *p66 Q13* ⑪

Traditional Danish

This old-school *smørrebrød* restaurant is just across the canal from Christiansborg Slot (home to the Danish parliament). Simply choose sandwiches, *frikadeller* (meatballs) and *sild* (herring) from the counter, and the attentive staff bring them to your table. Fried plaice and pickled herring are two of the top choices here, classically washed down with a beer and *snaps*.

Cafés & bars

❤ Bastard

Rådhusstræde 13 (42 74 66 42, bastardcafe. dk). Metro Rådhusplads or Central Station. ***Open*** *noon-midnight Sun-Thur; noon-2am Fri-Sat.* ***Map*** *p66 P14* ❷

Copenhagen's first board game café has a pub-like atmosphere, beers on tap, big plates of nachos to share and, more importantly, a huge library-like room full of board games to borrow for the afternoon/evening. If you don't know the rules to anything, just ask – games gurus are on hand to help.

▶ *In the same Huset building you can find a cinema showing quirky films, a bar and event spaces with occasional talks, and a music venue (huset-kbh.dk).*

Bertels Salon

Kompagnistræde 5 (33 13 00 33, www. bertelskager.dk). Metro Kongens Nytorv. ***Open*** *11am-10pm Fri-Sat; 11am-9pm Sun.* ***Map*** *p66 P14* ❸

Make like a Dane and have cake on a Thursday (for some reason, it's the traditional day to have cake served at work). American cheesecakes are the speciality here, and there are some 20 types on offer; we especially recommend the coconut-pineapple version. **Other location** Falkoner Allé 54, Frederiksberg (31 16 69 62).

❤ Ruby

Nybrogade 10 (33 92 12 03, rby.dk). Metro Kongens Nytorv. ***Open*** *4pm-2am Mon-Sat; 6pm-2am Sun.* ***Map*** *p100 P14* ㉒

One of the city's best-loved cocktail bars, Ruby is near Thorvaldsen's Museum in an old townhouse dating to 1740. She's seen a few things come and go over the years; these days her views take in politicians going to work instead of fishwives and farmers, and she's still selling cocktails, just like she was in 1882. Regularly changing cocktail menus include a version of a whisky highball that won the title of world's best scotch cocktail at Diageo World Class 2018. Look them up on Instagram (@rubycph) for a little insight on what to expect.

Ved Stranden 10

Ved Stranden 10 (35 42 40 40, www. vedstranden10.dk). Metro Kongens Nytorv. ***Open*** *noon-10pm Mon-Sat.* ***Map*** *p66 Q14* ㉖

This superb wine bar is just off the canal and has a sommelier service ready to find just the right wine for your tastebuds. Food is served, communal style, on a Monday from 6pm (100kr per person). Check the menu online first – there is only one choice. Other nights, just come for a drink or three and enjoy the great atmosphere alongside the well-heeled locals.

Zirup

Læderstræde 32 (33 13 50 60, www. zirup.dk). Metro Kongens Nytorv. ***Open*** *9.30am-midnight Sun-Wed; 9.30am-1am Thur; 9.30am-2am Fri, Sat.* ***Map*** *p66 P13* ㉗

Zirup is our choice of all the many friendly cafés on this pretty pedestrian street parallel to Strøget. It has a beautifully lit interior, and a good-value and slightly adventurous fusion menu (offering everything from stroganoff and curry to Mexican wraps), and there are tables outside when the weather permits. All in all, it's a very pleasant place to pass time. The Sunday morning hangover brunch should be available on prescription.

SLOTSHOLMEN & THE WATERFRONT

There is plenty to explore as you walk down HC Andersens Boulevard to the water. Styled as 'The Culture Quarter', the area to the left includes the excellent Nationalmuseet (*see p93*), full of Viking treasures, Københavns Museum (*see p74*) and Christiansborg Slot (*see p92*). To the right you'll walk past Ny Carlsberg Glyptotek (*see p75*), and as you reach the water, you'll discover BLOX (*see p91*), the home of the Danish Architecture Centre, Kalvebod Bølge and the Black Diamond (Det Kongelige Bibliotek or Royal Library). Modern buildings sit on this historic land and make a bridge between old and new, finding ways to explain the past and its relevance today.

The largest building on Slotsholmen is **Christiansborg Slot** (Christiansborg Castle, *see p92*), the modern-day parliament

Black Diamond *p96*

building that takes up the northern half of the island. For many centuries, the previous castles that stood on this site effectively were Copenhagen, so central were they to the lives and prosperity of the townsfolk and so important were they as a power base for the region.

Christiansborg's development can be divided into three stages: Absalon's fortress dating from 1167; the 17th century; and the current palace. The original building is long gone, but you can still see remnants of its foundations in the enjoyable **Ruinerne under Christiansborg** (Ruins under Christiansborg, *see p95*), a museum dedicated to the 850-year history of the castle site. The current palace is built directly above and houses the Danish parliament, **Folketinget**, where 179 members sit in a semi-circle in their party groups (of which Denmark has many), facing the Speaker.

Close by the Ruinerne museum is the equestrian arena, with entrances to two particularly enchanting royal attractions: the **Kongelige Stalde og Kareter** (Royal Stables and Coaches) and **Teatermuseet** (Theatre Museum, *see p95*). The stables offer a glimpse into an extravagant royal past, while the Teatermuseet is housed in the old Royal Court Theatre, designed by the French architect Nicolas Henri Jardin.

Continue across the equestrian arena to the archway beyond and you'll come to Frederiksholms Kanal, which is crossed by Marmorbroen (Marble Bridge). A few steps from the bridge is the magnificient **Nationalmuseet**. Housed in a sumptuous former royal palace and boasting some of the finest rooms in the city, Denmark's National Museum is the country's oldest historical collection, with its origins as Frederik II's Royal Cabinet of Curiosities (c1650). It focuses, naturally, on Danish culture and history, but there are also world-class Egyptian, Greek, Roman and ethnographic departments. All exhibits have excellent English captions.

Just north of Christiansborg Slot is the classical stuccoed mausoleum (by Gottlieb Bindesbøll) that houses the definitive collection of works by Denmark's master sculptor, Bertel Thorvaldsen (1768-1844; *see p83*). Immediately behind the museum is **Christiansborg Slotskirke** (Christiansborg Palace Church), one of CF Hansen's neoclassical masterpieces, with a columned façade and a beautiful white stucco interior and dome.

Børsen, on the other side of Christiansborg Slotsplads, is the oldest stock exchange in Europe, built between 1619 and 1640. It still serves as a business centre and Copenhagen's chamber of commerce and, as such, is not open to the public. However, the exterior of this Renaissance wedding cake is a riot of stonework, embellished gables and green copper. Above it towers one of Copenhagen's most recognisable landmarks – a fantastical 54-metre (177-foot) copper spire made of four intertwined dragon tails, built in 1625 to a design by Ludvig Heidtrider. The three gold crowns topping the spire represent the three Nordic nations: Denmark, Sweden and Norway. Børsen (which translates as 'the covered market') was built at the behest of Christian IV, who desperately wanted Copenhagen to become the financial capital of Europe (it didn't).

An unusually ostentatious altarpiece (for a Lutheran church) is the main draw of **Holmens Kirke**, dedicated to sailors. Across the street is a concrete building housing the **Nationalbanken** (National Bank), the work of Arne Jacobsen. It is not open to the public.

Sightseeing with Children

The city's top ten visitor attractions for kids

Copenhagen is a truly family-friendly city to visit with kids: museums often provide hands-on spaces, and playgrounds, play spaces and splash pads dot the city centre. Food options abound even for picky eaters, and bakeries and sausage wagons are a great low-cost option.

Rent a Christiania bike

Kids love the chance to travel a little differently, and getting around by cargo bike (*see p130*) is the way to do it in this city. If biking isn't your thing, riding the driverless metro – sitting at the front – usually gets the thumbs up.

The Nationalmuseet

Inside the National Museum (*see p93*), a large percentage of the ground floor is orientated towards children under ten, with play zones, dressing-up, role play and more, including the option to play Vikings on a boat in full costume, with wooden swords.

The harbour baths

Whatever age your children are, they can spend a happy sunny afternoon splashing at **Islands Brygge Harbour Baths** (*see p124*) or in the shallow children's pool. If city life is too busy, a day at **Amager beach** (*see p174*) is only 20 minutes away by metro from Central Station.

Hit the heights

Make it a mission to get a bird's-eye view of the city from as many spires as possible (and tire the kids out at the same time). The **Church of Our Saviour** (*see p123*), **Marmorkirken** (*see p115*) and **Rundetårn** (*see p81*) are all good options.

Discover Copenhagen's playgrounds

Copenhagen's playgrounds are a treat for all ages, with colourful and inventive play structures, manned offices, trikes to borrow and coffee stalls for parents. Danish play architects Monstrum are behind many of the very best designs. Try **Fælledparken**, with a choice of the Tower Playground or the Traffic Light cycling scooter park (you can often borrow small bikes); **Skydebanehaven** (Absalonsgade 12, just off Istedgade); **Nørrebroparken** (at the top of Jægersborggade, *see p157*); and **Superkilen** (*see p155*) just for a start.

The Louisiana

A whole wing at the Louisiana Museum of Modern Art (*see p170*) is dedicated to children's art, with workshops set across three floors allowing them to make their own paintings and sculptures. The education team thinks of everything – aprons are provided and there are drying racks so you can paint and come back later for dry artwork.

Copenhagen Zoo

► *Arken Museum for Moderne Kunst (see p176) has a studio for families, as does Statens Museum for Kunst (see p106), which runs weekend workshops for children.*

Copenhagen Zoo
Get up close with polar bears, pandas and more at the fantastic zoo (see *p146*). There are plenty of options for food and you don't even need to bring a pushchair or pram with you (handy if you're arriving by bike); you can rent a pull-along cart for the day.

Experimentarium
Hellerup's interactive science centre is huge and inventive, and the place to spend almost a whole day, creating experiments, playing with water, participating in dance videos and more. *See p171.*

Dyrehaven and Bakken
Another option for a day trip from the city is the family-friendly Dyrehaven deer park, and Bakken, the amusement park within it. It's also a short walk from Bellevue beach, for a full summer's day out. *See p171.*

Tivoli
If all else fails, there is always **Tivoli** (see *p70*). It's certainly a treat for all ages – but note that there are not many rides for under 5s, and it can be galling to spend money on entry to simply play in a playground (beautiful though it is!). For children over five and right through to teens, there are attractions, shows and food that they will love.

► *For suggestions on planning a family day out, see p25.*

Experimentarium

Another treat is the **Tøjhusmuseet** (Royal Arsenal Museum, *see p96*). Comprising an endless vaulted Renaissance cannon hall (the longest in Europe, modelled on the one in Venice), and a mind-boggling array of arms and armour in an upstairs display, this is probably the finest museum of its kind in the world.

Copenhagen's most beautiful 'hidden' garden, **Bibliotekshaven** (Library Garden), lies behind the old ivy-covered **Det Kongelige Bibliotek** (Royal Library), through a gateway on Rigdagsgården, opposite the entrance to Folketinget.

The Danes love nothing more than to juxtapose old and new, and architects Schmidt, Hammer and Lassen certainly created that in a dramatic form at the **Black Diamond**. Perhaps the best way to approach it is by walking through the old library's garden, so that you are suddenly confronted with the vastness of the new structure close up. The Kongelige Bibliotek is also attached to the **Dansk Jødisk Museum** (Danish Jewish Museum). Round the corner you'll find **Kayak Bar**, a relaxed open-air bar on the canal and floating beach where you can hire kayaks to explore the waterways in summer.

Sights & museums

Slotsholmen's museums and sights can be difficult to find, hidden behind seemingly closed doors with often hard-to-notice signs. It's a good idea to come on a Sunday afternoon when all the attractions are open at the same time – on Mondays they are typically closed, although some open on Mondays during the summer school holidays.

Bibliotekshaven
Søren Kirkegårdsplads 1 (33 95 42 00, no website). Metro Kongens Nytorv. ***Open*** *6am-10pm daily.* ***Admission*** *free.* ***Map*** *p66 Q15.*

Arranged in a square around a fountain and duck pond, the Library Garden blooms beautifully in summer – even the bronze of Søren Kierkegaard looks cheerful. You can see some of the old mooring hoops from Christian IV's time on the surrounding walls.

❤ BLOX
Bryghuspladsen (21 25 53 89, www.blox.dk). Central Station, harbour bus 991, 992. ***Open*** *8am-10pm daily.* ***Admission*** *free, apart from the Danish Architecture Centre, which is 110kr adults; 85kr reductions; free under-18s.* ***Map*** *p66 Q16.*

BLOX, one of the blockbuster buildings to come out of Copenhagen in recent years, was not universally well received when it opened in 2018. Its squat, block-like formation set right on the water's edge (in contrast to the celebrated light, high-ceilinged and graceful Nordic style) was not to everyone's liking; on top of that, having a Dutch architect design a building that was to house the best of Danish architecture appeared to be a misstep. That said, it's an interesting space, and if you love – really love – architecture, the exhibitions may well delight you. The Dansk Arkitektur Center (Danish Architecture Centre) shares the space with eateries and a gym in modern, multi-use fashion. A small design shop on the lower floor is also good for books and design items, and a playground at the back shows you what can be achieved with imagination and a small space (for a change, not by Danish super playground architects Monstrum). Best of all is the rooftop bar and restaurant, with great brunch deals and views of the water on a summer's day (*see p97*). Don't miss the website dac.dk for information on free guided walking tours with entry to the exhibitions (90 minutes, Saturday only) and a free app with architecture-themed walks around the city.

In the know
Kalvebod Wave

Take a right along the waterfront from BLOX and you'll find **Kalvebod Bølge**, an urban walkway in the water with bright orange climbing frames, a kayak launch spot and the ideal platforms to jump from in the summer. It was designed to liven up an otherwise fairly dull stretch of the waterfront; a seasonal floating bar **Green Island**, a few steps away, has jumped on the wave too...

Christiansborg Slot

Slotsholmen (33 92 64 92, www.christiansborg.dk). Metro Kongens Nytorv. ***Open*** *daily 9am-5pm Apr-Oct,; 10am-5pm Nov-Mar, closed Mon Nov-Mar. Tours (in English) 3pm daily.* ***Admission*** *95kr; 85kr reductions; free under-18s.* ***Map*** *p66 Q14.*

Christiansborg Slot is the castle to visit in Copenhagen – but be prepared for an onslaught of Danish history and a lot of walking. Those seeking a more contemporary take on castles and the royal family today might want to consider Amalienborg Slot instead (*see p112*). The current palace has its roots in Bishop Absalon's original 12th-century fortress that was badly damaged in 1259 by the avenging Wends. It was then burned to the ground in 1369 by an alliance of forces led by the Lübeckers against King Valdemar Atterdag. The fortress was then replaced by the first Copenhagen Castle. From 1416, when Erik of Pomerania moved in, the castle became the permanent home of the royal family (until they moved to Amalienborg Slot in 1794).

Christian IV had the place demolished in the early 17th century, replacing it with a typically over-the-top Baroque building, with its own chapel and very grand stables. During Frederik II's reign, the castle nearly fell to the Swedes, who, after a two-year siege, in February 1659 advanced towards it across the frozen sea, dressed in white cloaks to camouflage themselves. But the boiling oil, tar and water that the Danes rained down drove them back. Soon after, Frederik III built a new rampart where the Swedes had advanced. This became known as Vestervold (Western Rampart), and between it and Slotsholmen a new quarter, Frederiksholm, grew up.

BLOX *p91*

❤ Nationalmuseet

Ny Vestergade 10 (33 13 44 11, https://en.natmus.dk). Bus 1A, 2A, 9A, 11A,. ***Open*** *10am-5pm Tue-Sun.* ***Admission*** *95kr; 80kr adult with a child; free under-18s.* ***Map*** *p66 P15.*

Danish history and culture has so much to recommend it: not just an outsized modern design pedigree but also the drama, gold and blood lust of the Vikings, magical glimpses into prehistoric pasts via Bronze Age burials, and the colourful, exotic and shameful history of its colonies. All of these and more are on display at the excellent National Museum, which is well worth a visit for the Viking exhibits alone. These include a reworked permanent collection by designer Jim Lyngvild that opened late 2018. It puts you face to face with Viking beserkers, queens and their weaponry and jewellery. Costumes from the HBO Nordic series *The Vikings* are shown alongside them; the sense of drama is palpable.

The National Museum's main home is in Prinsens Palæ (Prince's Palace), just off a characterful canal on Slotsholmen. To the right, on the ground floor, is the **Prehistoric Wing**, showing Danish history from the reindeer hunters of the Ice Age to the Vikings. Here, you can marvel at archaeological finds from the Early Bronze Age unearthed in Denmark's bogs – the most impressive of which is the collection of large bronze horns, or *lurs*, played to appease the sun god. Also on this floor is the **Children's Museum**, a wonderful play area made up of several rooms where children can dress up, play act, jump into a boat and pretend to sail and travel the world. It's a great indoor playspace to hide out of the rain on a wet and windy day; the museum also has trails and entertainment for kids in English and Danish.

Upstairs, the **Medieval and Renaissance** department covers the pre- and post-Reformation periods, and majors on ecclesiastical and decorative art. Pieces here come from the era of the great Renaissance kings: Christian III, Frederik II and Christian IV.

The **Royal Collection of Coins and Medals**, though one of the more specialist sections in the museum, is intriguing. On the top floor is the museum's **Collection of Antiquities**, a mini take on the British Museum, with pieces from Egypt, Greece and Italy. On the same floor is a charming **Toy Museum**, which begins with a mention of a rattle in Saxo Grammaticus's *Gesta Danorum* and continues through early 16th-century German toys; a spectacular array of dolls' houses with lights and steps so smaller people can peek into all the windows; LEGO (of course); and toy soldiers.

The museum also has a good shop and an excellent café-restaurant, renowned for its brunches.

▶ *For more on the Vikings, take a day trip to Roskilde and visit the Vikingeskibsmuseet (see p179).*

In the know
Meet the locals

In July and August the 'Meet the Danes' tours (free with entry) are designed to give foreign visitors a local's take on *hygge*, work-life balance, cycling and more.

Viking exhibit

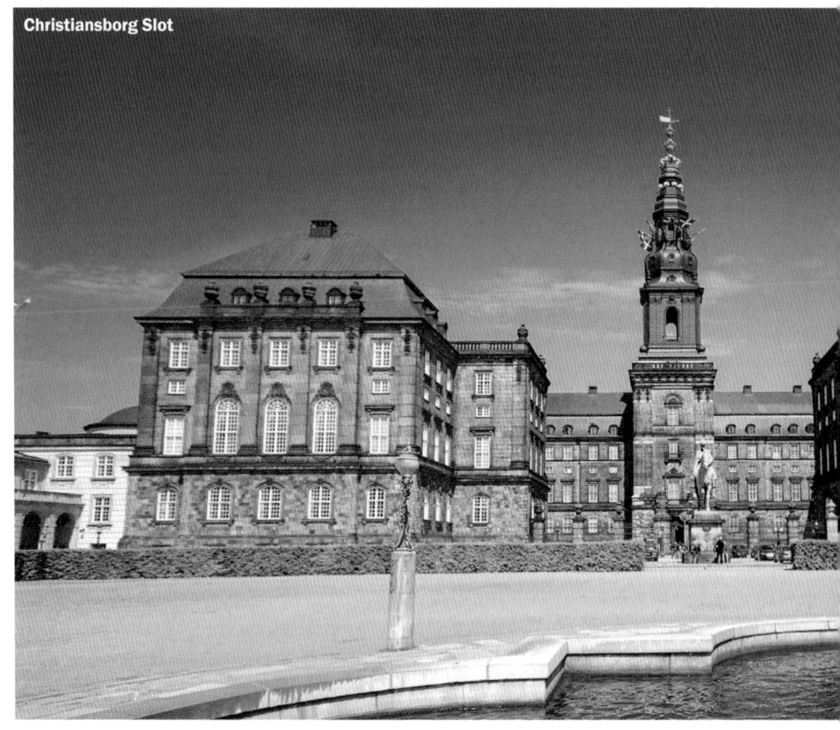
Christiansborg Slot

Frederik IV extensively modernised the castle between 1710 and 1729, but Christian VI tore it down in 1732. The Baroque replacement was one of the biggest palaces in Europe; its foundations alone cost three million rigsdalers, then equivalent to the entire value of Sjælland's arable land. But on the night of 26 February 1794, the whole lot burned down (bar the stables, which are still in use). The royal family finally gave up on Slotsholmen and bought Amalienborg Slot. Work on the next Christiansborg Slot started in 1803 and the building, a neoclassical masterpiece, was completed in 1828; however, that too was badly damaged by a fire in 1884.

You would hardly term present-day Christiansborg a castle. Nor is it especially graceful. But it is big. Its neo-Baroque granite and concrete façade was designed by Thorvald Jørgensen.

In the know
Just the ticket

A joint ticket is available for **Christiansborg Slot** (Royal Reception Rooms), the **Ruinerne under Christiansborg** and the **Kongelige Stalde** (Royal Stables). It costs 160kr (140kr reductions, free under 18s) and is valid for one month.

Christiansborg Slot: Folketinget

Rigsdagsgården (33 37 32 31, www.ft.dk). Metro Kongens Nytorv. ***Open*** *for open gallery sittings and guided tours, check website for details.* ***Admission*** *free.* ***Map*** *p66 Q14.*

Familiar to those who have seen TV drama series *Borgen*, the Folketinget is Denmark's parliament. A public gallery is open when parliament is in session, and there are English-language tours during the parliamentary recess in summer. Christiansborg also houses the High Court, several ministries, the Prime Minister's Department, the Royal Reception Chambers (De Kongelige Repræsentationslokaler) and the Queen's Reference Library.

Christiansborg Slot: Kongelige Stalde og Kareter

Christiansborg Ridebane 12 (33 40 26 76, www.christiansborg.dk). Metro Kongens Nytorv. ***Open*** *1.30-4pm Tue-Sun (Oct-Apr only). Guided tours in English at 2pm Sat.* ***Admission*** *40kr; 20kr-30kr reductions.* ***Map*** *p66 P14.*

Kongelige Stalde og Kareter

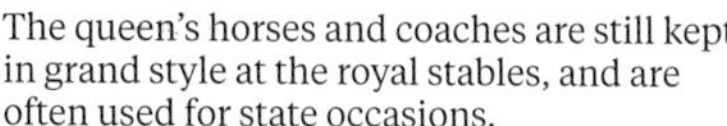

The queen's horses and coaches are still kept in grand style at the royal stables, and are often used for state occasions.

Christiansborg Slot: Ruinerne under Christiansborg

Christiansborg Slot, Prins Jørgens Gård 1 (33 92 64 94, www.christiansborg.dk). Metro Kongens Nytorv. ***Open*** *May-Sept 10am-5pm daily; Oct-Apr 10am-4pm Tue-Sun. Guided tours in English noon Sat.* ***Admission*** *60kr.* ***Map*** *p66 Q14.*

Housed in three large underground rooms are excavations of the older castles' foundations, including stonework from Absalon's fortress; remnants of Denmark's most famous prison, the **Blåtårn** (Blue Tower); and what is called Absalon's Well (though it's probably from the 19th century). The Blåtårn was used for several centuries to house prisoners of note – most famously Leonora Christina, daughter of Christian IV. She wrote what is considered the most important piece of 17th-century Danish prose, *Jammersminde*, while held here on suspicion of involvement in her husband's treasonous plot. Viewing this jumble of ancient masonry is like trying to put together the discarded pieces from several jigsaw puzzles, but the exhibition works hard to help you decipher the rubble (with English captions).

Christiansborg Slot: Teatermuseet

South wing of Christiansborg Slot, Christiansborg Ridebane 18 (33 11 51 76, www.teatermuseet.dk). Metro Kongens Nytorv. ***Open*** *noon-4pm Tue-Sun.* ***Admission*** *40kr; 30kr reductions; free under-18s.* ***Map*** *p66 Q14.*

Exhibits on show at the Theatre Museum include costumes, set designs and artworks. There's also a special cabinet of objects connected with the Royal Ballet choreographer Auguste Bournonville.

Christiansborg Slotskirke

Christiansborg Slotsplads (33 92 63 00, www.christiansborg.dk). Metro Kongens Nytorv. ***Open*** *10am-5pm Sun and daily in July.* ***Admission*** *free.* ***Map*** *p66 Q14.*

In the know
Colourful history

In 1990, the Danish business industry gifted Queen Margrethe 11 tapestries depicting the history of Denmark, to celebrate her 50th birthday. It took ten years to make them. They have been on display in the Great Hall since 2000 and are a colourful take on Danish history today.

This church was completed in 1829 and survived a fire in 1884, but the roof was destroyed by another fire that started during the Whitsun carnival in 1992. It was restored just in time for the 25th anniversary of Queen Margrethe's coronation in 1997.

Dansk Jødisk Museum

Det Kongelige Bibliotek, entrance via garden (33 11 22 18, www.jewmus.dk). Metro Kongens Nytorv, harbour bus 991, 992. ***Open*** *June-Aug 10am-5pm Tue-Sun. Sept-May 1-4pm Tue-Fri; noon-5pm Sat, Sun.* ***Admission*** *60kr; 50kr reductions; free under-18s.* ***Map*** *p66 Q15.*

This striking adaptation of the Royal Boat House was designed by Daniel Libeskind, responsible also for the Jewish Museum in Berlin and the new development at Ground Zero in New York. The museum is inspired by the Hebrew word *Mitzvah*, which loosely means 'compassion' and refers in part to the Danes' attitude towards the Jewish community during World War II.

Holmens Kirke

Holmens Kanal (33 13 61 78, www.holmenskirke.dk). Bus 1A, 26, 66. ***Open*** *10am-4pm Mon, Wed, Fri-Sat; 10am-3.30pm Tue, Thu; noon-4pm Sun.* ***Admission*** *free.* ***Map*** *p66 R14.*

Holmens Kirke is often used for royal occasions – Queen Margrethe and Prince Henrik were married here in 1967. Walk through the side door on the left of the altar and you'll enter a room dedicated to Denmark's naval heroes and graced by numerous ornate sarcophagi.

Det Kongelige Bibliotek (Black Diamond)

Søren Kierkegaards Plads 1 (33 47 47 47, www.kb.dk). Metro Kongens Nytorv, harbour bus 991, 992. ***Open*** *8am-9pm Mon-Fri; 9am-7pm Sat. Guided tours 3pm Sat.* ***Admission*** *Main building free; concerts vary.* ***Map*** *p66 Q15.*

This commanding parallelogram, made from glass, black Zimbabwean granite (cut in Portugal and polished in Italy), Portuguese sandstone, silk concrete and Canadian maple, was opened in 1999 and is known as the **Black Diamond.** Its reflective surfaces interact constantly with the sky and water, altering the building's colour by the second. The 500-million-kroner library houses 200,000 books, an exhibition space, a shop, a concert hall, an excellent restaurant (Søren K; *see p97*) and a café. The basement also holds the National Museum of Photography (40kr) and hosts occasional exhibitions from the Book Museum. The old library, the largest in Scandinavia, with its glorious reading room, is accessed through a glass walkway from the first floor. Bring a laptop and work in this enlightening space for free.

Thorvaldsens Museum

Bertel Thorvaldsens Plads 2 (33 32 15 32, www.thorvaldsensmuseum.dk). Bus 1A, 2A, 14, 26, 66. ***Open*** *10am-5pm Tue-Sun.* ***Admission*** *70kr; 50kr reductions; free under-18s; free to all Wed.* ***Map*** *p66 P14.*

The Thorvaldsens Museum, the oldest art gallery in Denmark, is a charming blend of celestial blue ceilings, elegant colonnades and mosaic floors. It isn't a modern museum in any way; you can get an audio guide, but mainly you will be strolling along corridors to see Thorvaldsen's incredible marble sculptures of the Greek gods without much guidance. It is worth persevering, however; at times it feels like a religious experience. His subjects include not only figures from mythology, epic studies of Christ and numerous self-portraits, but also busts of contemporaries such as Byron, Walter Scott and the Danish poet Adam Oehlenschläger. The great hall features absolutely enormous figures on horseback; Hercules, halfway up the stairs, is draped with a lion skin and looks truly god-like. It is a bit of a treat if you like sculpture. You can bring a pad and pencil, borrow a fold-up chair from the rack and do some sketches if you feel the urge. *See also p83* Denmark's Wandering Hero.

► *The admission fee allows visitors free entry to Nikolaj Kunsthal (see p77), to be used in the same 48 hours.*

Tøjhusmuseet

Tøjhusgade 3 (33 11 60 37, www.thm.dk). Bus 1A, 2A, 14, 26, 66. ***Open*** *10am-5pm Tue-Sun.* ***Admission*** *80kr; 70kr adult with a child; free under-18s.* ***Map*** *p66 Q15.*

The Royal Arsenal Museum is based in what was Christian IV's original arsenal building (1589-1604). On the ground floor, within walls 4 metres (13 feet) thick, are a vast number of gun carriages, cannons, a V-1 flying bomb from World War II and the tiniest tank you ever saw (from 1933). Upstairs, the glass cases, containing everything from 15th-century swords and pikes to modern machine guns, seem to go on forever. Many items, such as the beautiful ivory-inlaid pistols and muskets, are works of art, and the royal suits of armour are stunning.

Restaurants

Søren K

Det Kongelige Bibliotek, Søren Kierkegaards Plads 1 (33 47 49 49, www.meyersfb.dk/restauranter/sorenk). Metro Kongens Nytorv; harbour bus 991, 992. ***Open*** *11am-4pm, 5.30-11pm Mon-Sat.* ***Map*** *p66 R15* 12
Contemporary

This minimalist Scandinavian restaurant on the ground floor of the Black Diamond is a very popular lunch venue, and dining here is a great way to see the building's interior design. The food is refreshingly light and imaginatively prepared, with a focus on fish and vegetables. It's great value – the evening menu is 345kr for three dishes, while a business lunch is 220kr – and in a wonderful harbourside location.

Cafés & bars

DAC Café

Bryghuspladsen (32 57 19 30, dac.dk/en/explore/cafe). Central Station, harbour bus 991, 992. ***Open*** *10am-5.30pm Fri-Wed; 10am-8.30pm Thur. Entry requires a ticket from the Danish Architecture Centre (110kr adults, 85kr reductions, free under-18s).* ***Map*** *p66 Q16* 9

Three large rooftop terraces with water views make this a special place to eat (it's a shame you have to pay museum entry to get in, although they do offer entry plus a meal for 199kr). Enjoy light Nordic food – the ever-present *smørrebrød* of course, alongside delicate pastries, coffee and cake. Weekends from 10am-2pm see a lunch buffet including coffee and juice for 185kr that encompasses everything from skyr to bacon and eggs, mini pastries, pancakes, salmon rillette and a green salad.

Kayak Bar

Børskaj 12 (kayakbar.dk). Central Station or Kongens Nytorv; harbour bus 991, 992. ***Open*** *2-9pm Tue-Wed; 2-10pm Thur; noon-1am Fri-Sat; closed Sun.* ***Map*** *p66 R14* 16

This bar/café is lively right into the night in the summer, with music, events and a casual restaurant serving the likes of burgers, *moules* and soups (starting from around 75kr). It's a good place for a beer in the evening.

► *Next door at Kayak Republic (kayakrepublic.dk) you can hire kayaks or take a guided tour around the city's waterways.*

Øieblikket

Det Kongelige Bibliotek, Søren Kierkegaards Plads 1 (33 47 49 49, www.meyersfb.dk/restauranter/oieblikket). Metro Kongens Nytorv. ***Open*** *8am-7pm Mon-Fri; 9am-6pm Sat.* ***Map*** *p66 R15* 18

The Black Diamond's espresso bar is named after the magazine that Søren Kirkegaard used to edit. It's a popular lunch spot, offering decent sandwiches and soups, and good coffee, but the main draw is the view of Copenhagen's waterfront.

❤ Restaurant Smör

Nationalmuseet, Ny Vestergade 10 (53 61 14 16, restaurant-smor.dk). Bus 1A, 2A, 9A, 11A. ***Open*** *10am-5pm Tue-Sun.* ***Map*** *p66 P15* 21

This relaxed café-restaurant in the Nationalmuseet plays on its links with history and, of course, serves classic Danish food. À la carte *smørrebrød* cost around 95kr each (and you'll need at least two); you can also expect to find a good cheese plate, daily cakes and a good choice of beers, yes, even in a museum! The kids' menu is a little more limited and includes a set menu with a little dessert surprise. Locals love it.

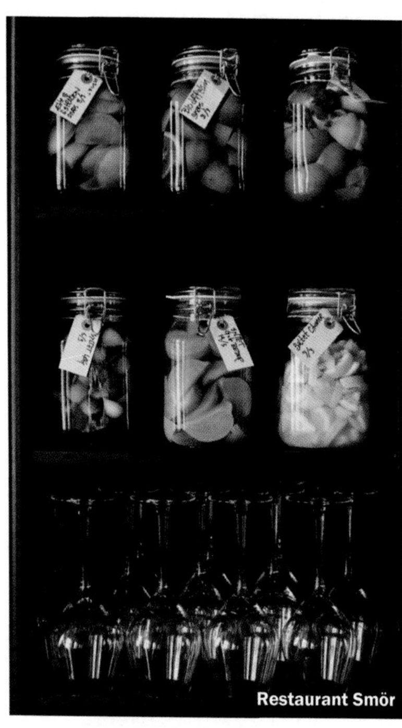

Restaurant Smör

North Central Copenhagen

North Central Copenhagen includes the Royal Palaces, Nyhavn and plenty of historic green spaces. Nørreport, where metros, S-trains and buses converge from all corners of the city, is its hub.

Start your day right with a coffee or brunch at nearby Torvehallerne, an excellent food market and a good spot to start a tour.

To the north, the Botanical Gardens offer an oasis from narrow cobbled shopping streets, as do the park and surrounds of the picture-perfect, Rosenborg Slot. These two attractions are part of the Parkmuseerne museum district, along with the Statens Museum for Kunst (SMK), the Hirschsprung Collection, the David Collection, the forthcoming Natural History Museum and the Workers Museum.

Beyond SMK and Østerport station, you reach Kastellet, the city's original fortress. *The Little Mermaid* sits on a windswept spot just beyond Kastellet, often surrounded by throngs of photo-taking daytrippers fresh from a cruise ship. Walk from here along the water towards the centre to find Instagram's favourite Copenhagen spot, Nyhavn, and the Royal Danish Playhouse beside it. All roads from here run to Kongens Nytorv, a grand square with fine buildings and wide streets that leads back to Strøget.

❤ Don't miss

1 Nyhavn to The Little Mermaid *p109*
Instagram your heart out at two of Copenhagen's most famous landmarks.

2 Marmorkirken *p115*
Marble-domed church with awe-inspiring interior.

3 Amalienborg Slot *p112*
Four rococo palaces round a grand cobbled square.

4 Rosenborg Slot *p105*
The city's fairy-tale palace.

5 Designmuseum Danmark *p114*
The works of the country's celebrated furniture designers.

6 Statens Museum for Kunst *p106*
Beautiful Danish art museum.

Nyhavn *p108*

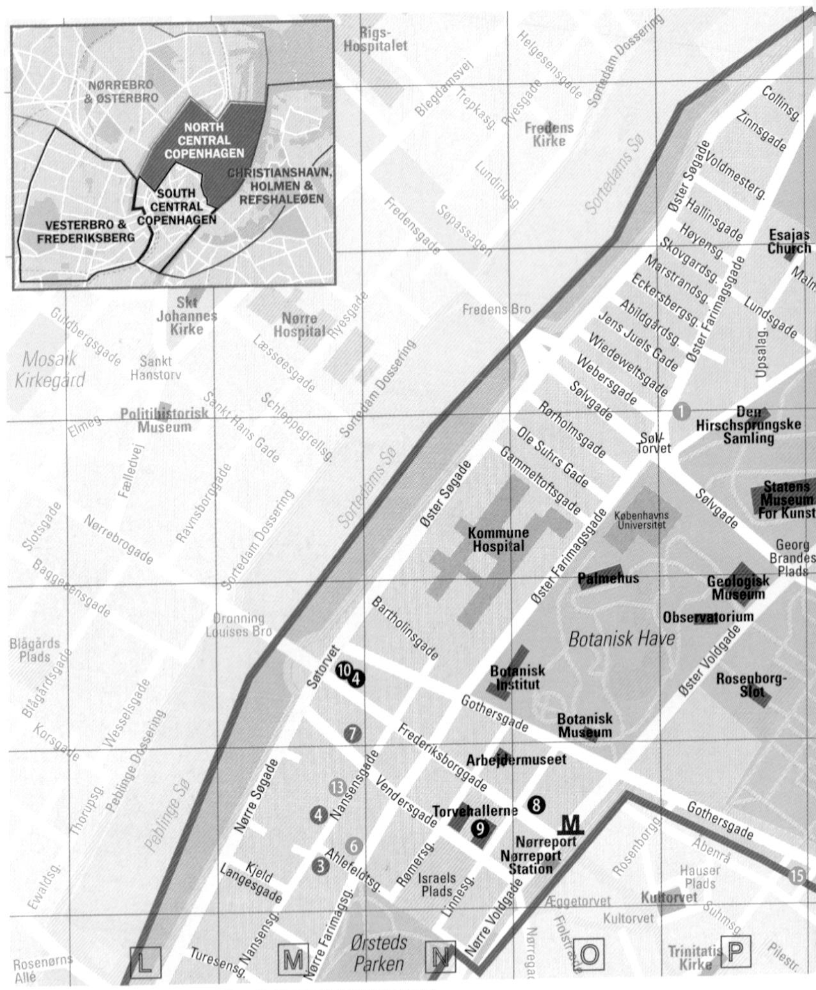

NORTH CENTRAL COPENHAGEN

Restaurants

1. Aamanns Etablissement *p107*
2. Almanak at The Standard *p108*
3. AOC *p116*
4. Cap Horn *p110*
5. Geist *p110*
6. Høst *p102*
7. Kokkeriet *p107*
8. Kong Hans Kælder *p111*
9. Marchal *p111*
10. MASH *p111*
11. Restaurant Ida Davidsen *p116*
12. Restaurant Rebel *p117*
13. Sticks'n'Sushi *p103*
14. Stud!o at The Standard *p111*
15. Sult *p107*

Cafés & bars

1. Apollo Bar *p111*
2. Balthazar Champagne Bar *p111*
3. Bankeråt *p103*
4. Bibendum *p103*
5. Café Atelier September *p107*
6. Klint – Designmuseets Café *p117*
7. Mikropolis *p103*
8. Oscar Bar & Café *p117*

Shops & services

1. Beau Marché *p107*
2. Bruun Rasmussen Kunstauktioner *p117*
3. Designmuseum Danmark Shop *p117*
4. Friluftsland *p104*
5. Løgismose *p117*
6. Magasin *p111*
7. Monies *p117*
8. Stilleben No.22 *p104*
9. Torvehallerne *p103 & p104*
10. Wood Wood MUSEUM *p104*

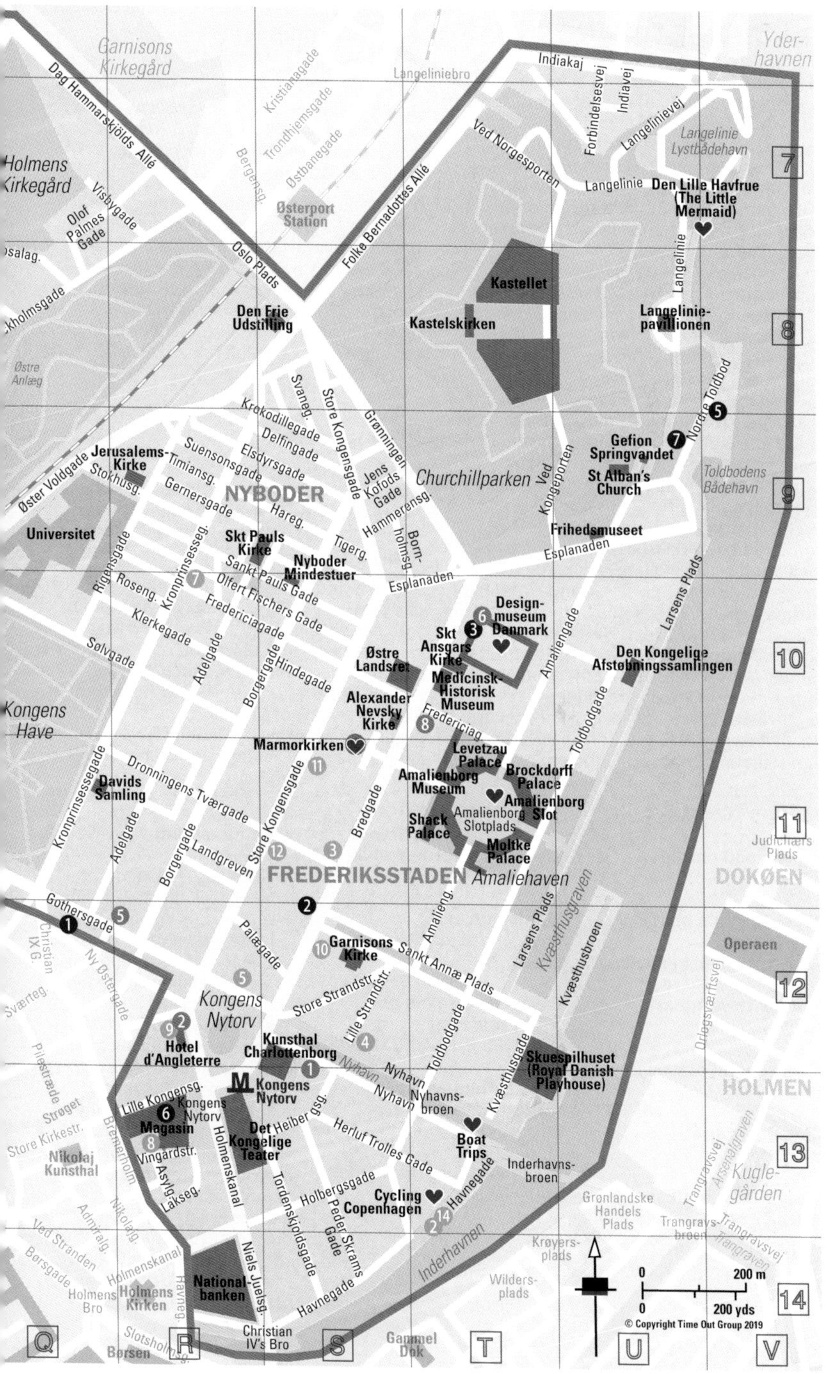
Garnisons Kirkegård
Langeliniebro
Yder-havnen
Indiakaj
Forbindelsesvej
Indiavej
Langelinievej
Langelinie Lystbådehavn
Dag Hammarskjölds Allé
Kristianiagade
Trondhjemsgade
Østbanegade
Bergensg.
Ved Norgesporten
Holmens Kirkegård
Visbygade
Olof Palmes Gade
Østerport Station
Folke Bernadottes Allé
Langelinie
Den Lille Havfrue (The Little Mermaid)
Oslo Plads
Kastellet
Langelinie
Kastelskirken
Den Frie Udstilling
Langelinie-pavillionen
Østre Anlæg
Svaneg.
Store Kongensgade
Grønningen
Krokodillegade
Delfingade
Elsdyrsgade
Nordre Toldbod
Gefion Springvandet
Jerusalems-Kirke
Suensonsgade
Timiansg.
Stokhusg.
Øster Voldgade
Gernersgade
NYBODER
Jens Kofods Gade
Hammerensg.
Churchillparken
Ved Kongeporten
St Alban's Church
Toldbodens Bådehavn
Hareg.
Universitet
Skt Pauls Kirke
Tigerg.
Born-holmsg.
Frihedsmuseet
Esplanaden
Nyboder Mindestuer
Rigensgade
Sankt Pauls Gade
Kronprinsesseg.
Roseng.
Olfert Fischers Gade
Esplanaden
Larsens Plads
Design-museum Danmark
Fredericiagade
Klerkegade
Skt Ansgars Kirke
Sølvgade
Amaliengade
Østre Landsret
Hindegade
Den Kongelige Afstøbningssamlingen
Adelgade
Borgergade
Medicinsk-Historisk Museum
Toldbodgade
Kongens Have
Alexander Nevsky Kirke
Fredericiag.
Marmorkirken
Levetzau Palace
Kronprinsessegade
Dronningens Tværgade
Brockdorff Palace
Davids Samling
Amalienborg Museum
Store Kongensgade
Bredgade
Amalienborg Slot
Amalienborg Slotplads
Shack Palace
Adelgade
Landgreven
Moltke Palace
Borgergade
FREDERIKSSTADEN
Amaliehaven
Kvæsthusgraven
Judichærs Plads
DOKØEN
Gothersgade
Christian IX G.
Amalieng.
Larsens Plads
Operaen
Ny Østergade
Palægade
Garnisons Kirke
Sankt Annæ Plads
Kvæsthusbroen
Orlogsværftsvej
Sværteg.
Kongens Nytorv
Store Strandstr.
Lille Strandstr.
Pilestræde
Hotel d'Angleterre
Kunsthal Charlottenborg
Nyhavn
Toldbodgade
Kvæsthusgade
Skuespilhuset (Royal Danish Playhouse)
Kongens Nytorv
HOLMEN
Strøget
Lille Kongensg.
Kongens Nytorv
Magasin
Heiber gsg.
Nyhavn
Nyhavns-broen
Store Kirkestr.
Bremerholm
Holmenskanal
Det Kongelige Teater
Herluf Trolles Gade
Boat Trips
Arsenalgraven
Nikolaj Kunsthal
Vingårdstr.
Asylg.
Lakseg.
Tordenskjoldsgade
Inderhavns-broen
Trangravsvej
Kugle-gården
Holbergsgade
Cycling Copenhagen
Havnegade
Grønlandske Handels Plads
Admiralg.
Nikolajg.
Peder Skrams Gade
Trangravs-broen
Trangravsvej
Trangraven
Ved Stranden
Inderhavnen
Krøyers-plads
Børsgade
Holmenskanal
National-banken
Niels Juelsg.
Havnegade
Wilders-plads
0
200 m
Holmens Bro
Holmens Kirken
Havneg.
0
200 yds
© Copyright Time Out Group 2019
Slotsholmsg.
Christian IV's Bro
Børsen
Gammel Dok
Q
R
S
T
U
V
7
8
9
10
11
12
13
14

NØRREPORT & AROUND

Head north beyond Nørre Voldgade (the northern boundary of the old city ramparts), and you'll arrive at an area dominated by two things: Nørreport station and the city's excellent covered food market, **Torvehallerne**. The latter opened in 2011 and is now a culinary focus for this part of the city and has done much to rejuvenate the surrounding area.

Just north of Israels Plads is **Arbejdermuseet** (The Workers Museum). The museum's entrance was once guarded by a statue of Lenin that looks as if it's come straight from a provincial Soviet town square, but the right-wing government of the noughties turned this into a political issue and the statue was moved to the back of the museum. The museum was updated recently and has a lot of family-friendly exhibitions about life in Denmark that go back to the 1880s.

The area south of Israels Plads is dominated by **Ørstedsparken**, a nice place for a stroll beside its large lake. The north-western side of the park is formed by Nørre Farimagsgade, where you'll find popular New Nordic restaurant **Høst**. **Nansensgade**, the next street up, is also worth visiting for its genteel atmosphere and traditional artisan shops, many of which are hidden away in unobtrusive basement spaces. On the corner sits **Ibsens Hotel** (*see p234*), its neon-red sign something of a local landmark.

Sights & museums

Arbejdermuseet

*Rømersgade 22 (33 93 25 75, www.arbejdermuseet.dk). Metro/train Nørreport. **Open** 10am-4pm Thur-Sun; 10am-7pm Wed. **Admission** 90kr; 65kr reductions; free under-18s. **Map** p100 N11.*

This atmospheric building, formerly the headquarters of the Social Democratic Party, has a wonderful period basement café and *ølhal* (beer hall). While the museum's aim – to show how Danish workers' lives have changed over the past century – is admirable, it is more geared up to Danes than international travellers and is regularly swarmed with school trips on weekdays.

Restaurants

Høst ♛♛♛

*Nørre Farimagsgade 41 (89 93 84 09, www.cofoco.dk/en/restaurants/hoest). Metro/train Nørreport. **Open** 5.30pm-midnight daily. **Map** p100 M11* ⑥ New Nordic

This ravishing two-storey restaurant located close to the lakes is as Nordic as they come, with raw aesthetics – think recycled wood, concrete floors and sheepskin rugs – and dishes made with local produce, such as lobster, beef and Danish cheese. It regularly features on lists of the world's most beautiful restaurants. Traditional Nordic recipes are given a modern twist, resulting

❤ Time to eat & drink

Classy food market
Torvehallerne *p103 and p104*

Copenhagen's best *smørrebrød*
Aamanns Etablissement *p107*

Drink with some art
Apollo Bar *p111*

For a special occasion
Geist *p110*

Michelin-starred
AOC *p116*

Superb interior design
SMK café *p106*

❤ Time to shop

Bohemian vintage chic
Beau Marché *p107*

Danish design
Designmuseum Danmark shop *p117*

Designer threads at a great price
Wood Wood MUSEUM *p104*

For anything you've forgotten to pack
Magasin *p111*

Fresh interiors inspiration
Stilleben No.22 *p104*

In the know
Getting around

This area is large and you might find it easier to explore by metro, bus and bike than on foot – but it depends what you plan to do. Nørreport is a connection point for buses, metro and S-trains. For Kastellet and *The Little Mermaid*, you could head for Østerbro station, just steps away from the sights, or take the harbour bus to the Nordre Toldbod stop, a short walk away. It is easy to cycle around this area but beware of other tourists stepping into the bike lanes – it can be very busy, particularly around the shopping streets and key attractions. Know that you have to jump off and push your bike on Strøget; the same does not go for the parallel streets.

in combinations such as scallops with horseradish and apple, cod with lingonberries and roasted chicken skin, and Norwegian lobster with sea buckthorn and carrots.

Sticks'n'Sushi

Nansensgade 59 (33 11 14 07, www.sticksnsushi.com/da). Metro/train Nørreport. ***Open*** *10am-10.30pm Sun-Thur, Sun; 10am-11pm Fri, Sat.* ***Map*** *p100 M11* ⓭ Japanese

One of Copenhagen's most accessible sushi restaurants (it was also the first), with branches all over the city. The menu varies depending on the fish available, but the quality remains generally high (as do the prices). Options include a good kids' menu and items for those who don't like raw fish. **Other locations** Øster Farimagsgade 16, Østerbro (35 38 34 63); Borgergade 13, Indre By (33 11 88 11); Gammel Kongevej 120, Frederiksberg (33 29 00 10); Bernstoffsgade 3, Tivoli (88 32 95 95).

Cafés & bars

Bankeråt

Ahlefeldtsgade 27-29 (33 93 69 88, www.bankeraat.dk). Metro/train Nørreport. ***Open*** *9.30am-midnight Mon-Fri; 10.30am-midnight Sat; 10.30am-8pm Sun.* ***Map*** *p100 M11* ❸

Monster brunches, great tortillas and pasta dishes, plus the quirkiest decor of all Copenhagen's cafés set this grungy boho cave apart. Brace yourself for a sobering encounter when you descend to the basement loos, as you're confronted by a ghoulish assortment of Gothic taxidermy tableaux.

Bibendum

Nansensgade 45 (33 33 07 74, www.bibendum.dk). Metro/train Nørreport. ***Open*** *4pm-midnight Mon-Sat.* ***Map*** *p100 M11* ❹

Copenhagen's first ever wine bar, Bibendum opened in 2001 and has sparked something of a trend. This cosy, sexy spot has an extensive range of wines by the glass (unusual in beer-minded Copenhagen) and a flirty cellar ambience. The charcuterie plates are excellent and the staff knowledgeable.

Mikropolis

Vendersgade 22 (32 13 79 97) mikkeller.dk/location/mikropolis. Metro/train Nørreport. ***Open*** *4pm-midnight Tue-Thu; 4pm-2am Fri-Sat* ***Map*** *p100 M10* ❼

If you see the name Mikkeller and you like beer, look no further. This bar is one of Copenhagen's many Mikkellers, known for their friendly style, great IPAs and relaxed Nordic-chic interiors (they are currently conquering New York, London and Bangkok too). The microbrewery is run by a former maths and physics teacher who started experimenting with hops one day in his Copenhagen kitchen; he's now one of the most cutting-edge brewers on the planet. A film about his life should be called *Breaking Beer*... that's what we think, anyway. This one fuses ten taps of beer, cocktails and a big spirit selection, so you don't need to stay true to any one thing. One of their best (and that's saying something). **Other locations** Viktoriagade 6; Warpigs, Kødbyen; Refshalesvej 169B.

❤ Torvehallerne

Frederiksborggade 21 (70 10 60 70, www.torvehallernekbh.dk). Metro/train Nørreport. ***Open*** *10am-7pm Mon-Thur; 10am-8pm Fri; 10am-6pm Sat; 10am-5pm Sun.* ***Map*** *p100 N11* ❾

Most definitely the right place to stop for a coffee, snack, lunch, dinner, food tour, food shopping and everything else in between. Torvehallerne's two halls plus outdoor market showcase everything from the delights created on Bornholm, Denmark's sunniest island, to specialist French cheeses, expertly chosen wine (which can otherwise be hit and miss in the city), pizza, *smørrebrød*, tapas, tacos and more. It's a particularly good spot if you are visiting as a family or in a group with picky eaters – you don't all have to eat the same type of meal. Recommended in particular: **Gorm's**, for thin pizzas; **Hija de Sanchez** (*see p140*); **Laura's Bakery**, for its excessive *wienerbrød* and great breakfast plates; and **Hallernes Smørrebrød**, particularly for the fried fish fillet with remoulade and capers.

Stilleben No.22 p104

Torvehallerne

Shops & services

Friluftsland

Frederiksborggade 50-52 (33 14 51 50, www.friluftsland.dk). Metro/train Nørreport. ***Open*** *10am-6pm Mon-Fri; 10am-3.30pm Sun.* ***Map*** *p100 M10* ❹ *Outdoor kit*

One of the most iconic Scandinavian souvenirs you can bring home is a super-stylish, super-durable Fjallraven Känken rucksack, and at this shop you can choose from all colours of the rainbow, as well as pick up quality outdoor kit, coats to help you brave the worst winter weather and all kinds of equipment, beautifully designed of course.

❤ Stilleben No.22

Frederiksborggade 22 (22 45 11 31, www.stilleben.dk). Metro/train Nørreport. ***Open*** *10am-6pm Mon-Fri; 10am-5pm Sat.* ***Map*** *p100 O11* ❽ *Homewares*

This premium interior design shop sells covetable items from artisan designers, including vases made on Bornholm, a large range of handcrafted ceramics and candle holders, and Tekla blankets and textiles. Prints, by the likes of local artist Anne Nowak, are sold with and without frames. Recommended.

❤ Torvehallerne

Frederiksborggade 21 (70 10 60 70, www.torvehallernekbh.dk). Metro/train Nørreport. ***Open*** *10am-7pm Mon-Thur; 10am-8pm Fri; 10am-6pm Sat; 11am-5pm Sun.* ***Map*** *p100 N11* ❾ *Food & drink*

The halls have plenty of shops to choose from, including bookshops with cookbooks in English and Danish, kitchen supplies stalls, food stalls that can vacuum pack cheese and offer travel-friendly pack sizes for hand luggage, and specialist ingredients and spice stores. A particular highlight is **Arla Unika**, an experimental cheese stall from Denmark's super dairy Arla, with cheeses named Northern Lights and Drunken Dog. *See also p103* under Cafés & bars.

❤ Wood Wood MUSEUM

Frederiksborggade 54 (35 35 62 64, www.woodwood.com). Bus 5C, 3A, 14. ***Open*** *10am-6pm Mon-Fri; 10am-4pm Sat; noon-4pm Sun.* ***Map*** *p100 M10* ❿ *Fashion*

Just over Dronning Louises Bro (Queen Louise's Bridge), this is another stellar Scandi brand's concept/outlet/samples store. For womenswear, menswear, accessories and homewares, not just from Wood Wood but also from other carefully chosen brands, it's a must do.

ROSENBORG SLOT & AROUND

North and east of Torvehallerne is **Parkmuseerne** – the Park Museum Quarter. First up is the **Botanisk Have & Museum** (Botanical Garden & Museum), a welcome (and free) green space in summer, with a balmy Palmehuset (Palm House) that provides refuge from the arctic frost of winter. Just to the north is the **Geologisk Museum** (Geological Museum), while further north still, the lakes of the **Østre Anlæg** park follow the line of the city's old defensive moat. Within the park are two fine museums: **Statens Museum for Kunst** is Denmark's national gallery and largest art museum, and **Den Hirschsprungske**

Samling (Hirschsprung Collection) displays art from the 19th and early 20th centuries.

Across from Statens Museum is the entrance to the oldest park in Copenhagen, **Kongens Have** (King's Garden) and **Rosenborg Slot** (Rosenborg Palace). A glimpse of this fairy-tale, 17th-century Dutch Renaissance castle in the heart of Copenhagen never fails to delight.

On Gothersgade is **Filmhuset** (Film House; *see p193*), the Danish Film Institute's (DFI) world-class complex devoted to Danish and international cinema, and on Kronprinsessegade is yet another treasure house of a museum, **Davids Samling**, a gorgeous collection of Danish, Islamic and European art.

At the north end of Store Kongensgade is **Nyboder**. While Kastellet was for centuries home to the army, the royal navy lived in the Lilliputian, ochre terraces of Nyboder, built during Christian IV's time to house over 2,200 naval staff (a purpose it still serves). There's a small museum, **Nyboders Mindestuer** (Nyboder Memorial Rooms).

Sights & museums

Botanisk Have & Museum

Gothersgade 128 (35 32 22 40, www.botanik.snm.ku.dk). Metro/train Nørreport. ***Open*** *Garden Apr-Sept 8.30am-6pm daily; Oct-Mar 8.30am-4pm daily. Palm house 1 Apr-30 Sept 10am-5pm Tue-Sun; 1 Oct-31 Mar 10am-3.30pm Tue-Sun.* ***Admission*** *free except the Palm House: 60kr adults, 40kr children 3-16.* ***Map*** *p100 O10.*

The Botanical Garden was laid out in 1871 to designs by HA Flindt, with a lake that was once part of the city moat as its centrepiece. You'll find examples of most of Denmark's flora, as well as those exotic plants that could be persuaded to grow this far north. The grounds also include the Natural History Museum of Denmark and the Geologisk Museum. These are a little old fashioned as they stand, but new state-of-the-art buildings and exhibitions are planned from 2022 when the new Natural History Museum is due to open.

In the know

Parkmuseerne

This collection of six museums – Statens Museum for Kunst, Davids Samling, Den Hirschsprungske Samling, Rosenborg Slot, the Natural History Museum of Denmark and Arbejdermuseet (The Workers Museum) – can be visited with a combined ticket costing 243kr (50% off typical prices), sold at all six venues; visit www.parkmuseerne.dk for details. The ticket also includes free entry to the Palmehuset in the Botanical Gardens; Davids Samling is free to all but the others cost approximately 95kr per museum.

Davids Samling

Kronprinsessegade 30-32 (33 73 49 49, www.davidmus.dk). Metro/train Nørreport. ***Open*** *10am-5pm Tue, Thur-Sun; 10am-9pm Wed.* ***Admission*** *free.* ***Map*** *p100 Q11.*

This art and antiquities museum is housed in what once was the home of its founder, Christian Ludvig David, a prominent lawyer whose collections spanned 18th-century European art, Danish Early Modern works, and Islamic art and artefacts. It is one of the ten most important collections of Islamic art in the Western world, covering the entire classical Islamic world, from Spain to India, and from the eighth to the 19th century.

Den Frie Udstilling

Oslo Plads 1 (33 12 28 03, denfrie.dk). Train Østerport. ***Open*** *noon-6pm Tue-Wed, Fri-Sun; noon-9pm Thur.* ***Admission*** *70kr, children under 12 free, 50kr reductions.* ***Map*** *p100 S8.*

Everything in The Free is about contemporary art – even the building's front relief, with an image of a child on Pegasus's back, is about freedom of movement. Founded in 1898, it's a beautiful building that plays host to contemporary installations, sculpture and artwork from Denmark and around the world, along with a great café.

Den Hirschsprungske Samling

Stockholmsgade 20 (35 42 03 36, www.hirschsprung.dk). Metro/train Nørreport. ***Open*** *11am-4pm Wed-Sun.* ***Admission*** *95kr; free under-18s.* ***Map*** *p100 P9.*

This art collection from the 19th and early 20th century is strong on the glorious Danish Golden Age (1800-50). It was created by tobacco manufacturer Heinrich Hirschsprung (1836-1908), who crammed the paintings and sculptures into his home on Højbro Plads. He donated the works to the Municipality of Copenhagen on condition that they be displayed in similarly intimate surroundings, hence the series of small rooms around three larger halls that make up the building.

❤ Rosenborg Slot

Øster Voldgade 4A (33 15 32 86, www.rosenborgslot.dk). Metro/train Nørreport. ***Open*** *2 Jan-15 Apr, 1 Nov-22 Dec 10am-3pm Tue-Sun; May, Sept, Oct, 26-30 Dec 10am-4pm daily; June-Aug 9am-5pm daily. Closed over Christmas.* ***Admission*** *115kr; 75kr reductions; free under-17s. 160kr Rosenborg & Amalienborg ticket (valid for 36hrs).* ***Map*** *p100 P10.*

Rosenborg was Christian IV's favourite residence and it's easy to see why. The fairy-tale palace, set in gardens much beloved by families, contains the Crown Jewels in the basement and rooms that are the exact opposite of Danish minimalism on all other floors. The intimacy of the decorations, plus the vast number of them, makes it great fun to explore.

The castle started as a small summer house. Christian extended it between 1606 and 1634, finishing with the octagonal staircase tower designed by Hans van Steenwinckel the Younger. Rosenborg is jammed full of the king's fancies: toys, architectural tricks, inventions, *objets d'art* and jewellery, which he gathered from across Europe like a regal Mr Toad. A source of great pride was the basement, where his orchestra would perform, the music travelling up through a complex system of pipes connected to his living quarters. These days, the basement houses the Treasury, the stronghold of the Crown Jewels – a collection in which quality, not quantity, is the watchword. The star piece is the Golden Crown of the Absolute Monarchy, decorated with sapphires, diamonds and rubies, made by Poul Kurtz in 1670, and used by Denmark's kings for 170 years. Christian IV's gold, pearl and jewel-encrusted saddle and crown (1595) are, as you'd expect, jaw-dropping. Other rooms in the basement display royal weapons and *objets d'art* of ivory and amber.

Rosenborg was a royal residence until 1838, when these collections were revealed to the public, along with the many rooms that had remained intact from the time of Christian IV (1588-1648) to Frederik IV (1699-1730); later rooms were re-created. The 24 rooms (plus six Treasury rooms) currently on show offer an insight into the lives of Renaissance kings that is perhaps unparalleled in Europe for its atmosphere and intimacy. Christian IV's toilet, covered in beautiful blue Dutch tiles, for example, is as fascinating a treasure as the jewels in the basement.

❤ Statens Museum for Kunst

Sølvgade 48-50 (33 74 84 94, www.smk.dk). Metro/train Nørreport. ***Open*** *10am-6pm Tue, Thur-Sun; 10am-8pm Wed.* ***Admission*** *120kr; 95kr reductions; free under-18s; 100kr adult with child.* ***Map*** *p100 P9.*

This beautiful museum, the best in the city, focuses on Danish art. The luminous, inspiring and astonishingly intimate portraits by the Danish masters from the Golden Age of the early 19th century figure prominently. Rooms are dedicated to CW Eckersburg and his pupils Christen Købke and Constantin Hansen. The landscapes of JT Lundbye, the stark portraits of Vilhelm Hammershøi, the powerful portraits of LA Ring and the

symbolist pieces by PC Skovgaard – as well as their forerunners from the 18th century, such as Nicolai Abildgaard and Jens Juel – are among the treats in the museum. The Skagen artists (Michael and Anna Ancher, PS Krøyer), who specialised in everyday scenes and light, summery landscapes, and the Fyn painters (Peter Hansen, Frits Syberg), are also well represented. No one before or since has quite captured the unmistakeable, crisp Danish light as these artists did, and their paintings often depict brutal, beautiful and compelling stories concerning 'real' people's lives.

In the new wing, 25 paintings by Henri Matisse, as well as works by Braque, Munch and Picasso, are highlights, as is the Danish modernist collection featuring the painters Harald Giersing and Karl Isakson, and sculptors Kai Nielsen and Astrid Noack. In the old wing, the Italians are well represented by Titian, Tintoretto, Filippino Lippi, Mantegna and Guardi; Dutch and Flemish masters from the 15th to 17th centuries include Rubens, Bruegel, Rembrandt, Van Dyck and Van Goyen; while Fragonard, Poussin and Lorrain are among the 18th-century French artists.

There's also a children's art studio with fantastic opportunities for painting, modelling, sketching and more (for an extra fee), often guided by artists and inspired by current exhibitions. Kids are kitted out with aprons before they begin. There is also a bookshop and a beautiful café, designed by artist Danh Vo, with classic Danish design furniture alongside Enzo Mari's 'do it yourself' pieces and Isamu Noguchi lamps. The green kitchen has its own bakery and serves a great

lunch as well as juices, tea, bread and the city's best museum coffee. You do not have to pay the admission fee to eat there.

Restaurants

❤ Aamanns Etablissement ♛♛

Øster Farimagsgade 12 (20 80 52 02, www.aamanns.dk). Metro/train Nørreport. ***Open*** *noon-4pm Mon-Sun; 6-11pm Wed-Sat.* ***Map*** *p100 P9* 1 *Modern Danish*

Visit this elegant, light-filled restaurant to sample Adam Aamanns' moreish open-topped sandwiches at lunchtime, or a heartier Modern Danish meal, based on local, seasonal ingredients (the likes of classic steak sandwiches or beetroot tartare) in the evening. If you're here for the *smørrebrød*, choose from inspired combinations such as cold-smoked Icelandic salmon with pickled radishes, or classic chicken salad with apple and fried chicken skin. Aamanns is generally recognised as serving the best *smørrebrød* in the city.

Next door, at no.10, is Aamanns Deli (20 80 52 01), where you can choose lunchtime *smørrebrod* to eat in at the small café table or take away. **Other location** Aamanns 1921, Niels Hemmingsens Gade 19-21 (20 80 52 04).

Kokkeriet ♛♛♛

Kronprinsessegade 64 (33 15 27 77, www.kokkeriet.dk). Train Østerport. ***Open*** *6pm-1am Mon-Sat.* ***Map*** *p100 R10* 7 *French/Danish*

Tucked away in Nyboder, this small, seductive restaurant has a Michelin star for its exceptional-quality Danish dishes that meld forgotten recipes and lively, contemporary cooking. Loved by locals, Kokkeriet serves vegan, vegetarian, pescatarian and light set menus, and a fun Tuesday option called the Tuesday Test, where guests can choose to add four experimental dishes to their large or small set menu.

Sult ♛

Filmhuset, Gothersgade 55(33 74 34 17, www.sult.dk). Metro/train Nørreport. ***Open*** *9am-10pm Mon-Fri; 10.35am-10pm Sat; 10.45am-7.30pm Sun.* ***Map*** *p100 P11* 15 *Global*

The Danish Film Institute's magnificent film centre has another draw. Here, skilful chefs successfully combine southern European food and global influences in handsome, modern, New York-ish surroundings (high ceilings, wooden floors, tall windows). *Sult*, which means 'hunger' in Danish, is named after Henning Carlsen's classic 1966 film of the same name. Weekend brunch is popular.

Cafés & bars

Café Atelier September

Gothersgade 30 (no phone; www.cafeatelierseptember.com). Metro/train Nørreport. ***Open*** *7.30am-6pm Mon-Fri; 9am-5pm Sat-Sun.* ***Map*** *p100 R12* 5

With coffee from Koppi, matcha tea from Marukyu Koyamaen Uji and avocado-fuelled brunches served all day every day, Atelier September is bright and beautiful, with an art-gallery feel and a small but perfectly formed breakfast and lunch menu. The place to take a break from design store browsing.

Shops & services

❤ Beau Marché

Ny Østergade 32 (55 77 14 30, beaumarche.dk). Metro/train Nørreport. ***Open*** *shop 10am-6pm Mon-Fri; 10am-5pm Sat. Café 8am-midnight Mon-Fri; 10am-midnight Sat.* ***Map*** *p100 Q12* 1

This chic and bohemian interior design store is a breath of fresh air after all the birch, pine and clean lines of the more modern interiors shops in the area. While those Scandinavian stylings are still super desirable, this place is more of an Aladdin's Cave of bright mohair blankets, vintage chairs, colourful vases and curios. The café/wine bar is a popular hang out with local media types and models.

KONGENS NYTORV & NYHAVN

Kongens Nytorv is an excellent starting point for a tour of the city, as Bredgade, Nyhavn and Strøget all branch out from it, and most of the other main sights are within a few minutes' walk. With the imminent opening of the city ring metro line, it will again be a hub for the city and its people.

The square is dominated to the south-east by **Det Kongelige Teater** (the Royal Theatre, Old Stage, *see p209*), which is used almost exclusively to show ballet. The main neo-Renaissance building, by Vilhelm Dahlerup and Ove Petersen, dates from 1872, although the theatre was founded in 1748. The Nye Scene was added in 1931, connected via an archway to the other side of Tordenskjoldsgade. The inscription outside, '*Ei blot til lyst*', is taken from the original building designed by Nicolai Eigtved and translates as 'Not just for pleasure'. This may suggest that productions are worthy affairs, but that doesn't stop most selling out way in advance.

Working clockwise round the square from the theatre, you come to Denmark's first department store, the grand **Magasin**, which replaced the Hotel du Nord in 1894 and now has a stylish Metro station outside its main entrance; **Hviids Vinstue**, a venerable drinking den dating from 1723; the eastern end of **Strøget**; and **Hotel d'Angleterre** (*see p233*).

On a corner of the square opposite the hotel is an ornate kiosk decorated with gold relief that depicts Denmark's early aviators. At no.4 is another of the square's finest buildings, the Dutch Palladian-style **Thotts Palais** (1685), named after a previous owner, Count Otto Thott. Today, the pink stucco palace houses the French Embassy.

East of Kongens Nytorv is **Nyhavn**, the city's most photographed and photogenic canal, lined with brightly coloured houses and with a rather checkered past. In winter there are Christmas stalls and fairy lights, while in summer it is packed with pavement cafés. At all times of year, you are more likely to meet other tourists than Danes down this stretch, but for its colour and hustle and bustle it's still worth a visit.

After the British bombardment of 1807, Nyhavn's so-called 'Palmy Days' of prosperity were brought to a rude end and the wealthy merchants moved out. By coincidence, Hans Christian Andersen moved in shortly after, and subsequently lived at three different addresses on the canal (*see p110*). During this time, Nyhavn's quayside saw service as one of the city's red-light districts, and as recently as the 1950s it was a disreputable place, lined with bars, knocking shops and old-school tattoo parlours. Today, the quayside is still a great place for a beer or two before heading elsewhere; a stroll north, for instance, will bring you to *The Little Mermaid, see opposite*.

Two charming shopping streets lead off the north side of Nyhavn: **Store Strandstræde** and **Lille Strandstræde**, both good for upscale antiques, clothes, art and ceramics. On the quieter south side, the main draw is the 17th-century Dutch Baroque palace of Charlottenborg, home to **Det Kongelige Kunstakademi** (Royal Academy of Fine Arts) since 1754. The former palace offers a changing programme of contemporary art exhibitions in the **Kunsthal Charlottenborg**. Further south-east, on waterside Havnegade, is **The Standard**, a striking teal-coloured restaurant/jazz club owned by New Nordic culinary pioneer Claus Meyer and jazz musician Niels Lan Doky.

In the know
Weak at the knees

In the centre of Kongens Nytorv is a faintly absurd statue (by Abraham-César Lamoureux, dating from 1687) of the square's patron, King Christian V, depicting him as a Roman general astride his horse. The weight of the gilded lead statue finally proved too much for the horse's legs and it had to be recast in bronze in 1946.

Sights & museums

Kunsthal Charlottenborg

Nyhavn 2 (33 74 46 39, www.kunsthalcharlottenborg.dk). Metro Kongens Nytorv. ***Open*** *noon-8pm Tue-Fri; 11am-5pm Sat-Sun.* ***Admission*** *90kr; 50kr reductions; free under-15s. Free after 5pm Wed.* ***Map*** *p100 S12.*

This huge gallery alternates between Danish and international exhibitions of contemporary art, architecture and decorative arts. The hall was built in 1883 at the request of an influential group of Danish artists and is now run by the Ministry of Culture.

Restaurants

Almanak at The Standard ♛♛

Havnegade 44 (72 14 88 08, www.thestandardcph.dk/almanak). Metro Kongens Nytorv, or bus 11A, 66. ***Open*** *noon-midnight Tue-Sun.* ***Map*** *p100 T13* ❷ New Nordic

❤ From Nyhavn to the Little Mermaid

***Map** p100 T13-V7*

Get your smartphone at the ready – have you even been to Copenhagen if you haven't taken a photograph of yourself at Nyhavn or in front of *The Little Mermaid*? These two sights are the city's best known and most photographed, and it's hard not to jump on the bandwagon. Grab a bike or some comfortable shoes (a warm coat is a good idea too) and get exploring. From Nyhavn, the lovely if windswept walk along the canal to *The Little Mermaid* takes in some of the city's best ancient and modern architecture and a few talking points too.

Starting at Nyhavn, walk to the water and head to the **Skuespilhuset**, the **Royal Danish Playhouse**. It's a good spot for a coffee, and you can browse costumes set out in the lobby too if that's your thing. Past the theatre, you'll find **Ofeliaplads**, a floating platform in the water that is used as a kind of outdoor beach in the summer, where kids play, deckchairs lounge and barbecue grills sizzle. Onwards along the waterfront, you'll walk past a few converted waterfront buildings to the green space of **Amaliehaven**. This garden has a beautiful fountain and a viewpoint through from the water to the green-roofed **Marmorkirken** (Marble Church, *see p115*) and **Amalienborg Square** (*see p112*). Across the water you can see the Opera House – there is culture and history everywhere you look.

It gets windier from this point, but keep walking, and look out for **Den Kongelige Afstøbningssamling** (the Royal Cast Collection), marked by a bronze replica of Michelangelo's *David*. Inside, 2,000 plaster casts of the world's most famous sculptures span a period of 4,000 years. Unveiled in 2018 and created by Virgin Islands' artist La Vaughn Belle and Danish artist Jeannette Ehlers, *Queen Mary* is a monumental sculpture referring to Danish colonialism in the Caribbean that sits a little further along the quay. The Mary in question is Mary Thomas, who led a labour revolt on St Croix in 1878 with three other women, burning down Frederiksted's town, sugar cane fields and plantations in the quest for freedom.

The next sight to spot is a huge mythical fountain (1908), the **Gefionspringvandet**, which shows a group of animals being driven by the Norse goddess Gefion. You can then walk or cycle past Nordre Toldbod, stopping at **Løgismose** (*see p117*) if you need gourmet food supplies or a picnic, continuing through **Langelinie Park** until you find *The Little Mermaid* perched on a slippery windswept rock surrounded by tourists. Commissioned by Carl Jacobsen of Carlsberg and created by Edvard Eriksen back in 1913, her body was modelled on the sculptor's wife, while the head was inspired by ballerina Ellen Price. Over the years she has lost her head, been covered in paint four times, lost her arms and been blasted off her rock; and yet today she's still here. The fact that the mermaid is small often disappoints people, as does the fact that there's not much to see at the end of the walk other than the mermaid. But if you enjoy a gentle 45-minute wander along the water mulling over her story – where a mermaid sacrificed her voice and her family to be able to walk and be with the person she loved – you might take something positive away. That, and a good selfie.

Hans Christian Andersen

The story of a man and a city

He may have been born a few hours away in Odense, but Denmark's greatest writer, Hans Christian Andersen, couldn't wait to leave and seek his fortune in Copenhagen. Andersen arrived on Monday 6 September 1819 (he had to walk the last few miles into town because he couldn't afford the full fare), a day so momentous that he marked it as his 'second birthday' every year thereafter.

He was virtually penniless when he arrived, yet he possessed an almost supernatural self-confidence. Andersen believed he was something special from an early age and immediately set about making something of his talents at the Royal Theatre. On his first visit, the very night he arrived in the city, he was so naive that he accepted a ticket from a tout as if it were a gift.

Andersen's confidence was shaken by the rejection of his ballet dancing, singing and acting skills, but slowly he built up contacts among Copenhagen's cultured bourgeoisie, who would sponsor his education and finance his early attempts at writing. These were not instantly successful, but his first published piece of any significance, a fantasy based on a walk on New Year's Eve across the city to Amager, was a moderate hit. It was all the encouragement his pathological need for recognition required. Poetry, plays and novels followed, few of which hold up to scrutiny today. But in 1835, almost as an afterthought, he published a small book of stories that would be the works for which he would be remembered.

Over 150 stories were to follow, many becoming world-famous. Tales such as *The Little Mermaid*, *The Emperor's New Clothes*, *The Snow Queen*, *Thumbelina*, *The Princess and the Pea*, *The Red Shoes* and *The Little Match Girl* remain widely read and translated, their messages and morals as universal today as when they were written. Copenhagen and its people often feature in these stories. When Tivoli Gardens opened in 1843, Andersen was among the first through the gates; in fact, it was after one of his frequent later visits that he was inclined to compose his celebrated story, *The Nightingale*.

Andersen travelled more widely in Europe than any other Dane of his time. He also never owned his own house, instead living at various addresses in Copenhagen and, in his later years, at the homes of aristocratic friends. He died, aged 70, in 1875 and is buried in Assistens Kirkegård (see *p155*).

► *There are statues of Andersen in Rådhuspladsen and Kongens Have, and plaques on his old residences in Nyhavn (nos.18, 20 and 67) and Vingårdstræde (no.6). And, of course, the city's symbol, The Little Mermaid statue, is inspired by one of his darkest fairy tales.*

The Standard's ground-floor restaurant (on the right-hand side of the building) is a showcase for New Nordic cuisine and style. The kitchen is very focused on the local and the seasonal. This translates as a fairly short menu, but you can always expect to find a good offering of fish and meat paired with local herbs and produce – perhaps fried scallops with Jerusalem artichokes, or beef tartare with dehydrated beetroot, and apple sorbet with almond crumble to finish. A five-course evening menu is 575kr without wine or coffee; lunches start at around 90kr for a single *smørrebrød* serving (two are recommended). The terrace is open with water views from April to September.

Cap Horn ♛♛

Nyhavn 21 (33 12 85 04, www.caphorn.dk). Metro Kongens Nytorv. ***Open*** *11am-10.30pm Mon-Thur; 11am-11pm Fri; 10am-11pm Sat; 10am-10.30pm Sun.* ***Map*** *p100 S12* 4 *Traditional Danish*

When Danes think of Nyhavn, they usually think of herring and *smørrebrød*, and for that you need a proper Danish *værtshus* (pub). Nowhere along this postcard-perfect but very touristy stretch of canal does it get better than Cap Horn. Situated in one of the beautiful old townhouses built by King Christian IV in the 17th century, the place oozes old-world atmosphere and was a popular haunt for sailors and ladies of easy pleasure before reaching its current rather more salubrious state.

❤ Geist ♛♛♛

Kongens Nytorv 8 (33 13 37 13, www.restaurantgeist.dk). Metro Kongens Nytorv. ***Open*** *noon-3pm, 5.30pm-1am daily.* ***Map*** *p100 R12* 5 *New Nordic*

Run by Copenhagen's charismatic superchef Bo Bech, Geist gets rave reviews for its small plates and experimental cuisine – think lobster tartare with yuzu and hibiscus; sliced avocado with lightly salted caviar; or wild duck with pumpkin and chestnut. Other highlights are the stylish contemporary decor with muted lighting and candles; friendly service; top-notch cocktails; and its legendary 'air in air in air tiramisu'.

Kong Hans Kælder 

Vingårdsstræde 6 (33 11 68 68, www.konghans.dk). Metro Kongens Nytorv. ***Open*** *6pm-midnight Wed-Sat.* ***Map*** *p66 R13* 8 *French/Danish*

Eye-wateringly expensive, Kong Hans was the first restaurant in the city to win a Michelin star. Its stylish, whitewashed, vaulted cellar rooms are tucked away down a small side street and haven't bowed to the pressure of New Nordic or experimental cuisine over the years: they stay true to their mission of high-quality French/Danish food. The cellar (*kælder*) space, dating from the 15th century, is said to be the oldest building in the city still in commercial use.

Marchal

Hotel d'Angleterre, Kongens Nytorv 34 (33 12 00 94, www.marchal.dk). Metro Kongens Nytorv. ***Open*** *7am-10.30am, noon-4.30pm, 6-10pm Mon-Fri; 7am-11am, noon-4.30pm, 6-11pm Sat, Sun.* ***Map*** *p100 R12* 9 *French*

This ornate room in the city's grandest hotel has decor perfectly matching a brilliantly executed menu of dishes such as grilled monkfish with potatoes, mussel sauce and mussels; and fried pigeon with sweetbread, truffle purée, beetroot and a 'mystery' sauce. Marchal was awarded a Michelin star in 2017.

MASH

Bredgade 20 (33 13 93 00, www.mashsteak.dk). Metro Kongens Nytorv, or bus 1A, 26. ***Open*** *noon-3pm, 5.30-10pm Mon-Wed; noon-3pm, 5.30-11pm Thur-Sat; 5.30-10pm Sun.* ***Map*** *p100 S12* 10 *Steakhouse*

MASH is indeed a 'Modern American Steak House' – and more. Head down a corridor lined with glass-fronted fridges stocked with steaks so deeply marbled and tender-looking you could scoff them raw, and into a vaguely 1980s setting of intimate leather booths, soft lighting and lots of red. Start with a signature margarita, followed by Gillardeau oysters, then a dry-aged Danish steak with onion rings, and an all-American cheesecake to finish.

Stud!o at The Standard 

Havnegade 44 (72 14 88 08, www.thestandardcph.dk/verandah). Metro Kongens Nytorv, or bus 11A, 66. ***Open*** *6.30pm-midnight Tue-Thu; noon-3pm, 6.30pm-midnight Fri, Sat. Set meal 800kr for 5 courses.* ***Map*** *p100 T13* 14 *Nordic/South American*

Another of Copenhagen's Michelin-starred delights, Stud!o is housed above Almanak at The Standard and offers exquisite lunches Thursday to Saturday, along with a wine-matched fine-dining experience of 12 seasonal courses each evening. For a quicker bite, the Stud!o Kitchen experience includes six courses and runs to an hour and a half. Expect the finest Nordic cuisine with a little South American seasoning courtesy of Patagonian head chef Damian Quintana, and such delights as scallop ceviche with apple and coriander; razor clam with nasturtiums and horseradish; and squid with gooseberries and kaffir lime.

Cafés & bars

❤ Apollo Bar

Kunsthal Charlottenborg, Nyhavn 2 (60 53 44 14, www.apollobar.dk). Metro Kongens Nytorv. ***Open*** *Canteen noon-2pm Tue-Fri. Bar 8am-5pm Tue; 8am-midnight Wed-Fri; 10am-midnight Sat; 10am-5pm Sun.* ***Map*** *p100 S12* 1

For an intimate drink on the harbourside, dodge the bright bars crowding Nyhavn and step into the art gallery's finest exhibit, the dark and beautifully styled Apollo Bar. The canteen serves one lunch option per day (typically vegetarian, for example, spicy tomato soup or chickpea curry) while the bar serves great-value breakfasts, delicious three-course vegetarian lunches and drinks to suit all.

Balthazar Champagne Bar

Hotel d'Angleterre, Kongens Nytorv 34, bar entrance on Ny Østergade 6 (33 12 12 62, www.balthazarcph.dk). Metro Kongens Nytorv. ***Open*** *4pm-2am Wed-Sat.* ***Map*** *p100 R12* 2

Contemporary style meets classic institution at Balthazar. This flash yet relaxed Hotel d'Angleterre bar, which opened in 2012, offers more than 160 different champagnes, as well as a menu of champagne cocktails. It's the spot to head to if you're discerning about fizz and like to feel grand.

Shops & services

❤ Magasin

Kongens Nytorv 13 (33 11 44 33, www.magasin.dk). Metro Kongens Nytorv. ***Open*** *10am-8pm daily.* ***Map*** *p100 R13* 6 *Department store*

Scandinavia's first department store remains its largest, with five floors of fashion, high-class cosmetics, household goods, books, fine food and two juice bars. If you're looking for somewhere to shop on a weekend afternoon (many shops close at 2pm), it's a fine place to start.

FREDERIKSSTADEN & KASTELLET

Frederiksstaden was the vision of Frederik V, who wished to celebrate the 300th anniversary of the House of Oldenburg in 1749 with a grand new building project. The king didn't fancy paying for it, so, instead, he donated the land on the condition that members of Copenhagen's nobility commission rococo architect Nicolai Eigtved to build a stylistically uniform quarter. Today, **Bredgade** is itself packed with treasures, some more obvious than others.

The main auction houses are based here, as are numerous art and antiques dealers from the higher end of the market, which makes for good window-shopping. A short way down Bredgade on the right is **Sankt Annæ Plads**, a quiet tree-lined square, with a statue of King Christian X at its head and a dull, red-brick church, Garnisonskirken, to the right. Another, far more impressive, church, Frederikskirken, better known as **Marmorkirken** (The Marble Church, *see p115*), is a short walk away.

Down Frederiksgade are the four rococo palaces surrounding a grand cobbled square that together make up **Amalienborg Slot** (*see p112*). This square is a delightful place to visit – not as grand as you might expect, but with fluffy-hatted soldiers guarding the corners looking as if they have stepped out of a storybook nonetheless.

Behind the mighty statue of Frederik V is Amaliehaven, a small harbourside park donated by the industrialist AP Møller in 1983. There is a lovely walk along the waterside here past the **Den Kongelige Afstøbningssamling** (Royal Cast Collection), the spectacular **Gefion Springvandet** (Gefion Fountain) and on to

In the know
The Royal Family

Denmark's queen, Margrethe Alexandrine Thorhildur Ingrid, was born in 1940, during the dark days of Germany's occupation of Denmark. In the 1960s, she studied at Copenhagen, Cambridge, Århus, London and the Sorbonne, her main subject being political science. She also spent time in the Women's Flying Corp and the WAAF in England. In 1967, she married a French diplomat, Henri, Comte de Laborde de Monpezat (now Prince Henrik), who died in 2018. They had two sons, Frederik, the wildly popular crown prince, was born in 1968, and Joachim, born a year later, in 1969.

Top 20

❤ Amalienborg Slot

Amalienborg Slotsplads (33 15 32 86, www. kongernessamling.dk/amalienborg). Metro Kongens Nytorv; Bus 1A, 15, 20E, 26, 350S. ***Open*** *May, Sept, Oct 10am-4pm daily; June, July and Aug 10am-5pm daily; Nov-Dec 11am-4pm Tue-Sun; Jan 10am-3pm Tue-Sat.* ***Admission*** *105kr; 70kr reductions; free under-17s.* ***Map*** *p100 T11.*

The four rococo palaces set round a grand cobbled square on Amalienborg Plads have been home to the royal family since 1794; today two of them are open to the public as museums, with the current royal family living in the other two. The palaces were originally built by four wealthy traders as part of Frederik V's scheme for the area; the royal family commandeered the buildings after a fire destroyed their previous home, Christiansborg. As you enter the square along Frederiksgade from Marmorkirken, the palaces are (clockwise from the left) **Levetzau Palace**, **Brockdorff Palace**, **Moltke Palace** and **Schack Palace** (originally Løvenskjold Palace).

The current Dronning (Queen) Margrethe II lives in Schack Palace (formerly Christian IX's palace). The Danes' unstinting love for their *dronning* is one of the great paradoxes of the national psyche, and after a tour around one of her palaces, you might well feel the same. It's an intimate, friendly and revealing experience, touring rooms that are human-sized, almost normal in their scope and decor, which feels highly suitable given that Danish people love equality and deeply mistrust elitism. It's also helped by the fact that Margrethe is a charming, modern, talented, conscientious and hard-working royal – with an actual job as a costume designer – and she smokes, too.

The Amalienborg Museum (within Levetzau Palace) features several private rooms and studies of the royal Glücksborg family from the late 19th and early 20th century. Note Frederik IX's pipe collection, Queen Louise's rococo drawing room and, right at the top, a number of lovely costumes and artworks by the current queen. A wander around these rooms reveals the evolution of the monarchy in Denmark over the past 250 years; it's hard not to contrast it with the pomp and ceremony of Buckingham Palace, and to imagine what it would be like to live there yourself. In truth, the palaces feel like an English stately home, intimate with a touch of grandeur, and are all the more charming for it.

In the know
Changing guards

A major photo op for tourists visiting Amalienborg is the changing of the guards, featuring the ever-present Royal Life Guards, whose duty it is to protect Queen Margrethe in the event of an attack. The guards stand in their blue, red and white uniforms beside their pretty red boxes day and night. The daily ritual begins at 11.30am at the barracks beside **Rosenborg Slot** (*see p105*), from where the soldiers process through the streets, with the military band playing a few tunes. The route takes them south-west to Kultorvet, down Købmagergade, left on to Østergade (part of Strøget), around Kongens Nytorv and up Bredgade, before taking a right into Frederiksgade and Amalienborg Slotsplads at noon. The queen's birthday, on 16 April, is the cause for more impressive pageantry and crowds.

The Little Mermaid (*see p109*). You may even bump into Queen Margrethe who walks her dachshunds here. Opposite the mermaid is the island of **Holmen** (*see p122*), home to the Danish navy for several hundred years.

Back on Bredgade, a few hidden treasures await. Just round the corner from Marmorkirken is **Alexander Nevsky Kirke** (*see p114*), the only Russian Orthodox church in Denmark. Copenhagen's small but beautiful neo-Romanesque Catholic cathedral, **Sankt Ansgar Kirke**, built in 1841, is next door. Immediately north of the cathedral is **Designmuseum Danmark**, Copenhagen's excellent design history museum, focusing on industrial design and applied arts, and with a section on 20th-century Danish furniture designers that has expanded hugely over the past decade.

Bredgade ends at a small park, **Churchillparken**, located in front of Kastellet, and named after Britain's wartime leader (there's a small, curmudgeonly bust of him here). Maintaining the British theme, you'll also find **St Alban's Church**, a perfect English Gothic flint church (bizarrely, part of the Anglican Diocese of Gibraltar), which looks as if it's been lifted straight from the Sussex Downs. Also here is **Frihedsmuseet** (Museum of Danish Resistance, www.frihedsmuseet.dk), due to reopen in a couple of years' time after a terrible fire in 2013. A new building is being constructed on the same site.

Frihedsmuseet is overlooked by **Kastellet**. Built by Frederik III in 1662 after the Swedish siege of 1658, this vast, star-shaped fortress with its five bastions was the base for the Danish army for many years. Ironically, it was right in front of Kastellet that the Germans landed many centuries later in 1940. These days, the path round the ramparts makes a good jogging track.

Sights & museums

Alexander Nevsky Kirke

Bredgade 53 (33 13 60 46, tours 29 61 39 08, www.ruskirke.dk). Bus 1A, 26. ***Open*** *varies; call for details. Tours by appointment only.* ***Admission*** *free.* ***Map*** *p100 S10.*

Denmark's only Russian Orthodox church is easily identified by its three incongruous gold onion domes. The church was built in 1881-84 at the behest of Princess Dagmar, daughter of Christian IX, who married Grand Duke Alexander, later Emperor Alexander III, and converted to Orthodoxy. Apparently, she needed somewhere to worship when she visited Copenhagen.

❤ Designmuseum Danmark

Bredgade 68 (33 18 56 56, www.designmuseum.dk/en). Metro Kongens Nytorv; bus 1A, 26. ***Open*** *10am-6pm Tue, Thur-Sun; 10am-9pm Wed.* ***Admission*** *115kr; free under-26s.* ***Map*** *p100 T10.*

Designmuseum Danmark

❤ Marmorkirken

Frederiks Kirke, Frederiksgade 4 (33 15 01 44, www.marmorkirken.dk). Bus 1A. ***Open*** *10am-5pm Mon-Thur, Sat; noon-5pm Fri, Sun. Tower tours 1pm Sat-Sun; 1pm daily 15 June-31 Aug.* ***Admission*** *free; dome 35kr; 20kr under-12s. Cash or MobilePay only.* ***Map*** *p100 S11.*

A visit to Copenhagen's inspiring Marble Church, down the street from the Design Museum and Amalienborg's palaces, is not to be missed. Enter the hushed atmosphere from the bustling street, and you immediately feel a sense of calm. Dazzling stained-glass window angels greet you as you step into the baroque church, while Veronica Hodges' installation of pink paper cherry blossoms tumble from the ceiling. They are part of the Cherish symposium highlighting the effect of climate change on seasonality, and have hung in the church since 2018. As you would expect, it is a sought-after place to get married (an option only open to those who live within a street or two of the church), and it also features on the city's Kulturnatten (Culture Night, *see p186*) when it hosts events. It is also an irregular venue for classical and chamber music; if you can get a ticket, go.

Although today it is one of Copenhagen's most breathtaking sights, the circular, domed Marmorkirken very nearly didn't get built. Work on the church, designed by Nicolai Eigtved as the focal point of a new quarter in the city, began in 1749 (when the king lay the foundation stone), but was halted in 1770 due to its exorbitant cost; the walls were still only 10-15 metres (33-50 feet) high. The Statens Museum for Kunst (*see p106*) has a painting by Frederik Sødring from 1835 showing the square where the church was due to be built as nothing but rubble, set alongside tenement buildings where white sheets flap in the breeze and the unloved, unfinished stones lie at angles amid mounds of grass.

It wasn't until the deep-pocketed industrialist CF Tietgen intervened in the late 1800s that the church was finished – in cheaper Danish Faxe marble, instead of the original Norwegian marble. It was topped with a 46-metre (150-foot) dome by the architect Ferdinand Meldahl; inspired by St Peter's in Rome, the dome is one of the largest of its kind in Europe. From the top you can see Sweden, and you can explore the height of the church and more on a guided tour most weekends.

In the know
Below the surface

Most recently, Marmorkirken has had a little extra turn in the spotlight in the Danish terrorist drama *Gidseltagning* (*Below the Surface*), where 15 passengers were held in a partially built metro station directly under the church.

Barracks at Kastellet

Denmark's largest and oldest museum of Danish and international design is housed round a grand courtyard in the old Frederiks Hospital, designed by Nicolai Eigtved (and, incidentally, is where Søren Kierkegaard died in 1855). The focus is on industrial design and applied arts, with a permanent collection featuring some 300,000 items – chairs dominate, but there are also textiles, carpets, clothing, ceramics, cutlery, silverware, glassware, art and other furniture on display. Objects range from the late Middle Ages to the present day, with particularly extensive sections on 20th-century Danish furniture designers, such as Arne Jacobsen and Finn Juhl, with English captions throughout. The shop (which has an excellent range of books on Danish design) and Klint café (*see p117*) are also well worth a visit, and can be entered without buying a ticket for the exhibitions.

Kastellet

Langelinie (no phone). Bus 1A. ***Admission*** *free.* ***Map*** *p100 T8.*

Built by Frederik III in 1662 after the Swedish siege of 1658, Kastellet was the base for the Danish army for many years and still houses troops in attractive red terraces inside the ramparts. Note that only the grounds are open to the public, not the buildings. It's a nice place for a walk on a sunny day, on the way to or from *The Little Mermaid*.

Restaurants

❤ AOC

Dronningens Tværgade 2 (33 11 11 45, www.restaurantaoc.dk). Metro Kongens Nytorv, or bus 1A, 26. ***Open*** *6.30pm-12.30am Tue-Sat.* ***Map*** *p100 S11* 3 *New Nordic*

The iceberg-white arches of this unusual-looking cellar restaurant could be chilly, but, in fact, the place oozes a cathedral-like serenity. The school of thought is: the cleaner the backdrop, the more sensory the food experience, and these dishes certainly make an impact. Head chef Søren Selin impresses with his precision cooking and generally Nordic flavour combinations. Sensory evenings offer a seven- or ten-course menu with matching wine; alternatively, there are regular four- to seven-course set menus to choose from. The restaurant holds two Michelin stars (one of only three in the city to hold two or more). Book well in advance; it seats about 40 people in total.

Restaurant Ida Davidsen 

Store Kongensgade 70 (33 91 36 55, www.idadavidsen.dk). Metro Kongens Nytorv, or bus 1A. ***Open*** *10.30am-5pm Mon-Fri.* ***Map*** *p100 S11* 11 *Traditional Danish*

Ida is the fifth generation of her family to run this 100-year-old lunch restaurant, concocting ornate *smørrebrød*. Home-made rye bread is piled high with toppings, such as home-cured

pickled herring with raw red onion and dill, smoked salmon and caviar, or silky beef tartare with a raw egg yolk plopped into the middle.

Restaurant Rebel

Store Kongensgade 52 (33 32 32 09, www.restaurantrebel.dk). Metro Kongens Nytorv, or bus 1A. ***Open*** *noon-4pm, 5.30pm-midnight Tue-Sat.* ***Map*** *p100 S11* ⓬ *French/New Nordic*

Martin Hylleborg and Natthee Thungnoi's buzzy bistro distinguishes itself from the rest of the contemporary Danish bistro scene by incorporating unconventional French flavours and methods into its dishes. Impeccable presentation and an elegant yet relaxed interior combine with the cooking to make this one of the most reliable modern restaurants in town. It was awarded a Michelin Bib Gourmand for its great-value, refined, Danish-produce-oriented food.

Cafés & bars

Klint – Designmuseets Café

Designmuseum Danmark, Bredgade 68 (22 52 22 86, www.designmuseum.dk). Bus 1A, 26. ***Open*** *10am-6pm Tue, Thur-Sun; 10am-9pm Wed.* ***Map*** *p100 T10* ❻

Designmuseum Danmark's elegant café is named after Danish furniture designer Kaare Klint. The popular lunch spot serves hearty Danish dishes – with salmon, rye bread, pickled herring, fish cakes and classic dessert *rødgrød* (berry coulis mixed with whipped cream) all appearing on the menu. It's very stylish, a lovely spot for a relaxed lunch and you don't have to pay entry to the museum to eat there.

Oscar Bar & Café

Bredgade 58 (33 12 50 10, www.cafeoscar.dk). Metro Kongens Nytorv; bus 1A, 26. ***Open*** *10am-10pm daily.* ***Map*** *p100 T10* ❽

A welcome refreshment stop, this light, spacious and relaxed establishment serves the usual beverages and sandwiches, plus a short menu of crêpes and a more substantial selection of beef, fish and pasta dishes. There are a few outside tables for summer.

Shops & services

Bruun Rasmussen Kunstauktioner

Bredgade 33 (88 18 11 11, www.bruun-rasmussen.dk). Metro Kongens Nytorv, or bus 1A, 26. ***Open*** *10am-5pm Mon-Fri; 10am-2pm Sat.* ***Map*** *p100 S12* ❷ *Antiques*

Denmark's premier auction house is one of the world's top ten auctioneers, serving the prime end of the antiques and arts market. Rasmussen's sales (usually themed) of art, antiques, furniture, wine and just about anything else take place at least a couple of times each week, and online each evening from 8pm.

❤ Designmuseum Danmark Shop

Designmuseum Danmark, Bredgade 68 (20 69 73 76, www.designmuseum.dk). Bus 1A, 26. ***Open*** *10am-6pm Tue, Thur-Sun; 10am-9pm Wed.* ***Map*** *p100 T10* ❸ *Interior design, fashion & books*

The Design Museum's shop sells an excellent selection of design books, ceramics, posters, postcards, textiles and jewellery.

Løgismose

Nordre Toldbod 16 (33 32 93 32, www.loegismose.dk). Train Østerport, or bus 1A. ***Open*** *10am-7pm Mon-Fri; 10am-5pm Sat.* ***Map*** *p100 V8* ❺ *Food & drink*

What started out as a wine importer attached to the renowned restaurant Kong Hans Kaelder has grown into one of the best gourmet supermarkets in town, with an eclectic mix of items, from Harvey Nichols tins and jars to delicious Valhrona chocolates.

Monies

Nordre Toldbod 17-19 (33 91 33 33, www.monies.dk). Train Østerport, or bus 1A. ***Open*** *9am-5pm Mon-Fri.* ***Map*** *p100 U9* ❼ *Accessories*

Spectacular formal jewellery by designer couple Gerda and Nikolai Monies, who use jade, bone, wood and amber, among other materials, to create truly original sculptural statements.

Christianshavn, Holmen & Refshaleøen

Christianshavn is the real Copenhagen, packed with historic streets and charming canals but without the hustle and bustle of the city centre. A few bridges lead to Christianshavn, and it's well worth a stroll down its cobbled streets to snap some shots of the colourful, old buildings. At its heart is the most renowned alternative area of the city: Christiania.

A self-declared independent state, founded by hippies in the 1970s, Christiania is where you'll find vegetarian cafés and stalls openly selling marijuana. But it's not all about the drugs. It's a colourful and vibrant place to visit, with houseboats, murals, lovely waterside walks and great live music venues.

Christianshavn links up with two islands to the north, Holmen and Refshaleøen. Holmen, a former military zone and dockyard, is the home of the Copenhagen Opera House. It connects Christianshavn to up-and-coming Refshaleøen, a creative, bohemian and foodie zone in the far north-east of the city, where you can eat the very finest New Nordic food, ski down a waste management plant, browse art installations at Copenhagen Contemporary, or just enjoy a coffee or glass of wine with a view of the water.

❤ Don't miss

1 Harbour swimming *p124*
Islands Brygge's swimming pool is perfect for a sunny day.

2 Christiania *p128*
Alternative architecture.

3 CopenHill *p133*
The best and quirkiest sport in the city.

4 Reffen *p43*
The city's best street food market, up in the far north of the city.

5 Vor Frelsers Kirke *p123*
Magnificent views from the top of the spire.

6 CopenHot *p130*
Hot tubs and harbour views.

Christiania *p128*

CHRISTIANSHAVN, HOLMEN & REFSHALEØEN

Restaurants

1 108 *p123*
2 Amass *p131*
3 Era Ora *p123*
4 Kadeau *p126*
5 Morgenstedet *p127*
6 Noma 2.0 *p131*
7 Restaurant 56° *p131*
8 Restaurant Kanalen *p126*
9 Spiseloppen *p127*
3 Café Nemoland *p129*
4 Café Wilder *p126*
5 Halvandet *p132*
6 Lille Bakery & Eatery *p132*
7 Luna's Diner *p132*
8 Parterre *p126*
9 Sofie Kælderen *p126*
10 Sweet Treat *p127*

Cafés & bars

1 La Banchina *p132*
2 Broens Gaddekokken/The Bridge Street Kitchen *p126*

Shops & services

1 Christiania Cykler *p129*
2 Nordatlantens Brygge *p127*

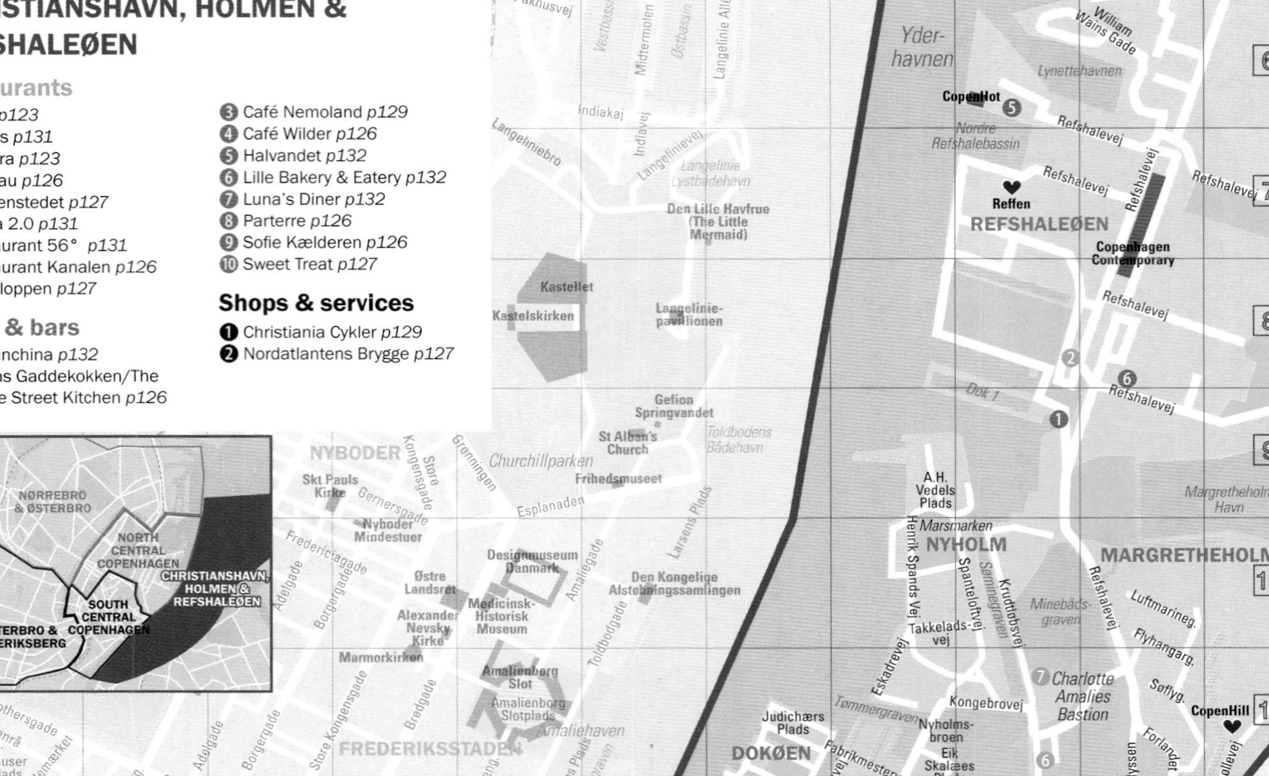

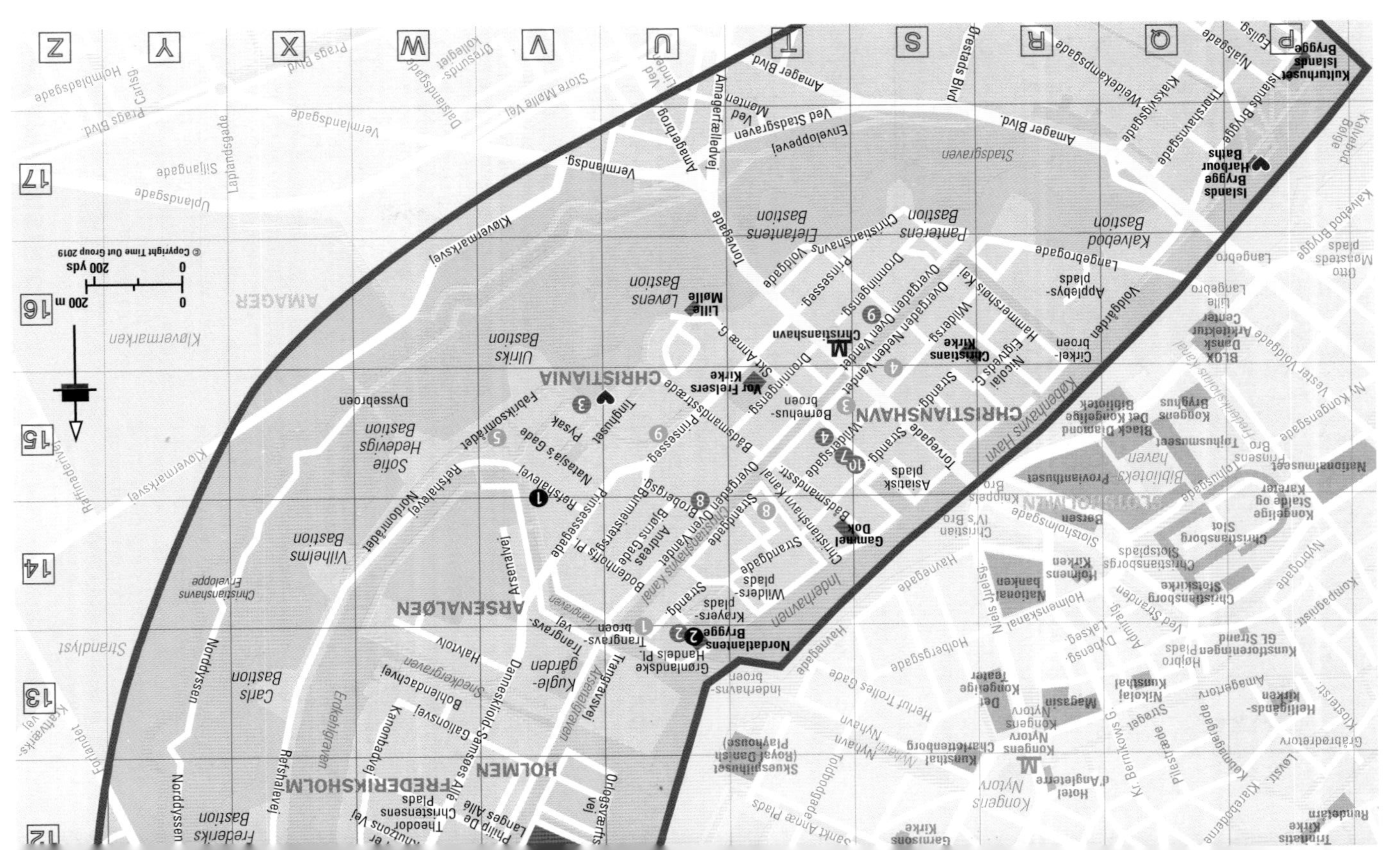
CHRISTIANSHAVN
CHRISTIANIA
HOLMEN
FREDERIKSHOLM
ARSENALØEN
AMAGER
SLOTSHOLMEN
Frederiks Bastion
Carls Bastion
Vilhelms Bastion
Sofie Hedevigs Bastion
Ulriks Bastion
Løvens Bastion
Elefantens Bastion
Panterens Bastion
Kalvebod Bastion
Kløvermarken
Vor Frelsers Kirke
Christians Kirke
Lille Mølle
Gammel Dok
Nordatlantens Brygge
Christianshavn
Kongens Nytorv
Islands Brygge Harbour Baths
Kulturhuset Islands Brygge
Nationalmuseet
Christiansborg Slot
Christiansborg Slotskirke
Børsen
Proviantshuset
Black Diamond Det Kongelige Bibliotek
BLOX Dansk Arkitektur Center
Tøjhusmuseet
Kongens Bryghus
Holmens Kirken
Nationalbanken
Det Kongelige Teater
Kunsthal Charlottenborg
Skuespilhuset (Royal Danish Playhouse)
Hotel d'Angleterre
Magasin
Nikolaj Kunsthal
Helligånds-kirken
Trinitatis Kirke Rundetårn
Kunstforeningen GL Strand
Garnisons Kirke
Kongelige Stalde og Karetter
Refshalevej
Prinsessegade
Torvegade
Amagerbrogade
Amager Blvd.
Vermlandsg.
Kløvermarksvej
Strandgade
Overgaden Oven Vandet
Overgaden Neden Vandet
Christianshavns Kanal
Inderhavnen
Københavns Havn
200 m
200 yds
© Copyright Time Out Group 2019

THE CANAL DISTRICT

Christianshavn was built to the east of Slotsholmen in the early 17th century to protect Christian IV's burgeoning city from attack, and to ease overcrowding within the city walls. The king's complex plan, inspired by Amsterdam's grid of canals, was eventually simplified for reasons of cost, and the district remains pretty much intact today following sympathetic renovation in the 1980s and '90s. Christianshavn's charming houses and courtyards also escaped most of the fires that ravaged Copenhagen over the centuries.

The dominant landmark in this area is the **Vor Frelsers Kirke** (Church of Our Saviour), whose fabulous 90-metre (295-foot) golden spire can be seen from most parts of the city centre. The district's other significant church is **Christians Kirke**, notable for its unusual interior, laid out in the style of a theatre.

One of Christianshavn's easily overlooked sights is **Lille Mølle** (Little Windmill), a windmill dating from 1669, situated on the ramparts south-east of Christiania. It was converted into a private home in 1916 and the interior has been perfectly preserved by the Nationalmuseet, which now owns the site. Currently opening hours are very limited, with guided tours taking place only on certain occasions, such as Culture Night (*see p186*) and the fourth Thursday after Easter (Great Prayer Day). However, next door is **Bastionen og Løven**, an excellent café from which you can at least view the windmill's exterior.

To the north of Christianshavn is **Holmen**, the old docklands area, which was built on reclaimed land in the 17th century. Holmen still has a naval base but the area has changed and now attracts students and arty types on summer evenings. It's a fascinating place, best explored by bicycle. The Henning Larsen-designed **Operaen** (Opera House, *see p206*) has put Holmen at the forefront of Denmark's cultural life.

To the south of Christianshavn, a short walk away, you'll come to **Islands Brygge Harbour Baths** (*see p124*), in the shadow of the bridge – a popular spot for a dip in summer.

Sights & museums

Christians Kirke

Strandgade 1 (32 54 15 76, www.christianskirke.dk). Metro Christianshavn, or bus 2A, 9A, 40. ***Open*** *10am-4pm Tue-Fri.* ***Admission*** *free.* ***Map*** *p120 S16.*

This rococo church, with a neoclassical spire, was designed by Nicolai Eigtved in 1755 for the German population of Christianshavn. Financed by a lottery, it was known for a long time as the Lottery Church.

❤ Time to eat & drink

Cosy and chic for lunch
108 *p123*

Food from everywhere
Reffen *p43*

Hipster-friendly pastries
Lille Bakery & Eatery *p132*

Superlative New Nordic
Amass *p131*

Swim, sauna and snack
La Banchina *p132*

Vegetarian treat
Morgenstedet *p127*

❤ Time to shop

Epic flea market
Kulturhuset Islands Brygge *p123*

Greenlandic jewellery meets Icelandic design
Nordatlantens Brygge *p127*

Iconic family bikes
Christiania Cykler *p129*

In the know
Getting around

If you are staying centrally, it's an easy cycle or walk from Nyhavn across the bridge to this part of the city, or, if you are staying elsewhere you can take the metro to Christianshavn station. To reach Refshaleøen or Holmen, by far the simplest route is to take the harbour bus from Nyhavn north (you can take a bike with you). It is three stops to the Operaen (Opera House) and four stops to Refshaleøen. You need to walk from the harbour bus stop to reach Reffen – it's a gentle 11-minute walk or three-minute cycle from the bus stop. In addition, the 9A bus runs from Central Station to the Operaen and Refshaleøen. Special buses are put on to coincide with show times at the Operaen. For details, see www.dinoffentligetransport.dk.

Vor Frelsers Kirke

❤ Kulturhuset Islands Brygge

Islands Brygge 18 (33 66 47 00, kulturhusetislandsbrygge.kk.dk). Waterbus Bryggebrøen. ***Open*** *8.30am-11pm Mon-Thu; 8.30am-midnight Sat-Sun.* ***Admission*** *free.* ***Map*** *p120 P18.*

Right on the harbour banks and next to the floating swimming baths, this culture house is a great bet if you're looking for good-value food, local or international music, yoga, children's culture or a bargain in one of their Sunday flea markets. The Kulturhuset is an official venue for the Copenhagen Jazz Festival.

Nordatlantens Brygge

Strandgade 91 (32 83 37 00, www.nordatlantens.dk). Waterbus Knippelsbro. Bus 2A, 9A, 350S. ***Open*** *10am-5pm Mon-Fri; noon-5pm Sat-Sun.* ***Admission*** *40kr; 30kr reductions; 20kr 12-18s.* ***Map*** *p120 U13.*

This cultural centre brings together the best of the Nordic region, focusing on cultural exhibitions from Greenland, the Faroes and Iceland. Art exhibitions, concerts, lectures, films and events fall under their remit; there is also a café selling Greenlandic snaps, cakes, Faroese beer and dried fish.

Operaen – Den Kongelige Opera

Ekvipagemeistervej 10 (33 69 69 33, www.kglteater.dk). Waterbus Operaen. Bus 9A. ***Open*** *9.30am-4pm Mon-Fri.* ***Admission*** *free.* ***Map*** *p120 V12.*

The waterfront Royal Opera House is worth exploring just for its art and architecture, regardless of whether you book performance tickets. It was designed by Henning Larsen and displays Danish art by the likes of Per Kirkeby and Per Arnoldi. Enjoy views of the city from the marble-clad foyer, or head to the rooftop restaurant for views of Amalienborg Palace and the Marble Church while you eat. Guided tours through the backstage areas and training rooms are available on request – see the website for full details.

❤ Vor Frelsers Kirke

Sankt Annægade 29 (32 57 62 25, www.vorfrelserskirke.dk). Metro Christianshavn, or bus 2A, 9A, 66. ***Open*** *Church 11am-3.30pm daily. Spire 10am-4pm Mon-Sat, 10.30am-4pm Sun. Closed 16 Dec-23 Feb.* ***Admission*** *Church free. Spire 35kr; 25kr reductions.* ***Map*** *p120 T15.*

This landmark church was built in 1682 by architect Lambert van Haven for Christian V, in the Palladian Dutch Baroque style, from red brick and sandstone. The extraordinary spire was inspired by the lanterns on the church of Sant'Ivo alla Sapienza in Rome and was completed, in pine with copper cladding and gilt decoration, in 1752. Don't believe stories about the spire's architect, Laurids de Thurah, throwing himself off the top because it wound the wrong way – he actually died in poverty seven years after its completion. On the day of its dedication, King Frederik V climbed to the top to receive a 27-gun salute as crowds cheered below. The spire is open to any visitors who feel they can conquer their vertigo and its 400 or so steps, which spiral ever narrower closer to the summit. The interior of the church is spacious but prosaic, in the typical Lutheran manner, though its immense three-storey organ (completed in 1698) is stupefying. Note that the spire is closed in winter and when there are high winds and bad weather.

Restaurants

❤ 108 ♛♛♛

Strandgade 108 (32 96 32 92, www.108.dk). Waterbus Nyhavn. ***Open*** *The Corner 8am-midnight Mon-Fri; 9am-midnight Sat-Sun. Restaurant 5pm-midnight daily.* ***Map*** *p120 U13* ❶ *New Nordic*

Another corner, another Michelin-starred restaurant; this time it's 108. The sleek and modernist restaurant serves up New Nordic, with an eight-course tasting menu for 1,150kr, including dishes such as brown beech mushrooms in a broth of whole roast chicken, toasted barley mousse with hazelnut and autumn truffles, and pumpkin seed ice-cream with pumpkin caramel. Menus are of course seasonal. Nestled right next door, **The Corner** is a great bet for lunch, breakfast or coffee at any time. They serve Tim Wendelboe coffee along with pastries, porridge and great sandwiches. It's recommended for a really special snack.

Era Ora ♛♛♛♛

Overgaden Neden Vandet 33B (32 54 06 93, www.eraora.dk). Metro Christianshavn, or bus 2A, 9A, 40. ***Open*** *noon-4pm, 6.30pm-midnight Mon-Sat.* ***Map*** *p120 T15* ❸ *Italian*

This beautifully decorated restaurant, which has held a Michelin star since 1997, serves only set menus, with a choice of fish or meat for the main course. The dedication of the chefs is evident in the complex yet light Umbrian dishes, using ingredients flown in from Italy. The wine list is as impressive (and expensive) as ever, and the service efficient and formal, making it the best Italian in town by a long shot. If your wallet doesn't stretch to these gastronomic heights, there's always its sister bistro **L'Altro** (Torvegade 62, 32 54 54 06, www.laltro.dk) across the canal.

Top 20

❤ Harbour swimming

***Open** 15 June-15 Sept daily, with lifeguard staffing 11am-7pm. **Admission** free.*

Copenhagen is a surprisingly good place for summer swimming, and you don't even have to go to the beach: just jump right into the harbour. In 2003, the construction of the open-air **Islands Brygge Harbour Baths**, 100 metres south of the Langebro bridge, opened up the harbour to city swimmers of all ages. Designed by Bjarke Ingels Group (BIG), the launch of these floating pools heralded the transformation from a city that used its waterways for transport and traffic to one that uses them for leisure. The opening of the baths followed a drive by local authorities to improve the quality of the harbour water, which is now as clean as that in the Øresund (and constantly monitored). Many areas have been awarded a Blue Flag.

Consisting of five pools (two for children) and with room for 600 people, the Islands Brygge baths have been an enormous success. Open from June to September, they mark the official start (and end) of summer for many locals, with regular outdoor events held nearby, an ice-cream van or two and a green space for picnics just next to it. In winter, you will still see hardy swimmers in the pools; they typically require membership outside the summer months.

There are two further floating swimming pools if Islands Brygge is too crowded: **Copencabana**, with three pools, at Vesterbro's Havneholmen (close to the Fisketorvet shopping mall, just south of Kødbyen); and **Koralbadet**, at Sluseholmen in the South Harbour, right at the end of the harbour bus line. You can also swim at **La Banchina** on Refshaleøen, where there is a sauna, and at a number of new harbours in the Sluseholmene/Teglhomen area along the Harbour Circle cycle route.

In the know
Safe swimming

Swimming in Copenhagen's harbour is only allowed at established bathing zones – there is still a lot of boat traffic in the water, including the regular harbour bus. Always respect the lifeguards and authorities at the harbour baths. If water quality is unsatisfactory, a red flag is raised and swimming pools are closed until the situation is rectified.

Kadeau

Wildersgade 10b (33 25 22 23, www.kadeau.dk). Metro Christianshavn, or bus 2A, 9A, 40. ***Open*** *noon-4pm, 6.30pm-midnight Tue-Sat.* ***Map*** *p120 S15* 4 *New Nordic*

Kadeau brings a little slice of Bornholm – a Danish island in the Baltic Sea, known for its culinary offerings and beautiful weather – to this airy, smart yet informal space. The two Michelin-starred restaurant makes much use of island herbs, meat, cheese, seafood and berries, with recent highlights from the tasting menu including Molbo oysters, white currants and rhubarb; salmon, elderflower and fig leaves; brown cabbage, caviar and forest mark; ox leek, blue cheese and bone marrow; and crème fraîche, raspberries and walnuts. A meal here doesn't come cheap, so be sure you understand the New Nordic concept (small plates, experimental dishes) before booking a table. The owners also run the similarly experimental **Pony in Vesterbro** (Vesterbrogade 135, 33 22 10 00, ponykbh.dk).

Restaurant Kanalen

Wilders Plads 2 (32 95 13 30, www.restaurant-kanalen.dk). Metro Christianshavn, or bus 2A, 9A, 40. ***Open*** *11.30am-4pm, 5.30pm-midnight Mon-Sat.* ***Map*** *p120 T14* 8 *Danish/French*

Tucked away beside the canals in a particularly idyllic corner of Christianshavn, Restaurant Kanalen (which means 'The Canal') strikes a happy balance between traditional and modern Danish cooking with a little French thrown in for fun. You'll find excellent herring and pork alongside more intricate dishes that blend the freshest local ingredients with deliciously light sauces and surprise ingredients from around the world. With alfresco dining in summer, sweet service and accessible prices, Kanalen is a great all-rounder.

Cafés & bars

Broens Gaddekokken/The Bridge Street Kitchen

Strandgade 95 (33 93 07 60, thebridgestreetkitchen.com). Metro Christianshavn, or bus 2A, 9A, 40. ***Open*** *11am-5pm Mon-Thur, Sun; 11am-8pm Fri-Sat.* ***Map*** *p120 U13* 2

This street food market right across the bridge from Nyhavn collects together the best of Copenhagen's cafés, with the likes of Grød, Gasoline Grill, Coffee Collective and California Kitchen among the stalls/booths represented. While they bill themselves as the location for world-class street food, in actuality it's not quite as vivid as that – think good coffee, burgers, hot dogs and *smørrebrød*. But it's a great spot for a beer in the summer or lunch at any time of year, and is easy on the pocket in the main.

► *For more diverse flavours, spices and an anarchic air, you should visit Reffen (see p43).*

Café Wilder

Wildersgade 56 (32 54 71 83, www.cafewilder.dk). Metro Christianshavn, or bus 2A, 9A, 40. ***Open*** *9am-11pm Mon-Thur; 9am-midnight Fri; 10am-midnight Sat; 10am-10.30pm Sun.* ***Map*** *p120 T15* 4

This lovely café-bar is located just a short walk from the chaos of Christiania. The food (salads and sandwiches) is fresh, cheap and simple, and the service is charming. This small, L-shaped room is usually crowded to bursting point with trendy, arty locals at weekends, so arrive early to be sure of a seat.

Luna's Diner

Sankt Annas Gade 5 (32 54 20 00, www.lunasdiner.dk). Metro Christianshavn, or bus 2A, 9A, 40. ***Open*** *9.30am-11pm Mon-Thur; 9am-midnight Fri-Sat; 9am-11pm Sun.* ***Map*** *p120 T15* 7

Close to Christiania and Our Saviour's Church, Luna's has tables on the streets on sunny days and is a bohemian, colourful spot that is open till late. The extensive menu includes sandwiches, breakfast, brunch, pasta and desserts, with reasonable prices (a cheeseburger is around 130kr); equally good for a snack, coffee or a beer.

Parterre

Overgaden Oven Vandet 90 (no phone; parterrechristianshavn.dk). Metro Christianshavn, or bus 2A, 9A, 40. ***Open*** *7.30am-6pm Mon-Fri; 8am-6pm Sat-Sun.* ***Map*** *p120 U14* 8

This charming café is a great stop for a simple breakfast (croissant plus rye bread and butter, boiled egg, cheese, chorizo, yoghurt and granola from 100kr), a similarly lovely lunch (avocado on rye, or a grilled goat's cheese sandwich), or a pastry and Swedish roaster Koppi's coffee at any time of day. Rustic and beautifully situated next to the canal, it's one of the city's most instagrammed breakfast spots. Great value too.

Sofie Kælderen

Overgaden Oven Vandet 32 (32 57 77 01, www.sofiekaelderen.dk). Metro Christianshavn, or bus 2A, 9A, 40. ***Open*** *2-11pm Tue-Wed; 2pm-midnight Thur; 2pm-3am Fri-Sat.* ***Map*** *p120 S16* 9

Another cellar by the canal, another treat: this time it's Sofie Kælderen, a relaxed and friendly restaurant near Christianshavns

Kanal and Torv, serving Danish/French food with seasonal menus including fish and meat of the day. Friday and Saturday nights see the cellar transform into a nightclub. It's a particularly nice place to spend a sunny afternoon dining or drinking beside the canal.

Sweet Treat

Sankt Annæ Gade 3A (32 95 41 15, www.sweettreat.dk). Metro Christianshavn, or bus 2A, 9A, 40. ***Open*** *7.30am-6pm Mon-Fri; 10am-5pm Sat, Sun.* ***Map*** *p120 S15* ⑩

This tiny pit stop is a favourite with smart creatives, who often stop off en route to work for a cup of their excellent coffee and a pastry or a boiled egg. But Sweet Treat is, as its name suggests, also great for those with a sweeter palate, serving what might be the best hot chocolate in town. There's also a wide range of teas, juices and smoothies.

Shops & services

❤ Nordatlantens Brygge

Strandgade 91 (32 83 37 00, www.nordatlantens.dk). Metro Christianshavn, or bus 2A, 9A, 40. ***Open*** *10am-5pm Mon-Fri; noon-5pm Sat, Sun.* ***Map*** *p120 U13* ❷ *Gifts & souvenirs*

The best source for Greenlandic handicrafts and information, this small shop attached to the Nordatlantens Brygge cultural centre sells books, jewellery, T-shirts, woollen sweaters (think Sarah Lund from *The Killing*), CDs, tote bags, exquisitely forged, hand-ground knives, art and – animal rights supporters, beware – seal-fur products.

CHRISTIANIA

Christiania is divided by the moat into two distinct areas – the main commercial centre, with its music venues, shops, restaurants and bars; and Dysen, a quiet residential district on the eastern side of the moat. 'Flower power' lives on here; walls are coloured with art and graffiti and a distinct scent wafts in the air. There are a number of cafés and restaurants; come by on a Friday or Saturday night to see the scene in full swing, grab a beer and visit music venue **Loppen** (*see p201*), or **Den Grå Hal**, Christiania's largest music venue (capacity 2,000), which has hosted gigs by the likes of Blur and Bob Dylan.

All of Christiania is open to tourists (except the private dwellings, of course). You can pass a pleasant afternoon in the quieter parts, inspecting the extraordinary variety of housing – from pyramids, railway carriages and tree houses, to sophisticated wooden chalets and the original 17th-century barracks. It's well worth taking the time to explore this remarkable community and, with a local guide, you'll see even more. Just head to the main entrance at 3pm in summer (weekends only the rest of the year), to find a guide to show you around.

▶ *For more on the history and contemporary life of Christiania, see p128.*

Restaurants

❤ Morgenstedet

Fabriksområdet 134 (no phone, www.morgenstedet.dk). Metro Christianshavn, or bus 9A, 40. ***Open*** *noon-9pm Tue-Sun.* ***No cards. Map*** *p120 V15* ⑤ *Vegetarian*

This cute clapboard cottage serves organic, vegetarian food at rock-bottom prices. Most of the produce comes from the owner's nearby farm and the menu changes daily. Depending on the season, expect the likes of wholesome potato gratins, bean stews and mushroom and tofu stir-fries. It's a great place to fill up while on a tour of the old hippie quarter – you can be sure you won't eat quite like this anywhere else in the city.

Spiseloppen

2nd floor, Loppen building, Bådsmandsstræde 43 (32 57 95 58, www.spiseloppen.dk). Metro Christianshavn/bus 9A, 40. ***Open*** *Jan-Apr 5-10.30pm Tue-Thur; 5-11pm Fri-Sat. May-Dec 5-11.30pm Tue-Sat.* ***Map*** *p120 U15* ⑨ *Global*

What do you get when you cross an Englishman, an Irishman, a Scotsman, a Dane, a Lebanese and an Italian? Spiseloppen's constantly changing rota of international kitchen staff create a different menu every night, but for once, this isn't a case of 'too many cooks'; the myriad influences at work here rarely fail to conjure something special (the vegetarian dishes are particularly impressive). The entrance to Spiseloppen, through an anonymous door and up some shabby stairs in one of

In the know
No pictures please

You'll notice signs around the Pusher Street part of Christiania asking you not to take photos. Take these signs seriously – locals won't take kindly to you ignoring them. However, beyond Pusher Street and its surrounding zone, you can normally get away with taking pictures of the fascinating alternative houses that line the water. Still, it's wise to check first with a local that it's OK before snapping away.

❤ Freetown of Christiania

Christiania, or the Freetown of Christiania to give it its full title, is a residential area unlike any other in Denmark. This mess of historic military buildings, makeshift housing and ramshackle businesses, which straddles the defensive moat and 17th-century ramparts to the east of Christianshavn, is home to families, musicians, artists and businesspeople; all of them free-thinkers.

This alternative neighbourhood has become one of Copenhagen's most-visited tourist attractions; it is open to the public, who love to wander among the home-made houses, workshops, street art, music venues and bars, and, even more than that, soak up its rebellious spirit.

The 7.7-hectare (19-acre) site that Christiania now occupies used to be an army barracks. When the army moved out in 1971, a group of like-minded Christianshavn residents decided to knock down the fence on Prinsessegade and use the land as a playground and open space. Meanwhile, an exhibition at Charlottenborg, *Noget for Noget* ('Give and Take'), which examined the hippie movement, and an alternative lifestyle newspaper, *Hovedbladet* (Head Magazine), galvanised Copenhagen's experimentalists. The paper ran an article on the barracks with various proposals for its use, one of which was as housing for the young. This was all the encouragement that hundreds of people from across Denmark needed, and soon the site began to fill up. Their mission statement centred on creating a self-governing society where community welfare was put in the hands of every individual, and where a self-sufficient economy should be built.

On 13 November 1971, the new residents founded what they like to call the Freetown of Christiania, although it was promptly declared illegal by the authorities. However, the number of residents had already grown to the extent that, despite their best and often most violent efforts, the police failed to clear the barricades.

In subsequent years, as the community formed its own system of government, built schools, shops, cafés, restaurants, various co-operatives and music venues, and embarked on recycling programmes and nascent solar- and wind-power projects, the debate about Christiania raged. The sale of soft drugs was ever-present, and the bulldozers and batons were never far away. Charity records, concerts, PR stunts and the election to the local council of some of its residents ensured Christiania remained in the headlines until eventually, in 1991, an uneasy truce was negotiated with the authorities. Christiania agreed to pay rent and cover the cost of water and electricity supplies, as well as to look after the buildings that were of historical importance, while the city council agreed it could continue as a 'social experiment'.

Today, a complex system of self-government is headed by the Common Meeting, with power devolved through 15 local Area Meetings. Decisions are arrived at via consensus, as opposed to majority vote, and new arrivals must be approved by the House Meeting.

The community earns money from its restaurants and bars, as well as the sale of its unique Christiania bicycles (*see p130* Cargo Collective) and handicrafts. The residents pay rent, which goes towards the upkeep of buildings, city taxes and services.

Nearly 1,000 residents live in Christiania, which, after some ructions, now follows common Danish law, although somewhat of a blind eye is turned towards the soft drugs trade. Christiania counts the frontman of the band Lukas Graham as one of its most famous sons.

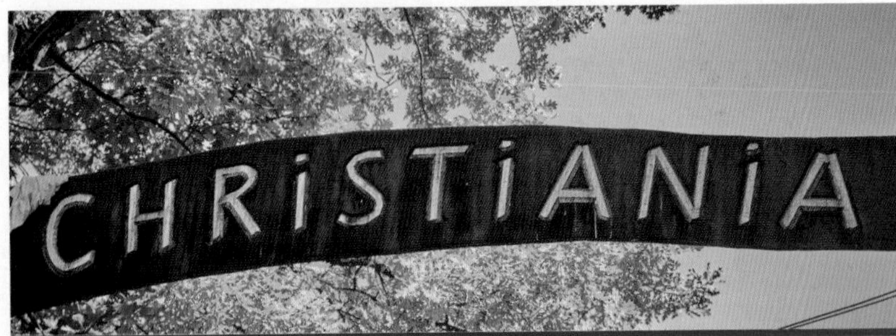

Christiania's warehouses, promises little, but once you enter its low-ceilinged, candlelit dining hall, its true worth becomes clear. Diners tend to be young and arty.

Cafés & bars

There are a number of cafés and bars within Christiania, some with no obvious name, most with outside benches and tables, and many of which are taken up by local dope smokers, students and teenagers.

Café Nemoland

Fabriksområdet 52 (32 95 89 31, www.nemoland.dk). Metro Christianshavn, or bus 2A, 9A, 40. ***Open*** *11am-midnight Sun-Thur; 11am-3am Fri-Sat* ***Map*** *p120 V15* ❸

One of the friendliest and most established cafés in Christiana, Nemoland café and cultural centre sells beer, wine, coffee and snack-style food, such as generous hamburgers for around 100kr. Entertainment is laid on in the form of live music, a pool table and chess sets, and there are plenty of colourful, pub garden-style tables outside, with a special no-smoking family garden.

Shops & services

❤ Christiania Cykler

Refshalevej 2 (70 70 76 80, www.christianiacykler.dk). Metro Christianshavn, or bus 2A, 9A, 40. ***Open*** *9am-5.30pm Mon-Fri; 11am-3pm Sat.* ***No cards. Map*** *p120 V15* ❶ *Bicycles*

Christiania Cykler's most interesting item is the idiosyncratic Pedersen bike. It's based on an early 20th-century design by Mikael Pedersen, who was tired of getting a sore backside from riding. He devised a swinging hammock-like leather seat, then built a pyramid-style frame to support it. Today, the shop builds 40 to 50 specially ordered Pedersen bikes a year, about half of which are shipped abroad. It also sells classic Christiania cargo bikes (*see p130* Cargo Collective) and offers a bike rental service.

REFSHALEØEN

Tucked away in the far north-east of the city, Refshaleøen (say it slowly: Refs–Hale–Œn) is by far the most dynamic, creative and edgy part of the city right now. Home to everything from tourist attractions to abandoned warehouses, an extreme watersports centre, Michelin-starred restaurants and a quirky spa, it is in the process of transformation from the city's furthest outpost, full of architecture students, to its most exciting hub. Gentrification is well on the way for this abandoned, former shipyard district, but it's not quite here yet – expect to see old industrial areas that don't look finished and streets still under construction as you wind your way towards the colourful **Reffen** (*see p43*) food market, quirky **CopenHill** (*see p133*) and any number of great places to eat. Often described as a little off the beaten path, it's still just 15 minutes by bike from

Christiania Cykler

Cargo Collective

The Christiania bike is a Danish design icon

Almost synonymous with the name 'cargo bike' in Denmark, the Christiania Bike (www.christianiabikes.com) has been an element of daily life in Copenhagen for over 25 years, and is one of the city's unofficial emblems. The bike was awarded the Classics Prize for the Danish Design Centre's Danish Design Awards 2010/11, where it was recognised as having 'proven its durability through many years of daily transport of shopping bags and children. The bicycle is a beautiful example of design that springs from a simple, good idea that stays viable due to function and charm.'

Invented in 1984 by Lars Engstrøm in the car-free commune of Christiania, the bike is essentially a back-to-front tricycle with a plywood box on the front for shopping or kids. The bikes have a fitted rain cover (with window), and Danish children are often carted to and from school in the front box, which comes complete with seats and safety belts; three or four youngsters can often be seen happily snuggled up together in the den-like space; alternatively, you might see cyclists with adult friends in the front, or even large dogs.

Copenhagen's flat terrain and safe bike lanes make for ideal conditions for the Christiania (a cargo-bike-based school run in Lisbon or San Francisco, say, would be decidedly more difficult). As well as using the bikes for school runs, locals use them for shopping, taking their dogs to the park, and moving tools, equipment, Christmas trees... whatever large items you might need to transport. Different models have different-sized and shaped boxes. Postmen even use a specially designed electric Christiania bike for deliveries, and entrepreneurial types have recently begun using them as mobile drinks and snack stalls.

Christiania bikes aren't cheap, costing between 10,800kr and 24,000kr – but you're paying for a high level of craftsmanship and a genuine alternative to the car. In this city, the bike soon pays for itself when you consider the savings in transport and petrol costs. If you're in Copenhagen with kids, and fancy carting them around in this most convenient and pollution-free way, the bikes can be rented from Baisikeli (*see p60* Bike Copenhagen) or from Christiania Cykler (*see p129*).

the centre of the city, and especially easy to reach by harbour bus from Nyhavn.

Refshaleøen has the Eurovision Song Contest in 2014 to thank for its revitalisation. Back in 1996, Burmeister & Wain (B&W) closed their shipyard on the island, which is annexed to the larger island of Amager, after occupying it for more than a 100 years. The abandoned buildings sat empty, but bit by bit, creatives looking for cheap space arrived. In 2010, the heavy metal festival CopenHell moved in, and the area started to welcome more music events, including Distortion and a Scandinavian reggae festival. The Eurovision Song Contest shone a brighter spotlight on which the area was transformed into Eurovision Island in 2014, and from then, the only way was up. Luxury flats are being developed on the approaches to the island, and with the combination of fine dining, art and urban adventure sports, it is a busy and enticing place to be at the weekend and especially in summer.

Sights & museums

Copenhagen Contemporary

Refshalevej 173A (29 89 72 88, www.cphco.org). Bus 40, 991, 992. ***Open*** *11am-6pm Tue-Sun.* ***Admission*** *100kr; 75kr reductions; free under-18s.* ***Map*** *p120 Y7.*

This spacious art gallery shows immersive installation art in its huge, light-filled rooms. The city's newest art centre, it has 7,000 sq m of space for international installation art in what was once the old welding hall of shipbuilders B&W. **CC Studio**, within the same building, hosts more intimate events, often with an interactive or family focus. On Sundays at 2pm there are special 30-minute family tours of the space and exhibitions.

❤ CopenHot

Refshalevej 325 (31 32 78 08, www.copenhot.com). Bus 40, 991, 992. ***Open*** *10am-10pm Tue-Sun.* ***Admission*** *see below.* ***Map*** *p120 X6.*

This is a Scandi spa experience like no other. Sit in a hot tub overlooking the harbour and look out across the water to Amalienborg Slot. Snuggle up on a winter's day in a hobbit-like wooden sauna hut, perched beside the water. Or rent a hot-tub boat with four of your friends and cruise the canals of the city with drinks and your favourite music. Bring a towel and swimwear, and you'll need to shower before you arrive. Saunas and spas have a minimum age of six and the hot tub boats require you to be 18 and a swimmer. On a Wednesday, Thursday and Sunday, the spa and sauna are open for public guests (300kr for 1.5 hours); the hot-tub boat is 2,200kr per boat (seating five) for a 1.5-hour tour. If you want to hire a spa or sauna privately, rates are 1,200kr-1,300kr per spa/sauna (seating up to six in the spa, 12 in the sauna). Book in advance.

Restaurants

❤ Amass ♕♕♕♕

Refshalevej 153 (43 58 43 30, www. amassrestaurant.com). Bus 40, 991, 992. ***Open*** *10am-midnight Tue-Fri, 1pm-midnight Sat.* ***Map*** *p120 X8* ② New Nordic

The opening of Amass in late 2013 generated the city's biggest culinary buzz since Noma (*see below*) first topped the World's Best Restaurant list nearly five years before. The two restaurants aren't unrelated: Amass is owned by Californian chef Matthew Orlando, a former Noma head chef who knows a thing or two about unusual flavour pairings (before Noma, he worked at NYC's Per Se and Heston Blumenthal's Fat Duck in the UK). It's not just an experimental stronghold; at its heart, Amass serves exquisite organic and sustainable food with a tight focus on locally sourced ingredients. There is even an 800-sq m garden at the premises to help accommodate the vision. Eating here, in an industrial loft-like space, is a real spectacle, and even more so in the 16-seat private dining room, set above the main restaurant. Staff are excellent at explaining each dish on the tasting menu: perhaps lobster, beetroot and elderflower; goose broth with sage; or fig-leaf cream with black orange and chestnut vinegar. It's all seasonal and experimental, and as entertaining for your eyes as it is for your taste buds. Along with a wine-matched tasting menu, it is possible to order à la carte and sit at a bar or counter seat (limited availability and on a walk-in, first-come, first-served basis). Book in advance to be sure you'll have a table.

Noma 2.0 ♕♕♕♕

Refshalevej 96 (32 96 32 97, noma.dk). Bus 40, 991, 992. ***Open*** *5pm-midnight Tue-Sat.* ***Map*** *p120 X11* ⑥ New Nordic

In its new location on Refshalevej, Noma 2.0 is still packing a punch as one of the world's best restaurants, after opening in February 2018. The *LA Times* said: 'You taste foods in ways you've never thought about tasting them before', while British *GQ* said: 'Noma is back. It's better than last time. It makes the old one look amateur in comparison.' From both top-tier restaurant critics and foodies, it's clear that this new location has only improved the world's best restaurant and sent it into the stratosphere.

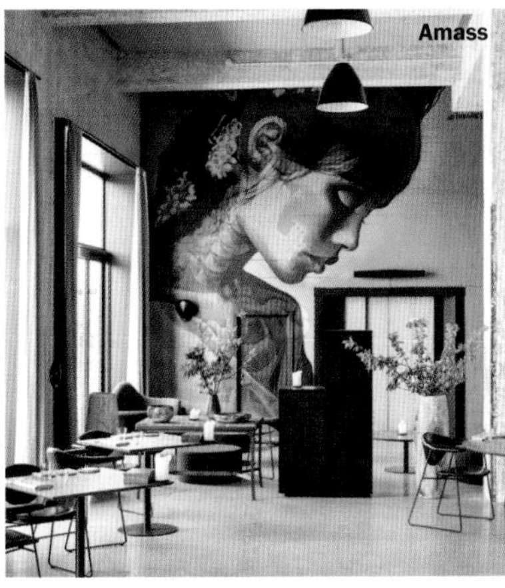
Amass

Designed by Bjarke Ingels Group, the building is set between two lakes on the site of an ex-military warehouse, with a culinary garden and greenhouses as part of the set up. Intimate and cosy, the restaurant seats 40 lucky, lucky customers with the most groundbreaking New Nordic cuisine imaginable: sea snail broth and kelp ice-cream being just two of the crazy dishes Mr Redzepi has served in the past. Sadly, you're not likely to get a table here as a walk-in – and, truthfully, unlikely to get a table here at all – bookings are taken via the website and you need to get in there quick, as soon as each season's dates are released. Best of luck – it's a life-changing place. And if you can't get in, there's always Noma's offshoot 108 (*see p123*) where the odds are more favourable.

Restaurant 56° ♕♕

Krudtløbsvej 8 (31 16 32 05, www. restaurant56grader.dk). Bus 9A, 40. ***Open*** *noon-3.30pm and 6pm-midnight Wed-Sat; 1-3.30pm Sunday.* ***Map*** *p120 X11* ⑦ Modern Danish

Set in the old naval dockyard and navy base at Holmen, Restaurant 56° is the ideal stop before a night at the opera. You'll find dishes such as herring, pork rillette, local Danish cheese and, where possible, vegetables and herbs plucked from its garden metres from the restaurant. It is all served in an atmospheric and friendly former gunpowder warehouse. Three-, four- and five-course menus are offered, matched with wine, or you can order a gourmet evening for a special occasion, which includes bubbles, snacks, six courses, wine and dessert. Reservations are accepted 60 days in advance and booking ahead online is recommended.

Cafés & bars

At the heart of Refshaleøen is Copenhagen's best street-food market, **Reffen** (*see p43*).

❤ La Banchina

Refshalevej 141A (31 26 65 61, www.labanchina.dk). Bus 40, 991, 992. ***Open*** *8am-8pm Sun-Wed, 8am-4pm, 6-11pm Thur-Sat.* ***Map*** *p120 X9* ❶

This simple 16-seat café has an outsized reputation in the city for its cosy vibe, sunbathing platform, swimming spot and little sauna. Enjoy pastries, bar snacks and coffee in the morning, or turn up for lunch or dinner with natural wine, and a vegetarian or seafood menu. No booking required, except for Thursday to Saturday nights, when you can enjoy a nine-course tasting menu with wine-matched food (595kr). Sustainability is key. The round wood-fired sauna is 50kr per person and looks right onto the water.

Halvandet

Refshalevej 325 (70 27 02 96, halvandet.dk). Bus 9A. ***Open*** *check www.facebook.com/halvandet as weather-dependent and typically only open in the summer and through to the end of Sept.* ***Map*** *p120 X6* ❺

Way out on the waterfront beyond Reffen, and all the better for it, Halvandet is the closest thing this cold, windy city has to a beach club. Swing in hammocks, down cocktails on a sunny day, swim in a new swimming area, or play any number of games from kayak polo to pétanque. Food served includes barbecues in the evening, burgers and sandwiches for lunch. If the weather is good, book ahead of time and reserve a mini cabana or sun lounger set for you and your friends. Reservations cost 1,200kr and are credited towards your account to use in the bar on the day.

❤ Lille Bakery & Eatery

Refshalesvej 213A (no phone, lillebakery.com). Bus 40, 991, 992. ***Open*** *8am-5pm Wed-Sun.* ***Map*** *p120 Y8* ❻

This much-raved-about artisanal bakery serves bread, breakfast and lunch and is worth following on Instagram (@lillebakery) so you can get a flavor of the place before arriving. Expect sausage rolls, sourdough bread, scrubbed pine tables and super-chic staff and customers. Run by ex-Noma and 108 sous chef Jesper Gøtz, the project got off the ground thanks to Kickstarter, and the promise to put flavourful and nutritious bread and pastries back on the table at affordable prices. Watch the bakers bake, and turn up for a supperclub-style dinner on occasional week nights; the focus is on seafood and seasonal produce. Dynamic and creative, the building itself is part of the Architecture School and used to be the shipyard apprentice school (attended by Jesper's father).

La Banchina

❤ CopenHill

Vindmøllervej 6 (no phone yet, www. copenhill.dk). Bus 40, 991, 992. ***Open & admission*** *check the website for details.* ***Map*** *p120 Z11.*

When it comes to fusing lifestyle, sustainability, architecture and design, Denmark is at the top of its game. And nowhere more so than at Amager Bakke, more commonly called CopenHill. This waste management plant is the focus of many a design and architecture journalist in 2019 when its ski slope and leisure facilities are due to open.

The power plant has existed on the site since the 1970s, and now sets new standards for environmental performance, energy production and waste treatment. Sustainability is so big in this city that waste has to be shipped in from Sweden to fuel it – the capacity (and the vision) here is vast. When the company behind it called for bids to design a new waste-to-energy facility in 2011, they specifically wanted to hear from architecture practices able to meld recreation with the power plant; in its location at the far end of Refshaleøen, this would give it a dual focus and change the public perception of how waste management should look.

Step forward Bjarke Ingels Group (BIG), never known to turn down a groundbreaking and creative challenge. While some other architectural firms suggested rooftop gardens, nobody else thought of a rooftop ski slope. As Denmark is sorely lacking in mountains, and has a population that loves outdoor sports, it was deemed a perfect fit.

BIG's plans included an idea to release a smoke ring every time 250 kilograms of carbon dioxide was released into the atmosphere from the plant, thus spreading awareness of waste and sustainability (the plant can be seen from many places in the city, and even from the shores of Sweden). As with many architectural ideas, it remains to be seen if the smoke rings will make it to the final functioning design, which at time of writing included juice bars, a 600-metre artificial ski slope, a dizzyingly high artificial climbing wall (the world's highest), an urban hiking area and running routes and paths with a view of the Øresund and Sweden. If adventure sports aren't your thing, you can still take a scenic stroll up the hill, and enjoy views of the sea with plenty of places to rest en route. The waste management plant has been in full operation since 2017 but the opening of the recreational facilities has been delayed by a number of months and is likely to happen mid 2019.

Amager Bakke is part of Copenhagen's drive to be the world's first carbon neutral capital and is designed to be the world's cleanest waste-to-energy plant. It is encouraging to see the buzz around the building in Copenhagen and abroad and to understand how waste management can feature in lifestyle design and family fun. CopenHill expects to see some 60,000 visitors in its first year and, combined with Refshaleøen's buzzing foodie scene and creative vibe, is likely to be one of the city's hot spots for quite some time to come.

► *The city's emergency facilities are reliable and on call at 112 should you have an accident.*

Vesterbro & Frederiksberg

Just to the west of the city centre, Vesterbro runs from Central Station along Istedgade to Enghave Plads and to the border with the newest central district, Carlsberg Byen. Once the red-light area of the city, there's still plenty going on after dark, with great dining in hipster-led Kødbyen and hidden cocktail bars. This being Copenhagen, even the local parks and squares have a dose of innovation to them – Enghave Park has been completely redesigned with global warming in mind, and is designed to be flooded. A stroll down Istedgade takes you along one of the city's most delightful independent streets, with excellent cafés and bakeries, second-hand stores, eco-boutiques, bike workshops and more to invite you in for a little colour and, of course, an introduction to excellent design.

Frederiksberg seems worlds away from its rowdy neighbour. Its wide, leafy avenues make this one of the city's most desirable residential areas, and its parks and zoo are popular destinations at weekends.

❤ Don't miss

1 Cisternerne *p147*
An incomparable art space under a city park.

2 Kødbyen *p141*
The city's most vibrant spot to eat out.

3 Copenhagen Zoo *p146*
Meet penguins, polar bears and elephants.

4 Istedgade *p139*
Vesterbro's hipster shopping street.

5 Værnedamsvej *p139*
Locals call this street 'Little France'.

Copenhagen Zoo tower *p146*

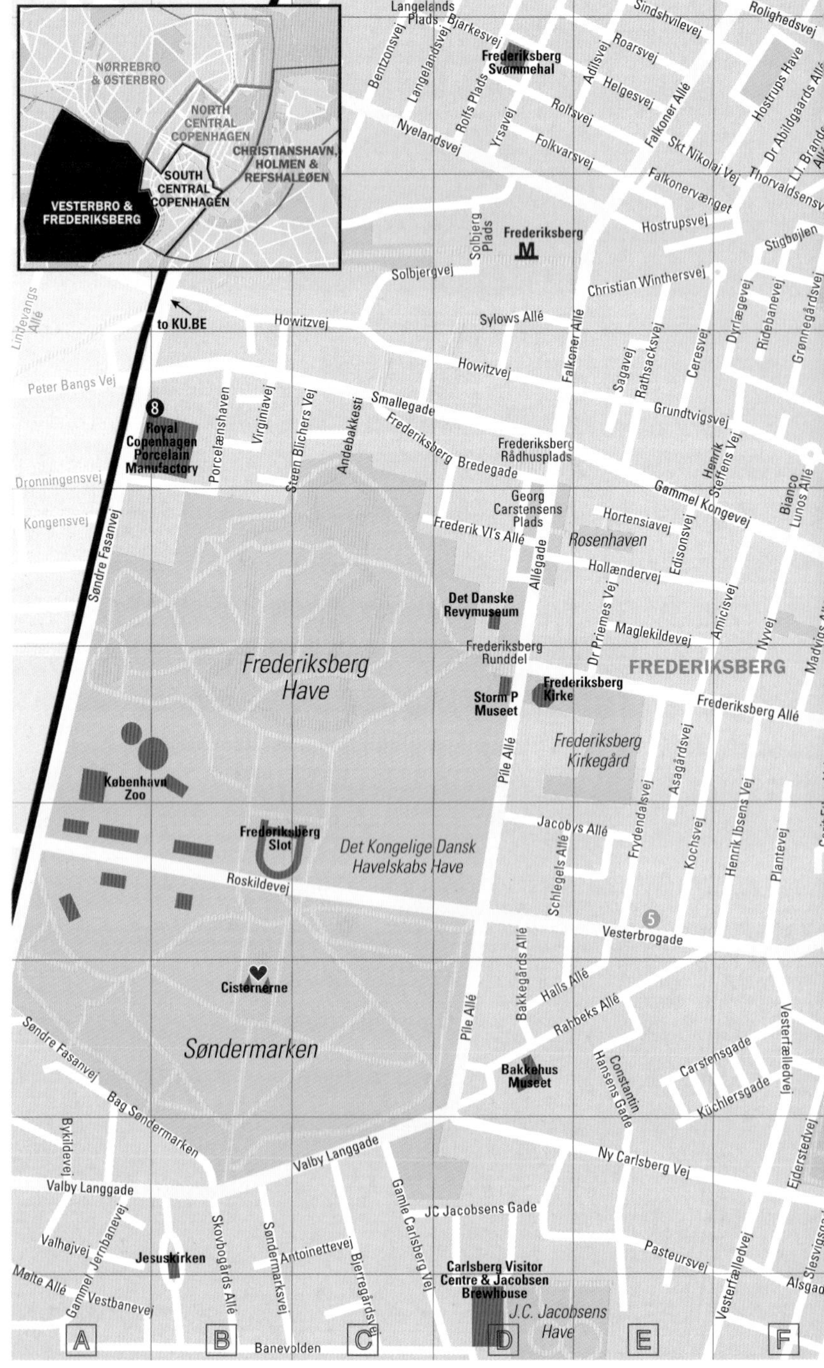
NØRREBRO & ØSTERBRO
NORTH CENTRAL COPENHAGEN
CHRISTIANSHAVN, HOLMEN & REFSHALEØEN
SOUTH CENTRAL COPENHAGEN
VESTERBRO & FREDERIKSBERG
to KU.BE
Frederiksberg Svømmehal
Frederiksberg
Royal Copenhagen Porcelain Manufactory
Frederiksberg Rådhusplads
Georg Carstensens Plads
Rosenhaven
Det Danske Revymuseum
Frederiksberg Runddel
Frederiksberg Have
Storm P Museet
Frederiksberg Kirke
FREDERIKSBERG
Frederiksberg Kirkegård
København Zoo
Frederiksberg Slot
Det Kongelige Dansk Havelskabs Have
Cisternerne
Søndermarken
Bakkehus Museet
Jesuskirken
Carlsberg Visitor Centre & Jacobsen Brewhouse
J.C. Jacobsens Have
Langelands Plads
Bjarkesvej
Bentzonsvej
Langelandsvej
Rolfs Plads
Yrsavej
Nyelandsvej
Sindshvilevej
Roarsvej
Adilsvej
Helgesvej
Rolfsvej
Folkvarsvej
Falkoner Allé
Skt Nikolaj Vej
Falkonervænget
Rolighedsvej
Hostrups Have
Dr Abildgaards Allé
Thorvaldsensvej
Hostrupsvej
Stigbøjlen
Solbjerg Plads
Solbjergvej
Christian Winthersvej
Lindevangs Allé
Howitzvej
Sylows Allé
Peter Bangs Vej
Porcelænshaven
Virginiavej
Steen Blichers Vej
Andebakkesti
Smallegade
Frederiksberg Bredegade
Sagavej
Rathsacksvej
Ceresvej
Dyrlægevej
Ridebanevej
Grønnegårdsvej
Grundtvigsvej
Henrik Steffens Vej
Dronningensvej
Kongensvej
Søndre Fasanvej
Gammel Kongevej
Frederik VI's Allé
Allégade
Hortensiavej
Edisonsvej
Bianco Lunos Allé
Hollændervej
Dr Priemes Vej
Maglekildevej
Amicisvej
Nyvej
Frederiksberg Allé
Pile Allé
Asagårdsvej
Frydendalsvej
Henrik Ibsens Vej
Jacobys Allé
Kochsvej
Plantevej
Schlegels Allé
Roskildevej
Vesterbrogade
Bakkegårds Allé
Halls Allé
Rahbeks Allé
Constantin Hansens Gade
Carstensgade
Küchlersgade
Vesterfælledvej
Bag Søndermarken
Bykildevej
Valby Langgade
Ny Carlsberg Vej
Eiderstedvej
Gamle Carlsberg Vej
JC Jacobsens Gade
Gammel Jernbanevej
Valhøjvej
Mølte Allé
Vestbanevej
Skovbogårds Allé
Søndermarksvej
Antoinettevej
Bjerregårdsvej
Pasteursvej
Slesvigsgade
Banevolden
A
B
C
D
E
F

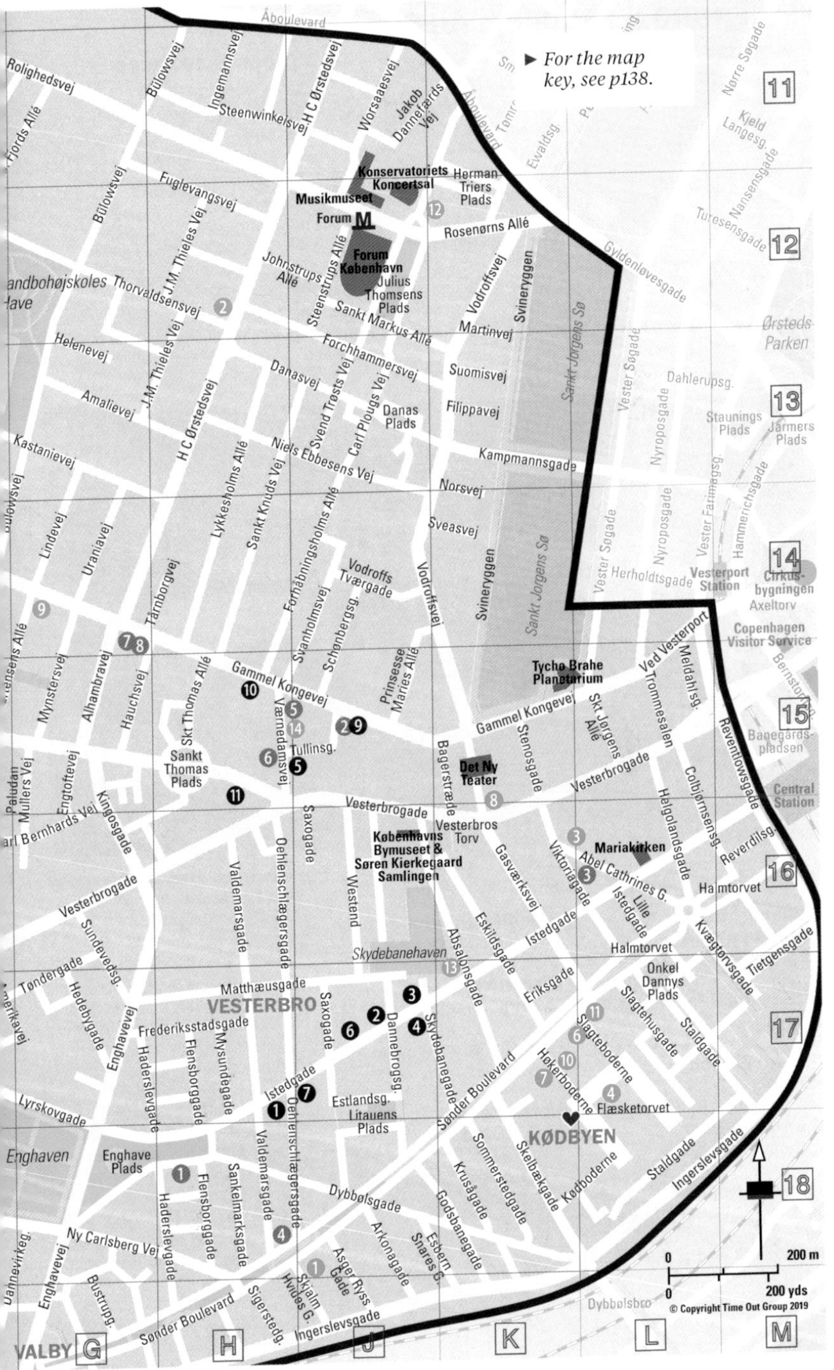
► For the map key, see p138.
Åboulevard
Rolighedsvej
Bülowsvej
Ingemannsvej
Steenwinkelsvej
H C Ørstedsvej
Worsaaesvej
Jakob Dannefærds Vej
Fuglevangsvej
Konservatoriets Koncertsal
Musikmuseet
Forum
Herman Triers Plads
Rosenørns Allé
Forum København
Julius Thomsens Plads
Johnstrups Allé
Steenstrups Allé
Thorvaldsensvej
J.M. Thieles Vej
Sankt Markus Allé
Martinvej
Vodroffsvej
Svineryggen
Sankt Jørgens Sø
Gyldenløvesgade
Helenevej
Forchhammersvej
Danasvej
Suomisvej
Amalievej
Svend Trøsts Vej
Carl Plougs Vej
Danas Plads
Filippavej
Kastanievej
Niels Ebbesens Vej
Kampmannsgade
Norsvej
Lykkesholms Allé
Sankt Knuds Vej
Forhåbningsholms Allé
Sveasvej
Lindevej
Uraniavej
Tårnborgvej
Vodroffs Tværgade
Svanholmsvej
Schønbergsg.
Prinsesse Maries Allé
Sankt Jørgens Sø
Tycho Brahe Planetarium
Ved Vesterport
Meldahlsg.
Mynstersvej
Alhambravej
Hauchsvej
Skt Thomas Allé
Gammel Kongevej
Værnedamsvej
Tullinsg.
Sankt Thomas Plads
Skt Jørgens Allé
Stenosgade
Trommesalen
Bagerstræde
Det Ny Teater
Vesterbrogade
Reventlowsgade
Engtoftevej
Kingosgade
Saxogade
Vesterbros Torv
Københavns Bymuseet & Søren Kierkegaard Samlingen
Mariakirken
Abel Cathrines G.
Colbjørnsensg.
Helgolandsgade
Reverdilsg.
Halmtorvet
Valdemarsgade
Oehlenschlægersgade
Westend
Gasværksvej
Viktoriagade
Istedgade
Lille Istedgade
Sundevedsg.
Eskildsgade
Skydebanehaven
Absalonsgade
Kvægtorvsgade
Tietgensgade
Tøndergade
Hedebygade
Matthæusgade
VESTERBRO
Eriksgade
Onkel Dannys Plads
Slagtehusgade
Staldgade
Enghavevej
Frederiksstadsgade
Mysundegade
Flensborggade
Haderslevgade
Dannebrogsg.
Skydebanegade
Sønder Boulevard
Slagteboderne
Høkerboderne
Flæsketorvet
Lyrskovgade
Estlandsg.
Litauens Plads
KØDBYEN
Enghaven
Enghave Plads
Sommerstedgade
Skelbækgade
Kødboderne
Ingerslevsgade
Sankelmarksgade
Dybbølsgade
Krusågade
Godsbanegade
Arkonagade
Esbern Snares G.
Asger Ryss Gade
Skjalm Hvides G.
Ny Carlsberg Vej
Bustrupg.
Sigerstedg.
Dybbølsbro
Vester Søgade
Nyropsgade
Dahlerupsg.
Staunings Plads
Jarmers Plads
Vester Farimagsg.
Hammerichsgade
Herholdtsgade
Vesterport Station
Cirkus-bygningen
Axeltorv
Copenhagen Visitor Service
Bernstorffsg.
Banegårdspladsen
Central Station
Nørre Søgade
Kjeld Langesg.
Nansensgade
Turesensgade
Ørsteds Parken
Ewaldsg.
VALBY
0 200 m
0 200 yds
© Copyright Time Out Group 2019
G H J K L M
11 12 13 14 15 16 17 18

VESTERBRO & FREDERIKSBERG

Restaurants

1. Absalon *p140*
2. Chai Wong *p148*
3. Cofoco *p140*
4. Fiskebaren *p140*
5. Formel B *p148*
6. Hija de Sanchez *p140*
7. Kul *p140*
8. Lê Lê *p142*
9. Mêlée *p148*
10. Mother *p142*
11. PatéPaté *p142*
12. Restaurant Radio *p149*
13. Sanchez *p142*
14. Les Trois Cochons *p142*

Cafés & bars

1. Brød *p142*
2. Central Hotel & Café *p142*
3. Democratic Coffee *p144*
4. Dyrehaven *p144*
5. Falernum *p144*
6. Granola *p144*
7. Hart Bageri *p149*
8. Meyers Deli *p149*

Shops & services

1. A Door *p144*
2. Cykelfabrikken *p144*
3. Dansk Made for Rooms *p144*
4. Donn Ya Doll *p145*
5. Dora *p145*
6. Es *p145*
7. Kyoto *p145*
8. Royal Copenhagen Factory Outlet *p149*
9. Soulland *p149*
10. Stig P *p149*
11. Tom Rossau Showroom *p149*

Carlsberg Visitor Centre & Jacobsen Brewhouse

❤ Time to eat & drink

A uniquely Danish experience
Absalon *p140*

Buttery breakfast pastries
Brød *p142*

Best for brunch
Sanchez *p142*

Charming bistro
Granola *p144*

Coffee perfection
Democratic Coffee *p144*

Glamorous cocktails
Lidkoeb *p197*

❤ Time to shop

Beautiful interior design
Dansk Made For Rooms *p144*

Bikes to die for
Cykelfabrikken *p144*

Eclectic homewares
Dora *p145*

Upmarket boutiques and high fashion
Kyoto *p145*, Soulland *p149*, Stig P *p149*

In the know
Getting around

As always, it's easiest to navigate this area on foot and by bike, especially if you are staying somewhere central. There is a new metro station due to open in Enghaveplads in 2019, which puts you at the far end of Istedgade; trains from Central Station also run to the station at Carlsberg Byen, which works if you plan to visit Carlsberg or Copenhagen Skatepark, in particular. Visit Carlsberg also runs a free shuttle bus from Central Station. An easy way to visit Cisternerne and/or Copenhagen Zoo is to take the free zoo shuttle bus also from Central Station.

VESTERBRO

Vesterbro has revelled in its trashy image since the 18th century, when it was the site of numerous music halls and drinking dens. Today it's still a leading light in the nightlife scene and home to concert hall Vega, that lures achingly hip acts from all over the world.

Meat markets, literal and metaphorical, have always been Vesterbro's speciality. Their trade was centred on **Værnedamsvej**, which is now one of the area's nicest streets, its cute food shops, boutiques and cafés, such as **Falernum** and **Granola** (*see p144*), giving it a Parisian feel. The city's remaining red-light area, such as it is, is right at the far eastern end of **Istedgade**, Vesterbro's main artery. For Vesterbro's plethora of fashion and design shops, head to the other (western) end of the street.

Hipsters flock to **Kødbyen** (*see p141*), just south of here; this is the regenerated Meatpacking District, whose low-rise former butchers' shops and slaughterhouses are now home to cool galleries, restaurants and nightspots (as well as a few remaining butchers), including late-night bar **Bakken** (*see p196*). Ikea's futures laboratory, **Space 10**, is in the main part of Kødbyen, and co-working spaces full of start-ups ensure that the area is always full of people with big ideas and open wallets.

Vesterbro proper has very few traditional tourist attractions; it's more about the nightlife and the shopping. **Tycho Brahe Planetarium**, on Gammel Kongevej, shows a variety of IMAX movies and puts on interplanetary displays. However, in the south-west corner of Vesterbro, where it meets Frederiksberg and Valby, sits the headquarters of what is Copenhagen's, and probably Denmark's, best-known international brand: Carlsberg. The **Carlsberg Visitor Centre & Jacobsen Brewhouse**, normally a must for beer buffs, is currently closed for renovation and will reopen in 2020, while the surrounding area, Carlsberg Byen, has a new hotel and several developments for shops and more. The area's vacant old warehouses are giving way to a new cultural, residential and commercial quarter, featuring green spaces, bike paths, 3,000 low-energy homes, and a range of new shops and cafés. The landmark **Elephant Gate** on Ny Carlsberg Vej – once the entrance to the brewery – will be preserved as part of the plan.

Tyco Brahe Planetarium

Sights & museums

Bakkehus Museet

Rahbeks Allé 23 (33 31 43 62, www.bakkehusmuseet.dk). Bus 26. ***Open*** *11am-4pm Wed-Sun.* ***Admission*** *50kr; free under-18s. No cards.* ***Map*** *p136 D17.*

This small, eclectic collection is housed in the former home of Knud Lyhne Rahbek, a literature professor and publisher in the early 19th century. The display includes everything from death masks to poet Adam Oehlenschläger's dressing gown.

Carlsberg Visitor Centre & Jacobsen Brewhouse

Gamle Carlsberg Vej 11 (33 27 10 20, www.visitcarlsberg.com). Train Enghave, or bus 18, 26 (plus a free shuttle from Central Station). ***Open*** *The museum is currently closed for renovation and will reopen in 2020.* ***Map*** *p136 D18.*

Take a self-guided tour through the various displays on the history of beer and the brewing processes used at Carlsberg. Naturally, visits conclude with a free sample in the bar of the Jacobsen Brewhouse. Guided tours are available at weekends.

Tycho Brahe Planetarium

Gammel Kongevej 10 (33 12 12 24, www.tycho.dk). Train Vesterport, or bus 9A. ***Open*** *noon-7.10pm Mon; 9.30am-7.10pm Tue-Sun.* ***Admission*** *(including IMAX screening) 160kr; 99kr under-13s.* ***Map*** *p136 K15.*

The Tycho Brahe Planetarium opened in 1989 in a cylindrical building designed by Knud Munk. It's named after the great Danish astronomer (1546-1601) who painstakingly catalogued the solar system – a crucial contribution to the understanding of the laws of planetary motion. IMAX films are screened during the daytime; there are tours and creative workshops during school holidays.

Absalon

Restaurants

❤ Absalon ♛

Sønder Boulevard 73 (no phone, absaloncph. dk). Bus 1A; Metro Dybbelsbrø. ***Open*** *7am-midnight Sun-Thur; 7am-1am Fri; 7am-2am Sat.* ***Map*** *p136 L16* ❶ Danish

A unique and rather wonderful experience, Absalon is open all day as a café in a former church and hosts regular events, including drop-in yoga classes and pub quizzes in the evening. The best of all is its community dinner where, for 50kr per head, you can enjoy home-cooked food from a single menu (ie there is no choice) eaten around a table in communal style. Get there early – 5pm – to make sure you have a seat. Beer and wine are served at the bar; dessert is extra.

Cofoco ♛♛

Abel Cathrinsgade 7 (33 13 60 60, www. cofoco.dk). Train København H, or bus 10, 14. ***Open*** *5.30pm-midnight Mon-Sat.* ***Map*** *p136 L16* ❸ French/Danish

Such has been the success of the Copenhagen Food Consulting people that their stable has now grown to nine restaurants (see website), all of them top quality. Cofoco and Les Trois Cochons (*see p142*) were among the first restaurants to make eating out fun and affordable in the Danish capital, and they continue to offer some of the most reliable cooking around. The interior at Cofoco is rustic, cosy and casual, with wooden tabletops and a blackboard marked up with the day's specials. The menu offers more than the usual confit and entrecôte, with dishes such as pork braised for 14 hours and served with lemon-scented jerusalem artichoke purée. Hearty portions, easy prices and an atmosphere of bonhomie make it perennially popular with locals.

Fiskebaren ♛♛

Flæsketorvet 100 (32 15 56 56, www. fiskebaren. dk). Train Dybbølsbro or København H. ***Open*** *5.30pm-midnight Mon-Thur; 5.30pm-2am Fri, Sat; 11.30am-midnight Sun.* ***Map*** *p136 L17* ❹ Fish

Located in the heart of Kødbyen, Fiskebaren is a shrine to the deliciousness of the deep. The vast, industrial space arranged round a U-shaped bar glows a deep-sea blue that seems exactly right for the food: plump, pearl-grey oysters from the icy depths of Limfjorden; Øresund mussels with raspberry and walnut vinaigrette; and white fish from Østersøen and chips from sweet Gotland potatoes with a hearty remoulade.

Hija de Sanchez ♛♛

Slagterboderne 8 (no phone, www. hijadesanchez.dk). Train Dybbølsbro or København H. ***Open*** *noon-8pm Mon-Thu; noon-10pm Fri-Sat; 11am-6pm Sun.* ***Map*** *p136 K17* ❻ Mexican

One of the stars of David Chang's *Ugly Delicious* Netflix series was ex-Noma pastry chef Rosio Sanchez's *taquería* in Kødbyen. Stop by on a summer evening to eat on the street (the margaritas are especially good) and expect to be queueing out of the door. The menu is short and the vibe is young and lively. No table reservations.

Kul ♛♛

Høkerboderne 16B-20 (33 21 00 33, www. restaurantkul.dk). Train Dybbølsbro or København H. ***Open*** *5-11pm Mon-Wed; 5pm-1am Thur-Sat.* ***Map*** *p136 K17* ❼ International/Grillhouse

With a menu formed of small dishes, Kul – meaning 'coal' in Danish – differentiates

❤ Kødbyen

www.kodbyen.kk.dk. Train Dybbølsbro or København H. ***Map*** *p136 K/L17.*

Copenhagen's meatpacking district, Kødbyen (pronounced *cool boo-en*), is Vesterbro's top zone for a good night out, whether you like cocktails or fine dining, dim sum or dancing until the early hours. The catch is – unlike Manhattan's Meatpacking District, all high heels, designer clothes and chic living – this little area is still a working food industry hub, with white-hatted butchers buzzing around in the mornings, and restaurant vans filling up with produce from the cash-and-carry all day. It is mixed-use in the truest sense of the word: Ikea's design and innovations lab **Space 10** is located here, along with the start-up office centre **Soho/Noho**, and it attracts people from all walks of life, hipsters and blue-collar workers alike.

Taking up all the space between the railway tracks and Sønder Boulevard, Kødbyen has three areas, white, brown and grey, named after the colour of the buildings there. The 'white' area is the main food zone, with restaurants and bars (*see below*). The 'brown' area is the oldest and has more of a nightlife focus, although its north-eastern half is a leisure and conference complex, **DGI** (www.dgi-byen.com), which includes a hotel, a leisure centre and an events space, **Øksnehallen** at Halmtorvet 11. The smaller 'grey' area has cultural venues, restaurants, offices as well as meat-related industries.

Where to begin on a night out at Kødbyen? Start with a drink or two at **Alfons** wine bar (Skelbækgade 42, alfonsvinbar.com); at the fringes of the area, just over Dybbelsbrø bridge, it serves natural wines, orange wines, beer and more in a casual, friendly space. Then, move on to find something to eat. **Hija de Sanchez** (*see p140*) is a renowned tiny food unit, only a touch larger than a food stall, serving tacos; next door, **Bollyfood** (Slagterboderne 10, bollyfood1716.dk) offers colour and spices on its Indian menu. **WarPigs** (Flæsketorvet 25, warpigs.dk), though best known for its beer, serves up Texan barbecue food to set you up for a long night out, while **Mother**'s sourdough pizzas are popular all through the day and night (*see p142*). If you're looking for a more upmarket meal, **Fleisch** (Slagterbodene 7, www.fleisch.dk) offers high-quality organic meat, while fish restaurant **Kødbyen's Fiskebar** (*see p140*), set up by ex-Noma restaurateur Anders Selmer, and has earned a Michelin Bib Gourmand for its fish-based menu. **Paté Paté** (*see p142*), the area's oldest restaurant, also has a good reputation, with a Spanish-Mediterranean flavor, a wine bar, restaurant and tapas bar.

You can continue the party without walking very far. Cocktail bars in the area include **Noho** (Flæsketorvet 28, noho.bar), **Magasasa** (Flæsketorvet 54, magasasa.dk), which serves cocktails and dim sum, and **1656** (Gasværksvej 33, 20 47 27 47), hidden behind a graffiti-scrawled door in true Copenhagen speakeasy style. In the main Kødbyen zone, nightclubs **Bakken** (*see p196*), **KB3** and **Jolene** (for both, *see p198*), keep the party going all night.

In the know
A word of warning

Turn up at Kødbyen too early and it will look something like a bike-strewn car park with a lot of closed restaurants. Bear in mind that the area is mid-regeneration, rather than the finished product. The best time to arrive is around 8pm, ideally with a dinner table pre-booked, although there are plenty of informal places to eat so you are unlikely to go hungry.

itself from other contemporary restaurants in Copenhagen by its focus on the grill. Chef duo Henrik Jyrk and Christian Mortensen create tasty offerings such as grilled wild shrimp with spicy avocado and coriander, and barbecued ribs with grilled baby gem lettuce – though the size of the plates means you'll need three or four per person to feel sated. The pared-back space includes some seating at the bar; but note that you'll feel the full effect of the grill if you sit there.

Lê Lê

Vesterbrogade 40 (53 73 73 73, www.lele.dk). Train København H, or bus 6A, 26. ***Open*** *5-10pm Mon-Thur; 5-10.30pm Fri, Sat.* ***Map*** *p136 K16* 8 *Vietnamese*

One of the city's best Asian restaurants, Lê Lê serves authentic, complex Vietnamese dishes – everything from soups and noodles to curries and rice dishes. The venue is cool too, with high ceilings and massive glass windows. It also offers takeaway, via **Lê Lê Street Kitchen** (at the same address), which has a handful of tables for eating in, and is a great place for a quick bite, especially if you're dining alone. **Other locations** Lê Lê Street Kitchens: Østerbrogade 56, Østerbro (33 22 71 31); Torvehallerne Hall 2 (53 73 73 95).

Mother

Høkerboderne 9-15 (22 27 58 98, www.mother.dk). Train Dybbølsbro or København H. ***Open*** *11am-1am daily.* ***Map*** *p136 K17* 10 *Pizza*

This Kødbyen pizzeria is super popular and runs a particularly good brunch operation at the weekend. The secret lies in the organic sourdough bases, quality toppings and authentic wood-fired oven, which combine to produce simply delicious pizzas. Starters and sides, such as bruschetta made from Manitoba flour, are also excellent.

PatéPaté

Slagterboderne 1 (39 69 55 57, www.patepate.dk). Train København H. ***Open*** *9am-midnight Mon-Wed; 9am-1am Thur, Fri; 11.30am-1am Sat; open Sun summer only.* ***Map*** *p136 L17* 11 *Mediterranean/Danish*

PatéPaté is a wine bar, restaurant, tapas bar and delicatessen that was opened in summer 2009 by the group that runs Bibendum (*see p103*) and Falernum (*see p144*). The restaurant's name was inspired by the building's previous incarnation as a liver pâté factory. Rustic cuisine is the name of the game, with lots of hearty meat and fish dishes, as well as an excellent wine list. Candlelight and homely decor create a convivial mood.

❤ Sanchez

Istedgade 60 (31 11 66 40, www.lovesanchez.com). Bus 14 or Enghave Plads metro station. ***Open*** *5pm-midnight daily.* ***Map*** *p136 K17* 13 *Mexican*

This intimate and friendly Mexican restaurant with a Danish bistro style has a very good reputation among locals. The weekend brunch is a great way to acquaint yourself with its bold flavours and delicious drinks; evening meals are a more refined and special affair, with prices to match. Run by Rosia Sanchez, ex-pastry chef at Noma, it's a definite foodie hangout in the city and a more formal version of her Kødbyen establishment (*see p141*).

Les Trois Cochons

Værnedamsvej 10 (33 31 70 55, www.cofoco.dk). Train Vesterport, or bus 6A, 9A. ***Open*** *8am-noon, 5.30pm-midnight Mon-Fri; 9am-3pm, 5.30pm-midnight Sat-Sun.* ***Map*** *p136 H15* 14 *French/Danish*

Run by the folk behind Cofoco (*see p140*), Les Trois Cochons produces similarly priced, good-value three-course French meals with locally sourced ingredients and an enjoyable lack of formality. Decor is a bit more luxe than at the sister restaurant, with chandeliers and generous armchairs that invite lingering. Dishes are a cut above the usual bistro offerings too, featuring the likes of rabbit cooked in smoked bacon, salsify and wine, or saffron-scented fish.

Cafés & bars

Other great bars in this area include **Duck and Cover** and **Lidkoeb** (for both, *see p197*).

❤ Brød

Enghave Plads 7 (33 22 80 07, www.facebook.com/Bageriet-BRØD-330089827074995). Bus 14. ***Open*** *7am-6pm Mon-Fri; 7am-5pm Sat-Sun.* ***Map*** *p136 H18* 1

Small but beautiful, this bakery is one of the very best in the city, with huge buttery croissants and plenty more to make your breakfast truly Danish and truly special. We also recommend their home-made chocolate spread, ideal for breakfast on one of their crusty loaves if you are self-catering.

Central Hotel & Café

Tullinsgade 1 (33 21 00 95, www.centralhotelogcafe.dk). Bus 9A. ***Open*** *8am-5pm Mon-Fri; 10am-5pm Sat; 10am-4pm Sun.* ***Map*** *p136 J15* 2

Situated on the border of eastern Frederiksberg, in a former shoe-repair shop, Central Hotel & Café is a one-room hotel with a cute coffee place below. The café, a

Skate Copenhagen

The city is a destination for skaters worldwide

Copenhagen has an active skateboarding scene that gets plenty of international interest. In fact, its annual **Copenhagen Open** (www.cphopen.dk, @copenhagenopen on Instagram), held in August, is one of Europe's largest professional skateboarding contests. Events are held in the main skateboarding areas across the city, but also in abandoned supermarkets, Tivoli Gardens and at the Town Hall. Even the city's mayor is right behind it – he's happy to see skateboard culture expand across the city as a way of using its public spaces in diverse and imaginative ways.

In the winter, the scene centres around the indoor **Copenhagen Skatepark** in Vesterbro (Enghavevej 78, 33 21 28 28, www.copenhagenskatepark.dk), while in summer, it's all about the impressive 4,000-square-metre facility at Østerbro's **Fælledparken**. Its outdoor skatepark spans 4,000 square metres (one acre) and was designed by Grindline. Also used by inline skaters, the park has a plaza-style street section, containing steps, handrails, flatbars and ledges; a large half-pipe; and a third mixed-terrain space, with bowls, quarter-pipes and ledges, often used for competitions.

There are a few other places where skateboarders congregate in the city, including **Israels Plads**, **Enghave Plads** and Red Square at **Superkilen** (*see p155*). The boardwalk at **Amager Strandpark** (*see p174*) can be fun on a sunny day, and there is a small area at **Reffen** (*see p43*), beside the food market. The indoor bowl in **Christiania** (*see p128*) is another option. For the low-down on all the best street spots (including a map that shows you options from street corners to school playgrounds worth visiting), head to skate shops **Circus Circus** in Nørrebro (Guldsbergsgade 16, 26 79 62 84, www.circuscircus.dk), **Street Machine** in the centre (Kronprinsensgade 3, 33 33 95 11, www.streetmachine.com), or **Sidewalk** in Vesterbro (Enghave Plads 10, 33 31 32 34, www.sidewalkshop.dk), where staff will be happy to let you know where's currently good to go.

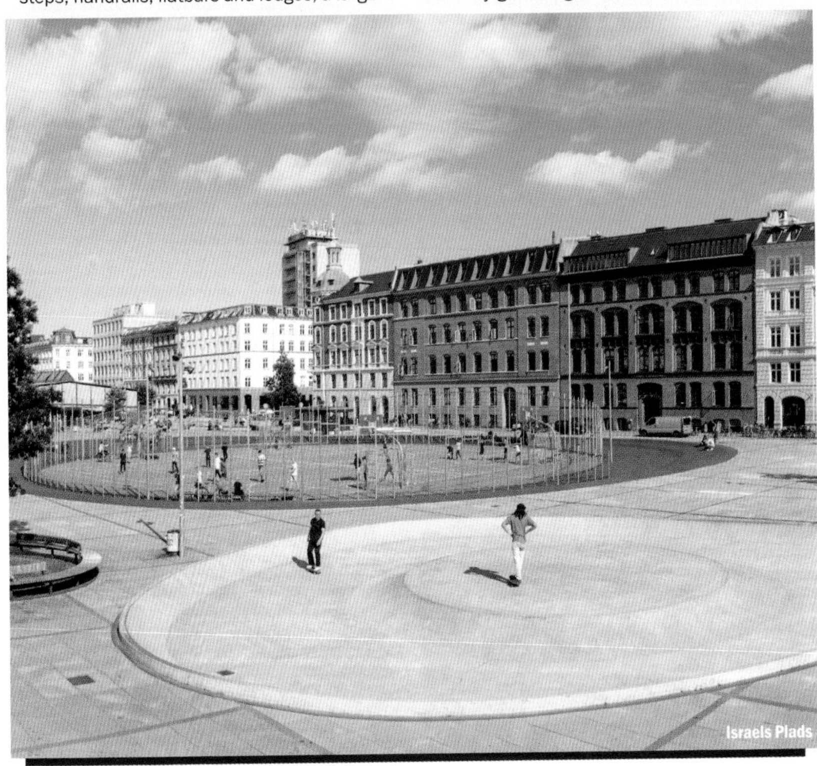

Israels Plads

favourite spot for locals to grab an espresso on the way to work, feels as if it's been around for decades; it is owned by local legend Leif Thingtved, who also owns Granola (*see p144*). As well as quality coffee (from Risteriet), there are teas, milkshakes and juices on offer, and sandwiches, pastries and ice-cream if you're feeling peckish.

❤ Democratic Coffee

Viktoriagade 19 (40 19 62 37, @ democraticcoffeebar). Bus 10, 14. ***Open*** *8am-4pm Mon-Fri.* ***Map*** *p136 L16* ❸

This tiny coffee shop, about the size of a living room, makes a cosy spot for a morning snack, just off Istedgade at the station end. The croissants are fresh and fluffy, the service is charming and the coffee is most definitely on point. If you're feeling super Danish, order a 'boller med ost' – a bread roll with cheese, and often jam as well. **Other location** in the city's main library, Krystalgade 15.

Dyrehaven

Sønder Boulevard 72 (33 21 60 24, www. dyrehavenkbh.dk). Train Dybbølsbro, or bus 10, 14. ***Open*** *10am-2am Mon-Thur; 9am-2am Fri-Sun (food served 10am-9pm Mon- Thur); 9am-9pm Fri-Sun.* ***Map*** *p136 H18* ❹

Owned by three young locals, this is an atmospheric spot that attracts small groups of sociable twenty- and thirtysomethings. The appeal is good design, a relaxed vibe, hearty food – classic dishes, such as *smørrebrød* and coq au vin – and well-priced drinks. The wood-panelled walls and bar, mounted deer heads, vintage pictures and separate dining cubicles give the bar a distinct 1970s feel. It's as popular for weekend brunch as it is for evening drinks.

Vesterbro Torv

Falernum

Værnedamsvej 16 (33 22 30 89, www. falernum.dk). Train Vesterport, or bus 6A, 9A. ***Open*** *noon-midnight Mon-Thur; noon-2am Fri, Sat; noon-11pm Sun.* ***Map*** *p136 H15* ❺

Located on one of the neighbourhood's nicest streets, this popular, cosy wine bar/café has plenty of character, thanks to its old wooden tables, candles and agreeable, loyal punters. The wine list is extensive and well thought out, and tapas are served in the evening. It's also a good spot for a light breakfast.

► *Falernum is part of a successful mini-chain that includes Bibendum and PatéPaté.*

❤ Granola

Værnedamsvej 5 (www.granola.dk, 31 31 15 36). Train Vesterport, or bus 6A, 9A. ***Open*** *7.30am-11pm Mon-Wed; 7.30am-midnight Thur-Fri; 9am-midnight Sat; 9am-5pm Sun.* ***Map*** *p136 H15* ❻

This French-style café has a strong following. The space evokes the 1930s with its retro decor, and it's a wonderful spot for breakfast, brunch or lunch, with classic French bistro food on the menu alongside Danish chicken salad and porridge. It also serves milkshakes and delicious ice-cream, and stocks an excellent range of top-quality tea and coffee.

Shops & services

A Door

Istedgade 101 (29 85 34 56, www.adoor.dk). Train København H, or bus 10, 14. ***Open*** *2-5.30pm Tue-Fri; 11am-3pm Sat.* ***Map*** *p136 H17* ❶ *Interior design*

It is not hard to find good homeware shops on Istedgade, and A Door, which sells trinkets, flower pots, rugs, candles, coffee and more, is one of the best. Tucked away on the Enghave Plads end of the street, it is well placed for a browse right after you've had breakfast at Brød.

❤ Cykelfabrikken

Istedgade 92 (27 12 32 32, www. cykelfabrikken.dk). Train København H, or bus 10, 14. ***Open*** *2-6pm Tue-Fri; 11am-3pm Sat.* ***Map*** *p136 J17* ❷ *Bike shop*

These well-designed, simple bikes are a perfect blend of track and Scandinavian upright frames. The stylish shop opened in 2009, and fits in perfectly on independent-heavy Istedgade.

❤ Dansk Made for Rooms

Istedgade 80 (32 18 02 55, www.danskmadefor rooms.dk). Train København H, or bus 10, 14. ***Open*** *11am-6pm Mon-Fri; 11am-4pm Sat.* ***Map*** *p136 J17* ❸ *Homewares/Accessories*

This light-filled design and homeware shop sells a choice selection of cushions, lamps, minimalist pots and trays, trendy headphones and graphics-led stationery and posters. It's a beautiful place to browse. If you have kids with you, send them to the next-door park to spare them touching the breakables.

Donn Ya Doll

Istedgade 55 (33 22 66 35) Train København H, or bus 10, 14. ***Open*** *11am-6pm Mon-Fri; 10am-4pm Sat.* ***Map*** *p136 J17* ❹ *Fashion*

Carefully edited multi-brand boutique stocking the likes of Henrik Vibskov, Nümph, and much more in a light two-roomed shop with a friendly and helpful owner. There's some beautiful jewellery too. Watch out for its occasional pop-up sales shop down the street.

❤ Dora

Værnedamsvej 6 (32 21 33 57, www.shopdora.dk). Bus 6A, 9A. ***Open*** *10am-6pm Mon-Fri; 10am- 5pm Sat; noon-4pm Sun.* ***Map*** *p136 J15* ❺ *Homewares/Accessories*

In line with the majority of homeware shops in Copenhagen, Dora has a distinct design focus, stocking a range of highly covetable candles, lamps, cushions, gadgets and storage, plus stationery from brands such as Flos, Georg Jensen and Made a Mano. Simple but fashion-forward jewellery is also for sale, alongside sunglasses from Han Kjøbenhavn, and there are items under 100kr too.

Es

Istedgade 110 (33 22 48 29, www.es-es.dk). Bus 10, 14. ***Open*** *11am-6pm Mon-Fri; 11am-4pm Sat.* ***Map*** *p136 J17* ❻ *Fashion*

This womenswear boutique offers a well-edited selection of stylish Scandinavian and other European brands. Clothes are classic and have a slow fashion edge; brands like Baum und Pferdgarten, American Vintage and Inwear sit alongside Marine Sixtine designer dresses, Yvonne Koné, Swedish Hope and Forte_Forte.

❤ Kyoto

Istedgade 95 (33 31 66 36, www.kyoto.dk). Train København H, or bus 10, 14. ***Open*** *10am-6pm Mon-Thu; 10am-7pm Fri; 10am-5pm Sat.* ***Map*** *p136 J17* ❼ *Fashion*

Kyoto was one of the pioneers of trendy new Vesterbro, and has been selling street-influenced menswear from its Istedgade outfit since 2001. It now sells both men's and women's clothing and accessories from its spacious showroom, with the likes of Maison Kitsuné, Rodebjer, Wood Wood, Woron and Norse Projects on its selective rails.

FREDERIKSBERG

Frederiksberg's appealing character may be partially the result of its distinct political status: like Christiania, Frederiksberg is a separate town within the city of Copenhagen (and a stark contrast to the alternative Freetown). An independent municipality of just over 100,000 people, it has its own mayor, town hall and administration. Apartments tend to be larger and more expensive than elsewhere in the city, especially those along Frederiksberg Allé, a long, wide, tree-lined boulevard that could have been lifted straight from an affluent arrondissement of Paris. Until the 19th century, Frederiksberg lay well outside Copenhagen, with views from its hill ('berg' means 'hill') over the fields – now Vesterbro – to the city beyond.

The district's most central area, around the concert hall and conference centre **Forum Copenhagen** (www.forumcopenhagen.dk), has undergone some rejuvenation in recent years. A regular host of design events and shopping expos, the Forum can be a hive of activity in the daytime even before playing host to music and events in the evening. Rosenørns Allé, in particular, has become livelier since the relocation here of the **Royal Danish Academy of Music** (*see p204*), which has been based in the former DR Radiohusets building since 2009.

However, most of Frederiksberg still has a unique sense of separateness from Copenhagen: true, the district's conservative character doesn't make for giddy nightlife, but it does have a few sights that are worth the short bus or Metro ride from the centre of town. **Gammel Kongevej**, one of the large streets running through it, is like the King's Road in London, lined with boutiques, cafés and designer bakeries; it's a lovely place for a stroll on a lazy afternoon. Note that shops open typically from 11am to around 4pm on a Saturday but may be open later on weekdays.

The heart of the quarter is **Frederiksberg Have**, a rambling park that was laid out in the formal French style in the 18th century, before being given a more informal English revamp at the turn of the 19th century. In the south-east corner is **Det Kongelige Danske Haveselskabs Have** (The Royal Danish Horticultural Garden), a formal, oriental-style water garden, created in 1884.

On the south side of Frederiksberg Have lies **Frederiksberg Slot** (Frederiksberg Palace), a royal summer residence used between the early 18th and mid 19th centuries. Beside Frederiksberg Slot is the **Zoologisk Have** (Zoological Garden),

Denmark's national zoo. Founded in 1859, it's one of the oldest in the world, and has a good reputation for its breeding programme.

Across Roskildevej, you'll find more greenery in the form of **Søndermarken**, a more informal but equally picturesque park, which also features one of Copenhagen's most unusual galleries, **Cisternerne** (*see p147*). Entrance to The Cisterns is gained via a Louvre-style glass pyramid in the park, opposite the rear of Frederiksberg Slot, and you can expect to discover any number of challenging avant-garde exhibitions in the extraordinary and atmospheric space beneath the park.

To the north-east of Frederiksberg Have is the **Royal Copenhagen Factory Outlet**, while close by you will find the modern cultural play space **Ku.Be** and the small, octagonal **Frederiksberg Kirke**, dating from 1734. This pretty Dutch Renaissance church holds regular concerts and has an altarpiece depicting the Eucharist, painted by CW Eckersberg, while in its cemetery is the grave of 19th-century poet Adam Oehlenschläger.

Moving south from here, and to the east of Søndermarken, is the **Bakkehus Museet**, a converted 17th-century house containing souvenirs of Denmark's early 19th-century Golden Age. It lies literally in the shadow of the old Carlsberg brewery (*see p139*), which is officially just over the border in Vesterbro.

Sights & museums

❤ Copenhagen Zoo

Roskildevej 32 (72 20 02 00, 72 20 02 80, www.zoo.dk). Bus 4A, 6A, 26. ***Open*** *July, Aug 9am-8pm daily. Mar 10am-4pm Mon-Fri; 9am-5pm Sat, Sun. Apr, May, June 9am-6pm Mon-Fri; 9am-8pm Sat-Sun. Sept 9am-6pm daily. Oct 9am-5pm daily. Jan, Feb & 1-14 Nov 10am-4pm Mon-Fri, 9am-4pm Sat-Sun; mid Nov-end Dec 10am-4pm Mon-Thur; 9am-8pm Fri-Sun.* ***Admission*** *195kr; 105kr 3-11s; free under-3s.* ***Map*** *p136 B16.*

If zoos are your thing, then Copenhagen's is one of the best: expansive, well-designed and with a renowned breeding programme. It's home to an impressive assortment of animals, including pandas, elephants, monkeys, tigers, lions, giraffes and gorillas. There are even polar bears, who can be seen both underwater and on land in the Arctic Ring enclosure: an awesome sight, as long you're comfortable seeing such large and endangered mammals in captivity. Perennially popular with families, the zoo also has plenty of interest for architecture buffs in the form of the zoo's 40-metre (131-foot) tower, the BIG-designed panda house, opened in 2019, and the Norman Foster-designed elephant house. The zoo was the focus of international controversy in February 2014 when it euthanised a healthy young giraffe due to space issues. The dead giraffe was dissected in front of a large crowd of onlookers and then fed to the lions.

Frederiksberg Have

Main entrance: Frederiksberg Runddel (no phone or website). Bus 8A, 26. ***Open*** *6am-sunset daily.* ***Admission*** *free.* ***Map*** *p136 D15.*

With its tree-lined paths, canals and lake, this is one of the city's most romantic spaces, particularly in spring. In its grounds are a Chinese pavilion, numerous statues and an impressive avenue of stately linden trees, dating from the 1730s. **The Royal Danish Horticultural Garden** (Det Kongelige Danske Haveselskabs Have, open 10am-sunset daily), located in the south-east corner of the park, features an oriental water garden, and is well worth a visit for horticultural inspiration; it's also one of the outdoor venues for the Copenhagen Jazz Festival (*see p185*).

Frederiksberg Slot

Roskildevej 28A (72 81 77 71, www.frederiksbergslot.dk). Bus 6A, 26. ***Open*** *Guided tours year-round except July & Dec, 1pm last Sat of mth.* ***Admission*** *Guided tours 100kr; free under-14s.* ***Map*** *p136 B16.*

Frederik IV was so taken with the villas he saw while on a visit to Frascati that, between 1699 and 1703, he instructed architect Ernst Brandenburger to build a palace in the Italian style. The two side wings, designed by Laurids de Thurah, were added in 1733-38, on the instruction of Christian VI. Today, the palace is home to the Danish Military Academy and, as such, is not open to the public other than for the occasional guided tour.

Frederiksberg Svømmehal

Helgesvej 29 (38 14 04 00, www.frederiksbergsvoemmehal.dk). Metro Frederiksberg. ***Open*** *Swimming pool 7am-9pm Mon-Fri; 7am-4pm Sat; 9am-4pm Sun.* ***Admission*** *45kr Swimming pool, 20kr under-15s; 175kr Spa.* ***Map*** *p136 D11.*

This local institution was built in the 1930s, making it one of Denmark's oldest swimming pools. The walls of the main pool area are decorated with colourful mosaics; there are multiple pools, a heated baby pool and a slide. Downstairs there is another pool with a slide ideal for kids. There's also a spa (bookable for a two-hour period, with saunas at a set time), with steam baths, saunas and cold plunge pools, plus a jacuzzi and a massage parlour. The place remains a popular spot for socialising and relaxing. Midnight swim sessions take place on the second Friday of the month and involve candlelit

Cisternerne

Søndermarken (30 73 80 32, www.cisternerne.dk). Bus 4A, 6A, 8A, 26. ***Open*** *16 Mar-1 Dec 11am-6pm Tue, Wed, Fri, Sun; 11am-8pm Thur.* ***Admission*** *70kr; 50kr reductions; free under-18s.* ***Map*** *p136 B17.*

There is something magical about hiding an art gallery under Frederiksberg Hill in the heart of Søndermarken Park. The Cisterns are a long-forgotten subterranean reservoir that once held Copenhagen's drinking water. Run as the Museum of Modern Glass Art from 2001 to 2013, partly connected to the city's status as European City of Culture in 1996, it is now the city's most avant-garde location for atmospheric, sometimes spine-chilling, but always inspiring art experiences/exhibitions.

As you walk through the green leafy park and along its sandy paths, look out for two crystal-shaped glass structures on the main lawn. These are the entry and exit points to this wonderful hidden gallery. Walk down the steep concrete steps into a world of vaulted ceilings reminiscent of a cathedral, and discover catacombs, light shows, echoing noises and stalactites.

Recent events have included 'The Water' in 2018, Japanese architect Hiroshi Sambuichi's first major exhibition outside Japan, which brought together pools of light, mirrors, wooden bridges and great puddles of water in a symphony of reflections and meditation. Eva Koch has projected video installations over the columns and walls in the space, while Christian Lemmerz filled the gallery with wax sculptures of huge candelabras. Danish artist group SUPERFLEX took over in 2019, flooding the main space to create an interactive, dystopian version of a climate-changed future.

In the know
Be prepared

It is dark down there, and might not be suitable for very small children, claustrophobics and those with accessibility needs – there is no lift. It can be cold even in summer, so dress appropriately; flat shoes are preferable.

swimming in the main pool plus saunas (book in advance via the website).

KU.BE

Dirch Passers Allé 4 (28 98 09 24, kube.frederiksberg.dk). Bus 34, 31. Metro Lidevang. ***Open*** *9am-9pm Mon-Fri; 10am-8pm Sat; 10am-3pm Sun. Playgrounds 9am-6.30pm Mon-Fri; 10am-6.30pm Sat; 10am-2.45pm Sun.* ***Admission*** *free.*

This inspiring cultural centre is aimed at families but has plenty to offer the wider community too, with a welcoming café, library, regular evening events and a huge indoor hard play area, made of climbing walls, semi-exposed tunnels, netting and more. Outside there is a garden ideal for sandwiches in summer. Modern and fresh, it's an example of urban architecture that brings together culture, health and movement.

Restaurants

Chai Wong ♕♕

Thorvaldsensvej 2 (27 52 35 65, www.chaiwong.dk). Metro Forum. ***Open*** *5pm-10pm Mon-Thu; noon-10pm Fri-Sat; 5pm-9pm Sun.* ***Map*** *p136 H12* ❷ *Pan-Asian*

This restaurant from the owners of Michelin-starred Kiin Kiin (*see p156*) is more relaxed – and more affordable – than its cousin, with black bistro-style tables, sofas to lounge on, dimmed lighting and a menu inspired by Asian street food. The delicious dishes might include char siu pork with glass noodle sesame; red curry with roasted duck; or slow-cooked pumpkin in coconut cream. There are also sharing plates and a takeaway menu.

Formel B ♕♕♕

Vesterbrogade 182 (33 25 10 66, www.formelb.dk). Bus 6A. ***Open*** *5.30pm-midnight Mon-Thur; 5.30pm-1am Fri, Sat.* ***Map*** *p136 E16* ❺ *French/Danish*

Several of Denmark's best-known chefs have passed through the kitchen of this small, marble-lined cellar restaurant at the western end of Vesterbrogade, and it's held a Michelin star since 2004. The concept is a riff on French and Danish classics, and they do it so well, taking the notion of modernism in cooking to a whole new level. It's not, strictly speaking, a fish restaurant, but that is where it shines. Try a dollop of caviar on a scoop of jerusalem artichoke ice-cream, then go on to more robust dishes, such as shellfish salad with rouille, skate wing with tarragon foam and pickled potatoes, or west coast turbot with braised veal tails. It draws the city's young and beautiful, so dress up and make a night of it.

Mêlée ♕♕

Martensens Allé 16 (35 13 11 34, www.melee.dk). Bus 9A. ***Open*** *5.30pm-midnight Tue-Sat.* ***Map*** *p136 G14* ❾ *Modern Danish Bistro*

Chinese pavilion, Frederiksberg Have

This is a *hyggeligt* little spot on a chichi residential street. In summer, there are a couple of tables outside, but it's best to be in the warm dining room to soak up the celebratory atmosphere. The wine list is carefully put together to match the hearty menu. Slabs of home-baked bread and butter accompany cod with pears and caper butter; lusty stews served straight from the pot come with mash.

Restaurant Radio

*Julius Thomsens Gade 12 (25 10 27 33, www.restaurantradio.dk). Metro Forum. **Open** Lunch noon-3pm Fri-Sat. Dinner 5.30pm-midnight Tue-Sat. **Map** p136 K12* ⓬ *New Nordic*

The epitome of New Nordic, both in terms of decor and food, this is the latest offering from celebrity chef Claus Meyer, owner of Meyers Deli (*see p149*) and co-founder of Noma (*see p131*). The small plates are conceptual offerings – think scallops with endive and seaweed – but most have flavours that are rich enough to satisfy unexperimental palates. Most of the produce used is organic. It's housed in the old Radio House, over the road from the Forum.

Cafés & bars

Hart Bageri

*Gammel Kongevej 109 (31 11 18 50, hartbageri.com) Bus 9A. **Open** 7.30am-6pm Mon-Fri, 8am-5pm Sat-Sun. **Map** p136 G14* ❼

It takes a certain sort of Englishman to set up a bakery in Copenhagen and achieve this level of success. Richard Hart is that man: ex-head baker at Tartine, his bakery, which opened in mid 2018, has drawn the crowds for its neat design and wonderful cakes, pastries and lunches. If you only eat one hot dog in the city, make sure it's from here. It's well placed for lunch after a leisurely stroll down leafy and gorgeous Gammel Kongevej.

Meyers Deli

*Gammel Kongevej 107 (33 25 45 95, www.meyersdeli.dk). Bus 9A. **Open** 7am-9pm Mon-Fri; 8am-9pm Sat-Sun. **Map** p136 G14* ❽

Claus Meyer is one of the leading foodie figures in Denmark. Entrepreneur, TV personality and restaurateur (he's the co-founder of Noma and recently consulted with local nurseries to help establish vibrant menus for under sixes), Meyer opened this magnificent deli-café in the heart of bourgeois Frederiksberg back in 2005. His healthy, innovative eat/heat/cook takeaways have proved popular with time-poor yuppie locals. **Other location** Meyers Bageri, Jægersborggade 9.

Shops & services

Royal Copenhagen Outlet

*Søndre Fasanvej 9 (38 34 10 04, www.royalcopenhagen.com). Metro Fasanvej, or bus 4A, 9A. **Open** 10am-6pm Mon-Fri; 10am-3pm Sat. **Map** p136 A13* ❽ *Homewares*

Cash-strapped fans of Denmark's most famous porcelain brand should head to its factory shop. You can buy discounted dinnerware and figurines that don't quite pass muster for the central Amagertorv shop, as well as discontinued items.

❤ Soulland

*Gammel Kongevej 41 (53 64 01 86, www.soulland.com). Train Vesterport, or bus 9A. **Open** 10am-6pm Mon-Fri; 10am-4pm Sat; noon-4pm Sun. **Map** p136 J15* ❾ *Fashion*

This gallery-like shop is the flagship of Soulland, the trend-led label of owner Silas Adler. As well as Soulland's streetwear-inspired garments, shoes and accessories, the shop stocks selected pieces from Acne Jeans, A Kind of Guise and Dana Lee. Menswear and womenswear are represented. It's impossible to walk down a city street in winter without spying one of Soulland's branded unisex beanies, which come in all colours of the rainbow.

❤ Stig P

*Gammel Kongevej 91C (70 22 86 18, www.stig-p.com). Train København H, or bus 9A. **Open** 11am-6pm Mon-Fri; 10am-5pm Sat. **Map** p136 H15* ❿ *Fashion*

Although it was founded back in 1969 (by Stig Petersen), this remains one of Denmark's most on-trend fashion boutiques. As well as wearable and relaxed T-shirts, tops, dresses and knitwear from the eponymous label, all Stig P branches stock clothing and accessories from cult brands such as Kokoon, Vanessa Bruno Athé, Sonia Rykiel, Rag & Bone and Sessùn. **Other locations** Kronprinsensgade 14, Indre By (33 14 42 16); Ravnsborggade 18, Nørrebro (35 35 75 00).

Tom Rossau Showroom

*Frederiksberg Allé 5 (71 94 00 00, www.tomrossau.dk). Train København H, or bus 6A, 26. **Open** 11am-6pm Tue-Fri; 10.30am-2pm Sat. **Map** p136 H15* ⓫ *Homewares*

Self-taught Danish designer Tom Rossau creates retro-inspired lamps from sustainable wood veneers. This flagship store showcases the full range (floor, pendant and table), as well as new shelving units and the TT01 Convertible coffee-cum-dining table. The large twisted birch veneer pendants, TR7, are particularly en vogue.

Nørrebro & Østerbro

Nørrebro and Østerbro, along with Vesterbro, are the main residential areas outside the city's ramparts and all have a flavour of 'real' Copenhagen about them that can be lacking in the city centre. Nørrebro is a diverse, pulsating and attractive neighbourhood, home to some of the coolest bars, restaurants and shops in town. Its cemetery, Assistens Kirkegård, is the final resting place for many famous Danes, as well as a popular sunbathing spot for the livelier locals. Østerbro is more sedate and well heeled, full of upscale boutiques, stylish cafés and smartly dressed couples pushing prams containing equally well turned-out children. Both districts abut the city's lakes, around which joggers pound the pavements with views of ducks and neon signs illuminated in the water.

❤ Don't miss

1 Danish design *p159*
Renting a flat in Østerbro can introduce you first hand to dazzling Danish interior design.

2 Boat trips on the lake *p162*
Grab a kitsch swan pedalo and have fun.

3 Jægersborggade *p157*
For independent shops, cobbles and great coffee.

4 Fælledparken *p161*
The green heart between these two districts, with playgrounds and picnic spots.

5 Superkilen *p155*
Hang out in a multicultural space, designed by Bjarke Ingels Group: BIG.

Multicoloured houses in Østerbro

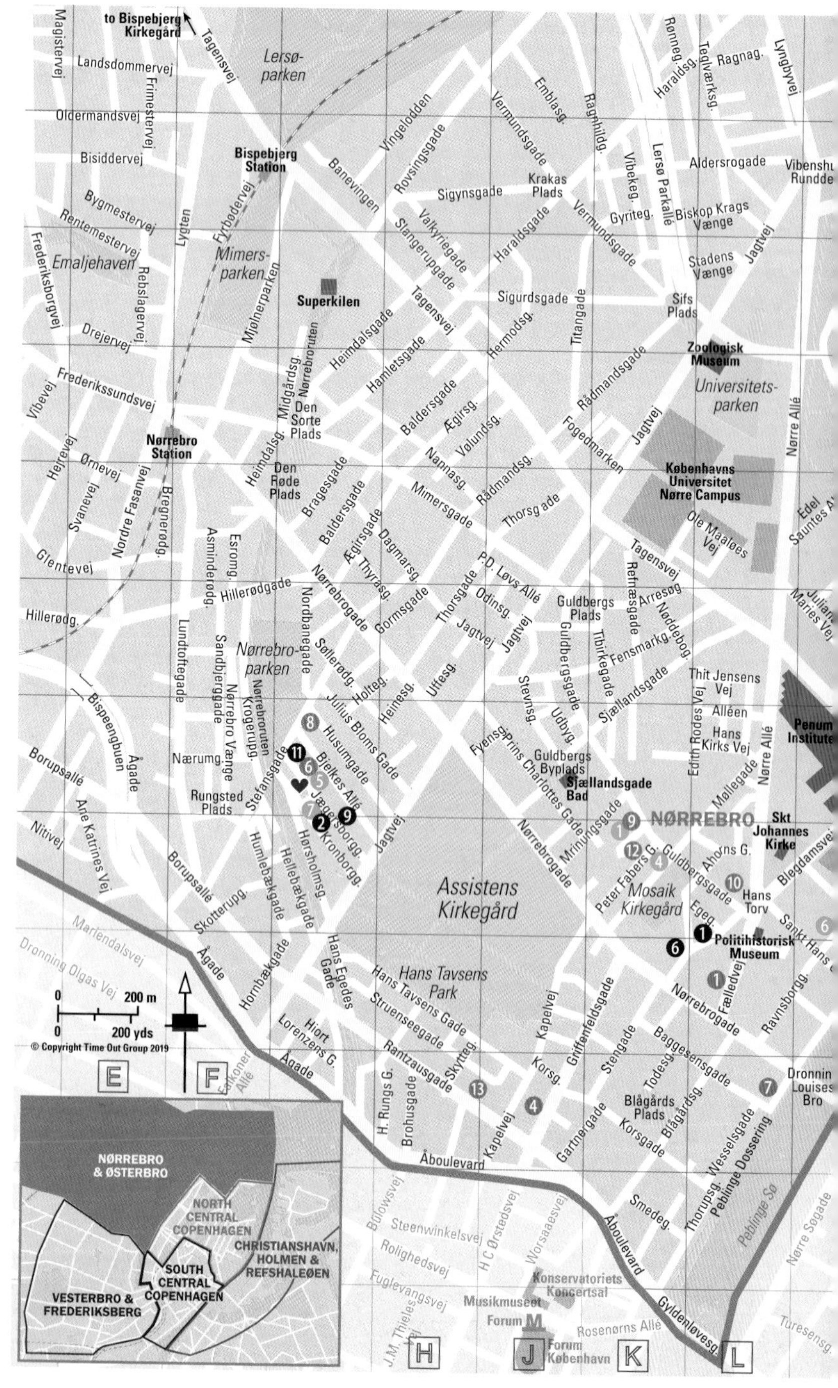
to Bispebjerg Kirkegård
Lersø-parken
Mimers-parken
Emaljehaven
Universitets-parken
Nørrebro-parken
Assistens Kirkegård
Hans Tavsens Park
Mosaik Kirkegård
Bispebjerg Station
Nørrebro Station
Superkilen
Zoologisk Museum
Københavns Universitet Nørre Campus
Penum Institute
Sjællandsgade Bad
Skt Johannes Kirke
Politihistorisk Museum
NØRREBRO
Den Sorte Plads
Den Røde Plads
Krakas Plads
Sifs Plads
Guldbergs Plads
Guldbergs Byplads
Rungsted Plads
Blågårds Plads
Hans Torv
Dronning Louises Bro
Peblinge Sø
Konservatoriets Koncertsal
Musikmuseet
Forum
Forum København
Magistervej
Landsdommervej
Frimestervej
Oldermandsvej
Bisiddervej
Bygmestervej
Rentemestervej
Frederiksborgvej
Rebslagervej
Drejervej
Lygten
Fyrbødervej
Mjølnerparken
Tagensvej
Banevingen
Vingelodden
Rovsingsgade
Sigynsgade
Valkyriegade
Slangerupgade
Vermundsgade
Emblasg.
Ragnhildg.
Rønneg.
Haraldsg.
Teglværksg.
Ragnag.
Lyngbyvej
Vibekeg.
Lersø Parkallé
Aldersrogade
Vibenshus Runddel
Gyriteg.
Biskop Krags Vænge
Stadens Vænge
Jagtvej
Haraldsgade
Sigurdsgade
Titangade
Hermodsg.
Heimdalsgade
Nørrebroruten
Midgårdsg.
Hamletsgade
Baldersgade
Ægirsg.
Vølundsg.
Rådmandsgade
Fogedmarken
Nørre Allé
Frederikssundsvej
Vibevej
Hejrevej
Ørnevej
Svanevej
Nordre Fasanvej
Bregnerødg.
Glentevej
Heimdalsg.
Bragesgade
Nannasg.
Rådmandsg.
Mimersgade
Thorsgade
Ole Maaløes Vej
Edel Sauntes Allé
Asminderødg.
Esromg.
Hillerødgade
Hillerødg.
Nørrebrogade
Nordbanegade
Baldersgade
Ægirsgade
Dagmarsg.
Thyrasg.
Gormsgade
Thorsgade
P.D. Løvs Allé
Odinsg.
Guldbergsgade
Tibirkegade
Refnæsgade
Arresøg.
Nøddebog.
Fensmarkg.
Juliane Maries Vej
Lundtoftegade
Sandbjerggade
Nørrebro Vænge
Krogerupg.
Søllerødg.
Holteg.
Heinesg.
Ullesg.
Stevnsg.
Udbyg.
Sjællandsgade
Thit Jensens Vej
Alléen
Hans Kirks Vej
Edith Rodes Vej
Bispeengbuen
Borupsallé
Ågade
Nærumg.
Stefansgade
Julius Bloms Gade
Husumgade
Bjelkes Allé
Jægersborgg.
Kronborgg.
Hørsholmsg.
Fyensg.
Prins Charlottes Gade
Møllegade
Ane Katrines Vej
Nitivej
Humlebækgade
Hellebækgade
Skotterupg.
Mriningsgade
Peter Fabers G.
Guldbergsgade
Ahorns G.
Egeg.
Bleqdamsvej
Sankt Hans G.
Marlendalsvej
Dronning Olgas Vej
Hornbækgade
Hans Egedes Gade
Hans Tavsens Gade
Struenseegade
Rantzausgade
Skytteg.
Kapelvej
Griffenfeldsgade
Korsg.
Stengade
Todesg.
Baggesensgade
Blågårdsg.
Fælledvej
Ravnsborgg.
Hiort Lorenzens G.
Falkoner Allé
H. Rungs G.
Brohusgade
Åboulevard
Gartnergade
Korsgade
Wesselsgade
Peblinge Dossering
Thorupsg.
Smedeg.
Nørre Søgade
Bülowsvej
Steenwinkelsvej
Rolighedsvej
H C Ørstedsvej
Worsaaesvej
Fuglevangsvej
J.M. Thieles Vej
Rosenørns Allé
Gyldenløvesg.
Turesensg.
0 200 m
0 200 yds
© Copyright Time Out Group 2019
E
F
H
J
K
L
NØRREBRO & ØSTERBRO
NORTH CENTRAL COPENHAGEN
CHRISTIANSHAVN, HOLMEN & REFSHALEØEN
SOUTH CENTRAL COPENHAGEN
VESTERBRO & FREDERIKSBERG

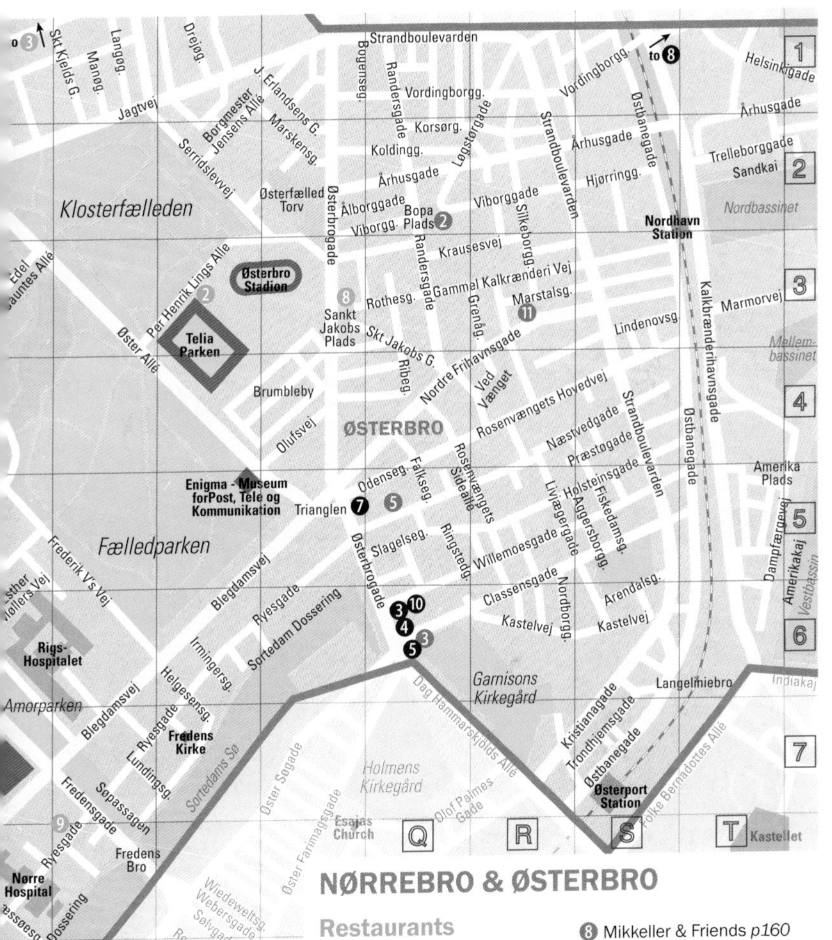

NØRREBRO & ØSTERBRO

Restaurants

1. Bæst *p156*
2. Geranium *p164*
3. Gro Spiseri *p164*
4. Kiin Kiin *p156*
5. Manfreds & Vin *p156*
6. Nørrebro Bryghus *p158*
7. Relæ *p158*
8. Le Saint-Jacques *p164*
9. Tigermom *p158*

Cafés & bars

1. Bip Bip Bar *p158*
2. Café Bopa *p164*
3. Dag H *p165*
4. Dupong *p158*
5. Gourmandiet *p165*
6. Grød *p158*
7. Kaffesalonen *p158*
8. Mikkeller & Friends *p160*
9. Mirabelle *p160*
10. Sebastopol Café *p160*
11. Souls *p165*
12. Tapperiet Brus *p160*
13. Tjili Pop *p160*

Shops & services

1. Acne Archive *p161*
2. Damernes Magasin *p161*
3. Ganni *p165*
4. Goods *p165*
5. Moshi Moshi Mind *p165*
6. Native North *p161*
7. Normann Copenhagen *p165*
8. Paustian *p165*
9. Den Sidste Dråbe *p161*
10. Søstjernen *p165*
11. Tú a Tú *p161*

Nørrebro

❤ Time to eat & drink

Afternoon tea by the lakes
Kaffesalonen *p158*

Beer on a sunny or not sunny afternoon
Nørrebro Bryghus *p158*

Fancy porridge, Danish style
Grød *p158*

Fashionable lunch
Manfreds & Vin *p156*

Picnic supplies for Fælledparken
Gourmandiet *p165*

Special evening meal
Gro Spiseri *p164*

Vegan food done properly
Souls *p165*

❤ Time to shop

Dream dresses
Ganni *p165*

Luxury homewares, Copenhagen style
Moshi Moshi Mind *p165*

Fabulous clothes for kids
Søstjernen *p165*

On-trend Scandi style
Acne Archive *p161*

Scandi clothes for men
Native North *p161*

In the know
Getting around

As always in Copenhagen, the best way to get around both Østerbro and Nørrebro is on foot or by bike. There are also multiple bus routes running through the area and established metro lines. Nørreport Station is a key point of entry for Nørrebro if you are coming by public transport; Trianglen and Østerport stations are the transport hubs in Østerbro.

NØRREBRO

Nørrebro is the epicentre of everything hip and hipster in the city and is especially good for nightlife, quirky bars and shopping. The area's ethnic mix is a major element of its appeal as an up-and-coming area. Centering around **Sankt Hans Torv**, there are three streets in particular that stand out: pedestrianised Blågårdsgade, Elmegade and **Jægersborggade** (*see p157*).

Recent years have seen a little more crime and violence on its streets in comparison to the rest of the city, but not enough for it to qualify as dangerous in any objective terms. It is ironic, then, that the main museum in Nørrebro is the **Politihistorisk Museum** (Police History Museum, *see p155*). This well-presented museum would potentially be of interest to foreign visitors but for the lack of any significant information in English.

Nørrebro also has two historic cemeteries. The Jewish cemetery, **Mosaisk Kirkegård**, on Peter Fabers Gade, is surrounded by a high wall and gates, and is open only for private visits arranged through the local Jewish community. **Assistens Kirkegård**, on the other hand, is open year-round and, for a place of eternal rest, is fairly lively; it's used by many as a local park and picnic place (rehearsing musicians are a common sight). City planners have developed it as an urban living room and it's a lovely place to wander on a sunny day, or to take pictures of blossom in spring. It's a stone's throw from Jægersborggade if you want a decent cup of coffee after paying your respects at Hans Christian Andersen's grave.

A newer Nørrebro public space, completed in 2012, is **Superkilen** (*see p155*), an urban park and playground. It's a fun place to take a stroll and the odd photo, particularly around the multi-lined hills and skateboard area in Red Square.

As well as its boutiques selling fashionable clothing and accessories, Nørrebro is known for its antiques shops. The trade is centred on **Ravnsborggade** (just south-east of Sankt Hans Torv) and its extension, **Ryesgade**, where every other store has a selection of vintage clothes, furniture, porcelain, art, glassware, silverware, gold or bric-a-brac. You'll also find boutiques and great casual eateries dotted along the road. Not far away is **Guldbergsgade**, a little night-time hotspot where some of the city's best places to eat and drink sit next to the Empire cinema.

On a summer's day, a walk by the lakes that separate Nørrebro from central Copenhagen can be a good way to explore the area. As night falls, grab a six-pack of Tuborg from a nearby supermarket and sit on Dronning Louises Bro, a popular gathering spot on summer evenings.

▶ *The tourist board's excellent Know Your Bro self-guided walking tour (www.nbro.io) takes you to all Nørrebro's best places and more with an insider's take on the area.*

Sights & museums

Politihistorisk Museum

Fælledvej 20 (40 32 58 88, www.politimuseum.dk). Bus 3A, 5C, 350S. ***Open*** *11am-4pm Tue, Thur, Sun.* ***Admission*** *50kr; free under-18s. No cards.* ***Map*** *p152 L8.*

As well as covering the history of the police force, with old uniforms, equipment and ephemera, the building houses the Museum of Crime, which documents Copenhagen's nefarious residents (including various infamous murderers) from past centuries (mostly in Danish only) and holds temporary exhibitions.

Sjællandsgade Bad

Sjællandsgade 12A (35 39 06 06, www.sjaellandsgadebad.dk). Bus 3A or 5C. ***Open*** *3-9pm Tue; 3-8pm Wed; 6-9pm Thur (aroma therapy sauna, mixed-gender); 4-8pm Fri (mixed-gender); 9am-3pm Sat; noon-1pm Sun (aroma therapy sauna, mixed-gender).* ***Admission*** *60kr sauna; 70kr aromatherapy in the sauna; 60kr bathing session.* ***Map*** *p152 J7.*

This old bathing house is a bit of a treat. Once the only place the people of Nørrebro could easily get a bath, it is now a quirky kind of spa run by volunteers, with a sauna and plenty of individual rolltop baths to relax in (take a swimsuit).

❤ Superkilen

Nørrebrogade 208 (no phone, www.superflex.net/superkilen). Bus 5C. ***Open*** *24hrs daily.* ***Admission*** *free.* ***Map*** *p152 G3.*

Stretching 750 metres (about half a mile) from Nørrebrogade to Tagensvej, Superkilen is Nørrebro's urban park, designed by artists' group Superflex, in collaboration with none other than Bjarke Ingels Group: BIG and German landscape architects Topotek 1. The park is a collection of global influences, to reflect the fact that the local neighbourhood is home to people from some 50 countries. It's divided into three main areas: **Red Square**, for music and sports; **Black Market**, with fountains and benches; and **Green Park**, for picnics, leisure and dog-walking. Local residents were asked to nominate objects for the park, resulting in a fountain from Morocco, benches from Brazil, swings from Iraq and a neon sign from a Russian hotel. Opened in 2012, it's due a refresh in 2019.

Superkilen *p155*

Restaurants

Bæst 

Guldbergsgade 29 (35 35 04 63, www.baest.dk). Bus 5C, 350S, 3A. ***Open*** *5-10.30pm Mon-Wed; noon-3am Thur-Sun.* ***Map*** *p152 K8* ❶ *Italian*

Nørrebro's renowned Italian restaurant made it to no. 8 in a list of the world's best pizza joints – in a list dominated by Italian pizzerias – and is run by ex-El Bulli, Noma, Relæ and Manfreds chef Christian Puglisi. It's inventive and interesting, run on organic and sustainable principles, and is warm and welcoming. Book in advance if you can. On the menu you'll find exquisite locally made mozzarella, charcuterie from some of the best pigs in the country (which is something indeed) and wood-fired pizzas. They even have a 'farm of ideas' 40km away where they keep the cows that produce the milk for the mozzarella.

Kiin Kiin ♛♛♛

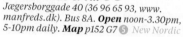

Guldbergsgade 21 (33 35 75 55, www.kiin.dk). Bus 5C, 350S, 3A. ***Open*** *5.30pm-midnight (last seating 8.30pm) Mon-Sat.* ***Map*** *p152 K8* ❹ *Modern Thai*

Chef Henrik Yde Andersen has put the five years he spent living in Thailand to good effect in this new three-storey restaurant, close to Sankt Hans Torv. Weary of being served the same five dishes in the city's Thai restaurants, Andersen's mission has been to get Danes eating new and interesting Thai food; vegetables and shellfish feature strongly in dishes such as orchid-lemongrass salad, and scallops with young ginger. The menu changes daily and there's a well-chosen wine menu for 775kr. Kiin Kiin is one of the few Thai restaurants in Europe to boast a Michelin star.

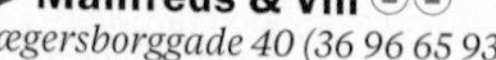

❤ Manfreds & Vin ♛♛

Jægersborggade 40 (36 96 65 93, www.manfreds.dk). Bus 8A. ***Open*** *noon-3.30pm, 5-10pm daily.* ***Map*** *p152 G7* ❺ *New Nordic*

Manfreds is more intimate and laid-back than its sister restaurant opposite, Relæ (*see p158*), though equally as scrupulous when it comes to sourcing ingredients. Most of the produce is organic and local, with biodynamic vegetables from Kiselgården,

❤ Jægersborggade

When it comes to hipster streets in Copenhagen, one in particular springs to mind: Jægersborggade. It's only a tiny cobbled street (not easy to cycle down in a hurry), but it has become a byword for independent shopping and is home to so many restaurants and bistros that you'll never go hungry again. New Nordic restaurant **Relæ** (*see p158*) and its sister spot, **Manfreds & Vin** (*see p156*), lead the charge in elegant dining, while popular chains **Grød** (*see p158*), **Meyers Bageri** (no.9, www.meyersmad.dk) and **Coffee Collective** (no.57, coffeecollective.dk) have all staked a spot on the street.

It's not just about food: the shopping here is exquisite. **Sneakers & Coffee** (no.30; sneakersandcoffee.dk) offers, well, take a wild guess, while **Gågrøn** ('Go Green'; no.48; www.gagron.dk) is great for sustainable products and design. There are tattoo artists, organic hairdressers, an acupuncturist and a cooking school, plus vintage fashion at **Tú a Tú** (*see p161*), and the extra special **Damernes Magasin** (*see p161*) for Ganni, Won Hundred, Sneaky Fox and plenty of other boutique-ready Danish designs for women. Make time to explore specialist spirits and unique Nordic drinks at **Den Sidste Dråbe** (*see p161*), pick up some items for a deli-style lunch at **La Dispensa** (no.25; www.ladispensa.dk), and grab some delicious caramels to take home as gifts at **Karamelleriet** (no.36; http://karamelleriet.com).

This little street of specialist shops has not always been the ideal place to spend a Saturday morning, however: 100 years ago it was reputedly the haunt of one of Copenhagen's worst child murderers.

roots from Lammefjorden, pork from Grambogaard, herbs from local forests, and wine – a big focus here– from organic and biodynamic vineyards. The emphasis is on sharing, with the menu consisting of small dishes – beef tartare with cress and rye bread, say, or charred onions with elderflower and Havgus cheese.

❤ Nørrebro Bryghus ♕♕

Ryesgade 3 (35 30 05 30, www.noerrebrobryghus.dk). Bus 5C. ***Open*** *noon-11pm Mon-Thu; noon-1am Fri-Sat; noon-10pm Sun.* ***Map*** *p152 M8* 6 *Gastropub*

This split-level, modern Scandinavian take on a microbrewery serves not just great home-brewed beers and ales, but also some good gastropub-style food. The monthly changing menu typically includes plenty of fresh fish, such as fried pepper mackerel with summer cabbage, plus a choice of roast meats. All washed down, of course, with some of the best beers in town.

► *Other good microbreweries include Mikkeller & Friends (see p160), Bryggeriet Apollo (Vesterbrogade 3, 33 12 33 13, ahb.dk/restauranter/bryggeriet-apollo) and Vesterbro Bryghus (Vesterbrogade 2B, 33 11 17 05, www.vesterbrobryghus.dk).*

Relæ ♕♕

Jægersborggade 41 (36 96 66 09, www.restaurant-relae.dk). Bus 8A. ***Open*** *dinner 5pm-midnight Tue-Sat; lunch noon-3pm Fri-Sat.* ***Map*** *p152 G7* 7 *New Nordic*

Not many restaurants would have the balls to serve you a raw, pickled carrot with a glass of champagne and call it an amuse-bouche. Then again, Relæ is no ordinary restaurant. Founded by Christian Puglisi (chef) and Kim Rossen (front-of-house), both previously at Noma (*see p152*), it looks quietly cool with an open kitchen and wrap-around bar, yet rocks to an eclectic sound track: a welcome antidote to more 'po-faced' restaurants. Relæ – which has a Michelin star – serves one meat and one vegetarian menu, both adventurous but accessible, featuring Nordic dazzlers such as barley porridge with cauliflower 'crumbs' and wild mushrooms, and silky slow-cooked veal heart with jerusalem artichoke purée.

Tigermom ♕

Ryesgade 25 (53 84 25 25, www.tigermom.dk) Bus 5C. ***Open*** *5.30-10pm Wed-Sat.* ***Map*** *p152 N8* 9 *Asian*

New to Ryesgade at the end of 2018, this superb Asian restaurant is great value and highly sociable. All the food is served family style and the limited menu is something you can rely on – Lisa Lov, Tigermom herself, has great taste and is on a mission to improve the quality of Asian food in the city. Everything is served with a mound of jasmine rice from Thailand and dishes include grilled octopus, organic Danish beef and authentic broth.

Cafés & bars

Bip Bip Bar

Fælledvej 7 (www.bipbipbar.dk). Bus 3A or 5C. ***Open*** *5pm-midnight Wed; 5pm-12am Thur; 5pm-2am Fri; 3pm-4am Sat; 11am-4am Sun.* ***Map*** *p152 L9* 1

Come to play, stay to drink – or the other way around. Nørrebro's premier retro gaming café invites you to play games such as SuperBomberman, table football or pinball machines, alongside the city's hipsters and retro games fans. Quirky, but what else did you expect?

Dupong

Griffenfeldsgade 52 (no phone, www.dupong.dk). Bus 3A. ***Open*** *7pm-1am Wed, 7pm-2am Thur; 7pm-3am Sat, Sun.* ***Map*** *p152 J10* 4

The city's first and only table tennis bar is a place to drink, watch, play and make friends. Wednesday and Thursday nights see happy hour running to midnight; cocktails, beer and great music get the crowds going at this colourful joint. Their Instagram feed @dupongbar gives you an idea of what to expect.

❤ Grød

Jægersborggade 50 (50 58 55 79, www.groed.com). Bus 8A. ***Open*** *7.30am-9pm Mon-Fri; 10am-9pm Sat, Sun.* ***Map*** *p152 G7* 6

This healthy porridge café is more exciting than it might sound, seeking as it does to redefine the concept of porridge via enticing recipes and the use of different grains. The menu changes regularly, but always includes oat-based breakfast-style porridge (maybe with blackcurrant sugar, fresh blood orange and walnuts). **Other locations** Torvehallerne (Hall 2, Stall A8); Nørreport (50 59 82 15).

❤ Kaffesalonen

Pebling Dossering 6 (35 35 12 19, www.kaffesalonen.com). Bus 5C. ***Open*** *8am-midnight Mon-Fri; 10am-midnight Sat, Sun.* ***Map*** *p152 L10* 7

Salonen is blessed with an ideal location close to the lakes, which allows it to expand onto a large floating deck during summer. It's the perfect place for a long, leisurely sundowner, followed by a selection from the accomplished French-Danish menu, or an ice-cream on a hot day.

❤ Danish design

You'll find classic Danish furniture everywhere in Copenhagen, from the chair you sit on in the library, to cool bars and restaurants. For accommodation, the **Hotel Alexandra** (*see p235*) is a delight. Several of the rooms are furnished with design classics by Jacobsen, Wegner, Ole Wanscher and Finn Juhl.

Østerbro and Nørrebro have fewer hotels than the rest of the city. But if you love design, why not rent an apartment, particularly in Østerbro, and you may well get to know first hand what Danish interior design is all about?

The first thing you'll notice is the elegant simplicity. Where is all the clutter? The answer: there is no clutter. Danes have impeccable taste, and the mantra is ingrained from a young age that it is worth saving for a piece of design furniture that you will prize and love forever over something cheap and functional.

Look closer and you might spy lighting by Louis Poulsen, a statement chair by Arne Jacobsen and knick-knacks on the shelf that almost certainly include a Kay Bojesen monkey or carved birds. Designed in the 1950s, their playful appearance works exceptionally well today.

Scandinavian maximalism is set to return as a key theme in interior design, after many years of serious restraint, so brace yourself for clashing colours and multivariant florals.

Product placement

If you want to create the same look at home, head for the second-hand and antiques shops on Ravnsborggade in Nørrebro, or the more exclusive dealers on Bredgade in Frederiksstaden. *Loppemarkeds* (flea markets) that take place from the spring to the autumn also sell vintage, second-hand interior design goods, furniture and fashion, at extremely good prices. Design temple **Illums Bolighus** (*see p78*) is another great place to start, with everything from elegant chopping boards to fashion and high-design Danish furniture.

Neighbouring **Royal Copenhagen** (*see p79*), sells contemporary and classic porcelain, glassware and silverware. Even if you can't afford a major purchase, it's well worth wandering through the gallery-style halls to be inspired and tempted by a Jensen stainless-steel watch, the perfect porcelain of Bing & Grøndhal, or the crystal creations of contemporary Danish craftsmen such as Michael Bang, Torben Jørgensen and Allan Scharf. Even the area outside the store has designer pedigree: the geometric patterns of the marble-paved fountain square were designed by Bjørn Nørgaard in 1996.

Other good shops for new furniture are **HAY House** (*see p85*) in the centre, and **Normann Copenhagen** (*see p165*) in Østerbro. For design-led electronics, meanwhile, head to the end of Strøget to Kongens Nytorv for **Bang & Olufsen**'s flagship store (*see p78*).

For inspiration on Scandinavian interior design and style, the excellent blog www.myscandinavianhome.com serves up charming home tours and shopping guides. And if you're interested in learning more about Danish design, make **Designmuseum Danmark** (*see p114*), on Bredgade, your first port of call. As well as housing an expansive collection of items, the museum also puts on dynamic temporary exhibitions and has a whole room showing the evolution of the Danish chair. Its shop is also an excellent place to buy books on Danish design (as well as posters and homewares), and you can sit in the stylish café – called Klint – to read them afterwards.

Hotel Alexandra

Manfreds & Vin *p156*

Mikkeller & Friends

Stefansgade 35 (35 83 10 20, www.mikkeller.dk). Bus 8A. ***Open*** *2pm-midnight Mon-Wed, Sun; 2pm-2am Thur, Fri; noon-2am Sat.* ***Map*** *p152 G7* 8

The second Copenhagen bar from this popular microbrewery has been drawing beer-loving crowds since 2013. With shiny turquoise floors, and custom-made benches and tables in unstained wood, the roomy bar is a calming space in which to sink some draught beer. Formed in 2010 by two students and their physics teacher, Mikkeller & Friends now brews some 40 different craft beers, all available on tap here. Cider, Mikkeller spirits and Three Floyds draught beer from the USA are also on offer, while food comes in the form of gourmet sausages and cheese. **Other location** Viktoriagade 8B/C, Vesterbro (33 31 04 15).

Mirabelle

Guldbergsgade 29 (35 35 47 24, mirabelle-bakery.dk). Bus 5C. ***Open*** *7am-9.30pm Mon-Sun.* ***Map*** *p152 K8* 9

Part bakery, part deli and part intimate and friendly restaurant, Mirabelle is a hipster haunt and much beloved in this part of Nørrebro. Enjoy anything from fresh pasta to delicious pastries in the Danish/Italian-influenced restaurant. Lunches and dinners are served as a series of sharing dishes for the table, and it's all organic, seasonal and quality driven. The kitchen works with next-door Bæst, and there are strong links with Manfreds and Relæ.

Sebastopol Café

Sankt Hans Torv 32 (35 36 30 02, www.sebastopol.dk). Bus 3A, 5C. ***Open*** *10am-midnight Mon-Sat; 10am-10pm Sun.* ***Map*** *p152 L8* 10

Sebastopol's French staples provide tempting, good-value options in this ultra-cool part of town. The cool, young clientele (musicians, journalists, advertising types and the like) provides constant visual entertainment. Sebastopol gets very crowded on summer weekends.

Tapperiet Brus

Guldbergsgade 29F (75 22 22 00, tapperietbrus.dk). Bus 5C. ***Open*** *3pm-midnight Mon-Thu; noon-3am Fri; 11am-3am Sat; 11am-midnight Sun.* ***Map*** *p152 K8* 12

This fashionable brewery, bar, shop and eatery is right next door to the Empire cinema in Nørrebro and across a courtyard from Bæst, so you have your night planned out for you pretty easily. The brewery does a monthly tour and tasting on a Saturday (check the website for details) but you don't have to be a big beer drinker to love its Nordic style, burgers, snacks and friendly ambience.

Tjili Pop

Rantzausgade 28 (35 35 90 20, www.facebook.com/cafetjilipop). Bus 3A. ***Open*** *9am-1am Mon, Sun; 9am-2am Tue-Wed; 9am-3am Thu; 9am-4am Fri-Sat.* ***Map*** *p152 J10* 13

Cosy and authentic, Tjili Pop is a bistro-bar with live music, a ramshackle, colourful appearance and good vibes all round. Rustic bowls of ratatouille and bread will set you back around 49kr, and regular music nights mean you're likely to discover something new every time you visit.

Shops & services

❤ Acne Archive

Elmegade 21 (33 14 00 28, www.acnestudios.com). Bus 3A, 5C. ***Open*** *11am-6.30pm Mon-Thu; 11am-7pm Fri; 10am-5pm Sat.* ***Map*** *p152 L8* ❶ *Fashion*

Fans of the Swedish high-fashion label will be pleased to hear that this spacious shop sells clothing and accessories from previous seasons at a discount – though that still requires a fairly fat wallet.

Damernes Magasin

Jægersborggade 29 (32 176 177, www.damernes-magasin.com) Bus 8A, 5A. ***Open*** *11am-5pm Mon; 11am-6pm Tue-Fri; 11am-4pm Sat-Sun.* ***Map*** *p152 G8* ❷ *Fashion*

This super-chic womenswear shop stocks the like of Stine Goya, Sneaky Fox tights and sustainable Woron lingerie, and has charming staff on hand to help you find the most minimalist styles and Copenhagen chic to suit you. Also has a well-stocked webshop online.

❤ Native North

Elmegade 3 (93 89 08 00, www.nativenorth.com) Bus 3A, 5C. ***Open*** *11am-6pm Mon-Fri; 11am-4pm Sat.* ***Map*** *p152 K9* ❻ *Fashion*

Fit right in on Nørrebro's hip streets with clothes from Native North. This menswear boutique stocks their own-brand T-shirts, shirts, trousers and jackets plus a few hard-to-find Korean brands, accessories and footwear.

Den Sidste Dråbe

Jægersborggade 10 (30 48 76 22, www.facebook.com/densidstedraabe) Bus 8A. ***Open*** *noon-6pm Tue-Fri; 10am-6pm Sat; noon-6pm Sun.* ***Map*** *p152 G8* ❾ *Alcohol*

The Last Drop is an exquisitely curated spirits shop with beautifully labelled liquor bottles, a retro feel and knowledgeable staff to help you find your way around Scandinavian gin, local and organic whisky, the best tequila you've ever had and some super-trendy spirits. **Other location** Istadgade 83.

Tú a Tú

Jægersborggade 56 (41 10 80 60). Bus 18. ***Open*** *11am-5.30pm Mon-Fri; 11am-4pm Sat; 11am-3pm Sun.* ***Map*** *p152 G7* ⓫ *Fashion*

There are plenty of options to choose from when it comes to buying pre-loved, vintage and sustainable fashion in this uniquely stylish city. Step into Tú a Tú on Jægersborggade, and you can find Marni sandals, Stine Goya jackets, Acne boots and more, often with the labels still on. It's a well-edited treasure trove and if it sounds like your kind of thing, follow them on Facebook (@tuatu.secondhand) or Instagram @tuatua_secondhand) and reserve their newest items as they come in.

ØSTERBRO

Østerbro, which runs from the eastern side of Nørrebro across to the docks on the coast, is dominated by Denmark's national stadium, **Parken**, home of **FC København**, the country's top football team, in Fælledparken. Bordered by Nørre Allé, Blegdamsvej, Østerbrogade and Jagtvej, **Fælledparken** is a vast green area with a small lake, multiple playgrounds and plenty of space to play just about any sport you could imagine. Its excellent skatepark (*see p143* Skate Copenhagen) is one of the biggest in Europe; other areas for wheely good fun include a special scooter park next

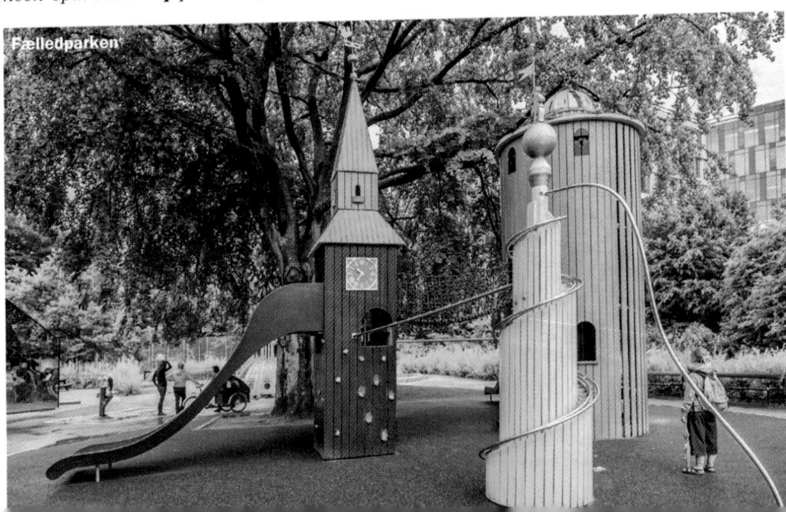
Fælledparken

❤ Boat trips

In summer especially, enjoying the water is something of a Danish pastime, and since water seems to be everywhere – from canals and the sea to the three artificial lakes dividing Østerbro and Nørrebro from the oldest part of the city – if you're not swimming in it, you might as well be floating along on top of it. Boat tours are a great way of seeing the sights.

Traditional tourist boats leave from Nyhavn and take trips up and down the waterfront with commentary, usually as far north as Refshaleøen and even as far south as Sluseholmen in the south. They are cost-effective, easy to find and a great way to orientate yourself. An even cheaper option is to take the **Harbour Bus** (991 or 992), also from Nyhavn, although you won't get a running commentary on what you're seeing.

CopenHot Sailing Hot Spa

Refshalevej 325 (31 32 78 08, copenhot.com). Departs from Refshalevej 325, 1432 Copenhagen. ***Open*** *tours all year; times vary. Book in advance online.* ***Rates*** *2,200kr per boat (up to 5 people).* ***Map*** *p120 X6.*

Tour the city's waterways in winter in a swimsuit without so much as a shiver. Along with a series of harbourfront saunas, this unique operation offers a 1.5-hour hot-tub sailing boat tour of the city, cruising the cold Nordic waters in a spa set at 40 degrees. Boat, skipper and optional music hook-up are provided. *See also p130.*

GoBoat

Islands Brygge 10 (40 26 10 25, en.goboat.dk). ***Open*** *9.30am-sunset. Duration from 1hr to 6hrs.* ***Rates*** *from 449kr (1hr) to 2,096kr (6hrs) per boat (up to 8 people).* ***Map*** *p120 P17.*

If you plan to take a picnic, hang out with some friends and a six pack of Tuborg, you could do what the locals do and grab a GoBoat. These self-drive motorboats are a regular sight on the city-centre canals and along the waterfront in summer, and can be hired from a station next to the Islands Brygge floating swimming pool (*see p124*).

Hey Captain

61 68 45 70, www.heycaptain.dk. Departs from Ofelia Plads, Copenhagen K. ***Open*** *tours Mar-Dec; times vary. Book in advance. Duration 1hr, 2hrs or 5hrs.* ***Rates*** *from 200kr per person; private tour from 2000kr (up to 12 people).* ***Map*** *p100 T12.*

Hey Captain

Small-group boat tours of the city's canals with a personal guide/skipper and a glass of wine or *gløgg*, or hot chocolate in winter. Boats seat up to 12. Expect to see palaces, bridges, Christiania from the water and *The Little Mermaid*, although routes may vary.

Netto-Bådene

32 54 41 02, www.havnerundfart.dk. Departs from Nyhavn. ***Open*** *tours all year; times vary. Duration 1hr.* ***Rates*** *40kr; 15kr reductions. No cards.* ***Map*** *p100 T13.*

Great value harbour and canal tours on the blue Netto boats.

Pedalos

Kaffesalonen, Peblinge Dossering 6 (35 35 12 19, kaffesalonen.com/baadudlejning). ***Rates*** *125kr for 1hr (2 people).* ***Map*** *p152 L10.*

Pedalos in the shape of swans (and one duck) are available at the Copenhagen Lakes Boat Rentals, by Dronning Louises Bro, and are fun on a sunny afternoon, especially with kids.

GoBoat

to the Tower Playground, which has play spaces that look like the city's skyline, and the Traffic Light park, a special fenced-off area where young children can play at riding bikes (sometimes available to borrow) along roads with traffic lights and pedestrian crossings. The park also has illuminated exercise paths, sports areas, a water splash zone (summer only), tree planting and a number of cafés to enjoy. A more practical open space than Copenhagen's other more historic or ornamental gardens, this is where locals come for a game of football or hockey, to play tennis, cycle, rollerskate, jog or skateboard. During the summer there are often free concerts here: larger-scale pop and rock concerts by big-name bands and artists take place in the big concrete stadium. To the west of Parken, across Nørre Allé, is the **Zoologisk Museum** (Zoological Museum, *see p163*); while to the east is **Geranium** (*see p164*), one of Copenhagen's best restaurants.

Østerbro itself is a prosperous residential area containing century-old apartment buildings and newer high-rise blocks. A good mix of shops, cafés and restaurants stretches along **Østerbrogade**, and the shops on **Nordre Frihavnsgade** and the bars on **Bopa Plads** and **Rosenvængets Allé** all cater for the well-heeled families of the area. Rosenvængets Allé is also home to gourmet organic butcher/café **Gourmandiet** (*see p165*), a popular brunch spot.

The north and east of Østerbro have seen significant development in recent years, with Nordhavn and its shiny offices, skyscrapers and apartments leading the way. This is also where you'll find the cavernous modern furniture store **Paustian** (*see p165*) and a couple of stylish restaurants, as well as Copenhagen's yacht basins. Nearby is **Svanemøllestranden**, a man-made beach that's much used in summer. In terms of innovative architecture, this is one of the most stimulating parts of the city – but bring a bike, the area is too big to cover on foot.

Sights & museums

Zoologisk Museum

Universitetsparken 15 (35 32 22 22, www.zoologi.snm.ku.dk). Bus 8A, 42, 150S, 184, 185. ***Open*** *10am-4pm Tue-Sun.* ***Admission*** *95kr; 50kr reductions.* ***Map*** *p152 L3.*

Though it's a little fusty – the mammals and birds from around the world that are displayed here are all stuffed – the city's natural history museum is still a good place to take children if the weather is bad, and includes the all-important dinosaurs, plus regular interactive exhibitions.

Gro Spiseri

Restaurants

Geranium ♛♛♛♛

Per Henrik Lings Allé 4, 8 (69 96 00 20, www.geranium.dk). Bus 3A, 8A, 14. ***Open*** *noon-4pm (last seating 1pm), 6.30pm-midnight (last seating 9pm) Mon-Sat.* ***Map*** *p152 O3* ❷ New Nordic

In 2011, chef Rasmus Kofoed earned himself the Bocuse d'Or award for culinary greatness, and in so doing firmly established Copenhagen's position as one of the most exciting places in the world to eat. Today, Geranium is the only restaurant in the city to have three Michelin stars. Kofoed – like every leading chef in Denmark these days – has if not an entire crusade, then at least a manifesto to shake things up a bit; in his case, a predilection for food that is 'light', 'lucid' and provides 'enriching challenges'. Geranium is in the immense parkland of Faelledparken, getting you closer to 'nature' and, if anything, an even finer plate of food. Dishes veer towards molecular gastronomy but remain recognisable and change with the seasons. Expect sybaritic intrigue along the lines of smoked potatoes, dried peas and lovage, and roast monkfish with 'elements of the sea and ocean'. It doesn't come cheap, though: if you decide to go for the wine pairing, you're looking at spending around 4,200kr per head for dinner.

❤ Gro Spiseri ♛♛♛

Æbeløgade 4 (52 22 28 79, grospiseri.dk). Bus 4A. ***Open*** *Jan, Mar 5.30-11.00pm Thu-Sat; Feb closed; Apr-Nov 5.30-11pm Thu-Mon. Book in advance.* ***Map*** *p152 M1* ❸ New Nordic

This unique dining experience takes place on one of Østerbro's rooftops in a location that was once used for car auctions. Since 2014 it has housed ØsterGRO, a rooftop farm, and it is now a dining project focusing on organic food. Chefs come from the likes of Noma, 108, Manfreds and Bæst and create shared, family-style meals served on a long table in the cosy greenhouse. The seasonal organic menu changes regularly and is accompanied by natural wines, beers and organic drinks. It's the perfect spot for a sundowner.

Le Saint-Jacques ♛♛

Sankt Jakobs Plads 1 (35 42 77 07, www.lesaintjacques.dk). Bus 3A, 14. ***Open*** *noon-3pm, 6-10pm Mon-Fri; noon-4pm, 6-10pm Sat; 5-10pm Sun.* ***Map*** *p152 P3* ❽ French

This reasonable and inviting French restaurant is set across the street from the national stadium, Parken, in a quiet square just off busy Østerbrogade. Impeccable service, crisp white linen tablecloths, and candlelight that flickers across the glittering gold of the religious icons on the walls ensure that locals return again and again for special treats or a well-earned blow-out. Home-smoked salmon is a speciality.

Cafés & bars

Café Bopa

Løgstørgade 8 (35 43 05 66, www.cafebopa.dk). Train Nordhavn, or bus 1A, 3A, 18, 40. ***Open*** *9am-midnight Mon-Wed; 9am-1am Thur; 9am-5am Fri; 10am-5am Sat; 10am-11pm Sun.* ***Map*** *p152 Q2* ❷

Dark and arty by day, pulsating by night, Bopa is at the heart of this leafy square's young scene. In summer the café spills out on to Bopa Plads, with deckchairs, rugs and pétanque. *See p196.*

Dag H

Dag Hammarskjölds Allé 36-40 (35 27 63 00, www.dagh.dk). Bus 1A, 14, 15E. ***Open*** *8am-11pm Mon-Fri; 10am-11pm Sat; 10am-10pm Sun.* ***Map*** *p152 Q6* ❸

This mainstay of Østerbro's café life on Lille Trianglen (Little Triangle, just along from the US Embassy) has an emphasis on the kitchen. The excellent food includes fancy burgers and Modern European dishes, as well as quality cakes and generous weekend brunch platters.

❤ Gourmandiet

Rosenvængets Allé 7 (39 27 10 00, www.gourmandiet.dk). Bus 1A, 3A, 14. ***Open*** *11am-6pm Tue-Thur; 11am-7pm Fri; 10am-3pm Sat.* ***Map*** *p152 Q5* ❺

This upmarket organic butcher's/café is a hit with the neighbourhood's residents, who come here for top-quality steaks and biodynamic wine. The walls are adorned with murals of pastoral scenes, while nicely arranged displays showcase the shop's tempting array of products, including organic charcuterie.

❤ Souls

Melchiors Plads 3 (34 10 01 01, www.soulscph.dk). Bus 3A. ***Open*** *10am-9.30pm Mon-Wed; 10am-10pm Thur, Fri; 9am-10pm Sat; 9am-8.30pm Sun.* ***Map*** *p152 S3* ⓫

Copenhagen's best vegan restaurant is a low-key, relaxed bistro, with açai bowls, smashed avocados, pickles, freshly pressed juices and more. The big ambition is to reduce the collective human footprint on the environment; the reality is that it's a great fun, easy-going place to eat meat-free.

Shops & services

❤ Ganni

Østerbrogade 50 (22 20 02 85, www.ganni.dk). Train Østerport, or bus 1A, 3A. ***Open*** *10am-6pm Mon-Fri; 10am-4pm Sat.* ***Map*** *p152 Q6* ❸ *Fashion.*

Fabulous colours, a boudoir feel and Scandinavian maximalism put Ganni on the map and in the pages of international lifestyle magazines every week. A fixture on beautiful boutique-led Østerbrogade.

Goods

Østerbrogade 44 (35 43 05 05, www.goodscph.com). Train Østerport, or bus 1A, 3A. ***Open*** *11am-6pm Mon-Fri; 11am-3pm Sat.* ***Map*** *p152 Q6* ❹ *Fashion*

This cool menswear shop is all about quality craftsmanship and cult brands, with knitwear from Folk and YMC, bags from Filson, jeans from Levi's Vintage, T-shirts from Our Legacy and sunglasses from Han Kjøbenhavn. It's the place to head if you want to look like a trendy local.

❤ Moshi Moshi Mind

Dag Hammarskjölds Allé 40 (35 38 70 79, www.moshimoshimind.com). Bus 37, 14. ***Open*** *11am-6pm Mon-Fri; 11am-3pm Sat.* ***Map*** *p152 Q6* ❺ *Fashion.*

Soft and wonderful cashmere, luxurious loungewear and the odd piece of desirable homeware can all be found in this dreamy shop, focused on living well with luxury and meditation in mind. Extremely stylish but not trying too hard, it's the epitome of contemporary Copenhagen.

Normann Copenhagen

Østerbrogade 70 (35 55 44 59, www.normann-copenhagen.com). Bus 1A, 3A, 14. ***Open*** *11am-5.30pm Mon-Fri; 10am-3pm Sat.* ***Map*** *p152 P5* ❼ *Homewares*

Homewares take centre stage in the former theatre building, with a huge range of effortlessly sleek and streamlined domestic designer products, from arty vases to achingly modern salad sets. Lighting is another strong point.

Paustian

Kalkbrænderiløbskaj 2 (39 16 65 65, www.paustian.dk). Train Nordhavn, or bus 26. ***Open*** *11am-6pm Mon-Fri; 10am-4pm Sat.* ***Map*** *p152 S1* ❽ *Homewares*

It's a bit of a trek to get over here, but Paustian's stunning warehouse – designed by Jørn Utzon of Sydney Opera House fame – makes the trip worthwhile. Inside, you'll find furniture by the likes of Aalto, Eames, Starck and Jacobsen. There's also a popular restaurant.

❤ Søstjernen

Østerbrogade 50 (35 55 46 90, www.sostjernen.com). Train Østerport, or bus 1A, 40E. ***Open*** *11am-5.30pm Mon-Thur; 11am-6pm Fri; 10am-3pm Sat.* ***Map*** *p152 Q6* ❿ *Children/Accessories*

Children's shoe shop Søstjernen – 'starfish' in Danish – is the brainchild of Katrine Leisner. Spend some time in the neighbourhood and you'll realise that her shop's cute sandals, chelsea-style boots and desert boots, from brands such as Angulus, Petit Nord and PéPé, are something of a uniform for the area's trendy toddlers.

Day Trips

Within an hour's travel of Copenhagen, you'll find great beaches, seaside towns, world-class cultural institutions and majestic castles. To the north, The Louisiana Museum of Modern Art, stunningly located next to the Øresund, is filled to the brim with world-class art. The upmarket suburb of Hellerup has a superb family science museum, while Helsingør and its castle is a draw for anyone who has read or seen *Hamlet*.

West of Helsingør, in the town of Hillerød, is Frederiksborg Slot, an early 17th-century Dutch Renaissance castle with elegant Baroque gardens.

To the south, another modern art gallery, Arken Museum for Moderne Kunst, sits on a sandy beach and is surrounded by sculptures. The island of Amager, just a short bike ride from central Copenhagen, has the DR Koncerthuset, a great beach, plus the Blå Planet aquarium.

Anyone with love for the Vikings should head west to Roskilde, where original Viking ships are set in a sensational museum looking out to Roskilde harbour where they once sailed.

With more time, LEGO fans will be richly rewarded by a trip to Billund, in particular to the LEGO House created from 21 gigantic LEGO bricks.

❤ Don't miss

1 Louisiana Museum of Modern Art *p170*
Inspiring modern art in a sensational location.

2 Forgotten Giants *p177*
The best excuse to get off the beaten track.

3 Vikingeskibsmuseet *p179*
Set sail on a Viking boat across the water.

4 Crossing the bridge *p175*
Two countries in one day, plus a particularly unusual food museum.

5 LEGO House *p179*
A BIG-designed paradise for kids of all ages.

Arken Museum for Moderne Kunst *p176*

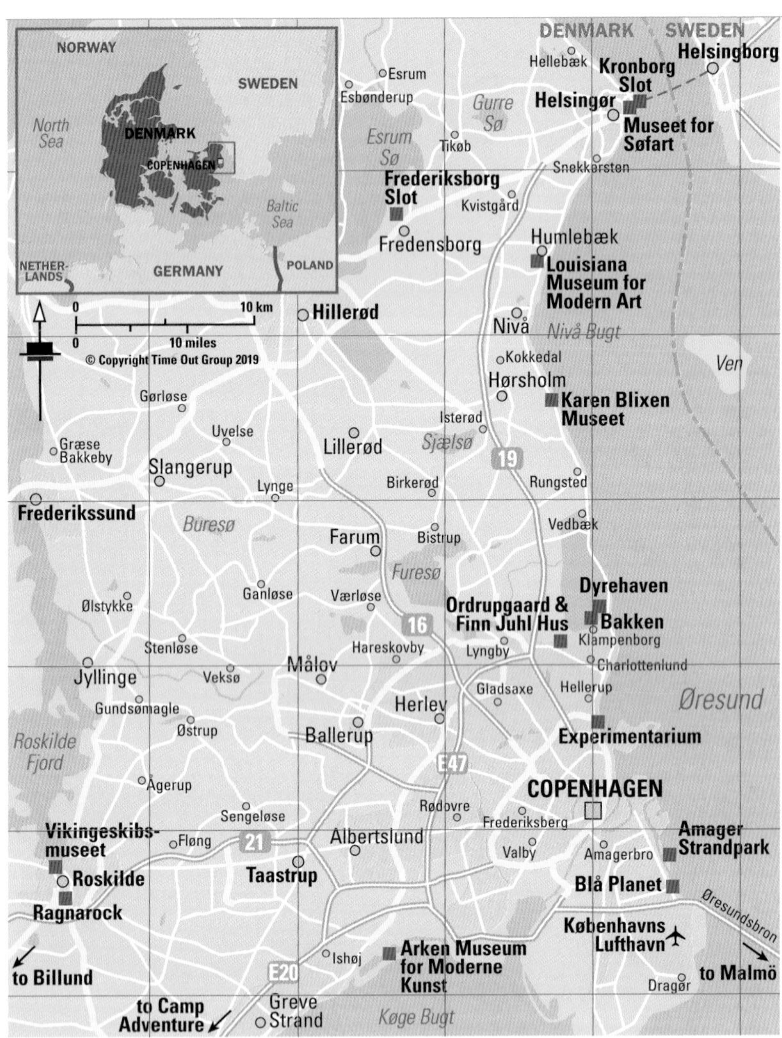

TO THE NORTH

The affluent coastal suburb of Hellerup, just north of the city centre via Østerbro, has some good shops and restaurants, but the star of the show is the superb **Experimentarium** science museum (*see p171*).

Continue northwards for **Charlottenlund Slot** (Charlottenlund Palace), the site of a royal residence since 1690, with grounds open to the public. **Charlottenlund Strand**, although small, is the nearest beach to Copenhagen heading north; most people continue to Bellevue Beach, although Charlottenlund has a large, landscaped grass area. It is a pleasant forest walk from Charlottenlund station. Arne Jacobsen fans might also want to head to Skovshoved nearby to eat ice-creams at his modernist-design petrol station, **Oliver's Garage** (*see p173*). As of 2020, culture vultures should visit the extended **Ordrupgaard** (*see p173*), which displays French Impressionist and Danish art from the 19th and 20th centuries. The museum's lovely grounds also contain the **Finn Juhl Hus**, the building where the Danish furniture designer spent the last few decades of his life.

Next is Klampenborg with the popular **Bellevue Beach**, as well as **Bakken** amusement park (*see p169*), which is on the edge of **Dyrehaven**, a 1,000-hectare (2,470-acre) former royal hunting ground which dates back to 1231. Nowadays, this rather serene deer park is to Copenhageners what Richmond Park is to Londoners. The park is closed to traffic; all the better for its large herds of free-roaming deer and the many walkers who come here from the city. Expensive horse-drawn carriage rides are also available.

The next major point of interest along the coast is **Rungstedlund**, the former home of the Danish novelist Karen Blixen, now the site of the **Karen Blixen Museet** (*see p172*). The internationally acclaimed author spent much of her life in Rungstedlund (except for 17 years in Kenya) and is buried in the gardens of the house, beneath a large beech tree, at the foot of Ewald's hill.

Between Rungstedlund and Helsingør are several small harbours, but the main attraction is the **Louisiana Museum of Modern Art** (*see p170*). There may be larger modern art collections in the world, but none is located in more blissful surroundings than Louisiana.

An additional 15 minutes north on the train brings you to **Helsingør** (often written as Elsinore). This port town is a popular day-trip destination for Swedes, being just a 20-minute ferry ride from Sweden's Helsingborg; many come here for the cheap(er) alcohol, and as a result it has a slightly downtrodden atmosphere, with booze shops aplenty, though its half-timbered houses and old cobblestone streets help to redress the balance. Many visitors, however, see little of the town itself, heading straight for **Kronborg Slot** (*see p172*) – a

Experimentarium *p171*

15-minute walk from the station, along the coast – and the **Museet for Søfart** (*see p173*), the National Maritime Museum of Denmark, right in front of it.

If you find yourself in Copenhagen for more than a few days and fancy a breath of old-fashioned seaside air, then a trip to the northern coast of **Zealand** (called Sjælland, locally) – with its classic fishing villages such as **Hornbæk**, **Gilleleje** and **Tisvildeleje** and glorious dune- and forest-backed beaches – could be just the ticket. Many Copenhageners have summer houses in the area (often available for rent via Airbnb and other websites), and much of the city decamps to the beach from late June to the end of July. On your way to the coast – about an hour's drive from Copenhagen, a little longer if you take the train – stop off at one of Denmark's most important castles, **Frederiksborg Slot** (*see p172*).

❤ Time to eat & shop

A slap up meal in a seaside setting
Den Gule Cottage *p173*

Art with a sea view
Arken museum's restaurant *p176*

Bird spotting
Café 8tallet *p176*

For art, fashion and interiors
The Louisiana Butik *p170*

Ice cream, architecture and a stroll along the harbour
Oliver's Garage *p173*

In the know
Getting around

Most of the options here are under an hour from Central Station by train and make for an easy day trip by public transport; the exceptions are Camp Adventure Tower, for which car rental is advised, and Billund, which takes three to four hours from central Copenhagen by train and not much less by car.

For Sweden, a train runs directly from Central Station to Malmö – you need to take your passport with you as there is a border control check on the train as you enter the country.

For information on trains, metro and bus routes from central Copenhagen, the website www.rejseplanen.dk is very useful (or download its app). It's often worth taking a bike with you on the train for further exploration.

❤ Louisiana Museum of Modern Art

Gammel Strandvej 13, Humlebæk (49 19 07 19, www.louisiana.dk). Train Humlebæk. ***Open*** *11am-10pm Tue-Fri; 11am-6pm Sat, Sun.* ***Admission*** *125kr; 110kr reductions; free under-18s.*

Founded in 1958 by the industrialist and art collector Knud Jensen, Louisiana contains more than 3,500 works (mainly painting and sculpture) dating from 1945 to the present. It began life as a purely Scandinavian affair – the first purchases were of works by Danish artists including Asger Jorn, Richard Mortensen and Robert Jacobsen – but the collection soon grew to encompass Auguste Herbin, Josef Albers, Naum Gabo and Alexander Calder; later, works by Dubuffet, Bacon and Rothko were added. Paintings by Picasso from several periods are among the highlights, while the 1960s Pop Art movement is well represented with pieces by Warhol, Lichtenstein, Oldenburg and Rauschenberg. The collection of 1970s German art is also strong. Louisiana is also famed for its dynamic temporary exhibitions and superstar retrospectives (Paul Klee, Ai Weiwei and Olafur Eliasson have all featured in recent years).

The existing 19th-century villa (called Louisiana after the original owner's three wives who, bizarrely, were all named Louise) has been added to over the years, and the resulting, much enlarged, complex is considered a major work in Danish modernist architecture.

Low key and horizontal, the 1950s additions are unpretentious and fit well in the environment, with floor-to-ceiling windows along long glass corridors looking out to the sculpture gardens, lawns and sea views. The whitewashed rooms with their large windows blur the divide between the indoor galleries and the outdoor sculpture park, creating a harmony between the buildings and their environment that counterbalances the frequently challenging nature of the works on display. And the light is wonderful too.

The south wing was added in 1982, with a corridor (now hung with Mortensen's colourful geometric paintings) connecting it to the old building. A subterranean wing opened in 1991. Lectures, film screenings and concerts are held regularly.

Children get their own wing, Bornehuset, with special workshops and activities. Wandering the grounds is a joy in itself at any time of year. In the garden, you'll find sculptures by some of the world's most iconic artists: Calder, Henry Moore, Joan Miró, Max Ernst and Giacometti, among others.

After you've had your fill of art, head to the café for a *smørrebrød*, beautiful views overlooking the Øresund, a terrace graced by one of Calder's sculptures and a log fire in winter. The large shop sells fashion, interior design, prints, toys and more handpicked from some of Denmark's best designers, and is an exceptional, if not exactly cheap, place to buy a souvenir that you won't be able to find elsewhere.

Sights & museums

Dyrehaven & Bakken

Dyrehavesbakken, Dyrehavevej 62, Klampenborg (39 63 35 44, www.bakken.dk). Train Klampenborg. ***Open*** *Amusement park 2nd Fri in Apr-2nd Sun in Sept times vary, but usually noon/2-10pm/11pm/midnight daily.* ***Admission*** *free. Rides (wristband) 269kr; 189kr children under 115cm.*

Dyrehaven is a beautiful deer park for a stroll, picnic, horse-drawn carriage ride and breath of fresh air from the city. It's a particularly popular place in autumn, when the leaves are falling. Nestled inside the forest, a short walk from Klampenborg station, you'll find Bakken ('the hill'), and the world's oldest amusement park. It has more of a funfair atmosphere than Tivoli and is much beloved by local families. There are 100 or so rides (which tend to be cheaper than Tivoli's), as well as 35 cafés and restaurants. Admission to the amusement park is free; prepaid ride wristbands are cheaper if you buy or reserve them online. Shows, guided walks and events at the park are generally free.

Experimentarium

Tuborg Havnevej 7, Hellerup (39 27 33 33, www.experimentarium.dk). Bus 1A, 21. ***Open*** *9.30am-5pm Mon-Thur; 9.30am-7pm Fri; 10am-7pm Sat, Sun.* ***Admission*** *195kr; 115kr reductions; free under-2s.*

This inventive science museum is filled with imaginative displays and hands-on experiments. Though aimed at children, it also attracts its fair share of adults, who are mesmerised by the technology (you can try a human-size gyroscope or programme robots). The museum renders mundane or esoteric topics – alternative power, genetics – fascinating and accessible. Be warned: the

In the know
Getting around

There are trains at least every 20 minutes heading north along the coast from Copenhagen Central Station via Nørreport. It takes 18 minutes to get to Klampenborg (for Dyrehaven, Bakken and Bellevue Beach); 30 minutes to Rungsted Kyst; 41 minutes to Humlebæk; and 56 minutes to Helsingør. For Louisiana, the cheapest option is a combined train/museum ticket for 210kr. To get to Hornbæk, catch a train from Copenhagen Central Station and change at Helsingør (about one and a half hours in total, one train per hour). To reach Gilleleje or Tisvildeleje, take the S-train (S-tog) from Central Station and change at Hillerød (one hour 20 minutes in total, around two trains per hour).

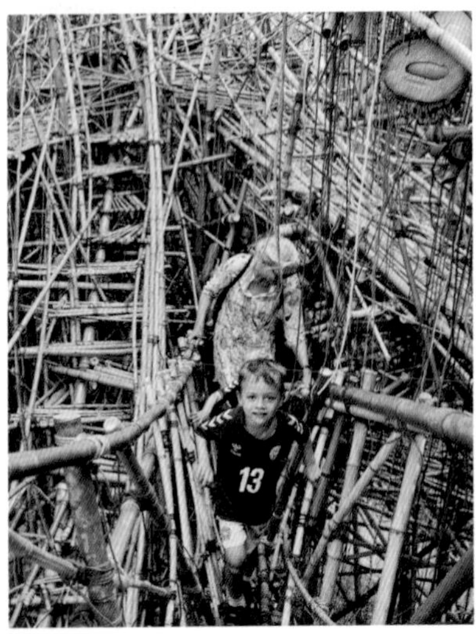

noise can be deafening. There is a toddler zone on the ground floor, but the museum is really orientated towards school-age children and older.

Frederiksborg Slot

Hillerød (48 26 04 39, www.dnm.dk). Train Hillerød. ***Open*** *Apr-Oct 10am-5pm daily. Nov-Mar 11am-3pm daily.* ***Admission*** *75kr; 20kr-60kr reductions.*

This early 17th-century Dutch Renaissance red-brick castle, with ornate spires and sandstone façade, stands on three small islands in Slotsø (Castle Lake), in the middle of the town of Hillerød. The castle is complemented by impressive baroque gardens and an English-style garden with its Bath House. Inside you can find Det Nationalhistoriske Museum (Museum of National History) charting Denmark's history through paintings. Since 1693, it's also been the chapel for Danish knights, whose shields hang on the walls; remarkably, it's also the local parish church.

Karen Blixen Museet

Rungstedlund, Rungsted Strandvej 111, Rungsted (45 57 10 57, www.karen-blixen.dk). Train Rungsted Kyst. ***Open*** *May-June and Sept 10am-5pm Tue-Sun. July-Aug 10am-5pm daily. Oct-Apr 1pm-4pm Wed-Fri; 11am-4pm Sat, Sun.* ***Admission*** *100kr; concessions 80kr; free under-14s.*

This simple early 19th-century house is set in 16 hectares (40 acres) of gardens that double as a bird sanctuary. The north wing has been preserved as if Blixen had just left, with her furniture, paintings and even her distinctive flower arrangements as they were when she lived here. There's also a gallery of Blixen's drawings and paintings, and a biographical exhibition, library and small cinema upstairs.

Kronborg Slot

Kronborg 2C, Helsingør (49 21 30 78, www.kronborg.dk). Train Helsingør. ***Open*** *Jan-Mar 11am-4pm Tue-Sun. June-Sept 10am-5.30pm daily. Apr, May, Oct 11am-4pm daily. Nov-Dec 11am-4pm Tue-Sun.* ***Admission*** *95kr; 85kr concessions; free under-18s. Combined ticket with Museet for Søfart (see below) for 25% off.*

Better known as 'Hamlet's Castle' or 'Shakespeare's Castle', this waterside Renaissance fortress – a UNESCO World Heritage Site since 2000 – has, over the centuries, served as a royal residence, a garrison, a tollbooth, a prison and a museum. It was constructed on the orders of Frederik II between 1574 and 1585, though the foundations date from a 1420s fortress built by one Eric of Pomerania. Shakespeare's famous play, *The Tragedy of Hamlet, Prince*

Frederiksborg Slot

of Denmark, was first performed in Kronborg in 1816 to mark the 200th anniversary of the Bard's death. It has been performed at the castle many times since, with acting legends Laurence Olivier, John Gielgud, Richard Burton and Derek Jacobi all taking to the courtyard stage here, as well as, in 2009, Jude Law. The best way to experience it is to come in August during the **Shakespeare at Kronborg** festival (www.hamletscenen.dk). Typically, the open-air plays are conducted in English with Danish subtitles on a screen.

Museet for Søfart

Ny Kronborgvej 1, Helsingør (49 21 06 85, www.mfs.dk). Train Helsingør. ***Open*** *July, Aug 11am-6pm daily. Sept-June 11am-5pm Tue-Sun.* ***Admission*** *120kr; free under-18s. Combined ticket with Kronborg Slot (see above) 25% discount.*

The Bjarke Ingels Group-designed National Maritime Museum of Denmark opened in 2013 on the doorstep of Kronborg Slot and has plenty to offer visitors who don't know much about maritime history, as well as those who do. Taking an innovative approach, BIG devised a space built around Helsingør's 60-year-old dock walls, creating an underground ship-shaped museum that is eight metres (26 feet) below sea level but filled with light. Ramped zigzagging bridges and gently sloping floors add to the overall seafaring effect in this dynamic museum whose themes include different aspects of life on the rolling seas. From three massive double-level steel bridges that unite the old and new elements of the site to benches based on ship's bollards and a hidden message based on Morse code, it's a site (and sight) that's well worth visiting. It all adds up to an absorbing look at man's universal desire for exploration and discovery.

Ordrupgaard & Finn Juhl Hus

Vilvordevej 110, Charlottenlund (39 64 11 83, www.ordrupgaard.dk). Train Klampenborg or Lyngby, or bus 388. ***Open*** *Park 8am-6pm daily. Museum closed until 2020.* ***Admission*** *Park free.*

This rather beautiful museum, surrounded by an art park, reopens in 2020 with an underground extension courtesy of Norwegian architects Snøhetta to showcase the museum's valuable French collection, with works by Manet, Renoir, Matisse and Gauguin. Through 2019, the art park will still be open for visitors. When the museum reopens, all access to the Zaha Hadid wing and to the museum's collection of 19th- and 20th-century Danish art will be restored, along with Finn Juhl's House in the grounds of the museum. The Danish furniture designer built the house in the 1940s, furnishing it with many of his own designs, and lived there until his death in 1989.

Restaurants

❤ Den Gule Cottage ♕♕

Tårbæk Strandvej 2, Klampenborg (39 64 06 91, www.dengulecottage.dk). Train Klampenborg. ***Open*** *Jan-Mar 12am-4pm, 4.30-9pm Tues-Sun; Apr-Dec noon-4pm, 4.30-9.30pm Tues-Sun.*

With a fairy-tale location in a thatched, half-timbered, 19th-century cottage, set beneath oak trees on lawns that roll down to Bellevue Beach, this tiny restaurant could probably get away with serving hot dogs (in fact, it used to be an ice-cream kiosk). But this is one of the cosiest restaurants in the region, serving elegant, modern Danish dishes made from fresh seasonal ingredients.

❤ Oliver's Garage

Kystvejen 24, Charlottenlund (no phone, Oliversgarage.dk). Train: Ordrup; Bus 1A. ***Open*** *winter 9am-8.30pm daily; summer 9am-10pm daily.*

Eat ice-cream with a side helping of architectural history at Oliver's Garage. The building was designed by Arne Jacobsen and was built as a Texaco gas station in 1937. It has a characteristic toadstool-shaped top, which some have said was the inspiration for his 1952 Ant chair. Totally renovated in 2013, the petrol station now has a 1950s diner feel and is a hang-out for anyone who likes burgers and ice-cream.

TO THE EAST

Amager is the island immediately to the east of central Copenhagen, reached via Langebro bridge from the city centre. Carry on beyond the lawns, cafés and floating harbour pools at Islands Brygge for a little over 20 minutes and you'll find the sea, and a great beach for a day out with the kids, **Amager Strandpark**. At the south end of the beach is the impressive, modern National Aquarium, **Den Blå Planet**, and a super cool swimming spot, **Kastrup Søbad**.

On the south-east coast of Amager, among salt flats and farmland teeming with birdlife, lies **Dragør**, with its maze of cobbled lanes and traditional yellow cottages. Like many coastal settlements in the area, it was founded upon the humble herring, and prospered during the 14th century as a fishing port. In the 19th century, it found a new lease of life as a centre for shipping and salvage, trading throughout the Baltic and as far away as England. That came to an end with the advent of steam ships, and since then little has changed here (which is part of its charm).

However, Dragør's sleepy idyll can be misleading. Property prices are high – the village is popular with affluent young professionals who commute into the city. They ensure that Dragør remains an improbably lively, almost cosmopolitan, village. There are also some smart shops on its short high street, as well as several good restaurants and beer gardens. The town has a marina, a small cinema and an equally small museum (Dragør Museum) in the town's oldest fisherman's house (dating from 1682). The Danish end of Øresund Bridge (*see p175*) is between Amager and Dragør.

In the know
The Øresund Bridge

Known just as 'The Bridge' by fans of the Danish drama series *Broen*, the Øresund Bridge connects the Danish and Swedish coasts over nearly eight kilometres (five miles) of sea from Amager to Malmö. Opened in July 2000, it is Europe's largest combined road and rail bridge and took five years to build in an architectural project by Hochtief, Skanska, Højgaard & Schultz and Monberg & Thorsen (Swedish/Danish/German). The design includes an artificial island, Peberholm, created so that part of the bridge could go underground and still allow ships to pass. It cost over 30.1 billion krone to build. During construction, 16 unexploded World War II bombs were found on the ocean floor, causing setbacks. It is a symbol of the connected nations (the greater Copenhagen area extends to southern Sweden) and many people commute daily between the two cities, which takes approximately 35 minutes end to end. But be aware that you do need a passport when you cross.

In the know
Getting around

It is really easy to reach Amager and Amager Strandpark from the city centre: by bike, it's a 30- to 40-minute ride; by metro to the Amager Strand station, it's about 40 minutes; by direct bus it takes about 50 minutes. To reach Dragør, it's a little under an hour by bike, around 40 minutes by train to Dragør train station, and about 50 minutes by bus (with changes). Once at either location, it's easy to explore on foot, or else take a bike on the train or metro and cycle while you're there.

Sights & museums

Amager Strandpark

Amager Strand Promenaden 1 (no phone, www.kk.dk/amagerstrandpark). Metro Øresund. ***Open*** *year-round.* ***Admission*** *free.*

This popular beach consists of 4.6 kilometres (3 miles) of imported yellow-white sand. You can swim in the sea, rent kayaks and cycle, skateboard or scoot along the tarmac promenade between the dunes and the water. There is a lagoon as well, always busy with watersports; 18 beach shops make sure

Crossing the Bridge

See two cities and two countries in one day

Copenhagen has more than enough sights to occupy you for at least a long weekend, but another city – smaller but equally scintillating – lies just 30 minutes away by car or by train (from Copenhagen Central Station). **Malmö** – Sweden's third-largest city – is worth the short trip via the spectacular Øresund Bridge. If you want to do two Nordic capital cities in a weekend, you can take an overnight train from Copenhagen to Stockholm (five to six hours each way), or a ferry to Oslo (seven to ten hours overnight), but will end up spending a lot of time in transit.

Malmö's cosmopolitan population includes some 24,000 university students, who give the city a vibrant energy. The place is particularly appealing during the summer, when its long sandy beach (a short walk west from the city centre) and beautiful parks really come into their own, and when its historic heart, centred around the lovely cobbled square of **Lilla Torg**, comes alive – especially at night. The city has a lively nightlife scene all year round, however; there are plenty of restaurants and bars on Lilla Torg and on **Södergatan** – the pedestrianised street that connects the Stortorget and Gustav Adolfs Torg squares. But if you want something a bit more memorable, head over to multicultural **Möllevången**, home to two well-established bar-restaurants favoured by the arty set: **Metro** (Ängelholmsgatan 14, 040 23 00 63, www.metropamollan.se), with a fusion menu and DJs at weekends, and **Grand Öl & Mat** (Monbijougatan 17, 040 12 63 13, www.grandolomat.se), a superb lunch and dinner spot with a stylish bar, set in an industrial complex.

Other highlights of Malmö include its atmospheric castle, **Slottet Malmöhus** (Malmöhusvägen 6, 040 34 44 00, www.malmo.se/museer), which is home to some top-notch museums, including art museum Malmö Konstmuseum, and Stadsmuseet, the city history museum; its 2-kilometre (1.25-mile), man-made, sandy beach, Ribersborgsstranden (known as **Ribban**); and some good shops – on Södergatan as well as around **Gamla Väster**, the old town. **Moderne Museet**, the city's modern art gallery, is ten minutes' walk from Central Station and also worth a visit, and for *fika* (coffee and cake), Korean food, fish or handmade chocolates, the city's revitalised food hall, **Malmö Saluhall**, is also a good stop.

If you want an authentically Swedish experience, a visit to the **Ribersborgs Kallbadhus** (Ribersborgs Cold Bath House; 040 26 03 66, www.ribersborgskallbadhus.se, 70 SEK – Swedish, not Danish kroner – is well worth a gamble. This charming wooden bathhouse, dating from 1898, is at the end of a short pier on the beach's eastern end and has segregated open-air deck areas (men to the left, women to the right) with modern saunas and bracing sea-water plunge baths. Note that nudity is the norm in the saunas. If you like the retro feel of this, then you'll also like nearby **Fiskehoddorna**, a row of pretty wooden huts where local fishermen sell their fresh catches every morning (except Sunday and Monday).

The most recent addition to the city has been in the Western Harbour area. A radical housing project, **Bo01**, has sprung up beside the sea, and won architectural plaudits from around the globe. The restaurants, harbour bathing deck, promenades, leisure facilities and shops here are a major attraction. At the centre of it all is the astonishing **Turning Tower** apartment block, designed by Spanish architect Santiago Calatrava. Completed in 2005, the 54-storey tower is the tallest building in Sweden and is renowned for its extraordinary external steel 'spine'.

Also extraordinary and also in the north of the city centre, **The Disgusting Food Museum** (Slagthuset, Carlsgatan 12) serves up 80 of the world's most notoriously disgusting foods, including *surströmming*, Sweden's noxious fermented herring, *hákarl*, Iceland's rotten shark delicacy, and durian from Thailand.

► *For more information, contact Malmö Tourist Office (Börshuset, Skeppsbron 2, 040 34 12 00, www.malmotown.com), located near Malmö Central Station and the harbour.*

that you are never far from an ice-cream, and there are toilets at strategic points along the promenade. But in general it feels underdeveloped, clean and very accessible.

Slightly further down the coast, and connected to Amager Strandpark by a long wooden bridge, is **Kastrup Søbad** ('the Snail'), a sculptural jetty where you can swim, sunbathe and picnic while being protected from the wind.

Den Blå Planet

Jacob Fortlingsvej 1, Kastrup (44 22 22 44, www.denblaaplanet.dk). Metro Kastrup. ***Open*** *10am-9pm Mon; 10am-5pm Tue-Sun.* ***Admission*** *170kr; 95kr reductions.*

The Blue Planet, northern Europe's largest aquarium, opened in 2013 in a stunning building designed by 3XN architects. Visitors can learn about sea life, and view hammerhead sharks in the Ocean Tank, colourful fish in the Coral Reef section, and piranhas in the Amazon area. It's always packed at weekends, on school holidays and rainy days.

Cafés & bars

❤ Café 8tallet

Richard Mortensens Vej 81A, Ørestad (32 62 86 28, www.timos.dk/restaurant-8tallet). Metro Vestamager. ***Open*** *11am-10pm Mon-Fri; 10am-10pm Sat; 10am-9pm Sun.*

Situated in an award-winning building designed by architecture firm BIG, the waterside Café 8tallet offers contemporary design and superb views of the Kalvebod Fælled nature reserve. It's a popular spot for brunch, but also serves generous *smørrebrød*, good coffee, tasty burgers and grander dishes.

TO THE SOUTH

The fourth of Sjælland's world-class art museums (after Louisiana Museum of Modern Art, Statens Museum for Kunst and Ny Carlsberg Glyptotek) is found in the suburb of Ishøj, 15 minutes by train south along the coast from Copenhagen. **Arken Museum for Moderne Kunst** was built to celebrate Copenhagen's year as European City of Culture in 1996.

Arken is next to **Ishøj Strand** (Ishøj Beach), an artificial but attractive seven-kilometre (four-mile) stretch of sandy beach, where you will be able to find one of the city's Forgotten Giants (*see p177*). There is also a sweet beach café nestled in the dunes, open for hot chocolate in winter and ice-creams in summer and set beside a playground.

Also to the south of the city, only easily accessible by rental car, **Camp Adventure Tower** is an ambitious modern wooden spiral viewpoint and treetop walk hidden in the heart of the Gisselfeld Kloster estate. Opened in spring 2019, it offers stunning views over woodlands.

In the know
Getting around

Zealand has an excellent public transport network, and Ishøj is just 17 minutes by train from the city. As you go further afield to seek the Forgotten Giants or to reach Haslev and Camp Adventure Tower, the best option is to hire a car.

Sights & museums

❤ Arken Museum for Moderne Kunst

Skovvej 100, Ishøj (43 54 02 22, www.arken.dk). Train Ishøj, then bus 128 or walk. ***Open*** *10am-5pm Tue, Thur-Sun; 10am-9pm Wed.* ***Admission*** *125kr; 110kr reductions; free under-18s.*

Arken is housed in an extraordinary concrete, glass and steel building designed by Danish architect Søren Robert Lund. His compelling and perplexing construction, with its echoes of marine architecture (both inside and out), won the design competition for the new gallery in 1988, and has the feeling of an abstract ship (*Arken* means 'The Ark' in Danish). Treats to look out for inside are dramatic high-ceilinged spaces, a specialist Nordic design shop (with pocket money options available), a huge light café and a family studio.

Arken's permanent collection of more than 350 pieces covers painting, sculpture, graphic art, media art and installation, with an emphasis on work since 1990. Many works are by Danes, but numerous foreign artists feature, including Damien Hirst, Grayson Perry and Katharina Grosse. One of the most famous pieces is the photograph *Flex Pissing/Björk er en nar* (aka *Bringing It All Back Home*) by Claus Carstensen and the art group Superflex (the mildly controversial 'Danish Art Mob'). The feeling here is significantly different from that of the Louisiana – it's not as extensive, for a start, and has a purely modern focus with a Danish angle. Set on a long sandy beach with pure blue water stretching across to Sweden, Arken shapes and sculpts the surrounding land as well. It also hosts superb temporary exhibitions of modern and contemporary Danish and international art, often transferred from other major European galleries. Past shows have included retrospectives of Picasso, Munch, Dalí, Miró, Warhol and Van Gogh. There's also a cinema and a concert hall.

❤ Forgotten Giants

► *To access a map, visit thomasdambo.com/works/forgotten-giants. As some of the giants are hidden in woodland areas, prepare yourself for a potentially muddy walk: boots and a waterproof coat are a good idea.*

In Old Norse manuscripts there are tales of trolls living in caves, mountains and on isolated rocks. These days you can seek them out in the countryside around Copenhagen. So if you go down to the woods today, you might just find six big surprises. But first, you'll need a treasure map.

Back in 2017, Danish artist Thomas Dambo had the idea of bringing art out of the museums in the city and using it as a way to encourage people to rediscover nature in unexpected and overlooked places around Copenhagen. In an era where overtourism is a grave concern in many of Europe's cities, Copenhagen being one of them, a focus on undiscovered spots is to be applauded. These special places are certainly photogenic and, as you have to work to find them, it feels like an accomplishment that not everybody can lay claim to.

Dambo felt that too many people live lives confined by their home, workplace and supermarket, and that we should all get out more; this is as true for tourists and travellers looking for the classic must-sees around the world as it is for locals living their daily lives. Created in conjunction with the municipalities of west Copenhagen, the six sculptures have certainly had the desired effect so far.

If you can hire a car, read a map and want an adventure that goes beyond the typical tourist trail, read on. The western suburbs of the city – Rødovre, Hvidovre, Vallensbæk, Ishøj (*see p176*), Albertslund and Høje Taastrup – are where you need to look. Hidden under bridges, behind trees and on hilltops, you'll discover Trine, Thomas, Tilde, Louis, Oscar and Teddy, Dambo's huge scrapwood trolls, all built with the help of local volunteers (and each named after a volunteer too).

Wild-haired Trine sits atop a hillside, gazing out to the distant sheep; sleeping Louis has a huge mouth that kids can climb into; cute-faced Tilde stands beneath a tree filled with 28 birdhouses; long-legged Thomas chills on a hill with a view; Teddy helpfully holds out his hand beside a stream, while Oscar hides under a bridge in classic troll fashion.

Scrambling across hillsides for the first look at one of them certainly gives you a sense of being in the great outdoors, with a little link to Scandinavia's mythic history.

Little Tilde

Camp Adventure Tower

Gisselfeld Kloster, Denderupvej 19, 4690 Haslev (38 15 00 30, www.campadventure.dk) Train Næstved, then bus 630R. The site is a 5-min walk from bus stop Sydmotorvejen (Ny Næstvedvej). Best by rental car. Parking 50kr. ***Open*** *Tower 10am-6pm daily. Adventure Park summer 10am-6pm daily; spring and autumn 10am-6pm Thur-Sun.* ***Admission*** *125kr; free under-7s.*

Around an hour south of Copenhagen by car (two hours by public transport), Camp Adventure is currently the largest high-rope course in Denmark with treetop climbs and aerial ziplines to enjoy, all in the heart of **Gisselfeld Kloster**, a great park surrounding a baronial mansion dating to 1575. Hans Christian Andersen's 'The Ugly Duckling' was written in and inspired by this fairy-tale landscape.

Opened in spring 2019, Camp Adventure's observation tower is the first of its kind in Scandinavia and consists of a 900-metre-long (half-mile) treetop walk with a 45-metre-high (147-foot) tower. Designed by Copenhagen's eco-architects EFFEKT, the tower and walk include a seamless spiral ramp accessible to all, with views of hills (a rarity in Denmark) as well as the historic forest, lakes and wetlands. Visually stunning, it looks set to feature on social media far and wide, and perhaps more importantly, open up this area south of the city to visitors. Architectural and design awards are already in the bag.

Cafés & bars

Ka'nalu

Skovvej 52, Ishøj (31 41 02 13, www.facebook.com/pg/kanalucopenhagen) Train Ishøj. ***Open*** *10am-5pm Tue-Fri; 10am-6pm Sat-Sun, closed Mon.*

There is no finer expression of *hygge* than a cosy afternoon spent at Ka'nalu while the wind/rain/snow (delete where applicable) howls outside. Styled as a Hawaiian beach café, it sells pastries, ice-cream from Hansens and Kødbyens Is, along with coffee, brunch and soft drinks.

TO THE WEST

Known internationally for its annual rock festival, **Roskilde** is an easy 25-minute train journey from central Copenhagen. It's an intriguing market town to visit, with a cathedral cemetery full of Danish monarchs, a charming town square and a couple of stellar attractions. **Ragnarock** celebrates the modern musical heritage of the town, a great modern temple to music with plenty of interactive exhibits. Referencing a different type of Ragnarok, the **Vikingeskibsmuseet** (Viking Ship Museum) sits overlooking the natural harbour that leads to the fjord where five Viking boats were discovered in 1962, sunk in the water. They date to 1070 and were deliberately scuttled by the Vikings to protect Roskilde from enemy attack by sea. The natural harbour is the reason the Vikings built a settlement here in the first place and it seems natural and poetic that their boats are still celebrated here today. Every summer, reproduction boats are taken out on the water to better understand the techniques and behaviour of the Vikings at sea.

Vikingeskibsmuseet

Billund, further west yet, through the island Fyn and on to Jutland, is the international hub and birthplace of LEGO. Those little plastic bricks have built an empire here – not just the offices but also LEGOLAND and LEGO House, the latter the recipient of a slew of architecture and design awards. It is a long trek from the city – achievable if you don't mind a six-hour round trip – and worth it if you love design, architecture and LEGO. Options to stay overnight in Billund abound (but book in advance), including LEGOLAND holiday village, Hotel LEGOLAND, campsites and Airbnbs.

In the know
Getting around

For Roskilde, trains run every five minutes from Central Station (25 minutes), while to Billund, trains run at least every hour (approximately three hours).

Sights & museums

❤ LEGO House

Ole Kirks Plads 1, Vejle (82 82 04 00, www.legohouse.com). Train Billund. ***Open*** *10am-7pm, check dates before visiting as they may vary.* ***Admission*** *229kr; free under-3s.*

Worth a visit for the architecture alone, which redefines not just the quiet backwater of Billund but how museums could and should be built, this Bjarke Ingels Group (BIG) masterpiece is made of 21 gigantic LEGO bricks stacked on top of each other, white on the outside and an explosion of colour inside. Allow yourself a full day to explore. Tickets have to be prebooked according to set times before you arrive.

Inside 'play agents' help with guided activities so you can build physical and digital models and make them work in different spaces. There really are no limits to this little plastic brick apart from your own imagination. Make cars and run them on loop-the-loop tracks. Build flowers and sit them alongside other flowers in a meadow. Build bugs. Create snowmen. Make your own LEGO man and take a picture of him in a digital scene. Create fish and scan them so they enter a digital aquarium. Everything is digitally connected with photo points all the way through that save your creative work to the LEGOHouse app, allowing your creations to travel with you. A highlight is the tree built through the centre of the museum, made of LEGO of course, showcasing growth, creativity and potential; a further room prebuilt with scenes from around the world shows LEGO life with trains and more running through it. Lunch is ordered using LEGO blocks in the main restaurant and delivered by robot – it's truly an immersive experience. In the basement, the Museum of LEGO showcases four generations of brand evolution, leading to this high point. There is also, of course, a LEGO Store and a series of playgrounds, all accessible without paying the entry fee.

LEGOLAND Billund Resort

Nordmarksvej 9, 7190 Billund (79 51 13 50, legoland.dk). Train Vejle. ***Open*** *30 Mar-14 Apr 10am-6pm Sat-Sun; 21 Apr-31 Aug 10am-6pm daily; Sept 10am-6pm Fri-Mon; 1 Oct-21 Oct 10am-6pm daily; 25 Oct-3 Nov 10am-6pm weekends only. See website for details. Closed Nov 4-last weekend in March.* ***Admission*** *from 341kr (best rates online).*

Go loopy over LEGO at the original LEGOLAND resort, a good three-hour train ride from Copenhagen. Themed around dragons, knights and princesses, there are plenty of rollercoasters for the kids to enjoy and fast food to eat. It's a little faded compared to the newer LEGO House, but there is a brand new hotel, LEGOLAND Castle Hotel, fresh for 2019. Book tickets in advance online for a 10% discount.

Ragnarock

Rabalderstræde 16, Musicon, 4000 Roskilde (46 31 68 54, museumragnarock.dk). Train Roskilde. ***Open*** *10am-5pm Tues, Thur-Sun; 10am-10pm Wed.* ***Admission*** *95kr, under-17s free.*

Whether you can floss or prefer to dance the Macarena, Ragnarock invites you to walk its red carpet and enter to discover stories of youth culture backed by music dating to the 1950s. Opened in 2016, the museum celebrates how music and youth culture have changed the world. Permanent exhibitions include light displays and the chance to participate in the world's largest choir.

❤ Vikingeskibsmuseet

Vindeboder 12, Roskilde (46 30 02 00, www.vikingeskibsmuseet.dk. Train Roskilde. ***Open*** *10am-4pm daily; during summer and school holidays 10am-5pm daily.* ***Admission*** *110-150kr; free under-17s; 120kr 50-min boat trips.*

Roskilde's glorious Viking boat museum tells the thousand-year-old story of the Vikings, in a beautiful space overlooking the sea where they once sailed. The museum is made of two main spaces: the Viking Ship Hall, where the five partially reconstructed boats stand, and the Boatyard, where archaeological work takes place alongside working boat builders, historical exhibitions and a collection of Nordic wooden boats. The Viking Ship Hall, designed by Professor Erik Christian Sørensen, has picture windows onto the water and, from the water itself, it looks as if the five ancient boats are still at sea. Back in 2013 they nearly were reclaimed by the water as high seas flooded the museum – but staff worked round the clock to keep the water from getting in.

The outdoor space shows reconstructions of boats in full scale and gives you a good idea of the precise craftsmanship that goes into such a beast. Even better, from May to September you can join a trip and sail on the fjord in a reconstruction ship.

Back in the main hall, you can dress up as a Viking, examine Viking handicrafts (or make your own during summer and school holiday workshops) and get a deeper understanding of Danish Viking culture. There is also a museum shop and a café serving Nordic cuisine. Overall, it is a great companion piece to the Nationalmuseet in Copenhagen and its Viking treasures (*see p93*).

Experience

Copenhell *p186*

Events	182
Film & TV	188
Nightlife	194
Performing Arts	202

Events

Our year-round guide to the best festivals, holidays and happenings in and around the Danish capital

---

Copenhagen has a wealth of annual events that hold great appeal for visitors. Summer is an especially exciting time to visit the city; this is when Danes peel back the layers and let loose with an array of music, sports and cultural festivals, typically held along the waterfront or in the heart of the city. The Copenhagen Jazz Festival and the Roskilde Festival are two of the best known, but Kulturhavn and Distortion also well and truly make their presence felt. In the colder months, events such as CPH:DOX, Fastelavn and Tivoli Christmas Season keep things cosy, festive and interesting.

Roskilde Festival p186

❤ Best events

Copenhagen Jazz Festival *p185*
Cut loose in underground bars, unique stages and city squares.

Copenhagen Pride *p186*
Celebrating the city's famously open-minded, egalitarian attitude.

Distortion *p184*
Europe's largest street party.

Kulturnatten *p186*
Museums and noble institutions throw their doors open and welcome you in.

Roskilde Festival *p186*
One of Europe's very best festivals, an easy train ride away.

▶ *For a list of annual public holidays and how these affect opening hours, see p245.*

Spring

CPH:DOX

Various venues (33 93 07 34, www.cphdox.dk). ***Date*** *Mar.*

Day and night for ten days in March, the city's many cinemas showcase more than 200 films, with directors often turning up to talk about their work after the screenings. This is the city's premier film festival: local, Nordic and international directors and films are celebrated across the city with parties, events and showings in creative and alternative venues.

Cherry blossom season

Various venues. ***Date*** *Apr.*

Bispebjerg Cemetery has become the most popular place to be in the city in early April when the cherry blossoms come out. Other popular locations include Langelinie Park, which holds a mini Sakura festival, and the Botanical Gardens. Go early.

Queen's Birthday

Amalienborg Slot. ***Date*** *16 Apr.* ***Map*** *p100 T11.*

The Danes are united by their fondness for their multi-talented Queen Margrethe II, and her birthday is cause for celebration across the country. The Queen herself makes an appearance on a balcony at Amalienborg Slot at noon, while the Royal Life Guards parade in their finest ceremonial dress.

In the know
Keeping up to date

The festivals and events listed here are just the highlights. For further details and precise dates, Visit Copenhagen (www.visitcopenhagen.dk) has an excellent English website with up-to-the minute listings and reviews of sporting and cultural events.

May Day

Fælledparken, Østerbro. Bus 1A, 94N.
Date *1 May.* ***Map*** *p152 N5.*

Head to Østerbro for this trade unions-led festival of the working man, complete with live music and ethnic food.

Copenhagen Marathon

All over Copenhagen (32 26 69 00, www.copenhagenmarathon.dk). ***Entry*** *695kr-750kr.* ***Date*** *3rd weekend in May.*

Professional and amateur runners from around the world pound the cobbles from Vesterbro to Nørrebro, Østerbro and Vester Voldgade. It's a flat race through some central districts with plenty of local support.

Ølfestival (Beer Festival)

Lokomotivværkstedet, Otto Busses Vej 5A (www.beerfestival.dk). Train Dybbelsbro, or bus 1A, 14. ***Tickets*** *125kr-450kr; available in advance online.* ***Date*** *late May.*

This is the country's leading beer festival, drawing crowds of over 10,000. Tastings, talks and, of course, monster hangovers are all part of the three-day event. Over 50 microbreweries, including Nørrebro Bryghus and Brooklyn Brewery, attend.

Summer

❤ Distortion

Various venues (www.cphdistortion.dk). ***Admission*** *free-550kr.* ***Date*** *late May-early June.*

Distortion is one of Europe's largest and loudest street parties, taking place over five days in early summer, and attracting more than 100,000 revellers every day. Split between a giant free street party, dance music club events and a weekend festival, you can decide how to take it. Stroll the streets of Vesterbro or Nørrebro with a six-pack of Tuborg in hand like the locals; bag tickets to the best venues for outrageous dance nights; camp at the festival venues and watch out for special events in one-off locations such as swimming pools and museums, leading up to a final party on Saturday afternoon/night.

Copenhagen Photo Festival

Various venues (www.copenhagenphotofestival.com). ***Tickets*** *varies.* ***Date*** *early June.*

This two-week festival showcases contemporary photography from established

❤ Copenhagen Jazz Festival

All over Copenhagen (33 93 20 13, www.jazz.dk). ***Date*** *early July.*

The summertime Copenhagen Jazz Festival is a huge affair, with 1,000-plus concerts held over two weeks in July at around 100 venues across the city. Lots of the events – which start at around lunchtime each day, and end in the early hours – are free, but you need to book early for any big names. Best of all, the atmosphere that imbues the city during the festival makes it a fantastic time to visit, even if you're not an aficionado.

Copenhagen's relationship with jazz goes back to the 1960s, when the likes of Dexter Gordon, Stan Getz and Ben Webster based themselves in a city that was seriously jazz-hot. These American musicians are so beloved that a new part of the city, Sluseholmen, has streets named after them. Half a century on, the definition of 'jazz' is thrillingly broad, embracing everything from New Orleans street bands, world music quartets and louche South American duos to the purer jazz sounds of Sonny Rollins, Herbie Hancock and Ornette Coleman (all past headliners), as well as huge vocal acts such as Dianne Reeves and Cassandra Wilson.

Venues vary from poky bars to illustrious classics including **Jazzhus Montmartre** (Store Regregade 19A, Indre By, www.jazzhusmontmartre.com) and the elegant, upscale **DR Koncerthuset** (*see p204*). Along the waterfront, enjoy concerts at the beautiful art deco **The Standard** (*see p108*) and at the **Kulturhuset Islands Brygge** (*see p123*).

It all combines to create a festival that's accessible to everyone. From parks, squares and gardens to waterside platforms and churches, from museums and galleries to cafés and bars, it's hard not to encounter some performance going on somewhere. In the long days of summer, whether picnicking in a park while watching a children's concert, or sitting in a cobbled square listening to local treasures, every aspect of the festival is a genuine delight.

If you prefer the bluesier, more melancholy sides of the genre, you might prefer the winter version: **Vinterjazz**, which takes place each February. It's a smaller, more low-key affair, but still brings around 400 concerts over a three-week period. Either way, you're sure to find something to your taste – even if jazz isn't your thing.

Danish and international names. Exhibitions and events take place in cultural institutions, galleries, museums and public spaces around the city – and many of them are free.

Copenhell

Refshaleøen (www.copenhell.dk). ***Tickets*** *1,640kr (3 days); 990kr (1 day).* ***Date*** *mid June.*

The city's primary rock and metal festival takes place out at Refshaleøen with an industrial backdrop for raw and ear-pounding sounds. Camping is right next door; beer gardens and parties are legendary.

Sankt Hans Aften

Various venues. ***Date*** *23 June.*

St Hans Night is one of the biggest celebrations of the festival calendar for Danes, who have marked the longest day of the year since pagan times with bonfires and songs. Gatherings are often held on beaches or in parks. Legend has it that the summer solstice is full of evil and the bonfires ward off witches en route to their homes in the mountains of northern Germany.

❤ Roskilde Festival

Roskilde (46 36 66 13, www.roskilde-festival.dk). Train Roskilde. ***Tickets*** *2,100kr (full festival incl camping); 1,0505kr (1 day); book in advance.* ***Date*** *late June/early July.*

Held over eight days, Roskilde rivals Glastonbury as Northern Europe's largest outdoor music event with crowds of 80,000 and headline acts that include the likes of The Cure, Cardi B and Robyn. The festival is famous for its relatively crime-free party atmosphere; for many teenage Danes, their first Roskilde Festival is an important coming-of-age milestone. A shuttle bus runs from Roskilde Station to the outskirts of this ancient town in the centre of Sjælland. Community spirit is at the heart of the festival.

Round Sjælland Yacht Race

Helsingør (www.sjaellandrundt.dk). Train Helsingør. ***Date*** *late June/early July.*

Sailors compete in one of Europe's major yacht races over three days.

Shakespeare at Kronborg

Kronborg Slot, Helsingør (49 21 69 79, www.hamletscenen.dk). Train Helsingør. ***Tickets*** *200kr-500kr.* ***Date*** *early Aug.*

Productions of *Hamlet* have been staged at Kronborg Castle since 1816. Laurence Olivier and his wife Vivien Leigh played here in 1937, but John Gielgud's 1939 *Hamlet* is generally regarded as the definitive performance. Since then, Richard Burton, Michael Redgrave, Derek Jacobi, Kenneth Branagh and Simon Russell Beale have all played notable Hamlets. The ten-day festival includes other Shakespeare plays, plus films and special productions for kids, with English as the main language.

❤ Copenhagen Pride

All over Copenhagen (www.copenhagenpride.dk). ***Date*** *mid Aug.*

Previously known as Mermaid Pride, this three-day festival is the event of the year for the city's LGBT community, drawing up to 40,000 participants in a huge parade that starts at Frederiksberg Town Hall and leads to Rådhuspladsen.

Copenhagen Cooking

Festival Centre at Israels Plads by Torvehallerne, as well as various venues around the city (www.copenhagencooking.com). ***Date*** *late Aug.*

Take a bite out of the local dining scene at Copenhagen Cooking, one of the world's leading food festivals. The ten-day event focuses on Danish culinary traditions, with key figures on the New Nordic scene – such as Rene Redzepi and Claus Meyer – normally playing a big part. Expect everything from crayfish parties to Greenlandic cuisine, pizza-making classes from local heroes Gorm's, and a seed exchange. Events are typically held in English.

Kulturhavn (Culture Harbour)

Islands Brygge, Amager (33 66 38 50, www.kulturhavn.dk). Metro Islands Brygge. ***Date*** *late Aug.*

On the penultimate weekend in August, over 80 events – from diving to dance, water polo to dragon boat races, and theatrical performances to fireworks – take place on and around the water beside Islands Brygge and up to Refshaleøen. Ride the harbour buses for free and try a plethora of watersports.

Autumn

❤ Kulturnatten

Various venues (33 15 10 10, www.kulturnatten.dk). ***Date*** *mid Oct.*

Every year on the first night of autumn half-term, Copenhagen opens its doors and exhibition spaces for Culture Night. Around 300 venues take part, including churches, galleries and other venues; many of the museums and palaces stay open until midnight, and even Parliament and the Supreme Court open their doors. There's usually a craft fair in Rådhuspladsen, performances on Strøget, countless concerts and performances, and rare displays of historic weaponry at the Tøjhusmuseet. This super-special event brings a singular atmosphere to the city.

Tivoli Halloween Season

See p70. ***Date*** *mid Oct-early Nov.*

Tivoli has opened its gates at Halloween since 2006, with special spooky activities for children and a Halloween market.

MIX Copenhagen (LesbianGayBiTransQueer Film Festival)

Various venues (www.mixcopenhagen.dk). ***Date*** *late Oct.*

Ten days of mainstream and underground LGBTQ films arranged by the Danske Film Institut, and shown at various cinemas around town, in the city's longest-running film festival.

Copenhagen Blues Festival

Various venues (www.copenhagenbluesfestival.dk). ***Date*** *late Oct.*

The city's leading blues festival features local and international blues musicians in more than 60 concerts over five days. Mojo, Huset and Amager Bio are among the 20 venues that take part.

Winter

Tivoli Christmas Season

See p70. ***Date*** *mid Nov-Christmas.*

Tivoli turns into a vast grotto with a Christmas market, ice-skating, Yuletide grub and an infestation of *nisser* (Danish Christmas elves).

Christmas Markets

Various venues (check www.visitcopenhagen.dk for updated information). ***Date*** *from late Nov.*

Like most European cities, Copenhagen is lit up with decorations at this time of year and several Christmas markets pop up around Nyhavn and the centre of the city, selling deer skins, wooden toys, *gløgg* and Christmas decorations. At the end of November, Father Christmas ('Juleman') parades through the city in the Great Christmas Parade.

Christmas

All over Copenhagen (www.visitcopenhagen.dk). ***Date*** *24 Dec.*

The Danes give a great Christmas, both in the privacy of their own homes, with elaborate rituals, feasting and decorations, and on a grander public scale. Like all Danes, Copenhageners celebrate on Christmas Eve. Having chopped down their own tree, Danes will decorate it with real candles. Once these are lit, the family dances around the tree holding hands and singing carols, before settling down to a traditional Christmas dinner of roast duck, potatoes and red cabbage followed by rice pudding with a hidden almond. The streets are empty and shops are closed.

New Year

Rådhuspladsen. ***Date*** *31 Dec/1 Jan.* ***Map*** *p66 N14.*

Rådhuspladsen is the place where locals gather on New Year's Eve for the traditional celebration. In recent years, the firework displays throughout the city have been ever more breathtaking. Be warned: the Danes are not too hot on firework safety.

Copenhagen Light Festival

All over Copenhagen (www.copenhagenlightfestival.org). ***Date*** *first 3 weeks of Feb.*

At the time of year when people in the north have forgotten what the sun feels like, this festival of light is the perfect event. For the first three weeks of February, the city is lit up with spectacular light exhibitions, and you can choose to see them by guided tour on a kayak, a Segway, walking tour, canal boat or on foot at your own pace.

Dining week

Various venues (www.diningweek.dk). ***Date*** *mid Feb.*

During week seven of the year, hundreds of the city's restaurants open their doors for special three-course meals, all for just 125kr. Eating out in this city is not known for its pocket-friendliness, and this is an incredible way to try new food and make the most of the city without hurting your bank account too much. Note: don't expect Noma to be included in the restaurant roster; it's more for mid-range restaurants.

Fastelavn

All over Copenhagen (www.scandinaviastandard.com/fastelavn-traditions-in-scandinavia). ***Date*** *late Feb/early Mar.*

Fastelavn is the Danish version of Carnival, at the start of Lent, though in a way it's more like Halloween. Children dress up in costumes and gather together, wielding sticks with which they beat the hell out of a sweet-filled wooden barrel. This is mild compared with what used to happen, when the barrel, containing a live cat, would be suspended from a tree by a rope so that the youths of a town could gallop past on a horse and wallop it until the bottom fell out. These days, whoever hits the barrel last before the sweets fall out is crowned the Cat King or Queen for the year.

Film & TV

From jumper-wearing detectives to documentary film festivals and Oscar-winning actors, the city isn't short on storytelling skills

---

The Danes have a prodigious moviemaking history. From the silent era of black and white film with piano accompaniment, through the Dogme collective, to the more recent spate of intelligent feature films and controversial documentaries – not to mention Nordic Noir, which has redefined the crime drama genre – Danish filmmakers have had an impact on cinema disproportionate to the country's size and population. This can be credited to the Danes' true love of and devotion to film, as well as government subsidies to create quality products for the international market.

There is also the famous Danish Film School (Den Danske Filmskole), with its steady flow of talented graduates, who have brought Danish cinema several notable triumphs during the last three decades. Lars Mikkelsen, his brother Mads Mikkelsen and Viggo Mortensen are three of the country's best-known Hollywood actors, while Sofie Gråbøl, Sidse Babett Knudsen, Nikolaj Coster-Waldau and Pilou Asbæk are a some of Denmark's small-screen actors who regularly feature on international screens, notably in *The Killing*, *Westworld* and *Game of Thrones*.

CPH:DOX *p192*

The Danish film industry

Denmark's filmmakers were among the key pioneers in European cinema, and in the decades leading up to World War II had a notable influence on its development. The establishment of the Nordisk Film Kompagni in 1906 galvanised the industry. **Nordisk Film** was the first studio in Europe to focus solely on feature films and it thrived (until the emergence of the American film industry, from around 1913), thanks to its technical superiority and the talent of its directors. As extraordinary as this may sound, in the early days of cinema Denmark was the world's biggest producer of films.

After facing near bankruptcy with the advent of sound, Nordisk Film – whose polar-bear logo is said to have inspired the use of a lion as MGM's symbol – re-established itself in 1929 as a producer of talkies. It remains the oldest working film studio in the world.

Among the most important innovators of early cinema were filmmakers **Benjamin Christensen** and **Carl Theodor Dreyer**. In front of the camera, the world fell in love with **Asta Nielsen**, one of the first great movie stars.

The popularity of cinema – particularly documentary, which is still one of Denmark's strongest genres – exploded in Denmark during the 1930s and, as a result, a film act was passed in 1938, establishing the Film Council, the Film Fund and the National Film Board.

Between World War II and the early 1980s, Danish cinema experienced something of a lull in international terms, with the country's filmmakers focusing their energies on television production. When feature films were made, they were often worthy social dramas or soft pornography (the industry having been de-restricted in 1969). Yet in this period, director **Henning Carlsen** created the masterful *Hunger* (1964), based on the novel by Knut Hamsun and now one of Denmark's film classics.

Government subsidies for film production started in the 1960s, and by the mid '70s most Danish films were made with some element of government aid. By 1989, an even more radical system was introduced, whereby a filmmaker could demand 50 per cent of the film's budget from the government (with no creative strings attached) if the producer could match it with private funding.

International success

In 1988, *Babette's Feast*, **Gabriel Axel**'s film adaptation of Karen Blixen's short story, won the Oscar for Best Foreign Language Film, which led the way to many more international successes for Danish cinema, including the unprecedented double triumph when **Bille August**'s *Pelle the Conqueror* won in the same category the following year. The film, adapted from Martin Andersen Nexø's novel telling the bleak tale of Swedish immigrants coping with life on 19th-century Bornholm, also won the Palme d'Or at Cannes. The great Swedish actor, Max von Sydow, received an Oscar nomination in the Best Actor category for his role in the film.

Enfant terrible

Danish cinema continued to hog the limelight in the 1990s with the international success of director **Lars von Trier**, and the advent of Dogme 95. Von Trier's successes over the last couple of decades have earned him a reputation for stylistic experimentation and provocative scripts, as well as problematic treatment of actors. He established his name on the international arthouse circuit with such films as *The Element of Crime* (1984) and *Europa* (1991), and his spooky 1994 TV series, *The Kingdom*. However, it was his 1996 feature, *Breaking the Waves*, that launched him on the world stage. A torrid and occasionally crudely manipulative film, it set the scene for his future relationship with the world's film critics, who continue to be polarised in their opinions of his work. Von Trier's 1998 Dogme release, *The Idiots*; his bleak 2000 musical *Dancer in the Dark*, which starred Björk; the 2009 horror *Antichrist*; and the 2013 *Nymphomaniac* have all been hugely controversial for their dark portrayals of violent sex and mental illness.

Dogme style

Von Trier was one of the filmmakers behind the internationally famous Dogme collective, a movement founded in Copenhagen by four Danish directors – von Trier, **Thomas Vinterberg**, **Søren Kragh-Jacobsen** and **Kristian Levring**. Dogme's mission was to discard the 'trickery' of modern filmmaking to refocus on the characters' emotional journeys.

The Dogme directors declared that Hollywood movies deceived their audience by mythologising the process of filmmaking. But to set themselves aside from all the other bleating, under-funded independent directors, they made it clear that their creed (called the Vow of Chastity) need not preclude Hollywood-sized budgets. As Vinterberg commented: 'The Dogme 95 Manifesto does not concern itself with the economic aspects of filmmaking. A Dogme film could be low-budget or it could have a $100m budget.' The 'Vow' included such draconian commandments as 'Shooting must be on location only', 'The director can receive no credit' and 'Films cannot be of a specific genre'. No dubbing, tripods, artificial lighting or optical effects were allowed either.

The movement spawned several notable successes, prime among them Vinterberg's second feature film, *Festen* (*The Celebration*, 1998), a disturbing tale of family secrets, set against the backdrop of a 60th birthday party.

However, the movement, which broke up in 2005, also had many critics, who saw it as a pretentious experiment that became as conventional as the genres it criticised.

Babette's Feast

21st-century productions

Resonant dramas such as *Facing the Truth* (2002), *Inheritance* (2003), *After the Wedding* (2006) and *In a Better World* (2010) are key examples of the intelligent and high-quality movies made by established directors such as **Nils Malmros**, **Per Fly**, **Susanne Bier** – who won the Oscar for Best Foreign Language Film in 2011 for *In a Better World* – and **Anders Thomas Jensen**, who continue to make waves internationally. Meanwhile, a new generation of young filmmakers is redefining genre-oriented films with forceful stories told in highly aesthetic packages, such as **Nikolaj Arcel**'s political thriller *King's Game* (2004), **Nicolas Winding Refn**'s raw and violent drug trilogy, which began with *Pusher* (1996), and **Christoffer Boe**'s modern romances such as *Allegro* (2005), and his thriller *Everything Will Be Fine* (2010). Winding Refn, in particular, has become a name to watch in Hollywood, with *Drive* (2011) and *Only God Forgives* (2013), both starring Ryan Gosling, earning the now US-based director international acclaim. He won Best Director for the former at the Cannes Film Festival in 2011.

CPH:DOX *p192*

More recently, the sparse police thriller *The Guilty* made a star of the lead actor **Jakob Cedergren**. Denmark's entry to the Foreign Language category of the 2018 Oscars, it was warmly received but didn't win (although it did win the Audience Award at the Sundance Film Festival). Brazilian director Joe Penna's *Arctic*, featuring Mads Mikkelsen and shot in nearby Iceland, premiered at the 2018 Cannes Film Festival to rave reviews.

Christian IV

Lars von Trier released his ultraviolent film *The House That Jack Built*, starring *The Killing*'s Sofie Grabøl alongside Matt Dillon. The director has been criticised for his unusual working practices and his production company was implicated in the #MeToo scandal in 2018; more than 100 people walked out of the movie premiere, finding its wanton violence and gore too much to take.

Palads *p193*

Documentary

Documentary is a major strand of Danish film, partly thanks to Copenhagen's ambitious CPH:DOX festival (*see p184* and *p192*). This success is also helped by public funding (administered by the Danish Film Institute) for the development and production of documentary films.

Three seasoned Danish documentary filmmakers – **Jørgen Leth**, **Jon Bang Carlsen** and **Anne Wivel** – can be said to have laid the groundwork for many of today's key players, who all play into the brand of Nordic humanism that is so well suited to this genre. Current documentary makers to note include **Mads Brügger**, whose *Red Chapel* comic documentary on Korea won Best Foreign Documentary at the 2010 Sundance Film Festival; and **Janus Metz**, best known for his controversial *Armadillo* (2010), about Danish soldiers in Afghanistan. US documentary director Joshua Oppenheimer, who directed the powerful and disturbing 2012 Danish-British-Norwegian film *The Act of Killing*, is also based in Copenhagen, where he works for the documentary production company Final Cut for Real (www.finalcutforreal.dk).

Small-screen successes

Television drama series have taken on an increasingly important role in Denmark's screen productions over the past decade. The well-respected national broadcaster **DR** (previously called Danmarks Radio) produced *The Killing*, *The Bridge* and *Borgen*, all exported internationally to huge acclaim. The publicly funded organisation gave its production departments a big push in the mid 1990s, sending several of its top dogs to Los Angeles to visit the sets of US dramas such as *24* and *LA Law*. They came back with fresh concepts that were injected into local productions, and the rest is screen history – and DR has a handful of Emmys to prove it.

What you might find strange is that while a lot of Nordic television makes its way across to BBC2 and BBC4 in the UK, there seems to be a reciprocal agreement in place. *Midsummer Murders* and *Inspector Morse* are regular evening features on Danish TV.

A lovely Danish television quirk is the *Julekalendar* (Christmas calendar), a family drama series told in 24 parts and shown every day through December up to Christmas. A close contender for seasonal favourite is the short film *Dinner For One*, an English black and white comedy sketch shown every New Year as tradition. You can find it on YouTube if you are keen to see what the fuss is about.

Nordic Noir

The huge success, at home and abroad, of a number of detective and political thrillers – namely *The Killing* (first series 2007), *Borgen* (first series 2010) and *The Bridge* (first series 2011) – is responsible for a new 'golden age' for Danish TV. These dramas can also be seen as follow-ups to a TV series from the late 1970s called *Matador*, which provided something of a springboard for drama in Denmark, and which is frequently re-aired on Danish television. Danish thrillers are celebrated for their gripping stories and plausible characters, as well as for their strong female leads – reasons why *The Killing* and *The Bridge* have both been remade (less successfully) in the US. In 2018 *Herrens vej* (*Ride Upon The Storm*) starring Lars Mikkelsen, won an Emmy; other more under-the-radar dark thriller series include *The Rain* (2018) and *Bedrag* (*Follow the Money*) (2016-18), whose lead actor **Esbem Smed** is hotly tipped for international success. For a country that feels overwhelmingly safe and secure, dramas full of crime, murders and drugs have a uniquely escapist feel.

Cinema-going and festivals

There are plenty of top-quality screens in Copenhagen's city centre, with a choice of multiplexes and arthouses, as well as the dynamic **Filmhuset** (*see opposite*). The vast majority of foreign films are shown in their original language, with Danish subtitles; but note that American and British family films are typically dubbed into Danish. Tickets usually cost around 100kr (80kr reductions). One of the perks is that you can take a beer in to the showing with you.

Copenhagen hosts several excellent annual film festivals. **CPH:PIX** (www.cphpix.dk) is the international feature film festival (the result of a merger between NatFilm Festival and Copenhagen International Film Festival). Held in September, the innovative ten-day festival screens some 180 films from around the world.

The International Documentary Film Festival **CPH:DOX** (www.cphdox.dk; *see p184*) has gone from strength to strength since it started in 2003. As the largest documentary film festival in Scandinavia, the ten-day event draws an engaged international crowd to Copenhagen every March, attracted both by the screenings and the professional seminars.

October's **MIX Copenhagen** festival (www.mixcopenhagen.dk; *see p187*) is one of the oldest LGBTQ+ festivals in the world, showing movies that bend gender and break sexual boundaries, challenge the gender debate and reflect a diverse world.

Filmhuset/Det Danske Filminstitut

Gothersgade 55, Indre By (33 74 34 00, www.dfi.dk). Metro/train Nørreport. ***Open*** *Café 9am-10pm Mon-Fri; 10.45am-10pm Sat; 10.45am-7.30pm Sun. Bookshop & Video Library 9am-9pm Mon-Fri; 10.45am-9pm Sat; 10.45-7pm Sun.* ***Map*** *p100 P11.*

This world-class film complex is devoted to Danish and international cinema. Among its facilities are a shop selling difficult-to-find film books, posters and DVDs, a restaurant, a documentary archive (open to non-members) and three cinemas.

Multiplexes

CinemaxX

Fisketorvet Shopping Center, Kalvebod Brygge 57, Vesterbro (70 10 12 02, www.cinemaxx.dk/ koebenhavn). Train Dybbølsbro. ***Tickets*** *70-105kr.*

This multiplex in a shopping mall has Copenhagen's biggest screen and an IMAX cinema (135kr).

Dagmar Teatret

Jernbanegade 2, Indre By (70 13 12 11, www.dagmar.dk). Train Vesterport. ***Tickets*** *115kr.* ***Map*** *p66 M14.*

A multiplex devoted to projecting quality films. The main cinema is decent, the smaller screens less so.

Empire Bio

Guldbergsgade 29F, Nørrebro (35 36 00 36, www.empirebio.dk). Bus 5A. ***Tickets*** *85kr.* ***Map*** *p152 K8.*

Nørrebro's local multiplex manages to show both arthouse movies and blockbusters. Comfortable double seats are available in the back row. The cinema is conveniently next to a couple of great eateries (Mirabelle, *see p160*, and Bæst, *see p156*) along with microbrewery Tapperiet Brus, if you want to make a night of it.

Imperial

Ved Vesterport 4, Indre By (70 13 12 11, www.nfbio.dk/biografer/imperial). Train Vesterport. ***Tickets*** *105kr.* ***Map*** *p136 L14.*

The Imperial is Copenhagen cinema par excellence. A large, old-fashioned auditorium (with just over 1,000 seats), it used to have the biggest screen in Scandinavia until the CinemaxX giant came to town. Many films premiere here.

Palads

Axeltorv 9, Indre By (70 13 12 11, www.nfbio.dk/biografer/palads). Train Vesterport. ***Tickets*** *105kr.* ***Map*** *p66 M14.*

Copenhagen's family multiplex is nicknamed 'the birthday cake' for its pink exterior.

Arthouse cinemas

Gloria

Rådhuspladsen 59, Indre By (33 12 42 92, www.gloria.dk). Train København H, or bus 11A, 14. ***Tickets*** *90kr.* ***Map*** *p66 O14.*

A small, underground arthouse cinema located in the heart of town.

Grand Teatret

Mikkel Bryggers Gade 8, Indre By (33 15 16 11, www.grandteatret.dk). Metro/train Nørreport, or bus 11A, 14. ***Tickets*** *90kr.* ***Map*** *p66 O14.*

This beautiful old building is home to a distinguished cinema (with six screens) showing an impeccable mix of international and arthouse titles.

Posthus Teatret

Rådhusstræde 1, Indre By (33 11 66 11, www.posthusteatret.dk). Metro Kongens Nytorv, or train København H, or bus 11A, 14. ***Tickets*** *85-90kr. No cards.* ***Map*** *p66 P14.*

Travel back in time in this tiny (90-seat) cinema, which from the outside could almost be mistaken for a puppet theatre.

Vester Vov Vov

Absalonsgade 5, Vesterbro (33 24 42 00, www.vestervovvov.dk). Bus 6A, 26. ***Tickets*** *105kr.* ***Map*** *p136 J16.*

Vesterbro's charming local cinema has a really cosy feel to it, with comfortable reclining airline seats in its two auditoriums.

IMAX

Tycho Brahe Planetarium Omnimax

Gammel Kongevej 10, Vesterbro (33 12 12 24, www.tycho.dk). Train Vesterport, or bus 9A. ***Tickets*** *160kr (entry plus film).* ***Map*** *p136 K15.*

This city landmark contains an exhibition space and also a spectacular IMAX cinema, showing family-friendly science and nature films.

► *For details of the city's planetarium, see p139.*

Nightlife

Cocktails, super-stylish nightclubs and some impressive live music venues make it easy to stay up late

For such a small city, Copenhagen's nightlife is surprisingly vibrant. Sure, there isn't the same diverse range of subcultural 'scenes' that flourish in other European capitals – crate-digging audiophiles are largely notable by their absence – but various forms of electronic music are well represented, with top-name international DJs being regularly booked at clubs such as Culture Box, Rust and Vega.

The city might be best known for its beer (and certainly has plenty of microbreweries where you can start your night), but it's also got a thriving cocktail scene to go along with its Michelin-level restaurants. If food and drink are your thing, you could do worse than plan for a night at Kødbyen, also known as the Meatpacking District, where butchers' shops and abattoirs have been transformed into cool bars and clubs. For a hipster-worthy night out, look to Nørrebro, where you can barhop down trendy streets and find an excellent variety of post-night-out snacks too. The city's authentic pubs – *bodegas* – offer a local (often smoke-filled) feel, frequented by oldies, students and everyone in between.

Vega *p199*

❤ Best night out

Arch *p197*
For posing.

Culture Box *p198*
For dancing.

G*A*Y Copenhagen *p198*
For the gay scene.

Lidkoeb *p197*
For cocktails.

Vega *p199*
For live music.

BARS & CLUBS

First-time visitors may find Copenhagen's party scene a little elusive. There are a few superb clubs and a multitude of ultra-stylish venues packed with armies of attractive punters, but the best nights are mainly promoter- rather than venue-led, which means it's possible to turn up at even some of the more dedicated clubs – including **Rust** and **Vega** – and find it's an off-night, the place lacking in both atmosphere and people.

Copenhagen is experiencing a blurring of boundaries in terms of pre-clubbing restaurant, café, bar and lounge venues that don't fit into the typical club mould, but which can be equally worthy of a night out in themselves. Kødbyen is just one example of an area where it's as easy to throw down a few cocktails before heading elsewhere as it is to spend the whole evening partying in the bar, if you don't have the inclination to move on.

The places listed here are the city's main nightlife venues, but clubs come and go and places fall in and out of fashion, so it's also worth checking the local press for updates on regular nights and one-offs. There are plenty of more informal places to party like a Dane in the city: on long, light summer nights, buying a six-pack of Tuborg and heading to Dronning Louises Bridge, or the wide streets and sunny central lawns of Sonder Boulevard is a popular tradition.

A word about stimulant use: it may not be as rampant as in other European capital cities, but toilets without lids and one-in-a-cubicle policies demonstrate that it's definitely present. Remember that security do search for drugs and will expel you immediately if they find any.

In the know
Dinner dating

Associated with **Meet the Danes** (www.meetthedanes.com), an organisation that arranges for visitors to dine with a local family to improve their understanding of Danish culture and customs, **Meet Gay Copenhagen** (www.meetgaycopenhagen.dk) offers dinners and socialising organised by local gay couples.

LGBT nightlife

Denmark has long been a great place for the LGBTQ community. In 2009, Denmark hosted the gay and lesbian sporting Outgames; Copenhagen Pride takes place every August; and the annual LGBT film festival, MIX Copenhagen, is held every October. With an open and accepting attitude to homosexuality, the city's nightlife scene is fairly mixed and its gay scene – concentrated in the Pisserenden part of the centre – is small. But what it lacks in size it makes up for with a warmth that few cities can match. Check out blus.dk to find out about local lesbian, gay, bisexual, transgender and queer events.

Lounge, cocktail & music bars

Bakken i Kødbyen

Flæsketorvet 19-21, Vesterbro (no phone, www.bakkenkbh.dk). Train Dybbølsbro or København H. ***Open*** *10pm-5am Thur; 8pm-5am Fri-Sat.* ***Map*** *p136 L17.*

Located in the Meatpacking District, Bakken is one of the hottest bar/clubs in the area. Its small, dark interior is packed with fashion-conscious revellers, who come to socialise, get drunk and move to the dance and indie-rock tunes provided by resident DJs.

Boutique Lize

Enghave Plads 6, Vesterbro (33 31 15 60). Bus 3A, 10, 14; Metro Enghave Plads. ***Open*** *8pm-3am Thur; 6pm-4am Fri; 8pm-4am Sat.* ***Map*** *p136 H17.*

Boutique Lize is a classic Vesterbro cocktail bar, rough around the edges but with drinks that draw the crowds. Happy hour is 8-11.30pm on Thursdays and 8-10pm on Fridays and Saturdays.

Café Bopa

Løgstørgade 8, Østerbro (35 43 05 66, www.cafebopa.dk). Train Nordhavn, or bus 1A, 3A, 18, 40. ***Open*** *9am-midnight Mon-Wed; 9am-1am Thur; 9am-5am Fri; 10am-5am Sat; 10am-11pm Sun.* ***Map*** *p152 Q2.*

A friendly café, bar and restaurant popular with locals. At weekends, DJs ensure the place is packed and sweaty. Disco and mainstream dance comprise the tunes. Unusually late opening hours are another plus, as are cheap cocktails.

Café Intime

Allégade 25, Frederiksberg (38 34 19 58, www.cafeintime.dk). Metro Frederiksberg. ***Open*** *4pm-2am daily.* ***Map*** *p136 D14.*

This pint-sized but eminently popular piano bar has been around since 1920, and these days draws everyone from older Marlene Dietrich obsessives to younger jazz connoisseurs. It's one of the stalwarts of the city's gay scene.

Centralhjørnet

Kattesundet 18, Indre By (33 11 85 49, www.centralhjornet.dk). Bus 1A, 14. ***Open*** *noon-2am Sun-Thur; noon-4am Fri, Sat.* ***Map*** *p66 O14.*

Copenhagen's most famous gay bar has been around for more than a century, offering a friendly pub atmosphere that's popular with everyone from the local 'countessa' to gay carpenters downing a pint or three after work.

Cosy Bar

Studiestræde 24, Indre By (33 12 74 27, www.cosybar.dk). Train Vesterport, or bus 5C, 6A, 14. ***Open*** *8pm-5am Wed-Sat.* ***Map*** *p66 N13.*

If you're still out and about after a long evening on the town, chances are you'll end up in this dark, boisterous and cruise-oriented gay bar, where the tiny dancefloor gets ridiculously packed at weekends.

Duck and Cover

Dannebrogsgade 6, Vesterbro (28 12 42 90, www.duckandcoverbar.dk). Train København H, or bus 6A, 26. ***Open*** *4pm-1am Tue-Wed; 4pm-2am Thur-Sat; 6pm-midnight Sun.* ***Map*** *p136 J16.*

One of the city's absolute finest cocktail bars (and that really is high praise), this cosy, dark and welcoming spot has the feel of a super-stylish retro living room, complete with expert bartenders, an award-winning inventive cocktail list and a great soundtrack. They brew their own aquavit – ask behind the bar if you're feeling brave, and expect a headache the next day.

Jailhouse Copenhagen

Studiestræde 12, Indre By (33 15 22 55, www.jailhousecph.dk). Train Vesterport, or bus 1A, 14. ***Open*** *Bar 3pm-2am Sun-Thur; 3pm-5am Fri, Sat.* ***Map*** *p66 N13.*

This two-level gay bar and restaurant is decorated with prison bars and jail-related paraphernalia and describes itself as the city's *hyggeligste* (cosiest) jail. It's not nearly as hardcore as it sounds: the downstairs bar is noted for being surprisingly relaxed, and staff are friendly and easygoing, despite being dressed in full prison-guard regalia.

❤ Lidkoeb

Vesterbrogade 72B, Vesterbro (33 11 20 10, lidkoeb.dk). Train København H, or bus 6A, 26. ***Open*** *4pm-2am Tue-Sat; 6pm-2am Sun; 8pm-2am Mon.* ***Map*** *p136 J15.*

Follow a discreet passageway that leads off Vesterbrogade to reach one of Copenhagen's bars of the moment. Housed in a three-storey, 18th-century building, Lidkoeb is renowned for quality cocktails (from 110kr each) and a welcoming vibe. Choose from the long, wooden ground-floor bar with fireplace and piano; the assembly room with balcony for smokers; or, at the top, a whisky lounge with a late-night feel. In the summer, tables in the garden under a canopy of fairy lights are a fun place to gather.

Nbar

Birkegade 10, Nørrebro (61 65 18 73, www.nbar.dk). Bus 3A, 5C. ***Open*** *3pm-2am Wed, Thur; 3pm-4am Fri, Sat.* ***Map*** *p152 L8.*

Serving speciality beers and fine cocktails, NBar is one of Nørrebro's cosy hipster hangouts. In summer, the terrace is a big draw, while in the winter quiz nights are held in the narrow candlelit bar. Wednesday is craft beer and boardgames night.

Oscar Bar & Café

Rådhuspladsen 9, Indre By (33 12 09 99, www.oscarbarcafe.dk). Metro Kongens Nytorv. ***Open*** *11am-11pm Sun-Thur; 11am-2am Fri, Sat.* ***Map*** *p66 N14.*

Take some sexy bartenders, mix with reliable café food and garnish with talented DJs spinning some of the funkiest house and dirtiest disco around, and you're some way to understanding the popularity of Oscar. The atmosphere here is gay, trendy but laid back, and people-watching is always at the top of the menu.

Clubs

❤ Arch

Nørregade 41, Indre By (41 14 14 33, www.archcph.com). Metro/bus Nørreport. ***Open*** *11pm-5am Thur; 11.30pm-5am Fri, Sat.* ***Map*** *p66 O12.*

Supersleek Arch is full of beautiful people and is owned by one of Denmark's biggest celebrities, Remee (for the uninitiated, he's a producer, composer and songwriter and once wrote a hit Eurovision song). His club is a playground for those who love style and want

In the know
Smoking

As a rule, you can smoke in *bodegas* (see *p200*) but not in other bars, clubs and restaurants.

to show off; music is mainly dance-oriented and top 40 smashes. Dress up.

Chateau Motel

Knabrostræde 3, Indre By (31 31 35 71, chateaumotel.dk). Metro/bus Rådhusplads. ***Open*** *11pm-5am Fri, Sat.* ***Map*** *p66 O13.*

Right in the heart of the city, this four-storey nightclub offers a little bit of everything, with a cocktail lounge, karaoke room, electro-focused main room and classic *bodega* room. One of the most popular places to party right now, there is free entry before midnight. Hip but not snooty.

❤ Culture Box

Kronprinsessegade 54, Indre By (33 32 50 50, www.culture-box.com). Bus 26. ***Open*** *varies; typically midnight-6am Fri, Sat.* ***Admission*** *varies; from 100kr.* ***Map*** *p100 R10.*

Copenhagen's premier techno palace regularly plays host to DJ legends such as Derrick May and Jeff Mills. The sound system has by far the most penetrating bass in town, the VJ shows are superb and the more sedate downstairs dancefloor is perfect for those who don't want to sweat on the main floor. The pre-clubbing bar next door, Cocktail Box, is open from 8pm.

❤ G*A*Y Copenhagen

Vester Voldgade 10, Indre By (33 14 13 30, (www.facebook.com/gaycopenhagennight club). Train Vesterport. ***Open*** *6pm-2am Thur; 8pm-5am Fri, Sat.* ***Map*** *p66 N14.*

Expect house DJs on Friday and Saturday nights, along with RuPaul's Drag Race viewing parties, Alice in Wonderland-themed parties and more. It's one of the key gay venues in town.

HIVE

Skindergade 45, Indre By (70 10 83 62, hivecph.dk). Metro/bus Rådhusplads. ***Open*** *11pm-late Thu-Sat.* ***Map*** *p66 O13.*

Close to Gammeltorv, this exclusive club has two lounges, tables with phone chargers, and DJs and dancing on Fridays. Saturdays see a 3D visual wall, secret tables, a dungeon and more – it's a little more conceptual. There is a dress code (err on the side of very stylish) and you may have to pay for a table. One of the city's most popular clubs. Copenhagen's club of the year in 2017.

The Jane

Gråbrødretorv 8, Indre By (61 69 21 64, www.thejane.dk). Metro/bus Nørreport. ***Open*** *8pm-3am Thu; 8pm-5am Fri-Sat.* ***Map*** *p66 P13.*

A nightclub-cocktail bar fusion, The Jane is cosy, retro and relaxed, with a Mad Men feel. Try pushing the old bookshelves, which open to reveal several other bar areas. DJs play from around midnight. Happy hour on cocktails typically until midnight on a Thursday.

Jolene

Flaesketorvet 81-85, Vesterbro (20 51 47 64, www.facebook.com/jolenebar). Train Dybbølsbro or København H. ***Open*** *10pm-4am Thu; 8pm-4.30am Fri, Sat.* ***Admission*** *varies.* ***Map*** *p136 L17.*

Of all the bars in the Meatpacking District, Jolene is probably the one that most lives up to its 'meat market' tag – albeit with a studenty, fun-packed vibe. A diverse line-up of DJs gets the tightly packed crowds moving, typically with techno on a Thursday.

KB3

Kødboderne 3, Vesterbro (33 23 45 97, www.kb3.dk). Train Dybbølsbro or København H. ***Open*** *8pm-late Thu-Sat.* ***Map*** *p136 K18.*

Until very recently, this warehouse-style club was a working meat freezer. The urban, gritty edge is still in focus (though it has been comprehensively redesigned) and you'll now find a 13-metre (42-foot) bar, cocktails, summer parties and an underground art house feel. It's the biggest nightclub in the Meatpacking District, and also hosts burlesque shows, films, concerts, album release parties and more.

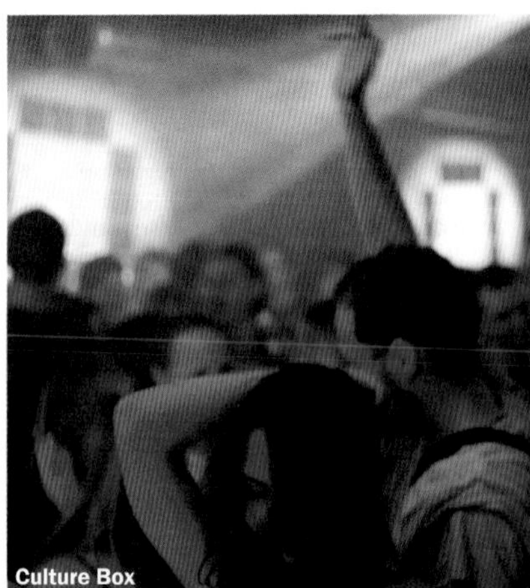
Culture Box

Rust

Guldbergsgade 8, Nørrebro (35 24 52 00, www.rust.dk). Bus 3A, 5C. ***Open*** *8.30pm-5am Wed-Sat.* ***Admission*** *varies according to events.* ***Map*** *p152 L8.*

Rust is one of the city's best venues for both concerts and clubbing, and an integral part of Copenhagen's nightlife. Its evolution over the years – from political café through to dubious rock club and, finally, the more polished venue seen today – is all the more impressive for its retention of an experimental edge and an ability to roll with the times. Expect to see anyone from Post Malone to Rufus Wainwright on its artist list; it specialises in indie rock, electronica and hip hop. When live music isn't on, the three-floor club is a little off mainstream and always busy on a Friday and Saturday night till late.

Sigurdsgade

Sigurdsgade 39, Nørrebro (www.sigurdsgade.com) Bus/metro Nørreport. ***Open*** *10pm-5am Fri, Sat.* ***Map*** *p152 K3.*

This music institution in outer Nørrebro is a welcoming and unpretentious place (no dress code, no table bookings) where people come ready to dance. Expect everything from hip hop, to soul, jazz and disco – anything to get your feet moving. It's a big place – capacity 500 – and weekends are full of partygoers.

Søpavillionen

Gyldenløvesgade 24, Nørrebro (33 15 12 24, www.soepavillionen.dk). Train Vesterport, bus 66. ***Open*** *Nightclub 11pm-5am Fri, Sat (check website for details).* ***Map*** *p152 L12.*

Reopened in summer 2019, Søpavillionen is one of the most iconic nightspots in the city, set in a fabulous pavilion building by Vilhelm Dahlerup, dating to 1895, and located right between the Peblinge Sø and Sankt Jørgens Sø. Intially built as the home of Copenhagen ice skating club, it now hosts a restaurant by day, with food from the ex-chef of Apollo Bar at Kunsthal Charlottenborg, and a nightclub on Friday and Saturday nights, and is run by the team behind Chateau Motel.

❤ Vega

Enghavevej 40, Vesterbro (33 25 70 11, www.vega.dk). Bus 3A, 10, 14. ***Open*** *Club 11pm-5am Fri, Sat. Concerts varies.* ***Admission*** *Club 60kr-150kr. Concerts 100kr-400kr.* ***Map*** *p136 G17.*

Opened in 1996 and housed in a listed landmark building dating from 1956, Vega is the queen of Copenhagen's nightlife. It features a large and small concert hall, Big Vega and Little Vega (1,200 and 550 capacity, respectively) – the latter doubles up as a nightclub; and the street-level Ideal Bar (*see p201*), a party institution in itself. The list of famous names to have played at Vega over the years is a testament to its popularity, from secret gigs by Prince and David Bowie to concerts from the likes of Björk. The interior is superb, the service professional and the DJs among the best in town.

Arch *p197*

Late-Night Bodegas

Meet the locals

If you're bored of ubiquitous, clean-lined Scandinavian aesthetics and expensive drinks lists, and if you're after a less-polished Copenhagen night-time experience, with jukebox tunes, local beers and random conversation, then you'll probably enjoy the atmosphere of a so-called *bodega*. The defining characteristics of these old-school local bars seem to be smoke-filled interiors (for some reason, these drinking dens are exempt from the smoking ban), old men propping up the counter, and affordable beer on tap, as well as simple snacks to munch on. The most popular *bodegas* (the meaning of the word is different to both the Spanish and US versions) have a worn-out charm and often a house-party feel after hours, when the old-timers are joined by students, musicians and artists keen to have a sociable (read: inebriated) time.

One of Copenhagen's best-known *bodegas* is **Eiffel Bar** (Wildersgade 58, 32 57 70 92, www.eiffelbar.dk). This Christianshavn institution – once a hangout for drunken sailors – has mirrored walls, well-priced Danish beer and Pernod, a 1950s jukebox and a diverse mix of customers, with a lively vibe on Thursday and Friday evenings.

Another good late-night bet is **Bo-Bi Bar** (Klareboderne 4, Indre By, 33 12 55 43), a central spot whose origins also lie in Copenhagen's maritime past – it's said to have been established by an American sailor in 1917, and the red-wallpapered interior has been a second home to artists, journos and office workers ever since. The hard-boiled eggs on the counter help to soak up the beer.

The neighbourhood of Vesterbro is home to several traditional *bodegas*, one of the most popular being **Freddy's** (Gasvaerksvej 28, 33 22 70 95). It's often packed on weekend nights, with revellers rocking out to '80s jukebox tunes. Walk west from here along Halmtorvet and Sønder Boulevard, and within ten minutes you'll come to **Dyrehaven** (*see p171*), the result of a makeover of an old-fashioned bar. This new-school *bodega* appeals to modern sensibilities thanks to its DJ nights, retro ambience and good-quality grub (not to mention smoke-free air), but it retains its *bodega* title through its *smørrebrod* plates, excellent beer and local vibe.

For a more sedate experience, head to neighbouring Frederiksberg to the eminently likeable **Vinstue 90** (Gl. Kongevej 90, 33 31 84 90). This local legend of a *bodega* opened its doors in 1916 and is now famous for its 'slow beer', poured from unpressurised kegs to produce an exceptionally smooth drink.

LIVE MUSIC

Touring international acts regularly make a stop in Copenhagen as they take on Europe. Typically you might see larger acts in the summer at festivals, including **Northside** (northside.dk) in Aarhus, **Heartland** (www.heartlandfestival.dk) at Egeskov Slot in Fyn, **Copenhell** (*see p186*) at Refshaleøen and **Roskilde Festival** (*see p186*), 20 minutes away.

Beyond these festivals (most of which you can buy day tickets for), **Vega** (*see p199*), **Rust** (*see p199*) and **Tivoli** (*see p205*) are key concert venues, hosting top-name acts; while **DR Koncerthuset** and the **Royal Arena** are major venues that host the likes of Shawn Mendez and Cher.

On a far more intimate level, live jazz can be found many nights of the week in the city's jazz clubs (*see right*) and during the twice-yearly jazz festivals (*see p185*).

Local music legends to look out for include Christiania's Lukas Graham, Tina Dico, MØ and The Raveonettes; along with probably the world's best-known drummer, Metallica's Lars Ulrich. Let's agree to not mention Whigfield or Aqua.

If you want to find out what's on, Ticketmaster.dk is one reliable source; Scandinaviastandard.com also posts an editor's pick of the month, including live music and club events.

Jazz, blues, folk & world

For more on the jazz scene in Copenhagen, *see p185*.

Alice

Nørre Alle 7, Nørrebro (50 58 08 41, alicecph.com). Bus 3A, 5C. ***Open*** *7pm-midnight daily.* ***Admission*** *varies.* ***Map*** *p152 L8.*

This Nørrebro venue, near Sankt Hans Torv, opened in 2018 as a fusion of two former music institutions, Jazzhouse and Global. Its arty feel and wide variety of live music and more makes it particularly appealing. With a capacity of 250, it hosts bands from home and abroad, encompassing nu-folk, jazz, global roots, experimental electronic, avant-garde rock and DJ-led club nights.

Copenhagen Jazz Festival *p185*

Black Diamond

Søren Kierkegaards Plads 1, Indre By (33 47 47 47, www.kb.dk). Metro Kongens Nytorv, harbour bus 991, 992. ***Open*** *8am-9pm Mon-Thur, 8am-9pm Fri; 9am-7pm Sat.* ***Admission*** *Main building free. Concerts vary.* ***Map*** *p66 Q15.*

Occasional international events at the Black Diamond are well worth checking out, with anything from progressive string quartets to Carl Nielsen's works for violin, top classical soloists and Klang, the city's avant-garde music festival taking place in its distinctive modern building.

La Fontaine

Kompagnistræde 11, Indre By (33 11 60 98, www.lafontaine.dk). Metro Kongens Nytorv, or bus 11A. ***Open*** *7pm-5am daily.* ***Admission*** *varies.* ***Map*** *p66 P14.*

Though it has a capacity of only 60 people, this cosy, low-key jazz venue is well known for its legendary jam sessions and late, late nights. It attracts music students and other jazz-lovers to its weekend swing and mainstream concerts.

Mojo

Løngangstræde 21C, Indre By (33 11 64 53, www.mojo.dk). Bus 11A. ***Open*** *8pm-5am daily.* ***Admission*** *varies.* ***Map*** *p66 O14.*

A grubby but friendly little blues venue, featuring live entertainment every night. Expect the likes of soul music on a Tuesday, with roots, African nights, blues jams and more through the rest of the week.

Rock & pop

Rust and **Vega** are arguably the city's best rock and pop music venues (*see p199*). In summer, don't miss the outdoor concerts at **Tivoli** (*see p205*).

Amager Bio

Øresundsvej 6, Amager (tickets Billetnet 70 15 65 65, information 32 86 08 80, www.amagerbio.dk). Metro Lergravsparken, or bus 5C. ***Open*** *varies.* ***Admission*** *varies.*

One of the largest concert spaces in Copenhagen, with a capacity of 1,000. The programme is strong on old-school rock, blues and country, with more than its fair share of middle-aged rockers on the concert list, alongside the likes of Jess Glynne.

Ideal Bar

Vega, Enghavevej 40, Vesterbro (33 25 70 11, www.vega.dk). Bus 3A, 10, 14. ***Open*** *10pm-4am Wed; 10pm-5am Thur-Sat.* ***Admission*** *from 100kr.* ***Map*** *p136 G17.*

Part of the Vega complex (*see p199*), this intimate, 200-capacity lounge bar hosts regular gigs by established Danish and international musicians, with indie-rock bands often on the rota. The venue also runs club nights and one-off parties.

Loppen

Sydområdet 4B, Christiania (32 57 84 22, www.loppen.dk). Metro Christianshavn, or bus 2A, 9A, 350S. ***Open*** *8.30pm-2am Sun-Thu; 9pm-2am Fri, Sat.* ***Admission*** *from around 100kr.* ***Map*** *p120 U15.*

Since opening in 1973, Loppen has built an excellent reputation for live music despite its rustic surroundings, and its predilection for rock predates the city's rock revival. The booking policy is adventurous, with everything from jazz to rock, but with a strong emphasis on alternative sounds. Loppen is a fully paid-up rebel of a venue, wallowing in the unique environment of Copenhagen's most hippie enclave.

In the know

Copenhagen distortion

Distortion started out by hosting mobile raves in unusual locations, but has since grown into Europe's largest street festival (see *p184*), with occasional one-off parties throughout the year. Visit www.cphdistortion.dk for details.

Performing Arts

Opera, Shakespeare and silent outdoor puppet shows

Copenhagen is known for its jazz scene, but it also has much to offer the classical music lover. Not only are there professional outfits such as the Danish National Symphony Orchestra – housed in the Jean Nouvel-designed DR Koncerthuset – but churches offer regular concerts too. The language barrier means that some theatre is inaccessible to visitors. But, as many of the city's directors come from abroad, it is possible for non-Danes to enjoy a night at the theatre. Opera fans, meanwhile, are in for a treat at the Operaen, set on the water in an impressive modern building. Dance has also been reinvigorated, both in terms of small modern dance venues and as a result of the reorganisation of the Royal Danish Theatre.

Nøddeknækkeren, Tivoli *p205*

CLASSICAL MUSIC & OPERA

Ensembles

Foremost among the professional choirs is **Musica Ficta** (www.ficta.dk), a chamber choir led by composer Bo Holten and performing mostly Renaissance and contemporary music. **Camerata Chamber Choir** (www.camerata.dk) is one of Denmark's oldest choirs; founded in 1965, it has attracted some of the best choral singers in the country, many of them students at the musical department of the University of Copenhagen. For something completely different, try **Concerto Copenhagen** (www.coco.dk), Scandinavia's leading Baroque orchestra and one of Europe's more interesting early music groups. More accessible are a number of **gospel choirs** (butenko.dk), and **Panum Koret** (www.panumkoret.dk), connected to the University of Copenhagen.

Festivals

Copenhagen hosts a number of performing arts festivals. In the summer, you can usually find organ festivals, a Baroque festival and Tivolis Koncertsal's season of mini festivals (from April to September). Every other year, national broadcaster **DR** puts on a competition for young ensembles and chamber musicians at DR Koncerthuset, while the **Copenhagen Summer Festival** (www.copenhagensummerfestival.dk) is an annual showcase for both young talent and established names in the classical music world. The festival takes place in late July/early August in the Charlottenborg Festival Hall in Kongens Nytorv, and boasts 12 concerts in 12 days, many with free admission.

❤ Best music venues

Black Diamond *p204*
Inspiring architecture and experimental performances.

DR Koncerthuset *p204*
Dubbed the best concert hall in Scandinavia.

Jazzhus Montmartre *p185*
Continuing a long tradition of jazz in the city.

Operaen *p206*
Anti-elitist opera for all ages.

Vega *p199*
Indie bands and Danish design.

Major venues

❤ Black Diamond

*Søren Kirkegårdsplads 1, Indre By (33 47 47 47, www.kb.dk). Bus 66. **Box office** 1hr before performances (tickets also available on the website). **Map** p66 Q15.*

The concert hall – called the Queen's Hall – in the Black Diamond (Den Sorte Diamant) is panelled with Canadian maple and ornamented with black tapestries woven with quotations from Hans Christian Andersen's fairy tales. The resident ensemble plays six times a year, with a repertoire covering everything from modern classics and newly composed works to experiments in the borderlands between musical styles.

❤ DR Koncerthuset

*Emil Holms Kanal 20, Ørestad (35 20 62 62, www.dr.dk/koncerthuset). Metro DR Byen. **Box office** noon-5pm Mon-Fri (tickets also available on the website).*

A little out of the city at Ørestad North, this blue box of a concert hall was designed by French architect Jean Nouvel and has four concert halls. Of these, Studio 1 seats up to 1,800 and has world-class acoustics; multiple magazines have crowned the space the best in Scandinavia and among the best concert halls of the millennium. It is the home of the Danish National Symphony Orchestra and the place to experience chamber music and choral performances. Recent touring acts include the likes of Gladys Knight, with comedians including Dylan Moran bringing their words to the stage.

KB Hallen

Peter Bangs Vej 147, Frederiksberg (tickets 70 26 32 67, kbhallen.dk). S Train KB Hallen, Metro Flintholm, bus 9A.

Small and lesser known, KB Hallen has an illustrious past – it hosted The Beatles back in 1964, and artists of the calibre of Louis Armstrong, Frank Sinatra and Miles Davis graced the stage here in days gone by. Today, following a fire, the hall has been reborn and is nearly back to its best; expect a mix of Danish pop and rock acts, and touring bands from all over the world.

Konservatoriets Koncertsal (Royal Danish Academy of Music)

*Rosenoerns Allé 22, Frederiksberg (72 26 72 26, www.dkdm.dk). Metro Forum, or bus 2A, 68. **Box office** (phone) 9am-3pm Mon-Fri. **Map** p136 J12.*

This Functionalist architectural gem, built in 1945 to a design by Vilhelm Lauritzen, housed the Danish Broadcasting Corporation's Radiohusets Koncertsal until 2008. After renovation work to modernise the building, it's

Tivoli

Rock and rollercoasters

Vesterbrogade 3 (33 15 1001, www.tivoli.dk). Train København H. **Shows** *Koncertsal usually from 7.30pm; check the website for details of lunchtime and afternoon concerts.* **Tickets** *typically 50kr plus entry to Tivoli. Koncertsal tickets may cost extra (around 225kr for a touring musical).* **Map** *p66 N15.*

Tivoli holds regular concerts and music events through the year, with live music every single day. International artists including Solange and A-ha have featured as part of its Fredagsrock shows, a unique summer event taking place on a Friday and attracting half a million fans every year. These summer night open-air concerts are free with entry to Tivoli and make **Plænen**, the theme park's outdoor stage, Denmark's most popular venue. On Thursdays in summer, the theme park has a special 'Little Friday' event showcasing upcoming Danish pop, rock and alternative artists in the same open-air space. The fun is not limited to these nights: Mondays have world music events, Tuesdays Danish classics, Wednesdays jazz, and Saturday nights involve a big band and late-night orchestra. It is worth timing your visit for the late afternoon, dining out at the park or taking a picnic, and settling in for an evening of entertainment; if there is a big name artist playing, book in advance.

The theme park has theatre on offer too – the oldest building in the park is the outdoor, Chinese-style **Peacock Theatre**, designed by Vilhelm Dahlerup (also responsible for Det Kongelige Teater) in 1874. The theatre's 'curtain' is a peacock's tail feathers, which fold back to reveal the stage. The theatre stages classical pantomime in the tradition of *commedia dell'arte*. The performances are complex, hard-to-follow shows, starring Pierrot, Harlequin and Columbine, but are worth a look if only to see this extraordinary theatre, operated by cords and pulleys. Ballet is also performed at the Peacock Theatre. Queen Margarethe is the costume designer and artistic director for the ballet theatre here.

More drama arrives every Saturday evening in the shape of a fireworks display. Throughout the summer (except for two weeks in mid July), you can also catch parades and performances by the Tivoli Youth Guard, a children's marching band, founded in 1844, and made up of 100 or so local boys and girls aged nine to 16. In their red uniforms, they look like tin soldiers marching through the park.

Rising talents and some of the world's biggest classical names take to the stage at the **Tivolis Koncertsal** (Tivoli Concert Hall), a beautiful 1940s hall that was renovated in 2005 to add a saltwater aquarium, restaurant and more. It seats 1,900 and is home to the Sjælland Symphony Orchestra; visiting orchestras, ballet companies, ensembles, comedians and soloists of world repute play here too. You can also expect to find occasional dinner and music nights, and musicals. You'll recognise the hall by the row of Danish flags along its roof. Christmas sees a regular revue take place – in English – when an uproarious cabaret show takes to the stage.

▶ *For details of Tivoli's history, layout and other attractions, see p70.*

Tivoli Youth Guard

Musicalen Midt Om Natten

DR Koncerthuset

now the venue for the Royal Danish Academy of Music's 200 annual public concerts, many of which are free of charge. The Academy's Concert Hall is also the winter residence of the Copenhagen Philharmonic Orchestra as well as housing the **Musikmuseet** (Music Museum; www.natmus.dk), open 10am-4pm weekends only.

❤ Operaen

*Ekvipagemestervej 10, Holmen (33 69 69 69, www.kglteater.dk). **Box office** 2-6pm Mon-Fri. **Map** p120 V12.*

This Henning Larsen-designed opera house opened in 2005 to widespread praise. Nine storeys high, it is home to two stages: the grandiose Main Stage and the smaller 'Takkeloftet', where you can expect to see anything from Tchaikovsky to hip-hop fusion on the programme, and especially productions that are accessible for younger viewers. The 2019 series includes Die Fledermaus, Turandot, a new interpretation of Cleopatra, and Tosca. Guided tours of the building can be arranged.

Church venues

Christianskirke

*Strandgade 1, Christianshavn (32 54 15 76, www.christianskirke.dk). Metro Christianshavn, or bus 2A, 40, 66, 350S. **Map** p120 S16.*

Concerts in this 16th-century church cover the full spectrum of musical genres, from gospel to chamber music, and are held throughout the year.

Garnisons Kirken

*Sankt Annæ Plads 4, Frederiksstaden (33 91 27 06, www.garnisonskirken.dk). Metro Kongens Nytorv, or bus 11A, 29. **Map** p100 S12.*

The venue itself is unremarkable, but this church hosts a number of enjoyable concerts throughout the year, including string quartets and chamber music in particular.

Holmens Kirke

*Holmens Kanal 21, Indre By (33 13 61 78, www.holmenskirke.dk). Metro Kongens Nytorv. **Map** p66 R14.*

Every Easter and Christmas, Holmens Kirke hosts performances of Bach's sublime Passions – both the *St John* and the *St Matthew* – and Handel's *Messiah*. There's also music throughout the evening on the annual Kulturnatten in October (*see p186*), and a variety of junior ensembles play through the year.

Kastelskirken

Kastellet 15, Frederiksstaden (33 91 27 06, www.kastelskirken.dk). Bus 15, 19. ***No cards. Map*** *p100 T8.*

This beautifully restored, yellow-painted church has superb acoustics and is used for recordings as well as concerts. Sometimes a military brass band performs on the square outside the church, mixing the usual military marches with the occasional ABBA number; more often, the free Sunday concerts highlight soloists and ensembles, organ music and brass groups.

THEATRE

The following listing are organisations and venues that are most relevant for English-speaking visitors to Copenhagen. More general information about what's on in the city can be found at **www.kultunaut.dk**, **www.berlingske.dk/aok.dk** and **www.cphpost.dk**.

Venues

Det Ny Teater

Gammel Kongevej 29, Vesterbro (box office 33 25 50 75, www.detnyteater.dk). Train København H. ***Box office*** *noon-6pm Mon, Tue; noon-7.30pm Wed, Thur; noon-8pm Fri, Sat; noon-3pm Sun.* ***Map*** *p136 K15.*

The misleadingly named New Theatre (it opened in 1908) is best known for staging Danish versions of blockbuster international musicals (*The Phantom of the Opera* was on in spring 2019), but it also has a restaurant, Teater Kælderen, where actors wait on tables and perform routines between servings.

Folketeatret

Nørregade 39, Nørreport (70 27 22 72, www.folketeatret.dk, tickets via teaterbilletter.dk). Metro/train Nørreport. ***Box office*** *10am-6pm Mon-Fri; 10am-2pm Sat.* ***Map*** *p66 O12.*

Despite starting out as a down-to-earth competitor to the Royal Theatre, the 'People's Theatre' – in existence for over 150 years – now offers an eclectic mix of more modern performances, including musicals, across three stages. Some of Denmark's biggest acting talent, including Paprika Steen and Lars Brygmann, tread the boards here.

Grønnegårds Teatret

Bredgade 66, Indre By (box office 33 32 70 23, www.groennegaard.dk). Bus 1A. ***Box office*** *mid June-Sept.* ***Map*** *p100 T10.*

Grønnegårds Teatret enjoys a unique outdoor location, nestling under linden trees in the garden of Designmuseum Danmark. The season runs throughout the summer and features a visit by the Royal Danish Ballet each July, with picnic baskets available from the museum's restaurant.

Improv Comedy Copenhagen

Frederiksholms Kanal 2, Indre By (22 17 34 69, improvcomedy.eu). Bus 9A; metro Kongens Nytorv. ***Shows*** *8pm Wed, Fri, Sat; 6pm Sun.* ***Map*** *p66 P14.*

This English-language comedy venue is relatively new to the city and puts on shows four nights a week, along with a major international improv festival each Easter. In 2017, it won the AOK 'Best Stage' award – some accolade – and it continues to go from strength to strength.

Skuespilhuset (Royal Danish Playhouse)

Sankt Annæ Plads 36, Frederiksstaden (box office 33 69 69 69, www.kglteater.dk). Metro Kongens Nytorv, or bus 11A, 29. ***Box office*** *2-6pm Mon-Sat.* ***Map*** *p100 T12.*

The waterside Skuespilhuset is in a wonderful spot just round the corner from Nyhavn and has done much to rejuvenate the area. Designed by Danish architects Lundgaard & Tranberg, who won a RIBA European Award for the building, it is the principal venue for dramatic theatre in Denmark. It also hosts a small number of music, dance and children's events. Most performances are in Danish. Recent productions have included *Who's Afraid of Virginia Woolf* (in Danish).

Companies

Copenhagen Theatre Circle

www.ctcircle.dk.

The only amateur English-language theatre group in Denmark, composed of non-professionals working in their spare time and aiming to stage at least one production per year.

London Toast Theatre

33 22 86 86, www.londontoast.dk.

The enormously successful LTT was established in 1982 by British actress, writer and director Vivienne McKee and her Danish

Child's Play

Entertaining options for kids

In addition to an annual festival of youth theatre (www.aprilfestival.dk), there are plenty of children's theatre groups in Denmark. These include **Det Lille Teater** (The Little Theatre, Lavendelstræde 5-7, Indre By, 33 12 27 13, www.detlilleteater.dk), Nørreport's **Anemonen** (Suhmsgade 4, 33 32 22 49, www.anemonen.dk) and Frederiksberg's **Comedievognens Broscene** (Lykkeholms Alle 11, 35 36 61 22, www.comedievognen.dk), which all offer theatre and puppet shows with particular appeal to children under 11 (check the age groups for each show to be sure). At this age, many shows are going to be enjoyable whether you speak Danish or not – expect colours, puppets and Danish versions of well-known comics and story books, including the likes of *The Very Hungry Caterpillar.*

Teater Hund (Toldboldgade 6, www.teaterhund.dk) is another Copenhagen-based theatre company for children and adults; check the programme in advance for age and language suitability.

The **Marionet Teater i Kongens Have** (Kronprinsessegade 21, Indre By, 35 42 64 72, www.marionetteatret.dk) puts on two puppetry performances daily during summer in the lovely Kongens Have. Bring a picnic and play in the dragon-themed playground afterwards.

With older children, a trip to the ballet can be an absolute joy. **Det Kongelige Teater, Gamle Scene** (*see p209*) is the place to see the best shows (*Alice in Wonderland* and *Cinderella* have recently been performed there), and Tivoli is also a good place for ballet shows with kids, if you can tear them away from the candyfloss and fairground rides. Meanwhile, the annual **Shakespeare at Kronborg** festival (*see p186*) includes silent outdoor puppet shows at Kronborg Castle, for age six and up, suitable whatever language you speak.

husband Søren Hall. Its eclectic English-language repertoire spans everything from the moderns and Shakespeare to stand-up comedy and murder mysteries. Its lighthearted Christmas cabarets have become a fixture of the Tivoli Christmas season.

Metropolis

33 15 15 64, www.metropolis.dk

Backed by the Danish Arts Foundation and supported by the long-standing company Københavns Internationale Teater, Metropolis's intention is to break the established notions of art and shake up the general image of performing arts. It's most visible in summer, when the group brings performances to city streets and untraditional spots in an attempt to interrogate where art fits into daily life.

DANCE

The Royal Danish Theatre's dance monopoly was broken in 1979 with the foundation of the Patterson independent dance group. In 1981, Patterson changed its name to Nyt Dansk Danse Teater (New Danish Dance Theatre). A year later, American dancer and choreographer Warren Spears joined the company and began a tradition of collaboration with choreographers and dancers from abroad, which has since become the lifeblood of contemporary Danish dance. Brit Tim Rushton took over as artistic director in 2001, shortening the company name to **Dansk Danseteater** (Danish Dance Theatre), and helped to popularise contemporary dance with lavish multimedia productions, such as *Requiem.*

Dansehallerne is the city's key company dedicated to modern dance, while the **Royal Danish Ballet** (based at the Royal Theatre) is recognised as one of the world's top five ballet companies.

Venues

Bellevue Teatret

Strandvejen 451, Klampenborg (39 63 64 00, www.bellevueteatret.dk). Bus 14, 85N, 185, 388. ***Box office*** *(70 20 20 96) 10am-4pm Mon-Fri.*

Since 2003, the seafront Bellevue Theatre – designed by Arne Jacobsen – has broadened its appeal by collaborating with Copenhagen International Ballet to produce the famous Summer Ballet under the careful direction of choreographer Alexander Kølpin. Newly developed musicals also feature on the programme, sometimes with accompanying English subtitles.

Dansehallerne

Office Valdemarsgade 1G; performances take place all over the city. (33 88 80 00, dansehallerne.dk). ***Map*** *p136 H16.*

The heart of the city's dance milieu, Dansehallernen is a national resource for dance and choreography and is dedicated to communicating ideas about politics, society and the human experience through movement. While its former home, Carlsberg Byen, is being redeveloped and a new location is sought, performances will take place in art galleries and other venues around the country.

Det Kongelige Teater, Gamle Scene (Royal Danish Theatre, Old Stage)

Kongens Nytorv, Indre By (box office 33 69 69 69, www.kglteater.dk). Metro Kongens Nytorv, or bus 11A, 29. ***Box office*** *2-6pm Mon-Sat.* ***Map*** *p100 R13.*

This 1872 neo-Renaissance building for the Royal Danish Theatre was designed by Vilhelm Dahlerup and Ove Petersen, with its 'new stage' – connected via an archway – added in 1931. The building was something of a second home for Hans Christian Andersen. It's now used mainly for traditional ballet performances and is the home of the Royal Danish National Ballet. The building also houses the Royal Danish Theatre's costume department.

Companies

Åben Dans Productions

35 82 06 10, www.aabendans.dk.

Åben Dans (Open Dance), based in Roskilde, is one of the most well-toured modern dance companies in Denmark. The majority of performances are accompanied by lectures, workshops and audience debates.

Danish Dance Theatre

35 39 87 87, www.danskdanseteater.dk.

Over the course of its 25-year history, Danish Dance Theatre has redefined modern dance and experimental ballet in Denmark with its high-quality productions. Shows are performed at the Operaen; in the summer, open-air events take place at the Louisiana Museum of Modern Art, as part of Louisiana Dance, and at the Copenhagen Police Headquarters as part of Copenhagen Summer Dance.

Royal Danish Ballet

www.kglteater.dk.

The artistic director of the Royal Danish Ballet is currently Nikolaj Hübbe, previously principal dancer of the New York City Ballet. Most productions are performed at the Old Stage of the Royal Danish Theatre (*see left*).

Breakfast med Bournonville, Det Kongelige Teater

Brunch og Ballet, Det Kongelige Teater

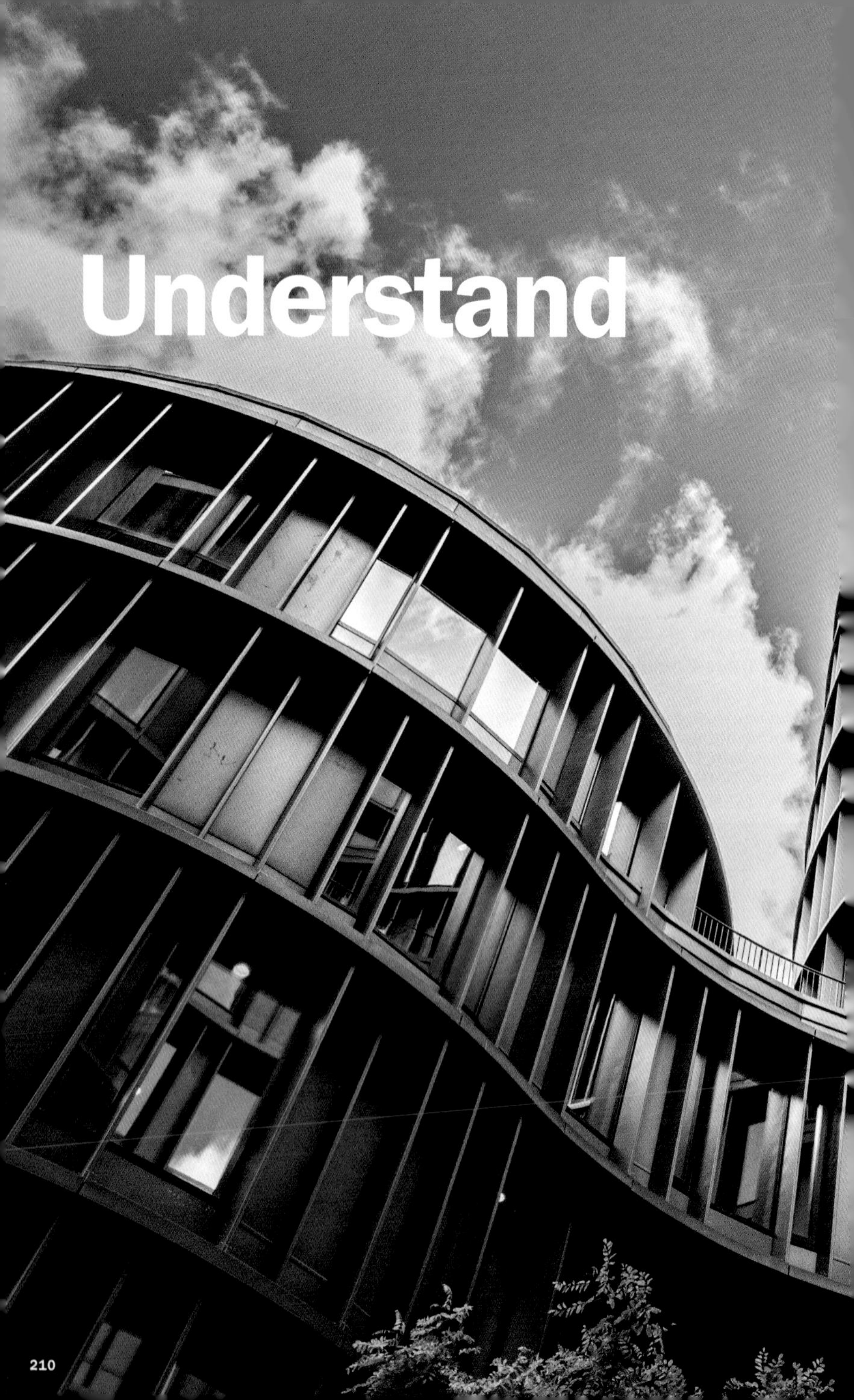

Understand

History 212

Design & Architecture 222

Axel Towers *p229*

History

From humble fishing village to international innovator

Copenhagen has not always been the capital of Denmark. In fact, it didn't take over as the royal seat until the early 15th century; up until that point it was a comparatively humble fishing village and place of defence against marauding pirates and Swedes. However, it grew in strength throughout the Middle Ages to become one of the wealthiest cities in northern Europe, a political powerhouse and cultural centre of great importance. At the peak of its glory, Copenhagen was ruled by one of the most fascinating and reckless of Renaissance kings, whose ambition and follies would eventually bring the country to its knees in the 17th century.

Yet, despite being set back by plague, city fires and hardship at various points over the following 200 years, Copenhagen re-emerged in the 19th century as a centre of culture, its 'golden age' producing writers and artists such as Hans Christian Andersen and Bertel Thorvaldsen, who would go on to become world famous and help to create a new Danish identity.

Havnegade, c1900

Evidence of human life in Denmark exists from tens of thousands of years ago in the form of discarded animal bones. But while the rest of Denmark busied itself with reindeer hunting, flint mining, the Bronze Age, the Viking Age, and the repelling of Charlemagne's advance on the southern border of Jylland (c800), Havn (Harbour), as Copenhagen was known, was little more than an insignificant trading centre for the copious quantities of herring that inhabited the Øresund. It was said that this pungent, oily fish – still a staple of the Danish diet – was so common in these waters that fishermen could scoop them into their boats with their bare hands.

The Vikings

The Vikings, who swept across northern Europe from southern Sweden around 800 AD, established the first Danish state and then rapidly expanded it by invading three of the Anglo-Saxon kingdoms, as well as Norway. The Vikings (meaning 'people from the fjord') even took Seville in 844 and stormed Paris in 845 and again in the 860s and 880s. The subsequent retaking by the nascent Danes of Skåne (or Scania, now southern Sweden, directly opposite Copenhagen) was to be the catalyst for the voracious expansion of Copenhagen 300 years hence, but at the time the villagers probably remained oblivious to their strategic potential. It is likely too that they remained unruffled by the conversion of the unifying Viking king, Harald I, Bluetooth – and eventually the entire country – to Christianity by a German missionary named Poppo around 965. Harald was mysteriously killed while relieving himself in the woods in 987, and many of his successors over the next 170 years met with a similarly murky fate.

Growing pains

In the 12th century, numerous churches blossomed on what was still an unappealing, boggy stretch of coast, among them Vor Frue Kirke (later the site of Copenhagen's current cathedral), and Sankt Petri Kirke (also still a site of worship). In 1238, an abbey of Franciscan Grey Friars was founded; its church (Helligåndskirken) still sits on Strøget, modern-day Copenhagen's main shopping street.

In the late 12th and early 13th centuries, King Valdemar and his sons Knud (Canute) VI and Valdemar II, the Victorious, reigned over a triumphant and expansionist Denmark, which not only conquered the Baltic Wends, but devoured Estonia and Holstein, and lorded it over Lübeck. This era

HRISTIAN DER ERSTE KO
NIG ZV DENNEMARCKEN
SCHWEDEN VND NORWE
GEN HERTZOG ZV SCHLES
WIG HOLSTEIN · K · FRIDER
DORTHEA GEBORN
BRANDEN BVRGK VN
CHRISTOFFERS VON
GELASSENE WIT
K· FRIDERICHS
Christian I and Dorothea

ended ignominiously with the loss of these Baltic territories in 1227. The second spurt of Copenhagen's growth occurred when Erik VII seized control of the town from the Church in 1417. Not only was the king now in charge, but he had become so fond of Copenhagen that he made it his home. This historic move ended the peripatetic tradition of Denmark's monarchy – wherever it laid its crown was its home.

In 1448, Christian I was crowned King of Denmark (later to become King of Sweden and Norway as well) in the first royal coronation to be held in Copenhagen. Inevitably, the city now became the economic, political and cultural focus for the nation. By 1500, the town revelled in riches as its guilds dominated those of the Hanseatic League, while the king too grew wealthy from the new tolls demanded of all who sailed from the North Sea through the narrow strait between Helsingør and southern Sweden on their way to the Baltic. There was no doubt that this was now Denmark's capital, and its leading citizens ruled via the Rigsråd (National Assembly), made up of clergy, prominent estate owners and the king. The Machiavellian Christian II, meanwhile, was politically astute enough to marry a sister of Holy Roman Emperor Charles V. However, he had a tendency to recklessness and was replaced, in 1522, by his uncle, who reigned as Frederik I.

Civil war and Reformation

During Frederik's rule, several popular uprisings – with Copenhagen as a particular hotbed – tried, unsuccessfully, to unseat the monarch and replace him with his exiled nephew, the pro-Lutheran Christian II. When Christian did finally return to Denmark, in 1531, it was as a prisoner to a country ruled entirely by Frederik.

Upon Frederik's death in 1533, the Catholic prelates intervened to postpone the accession of Frederik's son, Christian III, who also had Lutheran tendencies. However, unforeseen by the prelates, the Danish people were as keen on reformation (and the consequent redistribution of clerical property) as the rest of northern Europe, and they wanted Christian II back in power. His supporters in Copenhagen, both peasants and more prosperous townspeople, seized control of the town. Additional support from the German Lübeckers was to provoke one of the most damaging tiffs in Copenhagen's history: the Grevens Fejde (Counts' Feud) of 1534-36, Denmark's last civil war. The Germans' meddling and the accompanying peasants' revolt so concerned the bishops that they finally relented and allowed Christian III to take the throne and suppress Copenhagen. His coronation charter did, however, include the handing over of power to the aristocracy of the Rigsråd from the Crown. (Christian II, meanwhile, spent the rest of his life imprisoned in Sønderborg Castle, where he died in 1559.)

As things turned out, the bishops were to lose power anyway, as, in order to pay his own German mercenaries (without whom he would never have retaken Copenhagen), Christian III was forced to liquidate many of the Church's assets. As the final stroke of a coup that heralded the Danish Reformation of 1536, Christian III imprisoned the bishops.

The nobility benefited hugely from the transfer of money from the Church to their all-too-eager hands

In a display of the consensual diplomacy that still typifies Denmark's political machinations, Christian III offered the bishops the 'get-out' of conversion to Lutheranism, with the added sweetener that under the new doctrine they could marry and have children. Nearly all accepted. Lutheranism was now the official state religion of Denmark; Copenhagen celebrated with extravagant festivities. The nobility benefited hugely from the transfer of money from the Church to their all-too-eager hands, not to mention the exemption from taxes. Across Denmark, and especially in Copenhagen, this wealth was made manifest in grand Renaissance mansions.

The Sun King

Into this brave new world of wealth, expansion and optimism was born one of the great figures of Danish history. Christian IV, Denmark's 'Sun King', was a man possessed of heroic appetites. He ruled for 59 years (1588-1648) and is probably the nation's best-remembered monarch. He was a complex, highly educated man with interests in music, architecture and foreign affairs. He married Anna Catherine of Brandenburg; after she died in 1612, he went on to father a total of 24 children, half of them out of wedlock by a variety of mistresses.

It's hard to know where to begin in detailing the transformation that Copenhagen underwent during his reign. The city grew in all directions in the grandest of styles, with new buildings; a remodelling of its coastal access; improved defences and housing; the construction of entire new districts, bridges, churches, palaces, towers, observatories and theatres; and all the glittering hallmarks of the Renaissance. Upon his death, however, Copenhagen and Denmark would be a spent force, bankrupt, defeated, humiliated and seemingly doomed to an existence of debt and suppression by its enemies.

The problem was that the many ambitious construction projects undertaken during his rule were becoming a burden on the country's finances. When Christian came to the throne, Copenhagen had little industry to speak of. But, although he tried his best to establish industry in the capital, Copenhagen's products could never match the quality of those made by the best European craftsmen, which was a source of constant frustration and embarrassment to the king.

Christian's first priority was to cement Copenhagen's position as the major harbour of the region and, with this in mind, the channel between Sjælland and the small nearby island of Slotsholmen was straightened, narrowed and reinforced with wharfs. Slotsholmen was extended and, as the 16th century closed, a new armoury (Tøjhuset) and a new supply depot (Provianthuset) were constructed to maintain the fighting readiness of the navy. Further symbols of Christian's reign are found in the expanded palaces, prime among them Rosenborg Slot (Rosenborg Castle). But the most extraordinary of his creations is the Rundetårn (Round Tower), an observatory graced by a stepless spiral ramp.

Copenhagen-based international trading companies attempted to establish colonies in Africa and Asia, but they were as fleas on the shoulders of comparable Dutch and British enterprises. Instead, to raise money, Christian attempted to turn Copenhagen into the financial capital of Europe by ordering the construction of Børsen (Stock Exchange). But, despite the building's unquestionable architectural and decorative splendour, that too was a damp squib.

In 1523, Gustavus I of Sweden finally dissolved the Kalmar Union, which had unified the domestic and foreign policies of Denmark, Sweden and Norway (though the union of Denmark and Norway lasted until 1814). During Christian's reign, the increasing strength and confidence of Denmark's northerly neighbour were to threaten the very existence of the Danish state. At stake was control over access to the Baltic, which usually meant control of the region itself. In 1611, in a bid to protect the vital income he received from the Sound tolls (extorted at Helsingør Castle, the model for Shakespeare's Elsinore, north of Copenhagen), and to restore the Kalmar Union, Christian declared war on Sweden. The Kalmar War raged, with Denmark generally dominant, until 1613, when a peace accord brokered by the English concluded with a large ransom being paid by the Swedes to Denmark.

Danish triumphalism was short-lived, however, as Christian and his forces soon became embroiled in the Thirty Years War, in an effort to protect Danish interests on the north coast of Germany from Swedish expansion. The Danes' involvement in the war ended with a devastating defeat by the Swedes at the Battle of Lutter-am-Barenburg in 1626. The Danes got off more lightly than they deserved in the final peace settlement at Lübeck in 1629, in which Christian had to promise to take no further part in the war.

Christian's reign was to be marked by a third fateful conflict, Torstensson's War (1643-45). It was during this war that the 67-year-old Christian lost his right eye and received 23 shrapnel wounds. A much heftier defeat by united Dutch and Swedish forces ended the war, and a peace treaty signed in 1645 saw Denmark cede large areas of territory (chiefly, central parts of Norway, Halland and the islands of Gotland and Osel) to Sweden, and waive future Sound tolls. This was a dramatic and humiliating moment in Danish history. Thirty years followed in which Denmark barely survived as an independent state.

Christian didn't live to see his nation's darkest moment, however. He'd already been dead ten years when his successor, his second son, Frederik III, Prince Bishop of Bremen (who'd taken the throne after the death of his elder brother), started another Swedish-Danish war in 1658. The Swedes then forced the Danes to accept the humiliating Treaty of Roskilde, by which Denmark ceded Scania. Not content, King Karl Gustav of Sweden decided he wanted to take the whole of Denmark, and besieged Copenhagen in the winter of 1658-59. He led his German troops across the frozen sea surrounding Slotsholmen, but, in a last gasp of defiance, Frederik himself is said to have led the fight against Karl Gustav's army. This spirited defence, with cannon shot, bullets, boiling tar and water to melt the ice, gave time for a Dutch army to arrive and save the capital.

The fortuitous sudden death of Karl Gustav at the start of 1660 ended Sweden's ambition to conquer Denmark, but the price of the country's salvation was steep – Frederik was forced to capitulate control of the Sound (and its tolls), as well as all of Denmark's provinces to the east. Europe would never again allow Denmark, now a third of its former size, to hold power in the region.

Europe would never again allow Denmark, now a third of its former size, to hold power in the region

Once again Copenhagen picked itself up to rebuild and refortify, with the construction of a new rampart to protect Slotsholmen. Out of this came the new quarter of Frederiksholm. The impressive Kongens Nytorv square was laid out in 1670 and was soon surrounded with imposing Baroque houses and abutted by Nyhavn Canal – today one of the city's major tourist draws. An improved water supply, a company of watchmen and new street lighting complemented a fast-growing, modern capital whose population had doubled within 100 years to 60,000 by the early 18th century.

Fire and renewal

In 1711, during the reign of Frederik IV, Copenhagen was ravaged by plague in which 23,000 people died. It was also razed by fire twice during the century (in 1728 and 1795). The first fire broke out in Vesterport (the West Gate) on Lille Sankt Clemens Stræde and strong winds, negligible water supplies and general chaos ensured it travelled swiftly across town, destroying 1,600 houses, the town hall and the university, and leaving 15,000 people homeless. Happily, the building of the new five- and six-storey townhouses, and the grand public buildings that replaced the combustible low-rise wooden constructions of the 17th century, were strictly monitored by the building codes of the time: the capital was reborn more splendidly than ever before. The royal castle was also completely demolished and vast amounts of money were spent replacing it with the Baroque Christiansborg Slot.

To celebrate the 300th anniversary of the House of Oldenburg, headed since 1746 by Frederik V, work began in 1749 on a grand new quarter, Frederiksstaden. It was designed by the architect Nicolai Eigtved with wide, straight streets fronted by elegant, light, rococo palaces. At the heart of the new area was Amalienborg Plads, circled by four palaces that were financed by the noblemen of the town. In 1794, when another fire at Christiansborg levelled a large part of the palace, the royal family found themselves homeless. They commandeered the four Amalienborg palaces, employing CF Harsdorff to connect them with an elegant colonnade, and have lived there ever since.

The second fire of the century broke out on Gammelholm in 1795 and was even more destructive than the first, but again this only gave the city's architects and builders the chance to keep up with the fashion for the neoclassical.

One of those less likely to participate fully in the urban renewal of the city was the new king, Christian VII (1766-1808), who managed to rule for 42 years despite frequent and prolonged episodes of schizophrenia. In 1784, the 16-year-old Crown Prince Frederik, later Frederik VI, took power and acted as regent until the death of his father in 1808. By 1801 he probably wished he hadn't, as the first of two bombardments by the British navy took place.

During the 18th century, Denmark's neutrality proved increasingly irksome to the British. To protect itself from increased interference by the British navy, the Danes entered into an armed neutrality pact with Russia and its old foe Sweden. As a result, in April 1801, a British fleet under admirals Nelson and Parker sailed into the Øresund and began bombardment of the Danish navy. However, Denmark continued to profit from the trade that had so angered

Copenhagen Fire, 5 June 1795

Coronation of Christian VIII, 28 June 1840

the British, and anti-British fervour swept Copenhagen. That anger would be fuelled six years later when the British, under the Duke of Wellington, returned with a show of force that made the 1801 battle seem a mere fireworks display.

Napoleon was on the move across Europe and, with his fleet already destroyed by Nelson at Trafalgar, there were strong rumours in 1807 that the French were about to commandeer the Danish navy as a replacement. In fact, Frederik was preparing to defend his country from attack by the French in the south when he was visited by a British envoy, who offered him this ultimatum: surrender the Danish fleet to Britain, or the Royal Navy will come and take it. The Danes refused, and so the British sailed again on still-neutral Copenhagen and bombarded it for three days.

Understandably, the Danes then baulked at an alliance with the British, siding instead with Napoleon. It was a decision they were to rue in the painful years ahead when the British blockaded Denmark and Norway. Much of Norway starved, while Denmark fared little better, enduring great hardship until the defeat of Napoleon. The Treaty of Kiel (1814) saw Sweden (now in alliance with Britain) take control of Norway, which had been for 450 years as much a part of Denmark as Sjælland. A period of introspection, from which many say Denmark has never really emerged, followed, typified by the slogan: 'We will gain internally what was lost externally.'

Danish identity to the fore

Fortunately, this was to be a period of cultural growth for a country struggling to come to terms with a new identity based on little more than a shared language and religion. With all hope of playing a role on the international stage gone, and with little financial power to wield either (Denmark as a state was declared bankrupt in 1813 and later sold its colonies in Africa and India), the country instead began to extend itself in the arts and sciences. The storyteller Hans Christian Andersen (born in Odense, but a long-time Copenhagener), existentialist Søren Kierkegaard (the archetypal Copenhagener) and the theologian Nikolai Frederik Severin Grundtvig each contributed to the emergence of a defined Danish identity during the 19th century.

This was also to be a golden age for Danish art. Many painters learned their craft elsewhere in Europe before returning to Denmark to depict the unique ethereal light and colours of the Danish landscape. Among the most notable were Christen Købke, his mentor and founder of the Danish School of Art, Christoffer Wilhelm Eckersberg, JT Lundbye and Wilhelm Marstrand. Denmark's greatest sculptor, the neoclassicist Bertel Thorvaldsen, also returned to a hero's welcome after 40 years in Rome, while August Bournonville revitalised the Danish ballet at Det Kongelige Teater (Royal Theatre). Denmark also looked to its past to restore its sense of national pride, with the romantic poet Adam Oehlenschläger's mythologising the country's history in his epic poems, and the historical novels of BS Ingemann. As a counterbalance, the original Dagmar Teater (1883) and Det Ny Teater (1908) became known for their adventurous, modern programming.

In contrast to the aftermath of past wars, Copenhagen rebuilt only modestly following the British attack. The town hall was eventually reconstructed on the eastern side of Nytorv, while Christiansborg and Vor Frue Kirke were also repaired (Thorvaldsen's sculptures gracing the latter's interior). The 'corn boom' of the 1830s revitalised growth and the industrial revolution consolidated the city's revival, with a prosperous shipyard, Burmeister & Wain, starting up on Christianshavn in 1843. Tivoli Gardens opened in the same year. Frederiksberg also became an entertainment centre with its numerous skittle alleys, variety halls and dance venues. To help keep the revellers well oiled, the Carlsberg brewery expanded, moving to the suburb of Valby. Carlsberg's owner, Carl Jacobsen, would later use his profits to create a marvellous art collection, which he opened to the public in 1897 at what is now the Ny Carlsberg Glyptotek.

Democracy and growth

With such potent signs of the approaching modern age, Frederik VII knew that the days of absolute power were waning, and when, in March 1848, a demonstration culminated with a loud (but relatively peaceful) protest outside his palace, the king capitulated immediately. Denmark's first written constitution followed in 1849.

Copenhagen's political and artistic life may have been moving with the times during the mid 19th century, but the standard of living for most of its 130,000 inhabitants, crowded tightly in cellars and ever-higher tenements, had not kept pace with the higher echelons of society. Housing remained a dire problem, despite the progressive new terraces in Østerbro, and in 1852 the ban on construction outside the city's defences was lifted. In the latter part of the century a huge building boom saw swathes of land filled with inhospitable blocks of small 'corridor' flats (one-room properties arranged like the rooms of a hotel along one long corridor). Nørrebro and Vesterbro became notorious for the prevalence of such slum housing. Yet as soon as new housing popped up, the population expanded to

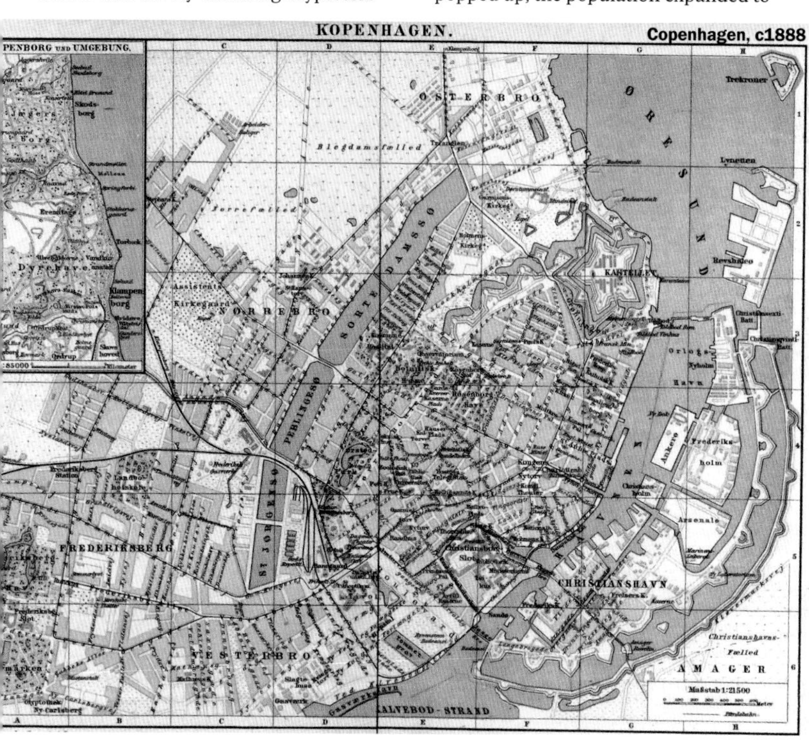

Copenhagen, c1888

fill it. By 1900, more than 400,000 people had moved to Copenhagen to escape the grinding poverty of rural areas. The council granted permission for the creation of a new open space, Ørsteds Parken, where the city's levelled ramparts once stood, together with the building of the Botanisk Have (Botanical Gardens), Statens Museum for Kunst (National Gallery) and a brand new observatory. Strøget, the city's main shopping street, flourished with the arrival of the major department stores Illum and Magasin du Nord. Electricity came to the capital in 1892 and was soon followed by electric trams (1897) flushing toilets (1908) and a vastly improved sewerage system.

In 1913, Copenhagen gained its international emblem, HC Andersen's *Den Lille Havfrue* (*The Little Mermaid*), a statue planted on some rocks in Langelinie, south of Frihavn.

Occupation and freedom

Despite its neutrality, Denmark was in Germany's pocket during World War I. It still, however, made provision for an outright attack by Germany, calling up 60,000 men to form a defence force, most of whom were stationed on the fortifications of Copenhagen. Fortunately, they weren't needed, and Denmark survived the Great War intact.

Between the wars, the pre-eminent figure to emerge in Danish politics was the Social Democrat Thorvald Stauning, who achieved the feat of transforming his party from near revolutionaries to true social democrats. A champion of inclusive politics and a tactical magician, Stauning appointed the first female government minister and helped revive the shaky Danish economy with the famous Kanslergarde Agreement of 1933, which allowed for the devaluing of the krone against the British pound and the subsequent resuscitation of Danish agriculture.

When World War II broke out in September 1939, Denmark braced itself to hold tight and sit out the conflict in peaceable neutrality, just as it had 25 years earlier. It was soon disabused of that notion, when, at 4am on 9 April 1940, Hitler's troops landed at Kastellet, fired a few shots on Amalienborg Slot (killing 16 Danes) and issued an ultimatum: allow Germany to take control of Denmark's defences or watch Copenhagen be bombed from the sky. After an hour and a half of deliberation, the Danish government and king agreed, and entered into a unique deal whereby the country remained a sovereign state, but Germany gained access to Norway, the Atlantic and Sweden. Denmark's Aryan genes ensured it was welcomed into the bosom of the Third Reich and, as a rich agricultural country, it was spared much of the brutality and suppression endured by neighbouring occupied states.

By the end of the war, the Danish Resistance numbered around 60,000. They were never called upon to fight, however, and documents unearthed after the war revealed that the German army had expected them to be far more troublesome than they were.

Post-war Denmark

After the war, Denmark faced several immediate domestic problems, which the founding of its welfare state would address. Culminating in the Social Security Act of 1976, the provision by the government (an endless series of coalitions dominated by the Social Democrats) of a safety blanket for the sick, the unemployed and the elderly has been one of Denmark's most widely admired achievements. Critics, however, point out that it was initially funded by foreign loans and has seen modern Denmark burdened by a vast public-sector workforce and a crippling income tax levied to pay for it.

Prior to 1976, however, with its capital more densely crowded than ever, the government sought to decentralise industry and intensify urban planning. An idealistic 'Finger Plan', in which the city's expansion would incorporate open spaces, was drawn up in 1947, but this was soon discarded to make way for more sprawling suburbs. Copenhagen's first tower blocks were built in 1950 at Bellahøj, but a public outcry curbed the extent to which they could be used to solve the perennial housing shortage. Instead, an urban renewal programme saw Adelgade and Borgergade, among other areas, refurbished. Much of Nørrebro and Vesterbro were also developed during the 1960s, and the latter would benefit from a second renewal programme at the end of the 20th century.

The use of cars increased exponentially in Copenhagen during this time and, as a result, Strøget was pedestrianised in 1962. During the 1960s, many citizens of Denmark (along with the rest of the West) embraced the sexual revolution. In June 1967, it became notorious as the first country in the world to legalise pornography. In 1968, Copenhagen's students, like those across the rest of the continent, grew restless. This being Copenhagen, though, their protest was hardly cataclysmic. Aside from storming the office of Copenhagen University's vice-chancellor and smoking all his cigars, the students caused little trouble.

Copenhagen's youth unrest lasted well into the 1970s, and its ultimate trophy still draws tourists from around the world.

In 1971, a group of squatters occupied Bådsmandsstræde Barracks, on the eastern side of Christianshavn. In protest against what they saw as oppressive social norms, the squatters announced the founding of the Free State of Christiania. The police moved in but underestimated the commune, whose numbers had been swollen by many like-minded hippies from across the country. Eventually the government gave in and allowed Christiania to continue as a 'social experiment', and its 1,000 or so inhabitants quickly began creating their own schools, housing, businesses and recycling programmes. The commune became well known across Europe for its tolerance of drugs.

A group of squatters occupied Bådsmandsstræde Barracks and announced the founding of the Free State of Christiania

Though Copenhagen's pre-eminence as a port came to an end with the advent of the superships (too big for the Øresund, they made instead for Gothenburg and Hamburg), in the 1970s the city nevertheless enjoyed full employment. That, in turn, led to a shortage of workers, and efforts were made to attract foreigners from southern Europe, Turkey and Pakistan, who tended to settle in Nørrebro and Vesterbro. As with London's docks, Copenhagen's waterside was to be redeveloped with expensive housing, exclusive restaurants and impressive new buildings for the city's cultural institutions, such as the Black Diamond national library extension, the Operaen (Opera House) and the new stage of the Royal Danish Playhouse.

Europe – to be or not to be?

In 1973, Denmark joined the European Common Market (as it was then known), mainly to secure its lucrative bacon and butter exports to the UK, but even after 20 years its membership was still the subject of heated national debate. Europe would twice more turn its attention to Denmark, which emerged from the margins of the European Union to stick a spanner in the works of the progression towards federalism. Denmark has never been a wholehearted member of the EU, and 51 per cent of Danish voters went a step further in June 1992, rejecting the pivotal Maastricht Treaty and causing

Queen Margrethe II

a mighty kerfuffle in the process. There were protests, some violent, on the streets of Copenhagen. In the end, after a re-vote in 1993, the Danes finally ratified the treaty (by a majority in favour of just 56.7 per cent), but only after they had been promised the right to abstain from common defence and currency commitments. In 2000, a referendum on whether to join the Euro was rejected by the Danes. The issue has taken more of a back seat in recent times, with the issues of immigration and social welfare coming to the fore.

A decade of national celebration began in 1996, with Copenhagen's tenure as Cultural Capital of Europe. This brought about several new arts projects, including Arken Museum for Moderne Kunst. The city saw major celebrations in 1997 for the 25th anniversary of the reign of Queen Margrethe. In 2000, the Øresund Bridge to Sweden opened, and in 2004, the Danish Royal Family celebrated the wedding of Crown Prince Frederik to the Australian commoner Mary Donaldson.

Early 2005 saw the re-election of Prime Minister Anders Fogh Rasmussen at the head of a Liberal-Conservative coalition in which the unsavoury power-brokers were the right-wing, anti-immigration Danske Folkepartie (Danish People's Party). Four years later, in 2009, Lars Løkke Rasmussen took over as prime minister, after Anders Fogh Rasmussen stepped down.

Denmark's first female prime minister, Social Democrat Helle Thorning-Schmidt, was elected in 2011, and the political climate moved to the left. However, Lars Løkke Rasmussen returned as prime minister again in 2015, following an election that saw the Social Democrats increase their share of the vote, but due to the nature of Danish multi-party politics, saw their opposing right-leaning bloc gain a parliamentary majority overall. All eyes are now set on the next general election, which is set for 2019 on or before 17 June.

► *For more on the current issues facing Copenhagen, see p28 Copenhagen Today.*

Design & Architecture

Classic minimalist design and forward-thinking sustainable architecture take centre stage

Danish design is renowned the world over, beyond all proportion to the size of the nation that fostered it. Collectors and designers flock to Copenhagen to find that original Jacobsen Egg chair or Henningsen lamp in the shops and showrooms of Bredgade and Ravnsborggade, to seek inspiration in the capital's excellent museums, or to clothe themselves in cool Danish threads. But why is Danish design so revered?

In the first half of the 20th century, a wave of Danish designers and architects emerged on the world stage, influenced in part by the radicalism of the Bauhaus, to change contemporary interiors and buildings forever. They looked anew at the style and function of everyday objects, as well as the materials used to make them, and created icons. Danish design has had a reputation to live up to ever since, and by and large it continues to surpass expectations, not just in furniture, product design and architecture, but also in the fields of industrial design, urban design, sustainability and fashion.

Cykelslange *p227*

Functionalism and International Modernism 1928-60

Functionalism was first conceptualised by the Swedish architect Gunnar Asplund in an exhibition in Stockholm in 1930, inspiring architects across Scandinavia to adopt the tenets of International Modernism. Architect **Kaare Klint** gave a succinct expression of the new Danish design philosophy when he said, 'The form of an object follows its function.' Denmark was a country late to industrialisation, and this, combined with its long heritage of quality craftsmanship, meant that it was in a perfect position to develop an exciting new design industry. The first project to create a major impact in the field of architecture was **Arne Jacobsen**'s **Bellavista** housing development (1934) and accompanying theatre **Bellevue Teatret** (1937). Taking inspiration from the German modernists, Denmark's master builder created in Bellavista an uncompromisingly modern development, with white surfaces and large windows (all apartments have sea views), in a posh coastal suburb north of Copenhagen. Jacobsen's lesser-known **Skovshoved Petrol Station**, situated on the route from Copenhagen to Bellevue, was also built in this era (in 1936) and today, as Oliver's Garage (*see p173*), is a great place to visit in the summer for superb ice-cream, along with an iconic view.

Throughout the 1930s, Klint (influenced by his father, PV Jensen Klint) wrote again and again in his notes that architecture and interior design should be unified in what he called 'the living life'. Function should be intrinsic to design, and styling should exist only to enhance practicality. Allying this idea with the traditional hallmarks of the best Danish work – industrial quality, outstanding craftsmanship and artistic flair – Klint produced a series of groundbreaking designs, and passed on his theories as a teacher at Copenhagen's Royal Academy of Architecture. Klint's students were advised that if, for example, they were making a chair, then its function (that is, comfort) should be the starting point – studying human proportions and posture, then applying this scientific rationale to the construction of the furniture should always be the primary objective. **Børge Mogensen**, **Mogens Koch** and **Hans J Wegner** were among his students; their production of simple, practical furniture swept across the country in the 1950s and their designs can be seen in homes all over Denmark to this day. This was also the era when 'Danish Modern' furniture became known internationally – but mainly through the works of **Finn Juhl** (1912-89), whose furniture was more sculptural and expressive than the pure functionalists, and almost a protest against their rigidity. The house that Juhl designed in 1942 can be visited at **Ordrupgaard** art museum (*see p173*); the designer lived there for over four decades and designed most of the furniture and interior details himself.

Arne Jacobsen took the notion of functional and stylistic unity to its extreme when he designed one of Copenhagen's most famous buildings: the **Radisson SAS Royal Hotel** (now Radisson Collection Royal Hotel), completed in 1960. With this building (the first and last proper skyscraper to be constructed in the centre of the city), Jacobsen embraced the principle of 'total design' with characteristically obsessive attention to detail, designing not only the building but also its lighting, furnishings and interior, right down to the cutlery in the restaurant. **Jørn Utzon**, meanwhile, won a competition to design one of the world's most famous buildings, Sydney Opera House, in 1957, marking a milestone in 20th-century architecture and putting Danish architecture solidly on the world map.

Early pioneers

Denmark is still reaping the benefits of this design explosion. The furniture of that era has been (and still is) hugely influential and remains in great demand, but there were a number of Danish pioneers who influenced concepts of modern functionalism before this.

The silverware created by **Georg Jensen**, for example, was revolutionary in its field. Trained as a sculptor and silversmith, Jensen opened his first silverworks in Copenhagen in 1904. From then until his death in 1935, he constantly challenged the conventions of silver design with creations that were both aesthetically pleasing and user-friendly. The cutlery, bowls and jewellery he created with the painter **Johan Rohde** were then at the vanguard of modern design, and today the Georg Jensen brand is as desirable as ever.

At the same time that Jensen was challenging cutlery conventions, fellow Copenhagener **Poul Henningsen** was innovating in the field of domestic lighting. 'From the top of a tram car, you look into all the homes and you shudder at how dismal they are,' he wrote. 'It doesn't cost money to light a room correctly, but it does require culture. My aim is to beautify the home and those who live there. I am searching for harmony.' So, in 1924, Henningsen designed a multi-shade lamp based on scientific analysis of its function. The size, shape and position of the shade

BIG in Copenhagen

Panda houses, power stations and play spaces

Bjarke Ingels Group, a Copenhagen-based firm of innovative architects, has made waves way beyond the borders of this small country. Not just influencers in the way Copenhagen has developed, their offices have designed Manhattan towers, art centres in Utah and Greenland and an energy company headquarters in China. Designs include public spaces that unite disparate cultures, environments that encourage interaction and playfulness, and buildings that bring colour and the environment together in unexpected and delightful ways.

Led by 17 partners, with the young and dynamic Bjarke Ingels at its helm (named one of the most influential people in the world by *TIME* magazine in 2016 at the age of 42), the architecture practice holds information-driven design at its core and is known for its playfulness and bold designs.

Within Copenhagen itself, BIG's playful style is in evidence in the city's public spaces, including **Superkilen** (*see p155*), designed alongside the artist collective Superflex to include play spaces, chairs, signs and more from diverse countries around the world; and the city's three floating **harbour baths** (*see p124*). Other recent triumphs include the giant panda enclosure at **Copenhagen Zoo** (*see p146*) and **CopenHill** (*see p133*), the urban sports area and ski slope atop the city's newest waste management centre – though not without controversy, a late opening and a dubious connection to a disgraced inventor.

Residential projects include the new neighbourhood of Ørestad: **VM Houses** (2005), inspired by Le Corbusier's Unité d'Habitation, led to the now highly coveted apartments of VM Mountain (2008). This was followed by **8Tallet**, a mixed-use housing development built in the shape of the figure 8 and notable for the way it uses the light and creates a sense of community; it won the Housing category at the 2011 World Architecture Festival.

Out of the city, the stunningly play-filled **LEGO House** (*see p179*) and the new subterranean **Danish Maritime Museum** (*see p173*), built into a dry dock, with gently sloping floors that resemble a ship, are also BIG buildings that particularly play to the imagination.

Detractors, of whom there are more than a few (tall poppy syndrome is a particularly Danish affliction), criticise BIG's designs for being childlike and glib, full of big ideas but unable to actually realise them, and for being made of less than top-of-the-range materials. Bjarke Ingels himself is a great showman, but is there depth to his vision, beyond his fantastic soundbites, they ask? But just as you don't make an omelette without breaking eggs, you certainly don't shake up the global architecture scene without taking a bold stance that annoys the establishment. His great achievements have been to put the fun back into architecture, making it more accessible, and putting sustainability and hedonism together to make a green scene people want to be part of. And there is certainly more to come.

With a new headquarters due to be built in Nordhavn, BIG still has its sights set on transforming the city's skyline. True to form, its initial designs have had the hackles up of architecture critics across the city; how it develops remains to be seen. For now, it's hard to imagine the city without the BIG touch – public spaces, the harbourside and key museums have all had a special sprinkle of magic on them and it has to be said that, like it or not, the Ingels touch has been part of the city's renaissance.

VM Houses

Designmuseum Danmark

determine the distribution of the light and the amount of glare. The PH lamp, which featured several shades to help correct the colour and shadow effect of the light, won a competition at the Paris World Fair, and Henningsen became a star. His lamps continue to light many Danish households, particularly the classic PH-Contrast (1962).

Other design trailblazers included silversmith **Kay Bojesen**, whose Grand Prix silver service (1938) was the template for aspiring cutlery designers, and the artist **Ebbe Sadolin**, with his plain white tableware, which was considered quite radical at the time.

Pushing the envelope

Two major talents to emerge in the field of furniture design in the 1950s were **Nanna Ditzel** (who kept working up until her death in 2005) and Jacobsen's contemporary, **Poul Kjærholm** (whose PK22 chair was influenced by Mies van der Rohe's designs). In the 1960s, **Verner Panton**, another of Jacobsen's former colleagues, addressed the frequent criticism levelled at designers – that their work was far too expensive and exclusive – and took on the challenge of pushing the boundaries of design aesthetics even further. Panton trained at the Royal Danish Academy of Fine Arts in Copenhagen, and initially worked in Arne Jacobsen's architectural practice. International attention soon centred on Panton's designs, based on geometric forms, and constructed from cheap, tough plastics that had previously only been used for industrial purposes. Combined with the use of vivid colours and outlandish shapes, Panton's inspirational style helped define the 'pop' aesthetic of the 1960s, with design icons such as the Flowerpot lamp, the Cone chair and the Panton chair. Although some contemporary critics dismissed Panton's work as a fad, before his death in 1998 it was reassessed and a new generation of designers saw it as being way ahead of its time.

Sound engineers

While their neighbours to the south in Germany aspire to owning a Mercedes and the Swedes keep up with the Jensens by buying a yacht, the Danes are a more modest bunch. But there is one luxury status symbol they all yearn for, and that's a state-of-the-art **Bang & Olufsen** sound system.

The company was founded in Western Jutland in 1925 by two engineers, Peter Bang and Svend Olufsen, in the attic of Olufsen's family house. They were the first to produce a radio that plugged directly into the mains instead of using batteries, and by the 1930s they had made a name for themselves with other firsts, including a push-button radio and a radiogram. The Germans destroyed the factory in 1945, but the pair rebuilt the business after the war.

Between launching their first TV in the 1950s and their first fully transistorised radio, the Beomaster 900, in the late 1960s, they made a global name for themselves through their radical yet simple designs and superior quality. In the 1970s and '80s, Denmark's furniture took a back seat while Bang & Olufsen and other industrial design brands, such as **Bernadotte & Bjørn** and **Jacob Jensen**, excelled. 'Bang & Olufsen is for those who discuss design and quality before price,' went the company's advertising campaigns and, accordingly, several B&O products made their way into the Museum of Modern Art in New York.

The Bang and Olufsen families continue to be involved in the running of the company, which, though it now has manufacturing plants all over the world, is still based in their home town of Struer.

Contemporary architecture

The designation of Copenhagen as the European City of Culture in 1996 prompted a period of intense development. Two major architectural works to come out of the event were **Henning Larsen**'s Impressionists gallery in the Ny Carlsberg Glyptotek (1996) and **Søren Robert Lund**'s ship-like **Arken Museum for Moderne Kunst** (1994-96). Neither was as spectacular as the **Øresund Fixed Link** tunnel and bridge, however, which joins Copenhagen to Malmö in Sweden, and opened in 2000.

The first decade of the 21st century also witnessed an invasion of global superstar architects working in Copenhagen. **Daniel Libeskind**, architect of the new building for the Twin Towers site in New York and the acclaimed Jewish Museum in Berlin, designed the **Jewish Museum** (2004) – housed in a converted 17th-century royal boathouse beside the National Library; **Jean Nouvel** designed the astonishing, long-delayed blue cube **DR Koncerthuset** (2009) for Danmarks Radio, in central Amager; and even **Norman Foster** has made his mark on the city, working on, of all things, an elephant house for **Copenhagen Zoo** (2007).

Local commentators call the current era the new 'Golden Age' for Danish architecture, and projects such as Henning Larsen's **Operaen** (2005); and **Lundgaard & Tranberg's** circular **Tietgen Students' Residence** (2006), inspired by traditional south-eastern Chinese housing, and 2008 **Skuespilhuset** (Playhouse; *see p207*) have demonstrated that Danish architects still have much to offer.

But it's **Bjarke Ingels** who has emerged as the new golden boy. The global starchitect, who was just 26 when he designed the **Islands Brygge Harbour Baths** (2002; *see p124*), heads architecture firm **BIG** (Bjarke Ingels Group), and has been behind some of Copenhagen's most talked-about projects (*see p225* BIG in Copenhagen). A slew of skyscrapers and arts projects in New York City are getting the BIG touch over the next few years; world domination is assured.

Design and sustainability

Copenhagen's urban design is much admired around the world, and, as a general rule, the city tends towards usable design and architecture that creates a better way to live, rather than elitist showpiece moneypits. There is no Gherkin in this city; instead, expect to see revolutionary bike bridges, such as the **Cykelslange**, that make getting around a lot easier. Icelandic/Danish artist **Olafur Eliasson** designed the beautiful **Circle Bridge** (2015), inspired by ships' masts, in Christianshavn. It's not just a usable work of art that honours the area's history, it's also designed so ships can pass under and through it.

BIG's **Superkilen**, a vast urban space in Nørrebro, was revolutionary when it opened in 2012, themed around diversity

Circle Bridge

Copenhagen's Historic Housing Projects

Hire a bike to discover Copenhagen's egalitarian spirit

Copenhagen has been at the forefront of residential housing design in the past decade or so, with contemporary projects on the island of Amager – such as Bjarke Ingles' VM Mountain and 8Tallet, and Lundgaard & Tranberg's Tietgen Students' Residence – inspiring architects and urban designers worldwide. Copenhagen was also a frontrunner for social housing projects during the 18th and 19th centuries – a time when urban expansion was attracting new workers to the city – and yesterday's forward-thinking urban designs are today's historic quarters.

Start the day at **Torvehallerne** (*see p104*), where you can pick up a coffee and a *snegle* (a cinnamon pastry in the shape of a snail) to fuel your bike ride or walk.

The next stops on this tour will be at two residential enclaves that were originally built as social housing projects for the city, in response to a cholera epidemic in the 1850s caused by cramped and unhygienic housing conditions. To find out more about this before starting the tour proper, head to the **Arbejdermuseet** (*see p102*), just two minutes' walk from the market. This museum aims to show how Danish workers' lives have changed since the 19th century.

The first historic housing project on the tour is **Kartoffelraekkerne** – 'potato rows' in English – consisting of a ladder of narrow streets built in very straight rows on an old potato-growing area on the border of Østerbro, between the lakes and Østre Anlæg park. All of the 480 terraced houses that make up this 19th-century development have front yards, and the area is now one of the most exclusive in the city – which makes the fact that it was built (by the Workers Construction Society in the 1870s) for the working classes a little ironic. The houses are in demand partly because of the charming and palpable sense of community here (you'll witness picnic tables in the street, for example).

From here, head north on the lakeside cycle lanes on Øster Søgade to Østerbro proper. Left off Østerbrogade, just before Sankt Jacobs Kirke, is Brumleby, another 19th-century residential district built for Copenhagen's working classes – this time by the Danish Medical Association. The rows of distinctive yellow-and-white terraced cottages were built between the 1850s and 1870s, making them one of Denmark's oldest social housing projects, and a model for subsequent projects. As with the potato rows, the houses are now among the city's most sought after.

After a spot of lunch – good options round here are **Café Bopa** (*see p164*) and **Dag H** (*see p165*) – head down towards Frederiksstaden, via Østerbrogade and Dag Hammarskjölds Allé, until you reach **Nyboder** (*see p105*), just past Østerport station. These ochre terraced houses, with their charming red roofs, were built for naval staff and their families in the 17th and 18th centuries, and still house some naval personnel today, though the majority are now occupied by civilians since the area was opened up to the general public in 2006. A small on-site museum, **Nyboders Mindestuer**, informs visitors about the district's history and the humble living conditions here in the first centuries after they were built.

With these historic social housing projects as a context for contemporary residential architecture, you might now like to cycle south along the harbourfront to Islands Brygge and Sluseholmen beyond it, to see where grain silos have been turned into contemporary housing units, and block after block of new-build apartments have sprung up round the water. **Sluseholmen**, at the end, is a modern canalside community founded with Amsterdam's spirit in mind. On the way, head over to **Christiania** (*see p128*) to look at some of the equally community-minded homes down by the water, many of which were built by hand; or stop by **Nokken**, on the edge of Amager Fælled just before you reach Sluseholmen, where a collection of eclectic and eccentric houses and summer houses sit by the water.

Kartoffelraekkerne

in a multicultural area, and featuring items including a black octopus slide from Japan and fountains from Morocco. Newer areas of the city being built include **Sluseholmen**, a former industrial area turned modern canal district modelled on Amsterdam, in the south of the city, and **Nordhavn**, in the north. Both are still in development. **Portland Towers** (2014) sit 52 metres high in Nordhavn and is a great example of repurposing former industrial buildings into architectural treats – the old silos are now eco-certified offices. Nearby, **The Silo** is an avant-garde raw steel-covered block of modern luxury apartments and a restaurant with incredible views on the top.

The National Aquarium in Kastrup, the **Blå Planet** (Blue Planet; 2013; *see p176*), was designed by 3XN with a landmark aluminium exterior, double-glazing units and a seawater cooling system to reduce energy consumption. It's the epitome of a new breed of Danish architecture that celebrates sustainability, water and the merging of Nordic tradition (simple lines, functional design) with the international tendency towards more flamboyant design.

New buildings to note include **Axel Towers** (2017), also known as the 'beer cans', a trio of buildings designed by Lene Tranberg from the award-winning Danish firm Lundgaard & Tranberg Arkitekter. A multi-use space, it includes a Michelin-starred restaurant, public gardens and offices. Also recent is the Danish Architecture Centre's new home, **BLOX** (2018). This controversial building is another mixed-use space which includes a large gym and playground, and is set right on the water in the city centre, at Bryghusplads. Designed by the Dutch architecture practice OMA under Ellen van Loom, it has certainly encouraged conversation, although local and international commentators have not been wholly supportive.

Daily life

There continues to be a strong emphasis on sustainability in Danish design. Investment pieces dominate interior design – durable, classic and always high quality. Green manufacturing processes, recycling and upcycling are also regular touchpoints. Energy-efficient housing made from hay and seaweed are in the works elsewhere in the country, while housing and offices are often powered by solar or wind energy. In Denmark, it's not enough for design to look good – it needs to be made with care and a consideration for the environment, be democratic and accessible to all, and above all, be useful.

▶ *For more on Danish design, see p159.*

Blå Planet

Plan

Magstræde

Accommodation	232
Getting Around	238
Resources A-Z	241
Vocabulary	248
Further Reference	249
Index	251

Accommodation

Copenhagen's hotel scene has rapidly expanded in the last few years, which, paired with multiple rental options from the likes of Airbnb, gives you plenty of choice, whatever your budget or taste. The city lays claim to one of the world's most luxurious hotels (the Nimb Hotel, next to Tivoli Gardens), as well as several that celebrate the city's acclaimed design heritage. Sky-high rates don't necessarily mean the roomiest spaces in town, but the prices are offset by exceptional design and, usually, a memorable breakfast buffet. If you're looking for more space or are travelling as a family, short-term rentals are a *hyggeligt* way to experience local life in the city.

Where to stay

This small but beautiful city is easily walkable, and the vast majority of hotels are only a short walk or cycle ride from the key historic sights, cobbled streets and trendy bars. Being so compact, there isn't really a 'bad' area to stay in; but note that hotels in Amager and Sydhavn are more oriented towards business trips and are a little further from the action. For a weekend trip, staying in Copenhagen K (**North Central** and **South Central Copenhagen**), **Østerbro**, **Nørrebro**, **Vesterbro** or **Christianshavn** makes most sense. **Nyhavn** is the best-known tourist area and prices are high as a result; staying a stone's throw away in Vesterbro lowers the price a little and puts you in the right area for nightlife. Just outside the city centre, **Kødbyen** has a new hotel with fantastic eating options on your doorstep, and a couple of hotels in the **Frederiksberg** area of the city parachute you into the most upmarket suburb of the city, with its wide and leafy streets.

CPH Living

In the know
Price categories

Accommodation in this chapter has been grouped according to price, but rates can vary wildly depending on season or room type within a single property. Categories are based on the cost of a double room in the summer (high season), service charge and tax included. Book in advance for the best deals and stay during the week rather than the weekend for the lowest rates.

Luxury	over 3,000kr
Expensive	2,000-3,000kr
Moderate	1,000-2,000kr
Budget	up to 1,000kr

Luxury

Copenhagen Admiral Hotel

Toldbodgade 24-28, 1253 Copenhagen K (33 74 14 14, www.admiralhotel.dk). Metro Kongens Nytorv. ***Rooms*** *366.* ***Map*** *p100 T12.*

At the Admiral, you could be forgiven for thinking you're sailing in the hold of some massive wooden galley. The tree-trunk-thick beams criss-crossing the huge lobby area and most of the rooms add to the maritime atmosphere of this waterside hotel, housed in a vast 18th-century warehouse. About half the bedrooms have sea views. At Salt, the bar and restaurant downstairs, you can touch the shrapnel scars on the beams from British naval bombardments in the 19th century, or agonise over which of the three different types of salt to pinch over your brasserie-style fare.

Hotel d'Angleterre

Kongens Nytorv 34, 1050 Copenhagen K (33 12 00 95, www.dangleterre.com). Metro Kongens Nytorv. ***Rooms*** *90.* ***Map*** *p100 R12.*

Copenhagen's stand-out five-star Hotel d'Angleterre is traditional to its core, and is the *grande dame* of the city's hotels. The Balthazar Champagne Bar is the definition of modern elegance. The massive 18th-century building contains 90 guestrooms, 60 of which are suites. Guests vary from international pop stars to pals of the royal family (Amalienborg Slot, the Queen's residence, is just round the corner). For a cool 22,500kr you too can feel like royalty, with a night in the Presidential Suite. The revamped spa and swimming pool (10m x 12m) are a real treat, while afternoon tea, served at 2.30pm, is a luxurious way to enjoy the art of Danish pastries.

Hotel Sanders

Tordenskjoldsgade 15, 1055 Copenhagen K (46 40 00 40, https://hotelsanders.com). Metro Kongens Nytorv. ***Rooms*** *52.* ***Map*** *p100 S13.*

New to the city in 2018, this sumptuous boutique hotel, owned by a former dancer from the Royal Danish Ballet, is a discreet and beautiful place to stay. Close to Kongens Nytorv and the Royal Danish Theatre, it is glamorous and central. The cocktail bar is a place to see and be seen. Rooms have wonderful light, modern but muted furnishings and a blend of plush fabrics and natural wood; some have sofa beds and can accommodate children. There is a restaurant along with the bar, and breakfasts enjoy waiter service. Understated and cool.

Hotel Skt Petri

Krystalgade 22, 1172 Copenhagen K (33 45 91 00, www.hotelsktpetri.com). Metro/train Nørreport. ***Rooms*** *288.* ***Map*** *p66 O12.*

Occupying a former department store in the Latin Quarter, this designer hotel is well located for sights and shopping. Rooms are hugely welcoming, with every feature you'd expect, including large, comfortable beds spread with soft, cool linen, and with a bold, bright (but not overwhelming) use of colour throughout. Ask for one of the 55 rooms on the higher floors with a balcony or terrace. The large atrium contains a swanky cocktail bar, while the street-level Petri Eatery is a popular stop for

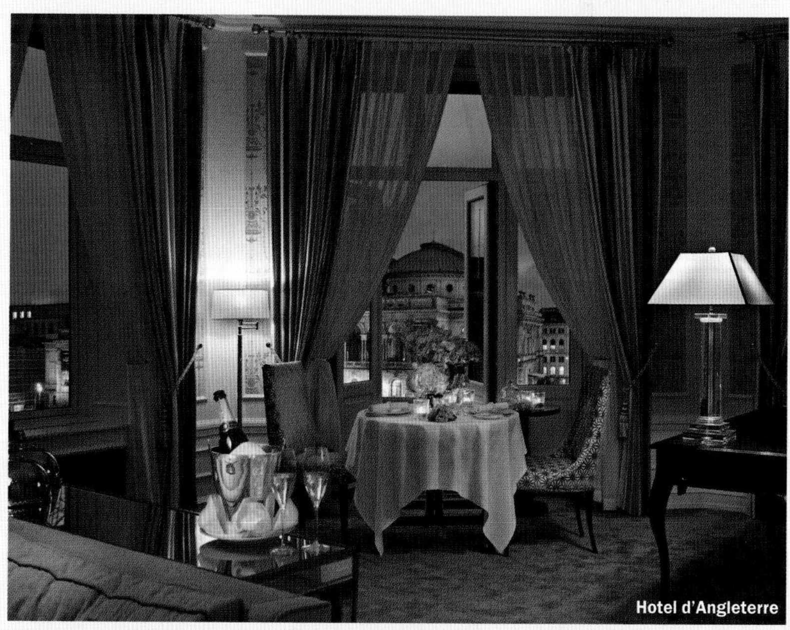
Hotel d'Angleterre

Apartment Rentals

Suite dreams

To get the true 'living like a local' experience, you can't beat renting an apartment in the city. Not only does this give you extra space, but you'll also get to experience typical Danish design (see *p159*), and have the option to dine at home, saving a welcome few kroner – Torvehallerne is a great place to shop for fine-dining ingredients for a stay-at-home feast.

What to expect in Danish apartments: bathrooms are typically tiny and feature showers rather than baths; double beds are usually made up with two single duvets, and furnishings are minimalist but super high quality as a rule. Ask your hosts if you can borrow bikes or if they can help arrange for bike rental to get the most out of the city.

► *The following operators offer rental apartments in Copenhagen: www.airbnb.com, www.booking.com, www.homeaway.com, www.kidandcoe.com, www.redappleapartments.com.*

power-shoppers on a break. Petri Restaurant is stylish and relaxed.

Hotel SP34

*Sankt Peders Stræde 34, 1453 Copenhagen K (33 13 30 00, www.brochner-hotels.dk). Metro/train Nørreport. **Rooms** 118. **Map** p66 N13.*

Set in the Latin Quarter, this hotels' highlights include well-designed rooms with lofty ceilings, a rooftop terrace and the organic breakfasts. The suites and penthouse provide lovely views of the old town. Extras include a bar that is better stocked with port than any other in the city, a private cinema-screening room, DJ sessions, tastings and jazz concerts, plus a daily wine hour. The hotel's three dining options include snacks in a café, burgers courtesy of Cocks & Cows, and a Nordic-infused restaurant with a greenhouse at its centre, right in the building.

Nimb Hotel

*Bernstorffsgade 5, 1577 Copenhagen V (88 70 00 00, www.nimb.dk). Metro/train København H. **Rooms** 38. **Map** p66 O17.*

The five-star Nimb has featured on several 'world's best hotels' lists since opening its doors in 2008. It is set in a converted 1909 Moorish-inspired building and has a cosy feel, with each individually decorated and art-filled room containing antique furniture, fireplaces, four-poster beds and top-notch linen. Spacious bathrooms and slick mod cons are further draws, and all the rooms look out over Tivoli Gardens (guests get complimentary entry passes). To top it all off, the hotel also contains a notable restaurant – Nimb Brasserie (*see p69*) – and a first-rate cocktail bar. With just 38 guestrooms (including eight suites) available, you'll need to book well in advance.

Expensive

71 Nyhavn

*Nyhavn 71, 1051 Copenhagen K (33 43 62 00, www.71nyhavnhotel.com). Metro Kongens Nytorv. **Rooms** 126. **Map** p100 T13.*

Perched at the end of Nyhavn within a splendid early 19th-century warehouse, this relaxed and well-regarded hotel enjoys a prime location. The small, modern bedrooms have managed to keep their character, thanks in part to their wood-beamed ceilings. When you check in, be sure to ask for a view over the water or you could find yourself facing the neighbouring building at the rear. Breakfasts are generally a cut above.

Central Hotel & Café

*Tullinsgade 1, 1610 Copenhagen V (33 21 00 95, www.centralhotelogcafe.dk). Train Vesterport. **Rooms** 1. **Map** p136 J15.*

You'll have to book well in advance to stay at this charming spot, which is located above a popular little café just behind Værnedamsvej (dubbed 'Little Paris' by locals). Consisting of just one room, it's an unusual operation, but perfect if you want to get away from chain hotels or the ubiquitous Scandinavian clean-lined design, and are travelling *à deux*. The room evokes the feeling of a vintage train interior, with lots of wood panelling and retro metal lamps. Breakfast at lovely Café Granola, half a block away, is included in the rate.

Hotel Ottilia

*Bryggernes Plads 7, Carlsberg Byen, 1799 Copenhagen (33 95 77 00, www.brochner-hotels.com/hotel-ottilia). Train Carlsberg. **Rooms** 100. **Map** p136 D18.*

Set across three buildings (some still under construction at time of writing), this is the first hotel in the Carlsberg Byen area of the city, steps from Vesterbro and close to the Carlsberg Brewery, Søndermarken and Copenhagen Zoo. Dark and seductive good looks characterise the rooms; a daily wine hour, optional organic breakfast and REN products add the cherry on the top. Superior double rooms, with fabulous windows and a lot of space, are the pick of the classic rooms; luxury suites are in the tower and include a living room and a round bedroom with turret windows. Finishes are beautiful and echo the history of the Victorian buildings.

Ibsens Hotel

*Vendersgade 23, 1363 Copenhagen K (33 13 19 13, www.ibsenshotel.dk). Metro/train Nørreport. **Rooms** 118. **Map** p100 M11.*

This friendly three-star hotel set in a 19th-century building has cosy design-oriented rooms.

A focus on local art showcases works by Nansensgade artists and artisans throughout the hotel: Krestin Kjaerholm's textiles decorate the lobby and Piet Breinholm's leather tags are used for the room keys. The location near Nørreport Station is about as central as you can get in Copenhagen, and it's a few minutes on foot to Torvehallerne market at Israels Plads. A number of up-and-coming and well-liked Nørrebro eateries, including Bæst, are also a short walk away. Guests have access to the Ni'mat Spa next door for just 250kr.

Manon Les Suites

Gyldenløvesgade 19, 1600 Copenhagen V (45 70 00 15, guldsmedenhotels.com/manon-les-suites). Train Vesterport. ***Rooms*** *84.* ***Map*** *p66 L12.*

Famed among locals principally for its superb pool bar scene, this all-suite hotel is just off the lakes in the central area of the city, close to Ørstedsparken and a short stroll from Torvehallerne. The hip, bohemian set up includes subway-tiled bathrooms, Balinese design accents, a superb gym, a rooftop area with sauna and steam room and a decadent tropical-themed pool and bar area. The first Friday of the month sees a pool party with DJs and more. Best for a couple travelling together; there are more family-friendly hotels in the city than this.

Nobis Hotel Copenhagen

Niels Brocks Gade 1, 1574 Copenhagen V (78 74 14 00, nobishotel.dk). Metro/train København H. ***Rooms*** *77.* ***Map*** *p66 O15.*

Located in the former Royal Danish Conservatory of Music, this exquisite hotel has high ceilings and shows off the most elegant design imaginable. In lively Vesterbro, a short walk from Tivoli Gardens, it has a fitness centre with sauna, hammam and plunge pool, along with a restaurant and bar. Rooms and suites are carefully and minimally designed, with custom-made contemporary fixtures and fittings.

Moderate

Absalon

Helgolandsgade 15, 1653 Copenhagen V (33 31 43 44, www.absalon-hotel.dk). Metro/train København H. ***Rooms*** *161.* ***Map*** *p136 L16.*

This classic Vesterbro hotel is close to Tivoli and the central station, with nightlife on the doorstep. Expect lush multicoloured boutique-style rooms and, in the most expensive Tricia Guild Suite, an explosion of modern floral Designers Guild wallpaper. Family rooms are larger and have a sofa bed as well as a double bed; other rooms sleep one or two, and further suites can sleep up to 4. Babysitting, bike hire, smart phones, umbrellas and luggage transfer to and from the airport are also available. Customised scents are used throughout the hotel. Breakfast is served; there is also a bar and room service for drinks and snacks, but not meals.

Bertrams Gulsmeden

Vesterbrogade 107, 1620 Copenhagen V (70 20 81 07, www.guldsmedenhotels.com). Metro Forum. ***Rooms*** *47.* ***Map*** *p136 G16.*

This intimate boutique hotel, in a central part of town, is furnished in Guldsmeden's signature fresh bohemian-Balinese style, with four-poster beds, Persian carpets, feather duvets and organic toiletries. Other pluses are a quiet courtyard garden, a sumptuous breakfast buffet and plenty of green credentials. This branch is child-free; other hotels in the Gulsmeden's chain welcome children and have more of a family-friendly appeal.

CPH Living

Langebrogade 1A, 1411 Copenhagen K. (61 60 85 46, www.cphliving.com). Metro Christianshavn. ***Rooms*** *12.* ***Map*** *p120 Q16.*

What better way to experience the life of the city than by staying in a floating hotel? This boutique boat – a former German-built barge – is moored by Langebro, a few short steps from the Islands Brygge Harbour Baths and GoBoat station. Decor is pared back and Nordic minimal; the large terrace up top is a good place to catch some rays on a sunny day. A free basic breakfast is included and coffee and tea are available around the clock; there is also a vending machine, free Wi-Fi, bike rental and luggage storage; there is no restaurant. One downside is that it can be noisy at night.

Central Hotel

Hotel Alexandra

HC Andersens Boulevard 8, 1553 Copenhagen K (33 4 44 44, www.hotelalexandra.dk). Metro Vesterport, metro/train København H. ***Rooms*** *61.* ***Map*** *p66 M14.*

A superb example of Danish style, the express intention of the owners is to create a small hotel where guests feel they are staying at the home of a Danish design-loving friend. Staff are all trained in design history; the experience is intentionally retro (with a 1950s and '60s theme), and fully focused on experiencing a certain slice of the city's culture. Rooms celebrate the likes of Finn Juhl, Hans J Wegner, Arne Jacobsen, Ole Wanscher, Nanna Ditzel and Børge Mogensen. The Panton Suite is an unforgettable floor-to-ceiling orange delight, dedicated to the designer Vernon Panton. Next door, the super-stylish restaurant Godtfolk serves Danish and international breakfast, dinner, snacks and more. A design-focused newspaper, the *Alexandra Chronicles*, introduces all the key concepts. It's walking distance from main attractions, and a pleasant half-hour stroll from Designmuseum Danmark.

Scandic Front
Sankt Annæ Plads 21, 1250 Copenhagen K (33 13 34 00, www.scandichotels.com/front). Metro Kongens Nytorv. ***Rooms*** *132.* ***Map*** *p100 T12.*

Grab a front-row seat with views of the waterfront, Langelinie pier, the Opera House and the Royal Danish Playhouse at this luxurious Scandic outpost. Steps from the Amalienborg palaces, the hot pink and cosy grey hotel is decorated with the finest designer furniture, combining comfort and extravagance. There is also a restaurant, bar, rental bikes and a gym. Families are welcome. Ask for a room overlooking the water for the best views from the huge windows. The morning breakfast spread is something to look forward to. Scandic is a reliable, well-priced and much-loved chain across Scandinavia.

Scandic Kødbyen
Skelbækgade 3A, 1717 Copenhagen V (72 18 33 40, www.scandichotels.com/kodbyen). Train Dybbølsbro. ***Rooms*** *370.* ***Map*** *p136 K18.*

New in 2018, this Scandic hotel is the best located in the city if you're wanting to explore the nightlife of the Kødbyen/Meatpacking District. Expect clean, Nordic-styled rooms, most sleeping two but with options for up to seven guests in larger suites. The hotel also has a grill restaurant with an Argentinian flavour, and a coffee shop, and breakfast is included. The location is the key draw: it's outside the main tourist zone of the city but with walking distance of Vega, Tivoli and the waterfront, with the diverse cafés, restaurants and cocktail bars of hipster-fave Kødbyen right outside the door.

Budget

Allegade 10
Allegade 10, 2000 Frederiksberg, Copenhagen (33 31 17 51, www.allegade10.dk). Metro/train Frederiksberg/Frederiksberg Allé. ***Rooms*** *12 plus 1 apartment.* ***Map*** *p136 D14.*

Dating to 1780, this mini-hotel is one of the city's oldest, and is well placed for exploring upmarket Frederiksberg, the zoo and all the city's key attractions. Rooms are cute and homely, with high ceilings, pretty chandeliers and oil paintings on the walls. The restaurant has a special nod to the past, with pictures of Denmark's royal family; for an authentically Danish experience, take brunch or a lunch of *smørrebrød* in the hotel's restaurant.

Axel Gulsmedan
Colbjørnsensgade 14, 1652 Copenhagen (33 31 32 66, guldsmedenhotels.com/axel-hotel-copenhagen-vesterbro). Metro/train København H, train Vesterport. ***Rooms*** *202.* ***Map*** *p136 L16.*

One of the five Gulsmedan boutique hotels in Copenhagen, Axel is known for its cosy feel and its spa. Close to both Central Station and Tivoli Gardens, it is in a good location for eating out, sightseeing and cocktail bars. Room types include doubles, twins, a family suite with a 4-poster bedroom connected to a bunkbed room, and a pair of show-stopping rooftop suites. The hotel's spa has steam room, sauna, cold-water tub and hot tub.

Citizen M
HC Andersens Boulevard 12, 1553 Copenhagen (89 88 07 77, www.citizenm.com). Metro/train København H, train Vesterport. ***Rooms*** *238.* ***Map*** *p66 M14.*

Brand new at the end of 2018, this budget boutique hotel is just off the main town hall square and in the former Dagmarhus building. Fresh and modern in approach, it has a barista and mixologist available 24/7, plus Vitra furniture, extra-large beds, powerful rainshowers as standard in the bathrooms and tech to control your in-room experience, along with Macs to borrow if you need.

Danhostel Copenhagen City
HC Andersens Boulevard 50, 1553 Copenhagen V (33 11 85 85, group booking 33 18 83 32, www.danhostelcopenhagencity.dk). Metro/train København H. ***Rooms*** *192.* ***Map*** *p66 P16.*

Tagged as 'the largest designer hostel in Europe', this five-star establishment opened in 2004 with Scandinavian furniture and a sharp, modern look. Located just five minutes' walk from landmark attractions such as Tivoli and the Royal Library, it also has a fantastic view over Langebro bridge.

Generator Copenhagen
Adalgade 5-7, 1304 Copenhagen K (78 77 54 00, generatorhostels.com/Copenhagen). Metro Kongens Nytorv/Nørreport, train Nørreport. ***Rooms*** *100+* ***Map*** *p100 Q11.*

Just off Kongens Nytorv in the heart of the city, this design hostel in a Philippe Starck development is close to great shopping, bakeries and key attractions and has a large bar with cheery bar staff to help your stay go with a swing. Private double, twin and quad rooms are available along with shared dorms. Breakfast and snack food is served in the bar area and on the outdoor terrace; bikes can be rented, tours can be booked and there is a pétanque court and shuffleboard if you're in the mood for games.

Wake Up Copenhagen Bernstoffsgade
Bernstoffsgade 35, 1577 Copenhagen V (44 80 00 00, www.wakeupcopenhagen.com). Metro/train København H, train Central Station. ***Rooms*** *585.* ***Map*** *p66 O17.*

This budget hotel is round the corner from the city's main station and is well located for exploring the heart of the Copenhagen. Designed by Danish architect Kim Utzon, it has a light and minimalist feel and has Green Key environmental certification, with Wi-Fi included and bike rental and breakfast on offer. Of Wake Up's three central budget hotels in the city, this is the newest (it opened in 2018). Family rooms with connecting doors are available; the largest rooms are 15 square metres (160 square feet).

COME HERE, YOU

Getting Around

ARRIVING & LEAVING

By air

Copenhagen Airport *Central switchboard 32 31 32 31; flight information: www.cph.dk.*
The airport website gives live information on arrival and departure times.

Copenhagen Airport (Københavns Lufthavne, also known as Kastrup) is often voted best in the world by air passengers. It receives direct flights from around 169 cities around the world, and 29.2 million passengers passed through in 2017.

Flight time from London is about 1.5hrs. Direct flights from New York take 7.5hrs, while the journey time coming from LA or San Francisco is approximately 10.5hrs. International and domestic flights both arrive and depart from Terminals 2 and 3.

Metro and train

To get to central Copenhagen from the airport, the easiest option is to take public transit – Metro or train. The **Copenhagen Metro** runs to and from the airport 24hrs a day, 7 days a week. All trains from the airport go in the same direction (M2 to Vanløse). The station is located in Terminal 3 – just walk straight ahead out of the arrivals hall and head up the escalator. It takes roughly 14mins to reach the centre (Nørreport), and you need a 3-zone ticket, which at the time of writing costs 38kr. You can buy tickets from the machines located just before the Metro platform (beyond the airline check-in machines); the machines take credit/debit cards and coins (no notes). For additional information, visit www.m.dk.

If you're staying near Copenhagen Central Station (København H), you might find it easier to take the mainline **DSB regional train** from the airport; it also leaves from Terminal 3 and the cost is the same.

Taxi

There are plentiful taxis at Terminals 1 and 3; the fare to the centre of the city should be around 250kr-300kr, depending on traffic. Tips are not expected in Danish taxis.

Bus

Local buses (5A goes to both Rådhuspladsen and Copenhagen Central Station) run from Terminal 3 every 10 to 20mins (the night bus is twice an hour), but most visitors take the Metro as the bus fare is only slightly cheaper and the journey longer. For further information on bus services, contact **Movia** (*see p239*).

By rail

DSB (*see p239*) connects Copenhagen with most of continental Europe's capitals. It also connects to the UK, though you have to change trains either in the Netherlands or in Germany. All international trains arrive and depart from Central Station (Hovedbanegård).

By road

The Danish capital is 300km (186 miles) from the German border, and only 30mins' drive to Malmö in Sweden. **Eurolines** runs express coaches to and from Copenhagen.

Danish Road Directorate *(72 44 33 33, Traffic Information Centre 70 10 10 40, www.vejdirektoratet.dk).* ***Open*** *Traffic Information Centre 24hrs daily.*
Route, roadworks and traffic info.

By sea

There are direct ferries between Copenhagen and Oslo in Norway (16hrs) and Swinoujscie in Poland (10hrs). In addition, there's a ferry route from Helsingør (47km/28 miles north of Copenhagen) to Sweden; from Esbjerg (200km/124 miles west) to the UK; from Rødby (150km/93 miles south) to Germany; and from Frederikshavn or Hirtshals (450km/280 miles north-west) to Sweden and Norway.

DFDS Seaways *Dampfærgevej 30, Østerbro (33 42 30 00, www.dfdsseaways.dk).* ***Open*** *Phone enquiries 9am-5pm Mon-Fri, 11am-2pm Sat-Sun and public holidays.*
Copenhagen–Oslo; Esbjerg–Harwich.

Scandlines *Copenhagen office: Dampfærgevej 10, Østerbro (33 15 15 15, www.scandlines.dk).* ***Open*** *Phone enquiries 8am-6pm Mon-Fri, 9am-6pm Sat-Sun.*
Helsingør–Helsingborg.

PUBLIC TRANSPORT

Trains, Metro & buses

Copenhagen is blessed with an efficient network of local buses (Trafikselskabet Movia), trains (S-tog) run by Danish State Railways (De Danske Statsbaner, **DSB**; *see p239*), and the smart Metro system, which is in the process of being extended.

The **Metro** has 2 lines, M1 and M2, plus a City Ring. The main M lines run from Vanløse in the north-west to Vestamager and the airport, respectively. Both lines run through Nørreport, Kongens Nytorv and Christianshavn. The driverless, automatic trains run roughly every 4-6mins (every 15-20mins at night), 24hrs daily. For fares, *see right*.

From summer 2019, the new 'City Ring' offers more routes around the city by Metro. The first new line is the Circle Line, linking Frederiksberg, Central Station, Nørrebro, Østerbro's Trianglen and Kongens Nytorv, with 17 stations in total. From 2020 lines will also run to Sydhavn and Nordhavn. For further information about the Metro, call 33 11 17 00 or visit www.m.dk.

The **S-tog local train** system is made up of 7 lines, 6 of which pass through Central Station (København H).

Handily, the buses, S-tog trains and the Metro all use the same ticket system and zoned fare structure. There's a map of the S-tog system and Metro lines on p255 of this guide.

Trains and buses run from 5am Mon-Sat (from 6am on Sun) until around 12.30am, although some buses do run through the night.

Movia *Gammel Køge Landevej 3, Valby (70 15 70 00, www.moviatrafik.dk). Train Valby.* ***Open*** *Phone enquiries 7am-9.30pm daily. No cards.* ***Map*** *p250 O12.*
The Movia office can supply journey plans, timetables, discount cards and lost property information. They also recommend the website www.dinoffentligetransport.dk.

Fares & discount cards

The Copenhagen metropolitan area is split into 7 zones, rings radiating out from the centre of the city. The basic ticket allows passengers to travel within 2 zones on a variety of transport: buses, trains and the Metro. It costs 24kr (12kr 12-15s; free under-12s when travelling with an adult, though no more than two under-12s can travel on one adult ticket). As the 2 central zones include almost every attraction, hotel, restaurant and bar covered in this guide, it's unlikely that visitors will need to buy anything more than this basic ticket (apart from when travelling to and from the airport, when a 3-zone ticket is needed, *see p238*).

Such a ticket also allows transfers between buses and trains. All tickets are stamped with the date, time and departure zone. From the stamped time 2- and 3-zone tickets are valid for a period of 1hr; 4- to 6-zone tickets can be used for 1.5hrs; all-zone tickets are valid for 2hrs.

Tickets are sold at all railway station ticket offices. They can also be purchased from machines at stations, and from bus drivers. 7-Eleven kiosks at the train and Metro stations also sell tickets. Coloured zone maps can be found at bus stops and in railway stations.

Children

Two children aged under 12 can travel free when accompanied by an adult. Children aged 12-15 pay the child fare or can use a child's discount card. Two 12-15s can travel on one adult ticket or on one clip of an adult's discount card.

Rejsekort

Rejsekortet, a travel card popular with commuters and frequent travellers in Denmark, offers the best rates for public transport. Foreign visitors can opt for Rejsekort Anonymous, which does not require an address in Denmark or any personal details. You can buy it at Copenhagen Central Station's ticket office and several other places. Users tap in and out at blue points throughout their journey. The card itself costs 80kr, and when you buy it, it will come charged with 100kr for your future travels. Find out more information at www.dinoffentligetransport.dk.

City Pass

This ticket allows unlimited travel within zones 1, 2, 3 and 4 for 24, 48, 72 and 120hrs on Copenhagen's buses and trains. It costs 80kr (40kr 12-16s) for 24 hrs and must be clipped in the yellow machines in buses and stations at the start of the journey. No more than 2 children under 12 can travel free with an adult holding a 24-hr ticket. The ticket can be bought from manned rail stations. An all-zone 72-hr City Pass costs 200kr (100kr 12-16s).

Copenhagen Card

As well as free admission to 86 museums, galleries and sights, the Copenhagen Card offers unlimited travel by bus and train within Greater Copenhagen. Cards are available in 4 formats: 24, 48, 72 or 120hrs, costing €54, €77, €93 and €121, respectively (note: euros, not kroner). Children's versions cost around half the price of an adult card. The card can be bought from DSB ticket offices in Rådhuspladsen and Toftegårds Plads. It can also be purchased at main stations, most tourist offices and from many hotels (the full list can be found online); you can also buy online at copenhagencard.com.

National rail system

For mapping out journeys and itineraries, **DSB** has an excellent integrated journey planner on its website (www.dsb.dk) for rail (and bus) journeys within Denmark. The journey-planning website **Rejseplanen** (www.rejseplanen.dk) is also useful for finding train departure times. Both websites have English versions.

DSB *Central Station (Customer Service 70 13 14 15, www.dsb.dk).* ***Open*** *8am-6pm Mon-Fri and 8am-3pm Sat-Sun.* ***Map*** *p66 M15.*

Waterbuses

The municipal harbour buses are a cheap alternative to the commercial canal tours that run along the harbourfront, and a useful way of getting from Indre By (the inner city) to Holmen or Amager, though timetables can be fairly limited.

There are 3 routes, which go along or across the harbourfront:

route **991** starts at Refshaleøen and stops at Nordre Toldbod, Holmen North, Opera, Nyhavn, Knippelsbro and the Black Diamond, Bryggebroen and Teglholmen. Route **992** goes the other way, stopping at exactly the same places. There is a third line, route **993**, that serves as a shuttle service between Nyhavn, Experimentarium and Operaen; it runs 9am-6pm Mon-Fri, and between the Operaen and Nyhavn only 6pm-11pm.

Harbour buses are operated by **Movia** (*see p239*) and are integrated into the public transport system, so ticket prices are the same as Metro and S-tog train tickets (*see p239*). Check timetables at dinoffentligetransport.dk.

Strömma (www.stromma.dk) also runs 3 hop-on, hop-off waterbus routes around the harbour area. 48-hr tickets cost 105kr (53kr 6-15s, free under-6s).

TAXIS

Taxis can be flagged down just about anywhere in Copenhagen. If the yellow 'Taxa' light on the roof of the car is illuminated, the taxi is available for hire. The basic fare is 40kr plus 8.50kr per km (rising to 13kr at weekends and up to 17kr at night). Fares include a service charge, so there's no need to tip. Cabs accept credit cards.

DRIVING

When it comes to driving, we have one word of advice: don't. The Danes, or rather their government, detest private cars and do everything to discourage their use.

If you can't do without wheels, here are some tips. The Danes drive on the right. When turning right, drivers give way to cyclists coming up on the inside and to pedestrians crossing on a green light. You must drive with dipped headlights during the day. Drivers have to pay for parking at most places within the city centre from 8am on Mon to 5pm on Sat; only Sun parking is free of charge.

Car hire

Avis, **Budget Rent a Car** and **Europcar** all have offices at Copenhagen Airport, Terminal 3 (*see p238*) and in the city centre.

Breakdown services

Falck *Emergency 70 10 20 30, www.falck.com.* ***Open*** *24hrs daily.*

CYCLING

Cycling is very popular. In summer you can borrow a City Bike (Bycyklen; www.bycyklen.dk) from one of the many ranks throughout the city centre (*see p60* Bike Copenhagen). It is also easy to rent a Donkey bike by the hour from the street – just download their app and look out for the orange bicycles.

Bike hire

Baisikeli *Ingerslevsgade 80, Vesterbro (26 70 02 29, www.baisikeli.dk). Train Dybbølsbro.* ***Open*** *10am-6pm daily. Rates 50kr-110kr/6hrs; 80kr-140kr/24hrs; 270kr-500kr/wk. No deposit.* ***Map*** *p136 L18.*
This laid-back, ethical bike-hire place has competitive rates. No deposit is required, but customers need to bring a valid passport or driving license. Profits go towards financing the collection and shipment of used bicycles to Africa (hence the name: *baisikeli* means bicycle in Swahili). It also has a good bike shop attached, and a nearby café.

Copenhagen Bicycles *Nyhavn 44, Indre By (35 43 01 22, www.copenhagenbicycles.dk). Metro Kongens Nytorv.* ***Open*** *9.30am-5.30pm daily. Rates 110kr/6hrs; 120kr/24hrs; 430kr/wk. Deposit (cash) 1,000kr.* ***Map*** *p100 T13.*

Københavns Cyklebørs *Gothersgade 157, Indre By (33 14 07 17, www.cykelboersen.dk). Metro/train Nørreport.* ***Open*** *10am-5.30pm Mon-Fri; 10am-2pm Sat, Sun. Rates 90kr-115kr/day; 450kr-700kr/wk. Deposit 300kr-500kr.* ***Map*** *p100 N10.*

Organisations

Dansk Cyklist Forbund *Rømersgade 5-7, Indre By (33 32 31 21, www.cyklistforbundet.dk). Metro/train Nørreport. Secretariat 10am-noon, 1pm-3pm Mon-Fri. Bike shop 10am-6pm Mon-Fri; 11am-3pm Sat.* ***Map*** *p100 N11.*
The Danish Cyclists Federation has cycling maps, an excellent website and runs cycling tours.

WALKING

Compact, flat Copenhagen is the ideal walking city. Even the main shopping street, Strøget, is pedestrianised. For organised walking tours, *see p62*.

Resources A-Z

Travel Advice

For up-to-date information on travel to a specific country – including the latest on safety and security, health issues, local laws and customs – contact your home country government's department of foreign affairs. Most have websites with useful advice for would-be travellers.

AUSTRALIA
www.smartraveller.gov.au

CANADA
www.voyage.gc.ca

NEW ZEALAND
www.safetravel.govt.nz

REPUBLIC OF IRELAND
foreignaffairs.gov.ie

UK
www.fco.gov.uk/travel

USA
www.state.gov/travel

ACCIDENT & EMERGENCY

Emergency *112*
Fire, ambulance or police.

Medical Helpline *1813*
National emergency line for out-of-hours medical issues.

Police *114*
Non-emergency.

ADDRESSES

Addresses in Denmark are formatted with the street name first, followed by the number.

AGE RESTRICTIONS

Drinking alcohol in a bar 18
Driving 18
Buying/smoking cigarettes 18
Sex 15

ATTITUDE & ETIQUETTE

Danish people have a reputation for being cold. They are not – it's just that they are more likely to wait until you ask for help or directions than offer it unbidden. Usually, all you have to do is ask. Danish people are humble, modest and reserved in general, and a lot of fun as well. They also tend to be very direct – it's a cultural norm in these parts to be told the unvarnished truth. Take it on the chin and know that it isn't meant harshly – sugar coating things is not the way things are done here. Bring a positive attitude and it will be reflected back at you.

Culturally, Copenhagen is a little quieter in volume than many major European cities – talking loudly on your phone might be frowned upon and being noisy in public spaces marks you out as a tourist. Remember that everyone speaks great English in this city, so it's best not to criticise it loudly in public.

In terms of serious etiquette breaches, most Danes are forgiving, especially with tourists who apologise. Make sure you understand the rules of the road before jumping on a bike in the city, signal clearly and try to avoid rush hour on the bike lanes (8am-9am and 4pm-5pm) or expect to be sternly reprimanded.

CLIMATE

The climate in Denmark isn't particularly severe. In midsummer it hardly gets dark at all and the evening light can last well past 10pm. However, winter is cold, wet and dark and some tourist attractions are closed. Tivoli, for example, is closed for most of the winter aside from Halloween and Christmas. Spring kicks off in late April, but can take a while to warm up. May and June are usually fresh and bright, with reasonable temperatures. Summer peak season is in July and August, when Copenhagen offers plenty of festivals and open-air events. July is also when all of Copenhagen migrates to the seaside for its summer holidays, so the city can seem quieter and many top restaurants and some other businesses are closed (*see also p245*).

CONSUMER RIGHTS

The Consumer Complaints Board (www.en.kfst.dk/consumer/the-consumer-complaints-board/, 41 71 50 98) handles consumer complaints relating to goods and services. There is a small fee (160kr) to submit a complaint, and the issue must concern goods or services costing over 500kr (depending on the goods or service).

CUSTOMS

Those aged 16 or over can import wine and beer from inside the EU, but you have to be aged 18 or over to import spirits and tobacco. From outside the EU you must be 17 or over to use the alcohol and tobacco allowance, including beer.

It is forbidden to import fresh foods into Denmark unless they are vacuum-packed.

Although duty-free goods within the EU were abolished in 1999 and there is now no legal limit on the quantities of alcohol and tobacco travellers may import into most EU countries (provided they are for personal use), Denmark, Finland and Sweden will continue to impose limits for the foreseeable future.

For enquiries about customs regulations, phone 72 22 18 18 or check the website www.skat.dk which is also available in English.

DISABLED TRAVELLERS

Facilities for disabled travellers in Copenhagen are generally excellent, compared with other European capitals. The website www.godadgang.dk/gb/main.asp has information in English on hotels and attractions in Copenhagen from an accessibility perspective.

Much Danish tourist literature, including the Visit Copenhagen website (www.visitcopenhagen.com), lists places that are wheelchair-accessible plus useful information on specific facilities for the disabled.

The following Danish organisations may prove helpful:

Dansk Handicap Forbund *Blekinge Boulevard 2 DK-2630 Taastrup (39 29 35 55, www.danskhandicapforbund.dk).* ***Open*** *Phone enquiries 10am-3pm Mon-Thur; 10am-1pm Fri.* Staff members speak English and may be able to help tourists, but members have priority.

Socialstyrelsen *Edisonsvej 1, 1st floor, 5000 Odense C (72 42 37 00, www.socialstyrelsen.dk).* ***Open*** *Phone enquiries 9am-3.30pm Mon-Thur; 9am-3pm Fri.* Socialstyrelsen ('Right to Use') can give information about a variety of subjects relating to physical disability in Denmark.

DRUGS

Hard and soft drugs are illegal in Denmark. Typically, the punishment for possession of small amounts of cannabis for personal use is a fine. Larger quantities generally result in a prison sentence. Christiania, the city's legendary hippie commune, has an extremely tolerant attitude towards drug use; weed is sold openly on the street and the area is not policed.

ELECTRICITY

Denmark, in common with most of Europe, has 220-volt AC, 50Hz current and uses two-pin continental plugs. Visitors from the UK will need to buy an adaptor for their appliances, while North Americans won't be able to use their 110/125V appliances without a transformer.

EMBASSIES & CONSULATES

Several embassies – including the British, Irish and US ones – are located in the area around Østerport train station, on the border of Østerbro and the city centre.

British Embassy *Kastelsvej 36-40, off Classensgade, Østerbro (35 44 52 00, www.britishembassy.dk). Train Østerport.* ***Open*** *9am-5pm Mon-Fri. Visa dept (by appt only) 9am-11am Mon-Fri.* ***Map*** *p152 R6.*

Canadian Embassy *Kristen Bernikowsgade 1, Indre By (33 48 32 00, www.canadainternational.gc.ca). Metro Kongens Nytorv.* ***Open*** *8.30am-noon, 1pm-4.30pm Mon-Fri.* ***Map*** *p66 Q13.*

Irish Embassy *Østbanegade 21, Østerbro (35 47 32 00, www.embassyofireland.dk). Train Østerport.* ***Open*** *10am-12.30pm Mon-Wed, Fri; 10am-12.30pm, 2.30pm-4.30pm Thur.* ***Map*** *p152 S6.*

US Embassy *Dag Hammarskjöld Allé 24, Østerbro (35 41 71 00, dk.usembassy.gov).* ***Open*** *Phone enquiries 8.30am-5pm daily.* ***Map*** *p100 Q7.*

For all other embassies, see http://embassy.goabroad.com.

HEALTH

All temporary foreign visitors to Denmark are entitled to free emergency medical and hospital treatment if they are taken ill or have an accident. Citizens of EU countries should obtain a European Health Insurance Card (or equivalent) before travelling. The EHIC entitles you to state-provided medical treatment that may become necessary during your trip. Any treatment provided is on the same terms as Danish nationals. Before you consult a doctor or hospital make sure that they accept the EHIC. Any costs incurred for private healthcare are non-refundable and not covered by the EHIC, but may be covered by travel insurance. For more information, visit www.gov.uk/european-health-insurance-card.

It is imperative for British citizens to check their entitlement to the EHIC health provision before travel – at time of writing, healthcare arrangements are in flux due to Brexit. The best advice is to check on the NHS

Local Weather

Average monthly temperatures and rainfall in Copenhagen

	High (°C/°F)	Low (°C/°F)	Rainfall (mm/in)
January	2 / 36	-2 / 28	40 / 1.57
February	4 / 39	-3 / 27	20 / 0.78
March	5 / 41	0 / 32	40 / 1.57
April	10 / 50	2 / 36	30 / 1.18
May	16 / 61	7 / 45	40 / 1.57
June	19 / 66	11 / 52	60 / 2.36
July	21 / 70	13 / 55	60 / 2.36
August	21 / 70	12 / 54	60 / 2.36
September	17 / 63	10 / 50	60 / 2.36
October	12 / 54	7 / 45	50 / 1.97
November	7 / 45	3 / 37	60 / 2.36
December	4 / 39	0 / 32	50 / 1.97

website or fco.gov.uk to get the most up-to-date information.

Citizens of non-EU countries should have adequate health insurance before travelling.

Dentists

Tourist offices (*see p247*) can refer foreign visitors to local dentists.

Emergency Dental Service *Oslo Plads 14 (1813, www.tandvagt.dk). Train Østerport.* ***Open*** *8pm-9.30pm Mon-Fri; 10 am-noon, 8-9.30pm Sat, Sun.* ***Map*** *p152 R7.*

Doctors

Lægelinien *(25 96 93 75, www.laegelinien.dk).* Telephone consultations and prescriptions from 130kr; hotel and house calls from 1,200kr.

Pharmacies

Look for the green 'a' '*apotek*' sign.

City Helse *Vendersgade 6, Indre By (33 14 08 92, www.cityhelse.dk). Metro/train Nørreport.* ***Open*** *9.30am-5.30pm Mon-Thur; 9.30am-6pm Fri; 9.30am-2:30pm Sat.* ***Map*** *p100 N11.* City Helse stocks a good selection of health food and natural medicine.

Steno Apotek *Vesterbrogade 6C, Indre By. (33 14 82 66). Metro/train København H.* ***Open*** *24hrs daily.* ***Map*** *p66 M15.*

ID

To access much of Denmark's social system, it is necessary to have a Yellow Card or ID card. It is only available for those who live in Denmark.

INSURANCE

Comprehensive travel insurance is recommended for all travellers. This includes EU nationals who are entitled to use the Danish healthcare service (*see p242* Health), as private travel insurance can also cover you for stolen or lost cash or valuables and for repatriation should it be necessary. Although there are generally no activities that would require extra cover in Copenhagen, it is important to check that your coverage is adequate before travelling.

LANGUAGE

Danish is the national language and is spoken everywhere. *See p248* Vocabulary. For language classes, *see p246*. English is spoken widely by people of all ages.

LEFT LUGGAGE

Travellers can avoid schlepping their bags unnecessarily around town by using one of several left-luggage options.

Copenhagen Airport Terminal 2 (www.cph.dk/en/practical/luggage/luggage-deposit) has baggage lockers by Parkeringshus 4 (P4), costing 60kr-120kr for 24hrs. Pay by credit card for a period of 4hrs-24hrs. You can also pay for storage for up to 7 days.

Copenhagen Central Station has luggage storage by the exit to Istedgade. Lockers cost 60kr-70kr for 24 hrs, depending on the size, and there is a staffed facility costing 65kr-75kr per 24hrs. Storage is available for up to 10 days.

Luggage Hero (luggagehero.com) stores your bags in certified hotels and shops from €1 and not more than €10 per day (quoted in euros, not kroner). Insurance is included and you pay online (so cash is not necessary).

LEGAL HELP

Copenhagen Legal Aid *Stormgade 20, 1st floor, 1555 Copenhagen V (www.copenhagenlegalaid.com/front-page, 33 11 06 78).* They provide legal advice to any citizen, Danish or not, in the city. Visit them personally or call 6.30pm-9pm Mon-Thu, 6.30pm-8pm Fri. Telephones are open from 7:30pm.

LGBT

Equality-driven Copenhagen is welcoming to LGBT travellers and prides itself on being one of the most LGBT-friendly destinations in Europe. The tourist board offers plenty of frequently updated advice on its website, www.visitcopenhagen.com/gaycopenhagen.

There are a couple of key LGBT events celebrated widely in the city. **Copenhagen Pride** (*see p186*) takes place in Aug with a parade running from the city center to City Hall Square. Oct sees **MIX Copenhagen** LGBTQ film festival (*see p187*).

LGBT Danmark – Landsforeningen for Bøsser, Lesbiske, Biseksuelle og Transpersoner (LGBT) *Nygade 7, Indre By (33 13 19 48, www.lgbt.dk). Bus 11A, 14.* ***Open*** *Phone enquiries 2-5pm Thur.* ***Map*** *p66 O13.* Denmark's national association for gays, lesbians, bisexuals and transgender persons was founded in 1948, and prides itself on being at the vanguard of gay politics.

Stop Aids *Vestergade 18E (88 33 56 00, www.aidsfondet.dk). Bus 11A, 14.* ***Open*** *Phone enquiries 10am-4pm Mon-Thur; 10am-3pm Fri.* ***Map*** *p66 N14.* Stop Aids has been promoting safe sex in Denmark since 1986. Its refreshing approach has included putting up condom-and-lube compartments in cruising parks, offering numerous free workshops and courses, distributing safe-sex kits in gay bars and at larger one-off parties, and providing free massages in exchange for a chat about safe sex.

LIBRARIES

Hovedbiblioteket *Krystalgade 15, Indre By (33 73 60 60, www.bibliotek.kk.dk). Metro/train Nørreport.* ***Open*** *8am-9pm Mon-Fri; 8am-5pm Sat; 11am-4 pm Sun (check website to confirm).* ***Map*** *p66 O12.* The central library has international newspapers, magazines in English and colour photocopying.

Det Kongelige Bibliotek *Søren Kierkegaards Plads 1, Indre By (33 47 47 47). Metro Kongens Nytorv.* ***Open*** *8am-9pm Mon-Fri; 9am-7pm Sat. Study rooms 9am-7pm Mon-Fri. Exhibitions 10am-7pm Mon-Fri, 10am-6pm Sat. All departments close at 7pm during July & Aug.* ***Admission*** *Main building & library free.*

Exhibitions free-50kr. Concerts vary. ***Map*** *p66 R15.* Denmark's national library also serves as a general research centre, a cultural centre and a meeting place.

LOST/STOLEN PROPERTY

The main lost property office is:

Copenhagen Police *Hittegodskontoret 1567, København V (38 74 88 22).* ***Open*** *9am-2pm Mon-Fri.* ***Map*** *p66 O16.*

Airport

If you lose luggage or other possessions on a plane, contact the relevant airline. Any lost possessions at the airport will be registered online at www.cph.dk and kept for 30 days before being moved to the police lost property office (*see p244*).

Buses & trains

If you lose something on a bus, call DOT general information (70 15 70 00; 8am-6pm Mon-Fri, 8am-6pm Sat-Sun). If you lose it on a train, call DOT general information (same number) every day 7am-8pm, and if on the Metro dial the same number Mon-Fri 8am-4pm.

Taxis

Call the taxi company. After a couple of days, items will be transferred to the central police lost property office (*see above*).

MEDIA

Newspapers & magazines

For a small population, there is a surprisingly large range of news sources. Copenhagen's newspapers and magazines focus of course on international issues as well as local ones, and typically have good coverage of the city.

Berlingske *(www.berlingske.dk).* A conservative, right-of-centre broadsheet with decent coverage of Copenhagen.

Børsen *(borsen.dk). Børsen* keeps tabs on the latest stock-market developments, economic predictions and the major players in the Danish financial world.

Ekstrabladet *(ekstrabladet.dk).* The country's best known tabloid newspaper, *Ekstrabladet* relies heavily on celebrity sleaze, opinionated editorials and endless reactionary campaigning.

Information *(www.information.dk).* Founded as 'the newspaper of the Danish Resistance' on the night of Denmark's liberation at the end of World War II. Today, the paper has no significant political leaning, its objective being to give its readers important background information on current affairs.

Jyllandsposten *(jyllands-posten.dk).* The most royalist and conservative of the national papers.

Politiken *(politiken.dk).* Once the paper of the Social-Liberal Party, *Politiken* now focuses on cultural issues. Strong on Copenhagen matters, with a good weekend section.

English-language press

Copenhagen Post *(www.cphpost.dk).* News coverage of Denmark and international issues in English.

The Local *(www.thelocal.dk).* Generally good coverage of Danish news, plus jobs and expat issues, in English.

Radio

Copenhagen's main radio stations are run by the state-owned **DR** (Danish Broadcasting Corporation, formerly called Danmarks Radio), which has a fine tradition of high-quality programming. Since 2017, they have been available on DAB and online.

P1 *90.8 MHz, www.dr.dk/radio/p1.* News, documentaries, political debates, education, general cultural, scientific and social programming.

P2 *88.0 MHz, www.dr.dk/radio/p2.* Classical music and jazz.

P3 *93.9 MHz, www.dr.dk/radio/p3.* Pop and chart music during the day, plus more alternative content at night. Broadcasts 24hrs a day.

P4/Københavns Radio *96.5 MHz, www.dr.dk/radio/p4kbh.* Features pop music, listeners' requests, phone-ins, local news and traffic reports.

P6 Digital-only channel with a focus on alternative music.

The Voice *104.9 MHz, radioplay.dk/the-voice.* A 24-hr chart/dance music station, The Voice is the only commercial station with more than a million listeners a week.

Television

Founded as a public service organisation and funded by individual licence fees, **DR** still dominates the television scene. It can be accessed online at www.dr.dk. Netflix is also widely available, with a small selection of Danish-language films and series (subtitled), and BBC Nordic and HBO Nordic offer subscription-based streamed TV shows too.

DR1 The first television channel in Denmark, DR1's strengths include news and current affairs, documentaries, and children's and youth programming. English-language programmes are subtitled not dubbed.

DR2 The little sister to DR1 and a slightly more alternative watch.

TV2 Despite introducing morning television and *Wheel of Fortune* to the Danes, TV2 pretty much resembles DR1, principally because TV2 is also a licence-financed station, with similar public-service obligations.

TV3/TV3+ *www.tv3.dk.* Targeting young people and families, TV3 is a commercial station that aims to provide quality light entertainment, with Danish soap operas and docu-soaps among the most popular programmes. Its sister channel TV3+ is the leading station for sport.

Kanal 5 Most of the programmes on Kanal 5 (a subscription channel previously known as TVDanmark1) are American sitcoms and soaps, though it occasionally broadcasts Danish docu-soaps.

MONEY

The Danish *krone* (crown) is divided into 100*øre*. There are coins in denominations of 50*øre* (copper), 1kr, 2kr, 5kr (all 3 silver in colour, the latter 2 with a hole), 10kr and 20kr (both brass). Notes come in 50, 100, 200, 500 and 1,000kr denominations. The abbreviation 'kr' and the crown symbol ♛ is used in this guide, though you may also see 'DKK' or 'KR' before the figure in question.

There is no limit to the amount of foreign or Danish currency you can bring into the country, though you will be required to explain the source of amounts over €10,000 (roughly 75,000kr).

Copenhagen is a largely cash-free city – you can pay for just about anything, whatever the amount, with a bank card. Contactless is generally preferred. The app Mobilepay (available only to those who have a Danish or Finnish bank account) is also in use all over the city, allowing for easy peer-to-peer payments. In some circumstances, for example at a flea market, payment is primarily by Mobilepay or cash.

Occasionally, in the most tourist-focused areas of the city, prices are given in euros, but payment is not typically accepted in euros outside these locations.

Banks & bureaux de change

Banks in Denmark tend to open 10am-4pm on weekdays, with late opening until 5.30pm on Thur. Some in the city centre have longer hours and open on Sat. Most will change foreign currency, as will bureaux de change.

Tax

Tax on goods (MOMS) in Denmark is levied at 25%. Non-EU residents are entitled to claim back up to 19% of the total price of any item bought in the country (providing that the purchase exceeds 300kr and that Denmark is their final EU destination before returning home). Visitors should ask shops to issue a Blue Tax Free Cheque for each purchase. These can then be stamped and handed in at the Global Blue desk in the Arkaden, between Copenhagen Airport's Terminals 2 and 3 (6am-9pm daily). For further information, contact Global Blue Danmark (32 52 55 66, www.global-blue.com).

OPENING HOURS

Most shops in Copenhagen open 10am-6pm Mon-Thur; 10am-7pm Fri; 10am-4pm Sat; and noon-4pm Sun (although in some areas only bakers, florists and souvenir shops will be open on Sun). Office hours are usually 9am-4pm Mon-Fri.

POLICE

In the unlikely event that you're a victim of crime, contact the Danish Police immediately. In emergencies, call 112 (free of charge), or dial 114 to be connected to your nearest local station. Open 24hrs, the Police HQ can direct you to your nearest station. These include Central Station (35 21 95 45; map *p66 M15*); and Halmtorvet 20, Vesterbro (38 74 88 22; map *p136 L16*). To connect with any local or sub-station in a non-emergency situation, dial the Police HQ switchboard (33 14 88 88) and they will connect you.

Police Headquarters *Polititorvet (33 14 14 48). **Open** 24hrs daily. **Map** p66 O16.*

POSTAL SERVICES

Most post offices open 10am-5.30pm Mon-Fri; 10am/11am-noon/2pm Sat. Copenhagen's largest post office is:

Post Office Pilestræde
*Pilestræde 58, 1112 Copenhagen K (www.postdanmark.dk). **Open** 8.30am-7pm Mon-Fri; 8.30am-2pm Sat, closed Sun. **Map** p66 P12.*

Postal rates

In addition to the rates below, express delivery services are also available. Contact any post office for details. Letters up to 50g cost 9kr within Denmark, and 27kr to other countries; letters up to 100g cost 18kr within Denmark and 27kr to other countries.

PUBLIC HOLIDAYS

All shops – including supermarkets – will normally be closed on public holidays and the majority of museums and galleries will either be closed or have limited opening hours. Note that as Christmas is celebrated on 24 Dec in Denmark, shops and attractions are closed on that day. They are also closed on 31 Dec for New Year's Eve. The following days are observed as public holidays across Denmark.

New Year's Day Nytårsdag *1 Jan*
Maundy Thursday Skærtorsdag *9 Apr 2020, 1 Apr 2021*
Good Friday Langfredag *10 Apr 2020, 2 Apr 2021*
Easter Sunday Påske *12 Apr 2020, 4 Apr 2021*
Easter Monday Påskedag *13 Apr 2020, 5 Apr 2021*
Common Prayer Day Store Bededag *8 May 2020, 30 Apr 2021*
Ascension Day Kristi Himmelfartsdag *21 May 2020, 13 May 2021*
Whit Sunday Pinsedag *31 May 2020, 23 May 2021*
Whit Monday Pinsedag *1 June 2020, 24 May 2021*
Constitution Day Grundlovsdag *5 June, from noon*
Christmas Jule *24-26 Dec*

RELIGION

There are close ties between Church and State in Denmark, and the Constitution declares the Evangelical Lutheran Church to be the national church. The Danish Folkekirken (People's Church) is funded by church members through a 'Church Tax', but in spite of the fact that most Danes (75.9%) are members, only a minority of Copenhageners would call themselves religious. Churches are often empty on Sun, and are mainly used at Christmas, Easter, or for private arrangements such as weddings. The second largest religious community in Denmark is Muslim; the third, Roman Catholic. The following churches hold services in English.

St Alban's Church (Anglican) *Churchillparken, Langelinie (www.st-albans.*

dk). Bus 1A, 15. ***Services*** *Holy Communion 10.30am Wed; 10.30am Sun.* ***Map*** *p100 U9.*

Great Synagogue (Orthodox Judaism) *Krystalgade 12, Indre By (33 12 88 68). Metro/train Nørreport.* ***Services*** *3 times a day with the largest congregation on Sat mornings. Check mosaiske.dk for times.* ***Map*** *p66 O12.*

Sakrementskirken (Roman Catholic) *Nørrebrogade 27, Nørrebro (26 70 46 76, sakramentskirken.dk). Bus 5A.* ***Services*** *5pm Wed (English); 10.00am Sun (Danish); 5.30pm Sun (English).* ***Map*** *p152 L9.*

Sankt Annæ Kirke (Roman Catholic) *Dronning Elisabeths Allé 3, Amager (32 58 41 02, saintanneschurch.dk). Bus 5C.* ***Services*** *in English: 5pm Sun and 4.30pm Sat.*

SAFETY & SECURITY

Copenhagen is generally safe compared with other cities in Europe and women can feel confident walking around the city alone. There are places where you should exercise caution late at night, however. These include side streets in Vesterbro, and the area around Rådhuspladsen stretching part of the way up Strøget – drunken violence is fairly common here at night. The area behind Central Station stretching along the first half of Istedgade is a hangout for alcoholics and junkies, but they are peaceable in the main. In the unlikely event that you're a victim of crime, contact the Danish Police immediately (*see p245* Police).

SMOKING

Smoking is banned in all indoor public spaces in Denmark, including public transport, cinemas and (most) cafés and restaurants, though some bars and small *bodegas* still allow smoking.

STUDY

Danish institutions for higher education have a friendly and open-minded policy towards international students. Exchange programmes provide links between Danish universities and their international counterparts, and in recent years exchanges have increasingly been developed through programmes such as Socrates/Erasmus, Lingua and Tempus, which are all supported by the largesse of the European Union. Some of the institutions also have summer schools and the largest universities and colleges have their own international offices.

Colleges & universities

The **University of Copenhagen** (35 32 26 26, www.ku.dk) is the city's flagship establishment. Founded in 1479, it is Denmark's oldest educational institution, and, with over 38,000 students, can also lay claim to being the largest.

The city has 2 business schools, **Copenhagen Business School** (38 15 38 15, www.cbs.dk) and **Niels Brock College** (33 41 91 00, copenhagenbusiness college.com).

Det Kongelige Danske Kunstakademi (www.kunstakademiet.dk), the Royal Academy of Fine Arts, offers a variety of fine-art courses and tutoring, as well as incorporating the **School of Architecture** (41 70 15 00, kadk.dk), the excellent **Danish Film School** (32 68 64 00, www.filmskolen.dk), the **National Drama School** (41 72 20 00, ddsks.dk) and the **Rhythmic Music Conservatory** (41 88 25 00, www.rmc.dk).

Det Kongelige Danske Musikkonservatorium (72 26 72 26, www.dkdm.dk), the Royal Danish Music Conservatory, offers classical music training.

Language classes

Berlitz *Borgergade 28, 1300 Copenhagen K, (70 21 50 10, www.berlitz.com).* ***Open*** *8am-9pm Mon-Fri.* ***Map*** *p100 R10.* Courses are taught by native speakers; most are tailored to individual needs.

KBH Sprogcenter *Valdemarsgade 16, 1665 Copenhagen V (33 21 31 31, kbh-sprogcenter.dk).* ***Map*** *p136 H16.* Offers language classes at all levels and has great social media feeds to help you learn and enjoy the quirkier side of the Danish language.

TELEPHONES

Danish phone numbers have 8 digits and there are no area codes.

Dialling & codes

The international dialling code for Denmark is 45. To dial Copenhagen from outside Denmark, dial the international code (00 in the UK, 001 from the USA) then 45 for Denmark followed by the 8-digit number.

To call abroad from Denmark, dial 00 followed by the country access code, the area code (minus the initial 0, if there is one), and then the local number. International codes are as follows: Australia 61, Canada 1, Irish Republic 353, United Kingdon 44, USA 1.

Mobile phones

Denmark is part of the worldwide GSM network, so compatible mobile phones should work without any problems.

TIME

Denmark observes Central European Time, 1hr ahead of Greenwich Mean Time, and 6hrs ahead of Eastern Standard Time. Danes typically use the 24-hr clock.

TIPPING

Service is included on hotel and restaurant bills, so tips should only be given for unusually good service. It's common practice to round up a bill. Similarly, it is not necessary to tip taxi drivers.

TOILETS

Public toilets are easy to find in libraries, department stores and train stations. Restaurants, cafés and museums have toilets for their guests. There is a public toilet at Torvehallerne serving the market square.

TOURIST INFORMATION

Danish Tourist Board *(32 88 99 00, www.visitdenmark.com).* If you plan to travel beyond the capital, check out the DTB's website – it's very useful for both practical advice and news about forthcoming attractions. The DTB doesn't encourage personal callers.

Visit Copenhagen Tourist Information Bureau *Vesterbrogade 4A, Tivoli & Rådhuspladsen (70 22 24 42, www.visitcopenhagen.dk).* ***Open*** *July, Aug 9am-8pm Mon-Fri; 9am-6pm Sat-Sun. Jan-Feb 9am-4pm Mon-Sat; 9am-2pm Sun. Mar-Apr 9am-4pm daily. May, June, Sept 9am-6pm Mon-Sat; 9am-4pm Sun. Oct-Nov 9am-4pm Mon-Sat; 9am-2pm Sun. Dec 9am-4pm Mon-Sat; 9am-2pm Sun. Phone enquiries 10am-4pm Mon-Fri, year-round.* ***Map*** *p66 M15.* The official Copenhagen tourist office is located opposite the Radisson Collection Hotel, across the road from Tivoli. It has a wealth of information on the city's attractions as well as a small souvenir shop.

VISAS & IMMIGRATION

Citizens of EU countries (outside Scandinavia) require a national ID card or passport valid for the duration of their stay in order to enter Denmark for tourist visits of up to 3 months within a period of 6 months. Tourists (EU citizens) can stay in the country for another 3 months if they are working or applying for a job. For stays lasting more than 6 months, you need a residency visa. US citizens require a passport valid only for the duration of their stay, but citizens of Canada, Australia and New Zealand require passports valid for 3 months beyond the last day of their visit. South African citizens need to apply for a tourist visa prior to leaving South Africa. For more information, contact the Danish Immigration Service on 35 30 84 90, or visit www.nyi danmark.dk, their multi-language advisory website.

WEIGHTS & MEASURES

Denmark uses the metric system. Decimal points are indicated by commas, while thousands are defined by full stops. In this guide, we have listed measurements in both metric and imperial.

WOMEN

Denmark is a country famously committed to equal opportunities for all citizens and a lot of effort has been made to achieve equal rights for women. Female visitors to Denmark are very unlikely to encounter any harassment problems. *See also p246* Safety & Security.

WORK

Even though most people in Denmark speak English, and many companies use English as a working language, it is still very useful to speak Danish if you want to find a job in Copenhagen. However, the current unemployment rate is very low so there are always some vacancies open to foreigners.

The Local (www.thelocal.dk/jobs) lists job vacancies for English speakers in the city.

The Confederation of Danish Industry runs a series of initiatives aimed at helping international people in Denmark. Their website and magazine *Expat in Denmark* (www.expatindenmark.com) is a good start if you want to understand life in the city. You can also visit their global talent site www.di.dk./globaltalent.

Work permits

All EU citizens can obtain a work permit in Denmark; non-EU citizens must apply for a work permit abroad and hand in the application to a Danish embassy or consular representation. The rules for obtaining work permits vary for different jobs – contact the Danish Immigration Service:

Udlændingestyrelsen *Ryesgade 53, 2100 Copenhagen Ø (35 36 66 00, www.nyidanmark.dk). Bus 3A, 6A.* ***Open*** *9am-3pm Mon-Wed; noon-5pm Thur, Sat; 9am-noon Fri.*

Useful addresses

The EU has a website (www.europa.eu) and helpline (00 800 6789 1011) providing general information on your rights, and useful telephone numbers and addresses in your home country. It also holds specific information on the rules for recognition of diplomas, your rights on access to employment and rights of residence and social security.

For general information about the Danish tax system, see the Skatteministeriet (Danish Ministry of Taxation) website (www.skm.dk) or contact SKAT (Customs and tax administration) with more specific questions.

SKAT *Sluseholmen 8B, 2450 Copenhagen SV (72 22 18 18, www.skat.dk).* ***Open*** *Phone enquiries 9am-5pm Mon; 9am-4pm Tue-Thur; 9am-2pm Fri.*

Vocabulary

Danish, Swedish and Norwegian share similar characteristics, and if you know one of these languages you should be able to get by in the others. And if you are fluent in German, you may also recognise a fair percentage of words. For everyone else, however, Danish is a difficult language.

The problem is pronunciation, which is full of idiosyncrasies, particularly the seemingly endless glottal stops and swallowing of parts of words. On top of that is the fact that a written word rarely sounds as it appears; phonetics is not your friend. Copenhageners are the worst offenders – they are the fastest talkers and are commonly said to speak 'as if they have a potato in their mouths'. Thankfully, the majority of Danes have excellent English and you can easily get by without learning any Danish at all. But, of course, a few basics are often appreciated: thanks (*tak*) is your key word – there isn't a word in this language for please.

Here's a brief guide to pronunciation and some useful basic words and phrases.

Vowels

- **a** *as in 'rather' or as in 'pat'*
- **å, u(n)** *as in 'or'*
- **e(g), e(j)** *as in 'shy'*
- **e, æ** *as in 'set'*
- **i** *as in 'be'*
- **ø** *a short 'er' sound*
- **o** *as in 'rot' or as in 'do'*
- **o(v)** *a short 'ow', as in 'cow'*
- **u** *as in 'bull' or as in 'do'*
- **y** *a long, hybrid of 'ee' and 'oo'*

Consonants

- **sj** *as in 'shot'*
- **ch** *as in 'shot'*
- **c** *as in 'send', but as in 'key' before a, o, u and consonants*
- **(o)d** *as the 'th' in 'those'*
- **j** *as the 'y' in 'year'*
- **g** *as in 'got', when before vowels*
- **h** *as in 'heart'*
- **k** *as in 'key'*
- **b** *as in 'bag'*
- **r** *a short guttural 'r' (less guttural after a vowel)*
- **w** *a 'v' sound*

Useful words & phrases

- **yes** *ja, jo* ('yer', 'yo')
- **no** *nej* ('ny')
- **thank you** *tak* ('tack')
- **hello** (formal) *goddag* ('godday'); **hello** (informal) *hej* ('hi')
- **goodbye** (formal) *farvel* ('fa-vel'); **goodbye** (informal) *hej hej* ('hi hi')
- **I understand** *jeg forstår* ('yie for-stor')
- **I don't understand** *jeg forstår ikke* ('yie for-stor ick')
- **do you speak English?** *taler du engelsk* ('tarler doo engelsk')?
- **excuse me** (sorry) *undskyld* ('unsgull')
- **go away!** *forsvind!* ('for-svin')
- **entrance** *indgang*
- **exit** *udgang*
- **open** *åben*
- **closed** *lukket*
- **toilets** *toiletter* (men *herrer*, women *damer*)

Days & months

- **today** *i dag*
- **tonight** *i aften/i nat*
- **tomorrow** *i morgen*
- **yesterday** *i går*
- **Monday** *mandag*
- **Tuesday** *tirsdag*
- **Wednesday** *onsdag*
- **Thursday** *torsdag*
- **Friday** *fredag*
- **Saturday** *lørdag*
- **Sunday** *søndag*
- **January** *januar*
- **February** *februar*
- **March** *marts*
- **April** *april*
- **May** *maj*
- **June** *juni*
- **July** *juli*
- **August** *august*
- **September** *september*
- **October** *oktober*
- **November** *november*
- **December** *december*

Numbers

- **0** *nul;* **1** *en;* **2** *to;* **3** *tre;* **4** *fire;* **5** *fem;* **6** *seks;* **7** *syv;* **8** *otte;* **9** *ni;* **10** *ti;* **20** *tyve;* **30** *tredive;* **40** *fyrre;* **50** *halvtreds;* **60** *tres;* **70** *halvfjerds;* **80** *firs;* **90** *halvfems;* **100** *hundrede;* **1,000** *tusind;* **1,000,000** *million*

Food & drink

- **apple** *æble;* **egg** *æg;* **peas** *ærter;* **orange** *appelsin;* **banana** *banan;* **bread** *brød;* **ryebread** *rugbrød;* **beans** *bønner;* **mushroom** *svampe;* **chocolate** *chokolade;* **lemon** *citron;* **steamed** *dampet;* **vinegar** *eddike;* **draught beer** *fadøl;* **fish** *fisk;* **cream** *fløde;* **trout** *forel;* **meatballs** *frikadeller;* **fresh** *frisk;* **fruit** *frugt;* **grilled** *grilleret;* **stew** *gryderet;* **green bean** *grøn bønne;* **vegetables** *grøntsager;* **carrots** *gulerødder;* **tomatoes** *tomater;* **garlic** *hvidløg;* **ice-cream/ice** *is;* **strawberry** *jordbær;* **coffee** *kaffe;* **cake** *kage;* **cabbage** *kål;* **potato** *kartoffel;* **meat** *kød;* **boiled** *kogt;* **cold** *kold;* **chicken** *kylling;* **salmon** *laks;* **lamb** *lamme;* **onion** *løg;* **marinated** *marineret;* **milk** *mælk;* **nuts** *nødder;* **beef** *oksekød;* **beer** *øl;* **oil** *olie;* **cheese** *ost;* **roasted** *ovnstegt;* **pepper** *peber;* **poached** *pocheret;* **fries/chips** *pommes frites;* **hot dog** *pølse;* **rice** *ris;* **smoked** *røget;* **raw** *rå;* **mustard** *sennep;* **herring** *sild;* **ham** *skinke;* **butter** *smør;* **fried** *stegt;* **sugar** *sukker;* **soup** *supper;* **pork** *svinekød;* **tea** *te;* **cod** *torsk;* **water** *vand;* **warm, hot** varm; **pastries** *wienerbrød*

Further Reference

BOOKS

Non-fiction

Booth, Michael *The Almost Nearly Perfect People* A riposte to all the Nordic hype, by a former editor of this guidebook.

Brandmark, Niki *The Scandinavian Home* Interiors inspiration from the queen of Scandinavian living blogs.

Christianson, JR *On Tycho's Island: Tycho Brahe and His Assistants, 1570-1601* Biography of the famous astronomer.

Crossly-Holland, Kevin & Jeffrey Allan Love *Norse Myths: Tales of Odin, Thor and Loki* A stunning illustrated take on the Viking myths for kids and adults alike.

Johansen, Signe *How to Hygge* The best of an outrageous number of books all about the Danish concept of *hygge*.

Johansen, Signe *Scandilicious* A beautiful and approachable cookery book about Scandinavian food, including Danish dreamcake.

Levine, Ellen *Darkness over Denmark: The Danish Resistance and the Rescue of the Jews* The remarkable story of the exodus of Danish Jews to Sweden during World War II.

Mad about Copenhagen collective *Mad About Copenhagen* The most up-to-date coffee table book about food, foodie movements and eating out in the city.

Monrad, Kasper, Philip Conisbee & Bjarne Jornaes *The Golden Age of Danish Painting* The works of 17 painters from the first half of the 19th century.

Poole, Roger & Henrik Stangerup *A Kierkegaard Reader* The leading resource on Denmark's leading philosopher.

Russell, Helen *The Year of Living Danishly: Uncovering the Secrets of the World's Happiest Country* An irreverent take on life in Denmark as an expat from the UK.

Sawyer, Peter (ed) *The Oxford Illustrated History of the Vikings* An enjoyable survey of the Vikings.

Spangenburg, Ray & Diane K Moser *Niels Bohr: Gentle Genius of Denmark (Makers of Modern Science)* An accessible analysis of the great Danish nuclear physicist.

Thoren, Victor E *The Lord of Uraniborg* Detailed biography of 16th-century astronomer Tycho Brahe.

Thurman, Judith *Isak Dinesen: The Life of Karen Blixen* Authoritative biography of one of Denmark's finest prose writers, and most famous daughter.

Wullschlager, Jackie *HC Andersen: The Life of a Storyteller* Comprehensive biography of Denmark's top tale-teller.

Fiction

Andersen, Hans Christian *The Complete Fairy Tales* More than 150 of the great Dane's best-loved fairy tales.

Blixen, Karen *Seven Gothic Tales* Blixen's darkly powerful masterpiece.

Ebershoff, David *The Danish Girl* The fictional story of the life of Lile Elbe, one of the first people to have gender reassignment surgery. Made into an Oscar-winning film.

Frayn, Michael *Copenhagen* Extraordinary play based on the visit of the great German physicist Werner Heisenberg to his erstwhile mentor and friend Niels Bohr.

Høeg, Peter *Miss Smilla's Feeling for Snow* Bestselling thriller set in Copenhagen and Greenland.

Shakespeare, William *Hamlet* The bard's Danish blockbuster – possibly the greatest play ever written.

Simpson, Jacqueline (ed) *Danish Legends* This collection comprises over 160 Danish folktales and legends.

Tremain, Rose *Music and Silence* Beautifully written fictional account of the latter years of Christian IV.

ONLINE

Apps

Apart from the obvious (Google Translate and Google Maps, of course), the following apps are useful.

Dot billet Good for transport.

DR For Danish TV on the go.

Memrise A good way to learn some Danish words before travel.

Rejseplanen Good for transport.

Scandinaviastandard.com Has a good Scandinavian travel app.

Websites

City of Copenhagen *www.kk.dk* The website of Københavns Kommune, the city authorities, with information on living and doing business in Copenhagen.

Copenhagen Post *www.cphpost.dk* Weekly news in English from the Danish capital.

Copenhagenize *www.copenhagenize.com* Mikael Colville Andersen's blog on 'Bicycle Urbanism for Modern Cities'.

Danish Youth Hostels Association *www.danhostel.dk* Search for a hostel and book online.

Danish Metereological Information *www.dmi.dk* Daily and long-term weather reports.

Danish Tourist Board *www.visitdenmark.dk* This national tourist board website has extensive information on Copenhagen.

Dejlige Days *https://dejligedays.com* Blog covering daily life in Copenhagen with plenty of useful links for those planning to move or stay for a long period.

DSB (Danish State Railways) *www.dsb.dk* Journey planner for train journeys within Denmark (in English).

The Local *www.thelocal.dk* Local news in English with a big expat focus.

Malmö Tourist Board *www.malmo.se* Information on the sights, attractions, restaurants, festivals and accommodation in this charming city.

Meet the Danes *www.meetthedanes.com* An organisation that arranges for visitors to dine with a local family to improve their understanding of Danish culture and customs.

My Scandinavian Home *www.myscandinavianhome.com* Award-winning lifestyle blog focused on interior design and architecture.

Rejseplanen *www.rejseplanen.dk* Useful site for journey planning within the city and country.

Scandinavia Standard *www.scandinaviastandard.com* Magazine-style blog with a great what's on section.

Visit Copenhagen *www.visitcopenhagen.dk* The regularly updated official website of the city's efficient tourist authority offers detailed information about the city's hotels, restaurants, cafés, bars, galleries, theatres, theme parks and museums, and many useful links.

FILMS & TV SERIES

Borgen *(TV series 2010-2013)* For a primer into how the country's government works, along with a whole lot more, this is a very entertaining place to start.

The Bridge *(TV series 2011-2018)* When a dead body is found half way between Denmark and Sweden on the Øresund Bridge, it falls to a cross-border team, half in Sweden, half in Copenhagen, to find the killer.

Copenhagen *(2014)* A sort of love story about a tourist visiting the city in search of his long-lost family, and a charming girl he makes friends with along the way.

The Guilty *(2018)* Minimalist film set in a police control room in Denmark.

The Killing *(TV series 2011-2014)* The definitive Nordic drama that kick-started the whole noir phenomenon.

Picture credits

Inside front cover 139 Nigar Alizada/Shutterstock.com; 2 (top), 16 (top) Martin Kaufmann; 2 (bottom) Elijah Lovkoff/Shutterstock.com; 3, 24 (top), 210 Sun_Shine/Shutterstock.com; 5, 18 (bottom), 62, 114, 135 EQRoy/Shutterstock.com; 6, 30 Mary Doggett/Shutterstock.com; 11 (top), 75 Kim Nilsson; 11 (bottom), 15 (middle), 57, 109 S-F/Shutterstock.com; 12 (top), 16 (bottom) Todamo/Shutterstock.com; 12 (bottom), 32 (top) balipadma/Shutterstock.com; 13 (top), 47, 170 Lousiana Museum of Modern Art; 13 (bottom), 93 Rikke Caroline Carlsen, Nationalmuseet; 14 (top), 162 Mikkel Schebye Johnsen/Hey Captain; 14 (middle), 31 (bottom) ephst/Shutterstock.com; 14 (bottom) Ron Graybill; 15 (top), 60, 128 badahos/Shutterstock.com; 15 (bottom), 26 (bottom left), 27 (middle), 40 (top), 69, 70, 71 (right), 203, 205 Tivoli Gardens; 17 (top), 226 olgagorovenko/Shutterstock.com; 17 (bottom), 185, 201 Kristoffer Juel Poulsen, Jazz.dk; 18 (top), 25 (bottom), 177 www.thomasdambo.com; 20 Ana Cecilia Gonzalez; 21 (top), 209 Det Kongelige Teater; 21 (bottom) CopenHot; 22 (top), 59, 143, 183, 231 Oliver Foerstner/Shutterstock.com; 22 (middle), 156, 225 laura zamboni/Shutterstock.com; 22 (bottom), 25 (top), 52, 104 Thomas Steen Sørensen; 23 (top) simona flamigni/Shutterstock.com; 23 (bottom), 44 (bottom) Chris Tonnesen/Andreas Raun Photography; 24 (middle) Olga Gavrilova/Shutterstock.com; 24 (bottom), 140 AriZelenko; 25 (middle) Mehdi Khalid/Shutterstock.com; 26 (top) ttwu/Shutterstock.com; 26 (middle) KN/Shutterstock.com; 26 (bottom right) photocritical/Shutterstock.com; 27 (top) ASTRIDKBH; 27 (bottom) RPBaiao/Shutterstock.com; 29 M.lim/Shutterstock.com; 31 (top) faithie/Shutterstock.com; 32 (bottom) Stephanie Braconnier/Shutterstock.com; 34 (top), 53 (top) oleschwander/Shutterstock.com; 34 (bottom) OLIVER-stockphoto/Shutterstock.com; 35 Sahar Mann/Shutterstock.com; 37 Lagkagehuset; 38 Ditte Isager; 39, 164 Gro Spiseri/Andrea Fjordside Pontoppidan; 40 (bottom) Claes Bech Poulsen; 41 (top), 160 Manfreds & Vin; 41 (bottom) Lille Bakery; 42, 78 DØP organic hot dog; 43 Rasmus G Srjersen; 44 (top) Grød; 45 (top) Lidkoeb; 45 (bottom), 79 (middle) Radiokafka/Shutterstock.com; 48 (top) Nakedcph; 48 (bottom), 85 HAY; 49 Devteev/Shutterstock.com; 50 (top), 103 Line Thit Klein/Stilleben No. 22; 50 (bottom) Dansk Made for Rooms; 51 Soulland; 53 (bottom) Discovering Destinations/Shutterstock.com; 54, 82, 112, 115 foto-select/Shutterstock.com; 58 Andrey Shcherbukhin/Shutterstock.com; 61 William Perugini/Shutterstock.com; 65 Atosan/Shutterstock.com; 68 footageclips/Shutterstock.com; 71 (left) Doubleclix/Shutterstock.com; 74 Kevin George/Shutterstock.com; 76, 143, 161 Kiev.Victor/Shutterstock.com; 79 (top) Heide Lerkenfeldt/Illums Bolighus; 79 (bottom) Søstrene Grene; 80 Telia/Shutterstock.com; 81 (top) Omar Ingerslev; 81 (bottom) Allard One/Shutterstock.com; 87 Summerbird; 89, 94, 106 Lepneva Irina/Shutterstock.com; 90 Anna50/Shutterstock.com; 91 David Trood; 92 Rasmus Hjortshøj; 95 (top) fotoliza/Shutterstock.com; 95 (bottom) trabantos/Shutterstock.com; 97 Restaurant Smör; 99 littlewormy/Shutterstock.com; 113 Evikka/Shutterstock.com; 116 Leonid Andronov/Shutterstock.com; 119 Dreamer Company/Shutterstock.com; 122 Adwo/Shutterstock.com; 124 JonLee/Shutterstock.com; 129 christianiacykler.dk; 131 Chris Tonnesen; 132 Anders Bendixen/La Banchina; 133 bmszealand/Shutterstock.com; 138, 227 Luisa Fumi/Shutterstock.com; 141 Guillaume Baviere/WikiCommons; 147 Color Chaser/Shutterstock.com; 148 Steffen Boss Jessen/Shutterstock.com; 151 Anastasia Vereftenko/Shutterstock.com; 154 ale de sun/Shutterstock.com; 157 Fred Romero/WikiCommons; 159 Hotel Alexandra; 163 Abdellah Ihadian; 167 Torben Petersen/Arken; 169 Adam Mørk/Experimentarium; 171 Dan Graham/Louisiana; 172 (top) PTCH/Shutterstock.com; 172 (middle) © Ordrupgaard. Photo Adam Mørk; 172 (bottom) © Ordrupgaard. Photo Andreas Omvik; 173 Arndale/Shutterstock.com; 164 Aeronautics/Shutterstock.com; 178 Werner Karrasch/The Viking Ship Museum in Roskilde, Denmark; 180 Morten Skovgaard ; 189 Jakobsteensennielsen/WikiCommons; 191 (top) Panorama Film/Det Danske Filminstitut/SuperStock.com; 191 (middle top) Rozbeh Zavari; 191 (middle bottom) CPH:Pix; 191 (bottom) alarico/Shutterstock.com; 195 PR/VEGA; 198 Henrik Duus; 199 ARCH; 206 DR Koncerthuset; 213 PhotoChrom Print Collection/WikiCommons; 214 WikiCommons; 217 De Agostini/Getty Images; 218 Johan Vilhelm Gertner/Rosenborg Museum/WikiCommons; 219 Meyers Konversationslexikon/WikiCommons; 221 Bill Ebbesen/WikiCommons; 223 Christoffer Chrintz/Shutterstock.com; 228 luis abrantes/Shutterstock.com; 229 A. Aleksandavicius/Shutterstock.com; 232 Henrik Smith/Cph Living ; 233 d'Angleterre; 235 Jon Norstrøm; 255 Metroselskabet og Hovedstadens Letbane

Index

8Tallet 225
42°Raw 83
71 Nyhavn 234
108 123
1656 141

A
Aamanns Etablissement 107
Åben Dans Productions 209
Absalon 140, 235
accident & emergency 241
Accommodation 232–237
Acne Archive 161
A.C. Perchs Thehandel 80, 84
The Act of Killing 192
addresses 241
Adler, Silas 48
A Door 144
After the Wedding 191
age restrictions 241
Agnete 87
airports 238
Akustikken 51
Alexander Nevsky Kirke 114
Alfons 141
Alice 200
Allegade 10 236
Allegro 191
Almanak at The Standard 108
Amager Bakke 133
Amager beach 90
Amager Bio 201
Amager Strandpark 143, 174
Amagertorv 77
Amaliehaven 109
Amalienborg Slot 18, 112
Amalienborg Square 109
Amass 131
Andersen, Hans Christian 110, 218
Anemonen 208
Antichrist 190
AOC 116
apartments 234
Apollo Bar 111
Arbejdermuseet 102, 228
Arcel, Nikolaj 191
Arch 197
architecture 222
Arctic 191
Arken Museum for Moderne Kunst 91, 176, 227
Armadillo 192
Arnold Busck 84
art collections 58
Assistens Kirkegård 155
Astas 50
August, Bille 190
Axel, Gabriel 190
Axel Gulsmedan 236
Axel Towers 73, 229

B
Bang Carlsen, Jon 192
Babette's Feast 190
Bæst 156
Baisikeli 240
Bakeries 38
Bakkehus Museet 139, 146
Bakken 91, 139
Bakken i Kødbyen 196
Balthazar Champagne Bar 111
La Banchina 124, 132
Bang & Olufsen 78, 226
Bankeråt 103
banks & currency exchanges 245
bars 45, 196. *See also* cafés and bars
Bastard 88
Battle of Lutter-am-Barenburg 216
Beau Marché 107
Bedrag 192
Beer Festival 184
Bellavista 224
Bellevue Beach 169
Bellevue Teatret 208, 224
Bernadotte & Bjørn 227
Bertels Salon 88
Bertrams Gulsmeden 235
Bibendum 103
Bibliotekshaven 91
Bier, Susanne 191
Bike Copenhagen with Mike 61
bike hire 61, 240
bike lanes 60
bike tours 61
Billund 178
Bip Bip Bar 158
Bishop Absalon 77
Bispebjerg Cemetery 184
Bjarke Ingels Group (BIG) 225
Black Diamond 91, 201, 96
Blå Planet 229
Blåtårn 95
BLOX 91, 229
blues 200
boat trips 14, 162
Bo-Bi Bar 200
bodegas 200
Boe, Christoffer 191
Bøf & Ost 82
Bojesen, Kay 159, 226
Bollyfood 141
Bonnén, Suste 87
books 249
Borgen 192
Børsen 89
Botanisk Have & Museum 105
Bournonville, August 218
Boutique Lize 196
Brdr. Price in Tivoli 69
breakdown services 240
Breaking the Waves 190
Bredgade 112
The Bridge 192
Bridge of Sighs 77
Brockdorff Palace 112
Brød 142
Broens Gaddekokken/The Bridge Street Kitchen 126
Brügger, Mads 192
Bruun Rasmussen Kunstauktioner 117
Bryggeriet Apollo 72
budget travel 24
Bungalow 50
Burmeister & Wain 219
buses 238
Bycyklen 61
Bye Bye Love 48
By Malene Birger 85

C
Café 8tallet 176
Café Atelier September 107
Café Bopa 164, 196
Café Europa 78
Café GL Torv 82
Café Intime 197
Café Nemoland 129
Café Norden 78
cafés 41
cafés & bars
Around Vesterport & Central Station 73
The Canal District 126
Christiania 129
East of Copenhagen 176
Frederiksberg 149
Frederiksstaden & Kastellet 117
Kongens Nytorv & Nyhavn 111
Nørrebro 158
Nørreport & Around 103
North of Strøget 83
Østerbro 164
Rådhuspladsen & Ny Carlsberg Glyptotek 74
Refshaleøen 132
Rosenborg Slot & Around 107
Slotsholmen & the Waterfront 97
South of Copenhagen 178
South of Strøget 88
Strøget 78
Tivoli 72
Vesterbro 142
Café Sonja 44
Café Victor 83
Café Wilder 126
Cakenhagen 72
Camerata Chamber Choir 204
Camp Adventure Tower 178
Canal District 122
Cap Horn 110
cargo bike 90, 130
car hire 240
Caritas Springvandet 77
Carlsberg Visitor Centre & Jacobsen Brewhouse 139
Carlsen, Henning 190
Casa Shop 85
cathedral 80
Cedergren, Jakob 191
Centralhjørnet 197
Central Hotel & Café 142, 234
Chai Wong 148
Charlottenlund Slot 168
Charlottenlund Strand 168
Chateau Motel 198
cheese 38
Cherry blossom season 184
children 25, 90, 208
Christensen, Benjamin 190
Christian I 214
Christian II 214, 215
Christian III 215
Christian IV 215
Christian V 108
Christian VII 217
Christiania 15, 24, 127, 128, 143, 221, 228
Christiania bike 90, 130
Christiania Cykler 129
Christiansborg Slot 88, 92, 94
Folketinget 94
Kongelige Stalde og Kareter 94
Ruinerne under Christiansborg 95
Teatermuseet 95
Christiansborg Slotskirke 89, 95
Christianshavn, Holmen & Refshaleøen 118–133
Christianskirke 206
Christians Kirke 122
Christmas 187
Christmas Markets 187
Churchillparken 114
Church of Our Saviour 90
cinemas 193
CinemaxX 193
Circle Bridge 227
Circus Circus 143
Cisternerne 14, 146, 147
Citizen M 236
City Pass 239
Civil war 215
classical music 204
climate 241
clubs 197
Cock's & Cows 42
cocktail bars 196
Coffee Collective 45, 157
Cofoco 140
Comedievognens Broscene 208
companies
dance 209
theatre 207
Concerto Copenhagen 204
Copencabana 124
Copenhagen
overview 58
Copenhagen Admiral Hotel 233
Copenhagen Airport 238
Copenhagen Bicycles 61, 240
Copenhagen Blues Festival 187
Copenhagen Business School 246
Copenhagen Card 62, 239
Copenhagen Central Station 243
Copenhagen Contemporary 130
Copenhagen Cooking 186
Copenhagen Food Tours 62
Copenhagen free walking tours 62
Copenhagen Jazz Festival 17, 185
Copenhagen K 58
Copenhagen Light Festival 187
Copenhagen Marathon 184
Copenhagen Metro 238
Copenhagen Ø 58
Copenhagen Open 143
Copenhagen Photo Festival 184
Copenhagen Pride 186
Copenhagen Skatepark 143
Copenhagen Summer Festival 204
Copenhagen Theatre Circle 207
Copenhagen Today 28–35
Copenhagen Zoo 91, 225, 227
Copenhell 186
CopenHill 12, 133, 225
CopenHot 130, 162
Cosy Bar 197

CPH:DOX 184, 192
CPH Living 235
CPH:PIX 192
Crown Prince Frederik 221
cuisine. *See* food
Culture Box 198
Culture Harbour 186
customs 241
cycling 10, 60, 240
cycling organisations 240
Cykelfabrikken 144
Cykelslange 227

D

DAC Café 97
Dag H 165
Dagmar Teatret 193
Damernes Magasin 161
dance 208
Dancer in the Dark 190
Danhostel Copenhagen City 236
Danish Architecture Tours 62
Danish Dance Theatre 209
Danish Film School 246
Danish Maritime Museum 225
Danish Road Directorate 238
Danish School of Art 218
Danish Tourist Board 247
Dansehallerne 208
Dansk Arkitektur Center 92
Dansk Cyklist Forbund 240
Dansk Danseteater 208
Dansk Jødisk Museum 91, 96
Dansk Made for Rooms 144
Davids Samling 105
Day Trips 166–179
Democratic Coffee 144
Den Blå Planet 176
Den Hirschsprungske Samling 105
dentists 243
department stores 52
design 17, 159, 222
Design & Architecture 222–229
Designmuseum Danmark 114
Designmuseum Danmark Shop 117
Det Danske Filminstitut 193
Det Kongelige Bibliotek 201
Det Kongelige Danske Kunstakademi 246
Det Kongelige Danske Musikkonservatorium 246
Det Kongelige Teater 108
DFDS Seaways 238
DGI 141
Dine with the Danes 39
Dining week 187
Dinner For One 192
Din Nye Ven 83
disabled travellers 241
The Disgusting Food Museum 175
La Dispensa 157
Distortion 184, 201
Ditzel, Nanna 226
doctors 243
documentary films 192
Dogme 95 190
Dogme collective 190
Domhuset 77
Donaldson, Mary 221
Donkey Republic Bike Rental 61
Donn Ya Doll 145
DØP organic hot dog stand 78
Dora 145
DR 192, 204, 244
Dragør 174
Dreyer, Carl Theodor 190
drinking 36, 44
Drive 191
driving 240
DR Koncerthuset 204, 227
drugs 242
DSB 239
DSB regional train 238
Duck and Cover 197
Dupong 158
Dyrehaven 91, 144
Dyrehaven & Bakken 171

E

East of Copenhagen 174
Eating & Drinking 36–45. *See also* cafés and bars, restaurants
Eckersberg, Christoffer Wilhelm 218
Eiffel Bar 200
electricity 242
The Element of Crime 190
Eliasson, Olafur 227
embassies & consulates 242
Emergency Dental Service 243
Empire Bio 193
Enghave Plads 143
ensembles
  classical music & opera 204
Era Ora 123
Es 145
etiquette 241
Europa 190
European Common Market 221
European Union 221
Events 182–187
Everything Will Be Fine 191
Experimentarium 91, 171

F

Facing the Truth 191
Fælledparken 90, 143, 161
Falernum 144
families 25
fares
  public transport 239
fashion designers 48
Fastelavn 187
FC København 161
Festen 191
festivals. *See* Events
  classical music & opera 204
Field's 53
film festivals 192
Filmhuset 105
Filmhuset/Det Danske Filminstitut 193
Film & TV 188–193
Finders Keepers 53
Finn Juhl Hus 168, 173
fire (1728 and 1795) 217
Fiskebaren 140
Fiskehoddorna 175
Fisketorvet 52
Le Fix 85
flea markets 53
Fleisch 141
Floss Bar 84
Flottenheimer 84
Fly, Per 191
folk 200
Folketeatret 207
Folketinget 89
La Fontaine 201
food 36
Forgotten Giants 18, 177
Formel B 148
Forum Copenhagen 145
Foster, Norman 227
Freddy's 200
Frederik I 214
Frederik III 216
Frederik IV 217
Frederik V 217
Frederik VI 217
Frederik VII 219
Frederiksberg 145
Frederiksberg Centret 52
Frederiksberg Have 145, 146
Frederiksberg Kirke 146
Frederiksberg Slot 145, 146
Frederiksberg Svømmehal 146
Frederiksborg Slot 172
Frederiksstaden & Kastellet 112
Den Frie Udstilling 105
Frihedsmuseet 114
Friluftsland 104
Frue Plads 80
Fru Nimb 72
Further Reference 249

G

Gågrøn 157
Gammel Kongevej 145
Gammel Strand 87
Gammeltorv 77
Ganni 48, 85, 165
Garage boutique 86
Garnisons Kirken 206
Gauguin, Paul 76
G*A*Y Copenhagen 198
Gefion Fountain 112
Gefionspringvandet 109
Geist 110
Gemyse Tivoli 69
Generator Copenhagen 236
Georg Jensen 78
Geranium 164
Getting Around 238–240
Getting Started 56–63
Ghost Tour 62
Gilleleje 169
Gisselfeld Kloster 178
La Glace 84
Gloria 193
GoBoat 162
Goods 165
Gorms 42
gospel choirs 204
Gourmandiet 165
Goya, Stine 48
Grabøl, Sofie 191
Gråbrødretorv 80
Grand Öl & Mat 175
Grand Teatret 193
Granola 144
Great Synagogue 246
Green Island 92
Grevens Fejde 215
Grød 42, 157, 158
Grønnegårds Teatret 207
Gro Spiseri 164
Grundtvig, Nikolai Frederik Severin 218
The Guilty 191
Guldbergsgade 155
Den Gule Cottage 173
Det Gyldne Tårn 70

H

Halvandet 132
Harald I 214
Harbour Circle 61
Harry's Place 42
Hart Bageri 149
HAY House 85
HC Andersens Boulevard 73
health 242
Heidi and Bjarne 51
Helges Ost 51
Helligåndskirken 77
Helsingør 169
Henningsen, Poul 224
Henrik Vibskov 86
Herrens vej 192
Hey Captain 162
Hija de Sanchez 140
History 212–221
HIVE 198
holidays 245
Holmen 122
Holmens Kirke 89, 96, 206
Hornbæk 169
Høst 102
Hotel Alexandra 235
Hotel d'Angleterre 233
Hotel Ottilia 234
Hotel Sanders 233
Hotel Skt Petri 233
Hotel SP34 234
The House That Jack Built 191
Hovedbibloteket 243
H. Skalm P. 50
Hviids Vinstue 108

I

I Blame Lulu 48
Ibsens Hotel 102, 234
ice-cream 39
ID 243
Ideal Bar 201
The Idiots 190
Illum 77, 78
Illums Bolighus 78
Illums Bolighus Tivoli 72
Imperial 193
Improv Comedy Copenhagen 207
In a Better World 191
Indre By 58, 62
Ingels, Bjarke 225, 227
Ingemann, BS 219
Inheritance 191
insurance 243
interior design 51
Isabel Marant 49
Ishøj Strand 176
Islands Brygge Harbour Baths 90, 124, 227
Israels Plads 143
Istedgade 139
Itineraries 20–27

J

Jacob Jensen 227
Jacobsen, Arne 159, 224
Jægersborggade 16, 157
Jailhouse Copenhagen 197
The Jane 198
Jarmers Tårn 73
jazz 17, 185, 200
Jazzhus Montmartre 185
Jensen, Anders Thomas 191
Jensen, Georg 224
Jewish Museum 227
Joe and the Juice 45
Jolene 198
Juhl, Finn 224
Julekalendar 192

K

Kadeau 126
Kaffesalonen 158
Kalmar Union 216
Kalmar War 216
Kalvebod Bølge 92
Ka'nalu 178
Kanslergarde Agreement 220
Karamelleriet 157
Karen Blixen Museet 169, 172
Kartoffelraekkerne 228
Kastellet 114, 116
Kastelskirken 207
Kastrup Søbad 176
Kayak Bar 91, 97

KB3 198
KB Hallen 204
Kierkegaard, Søren 76, 218
Kiin Kiin 156
The Killing 192
The Kingdom 190
King's Game 191
Kjærholm, Poul 226
Le Klint 79
Klint – Designmuseets Café 117
Klint, Kaare 224
Knud (Canute) VI 214
Københavns Cyklebørs 240
Københavns Museum 74
Købke, Christen 218
Købmagergade 80
Koch, Mogens 224
Kødbyen 17, 139, 141
Kødbyen's Fiskebar 141
Kokkeriet 107
Den Kongelige Afstøbningssamling 109
Det Kongelige Bibliotek 91, 96
Det Kongelige Danske Haveselskabs Have 145
Kongelige Kunstakademi 108
Den Kongelige Opera 123
Kongelige Stalde 94
Kongelige Stalde og Kareter 89
Det Kongelige Teater, Gamle Scene 209
Kongens Nytorv & Nyhavn 108
Kong Hans Kælder 111
Konservatoriets Koncertsal 204
Koralbadet 124
Kragh-Jacobsen, Søren 190
Kronborg Slot 169, 172
KU.BE 148
Kul 140
Kulturhavn (Culture Harbour) 186
Kulturhuset Islands Brygge 123
Kulturnatten 186
Kunstforeningen GL Strand 87
Kunsthal Charlottenborg 108
Kyoto 145

L

Lægelinien 243
Lagkagehuset 38
L'Altro 123
Langelinie Park 109
language 243
language classes 246
Larsen, Henning 227
Latin Quarter 80
Leckerbær 41, 50
left luggage 243
legal help 243
LEGO Flagship 79
LEGO House 179, 225
LEGOLAND Billund Resort 179
Lê Lê 142
Leth, Jørgen 192
Levetzau Palace 112
Levring, Kristian 190
LGBT 243
  nightlife 196
Libeskind, Daniel 227
libraries 243
Library Bar 73
Lidkoeb 197
Lilla Torg 175
Lille Bakery & Eatery 132
Lille Mølle 122
Lille Strandstræde 108
Det Lille Teater 208
The Little Mermaid 16, 109, 114
live music 200
Løgismose 117
London Toast Theatre 207
Loppen 201
Løs Market 51
lost property 244
Louisiana Museum of Modern Art 13, 90, 170
lounge bars 196
Lübeckers 215
Luggage Hero 243
Luna's Diner 126
Lundbye, JT 218
Lundgaard & Tranberg 227
Lundgaard & Tranberg Arkitekter 229
Lund, Søren Robert 227
Lutheranism 215

M

Maastricht Treaty 221
Mads Nørgaard 79
Magasasa 42, 141
Magasin 108, 111
Magasin du Nord 77
magazines 244
Malmö 175
Malmros, Nils 191
Manfreds & Vin 156, 157
Manon Les Suites 235
Marble Church 115
Marchal 111
Marionet Teater i Kongens Have 208
Marmorkirken 15, 90, 109, 112, 115
Marstrand, Wilhelm 218
MASH 111
Matador 192
May Day 184
media 244
Meet Gay Copenhagen 196
Meet the Danes 196
Mêlée 148
Metro 175, 238
Metropolis 208
Metz, Janus 192
Meyers 38
Meyers Bageri 157
Meyers Deli 149
Mikkeller & Friends 160
Mikkelsen, Lars 192
Mikkelsen, Mads 191
Mikropolis 103
Mini Me 52
Mirabelle 160
MIX Copenhagen 187, 192
Moderne Museet 175
Mogensen, Børge 224
Mojo 201
Moltke Palace 112
money 245
Monies 117
Monstrum 90
Morgenstedet 127
Mosaisk Kirkegård 155
Moshi Moshi Mind 165
Mother 142
Movia 239
Munthe plus Simonsen 86
Museet for Søfart 169, 173
museums. *See* sights & museums
music 200
Musica Ficta 204
music bars 196

N

Naked 86
Nansensgade 102
Nationalbanken 89
National Drama School 246
Nationalmuseet 13, 89, 90, 93
Native North 161
Naturli 51
Nbar 197
Netto-Bådene 163
New Nordic cuisine 39
newspapers 244
New Year 187
Niels Brock College 246
Nielsen, Asta 190
Nightlife 194–201
Nikolaj Kunsthal 77
Nimb Brasserie 69
Nimb Hotel 234
Nobis Hotel Copenhagen 235
Noho 141
Nokken 228
Noma 2.0 131
Nordatlantens Brygge 123, 127
Nordhavn 229
Nordisk Film 190
Nordisk Korthandel 86
Nørgaard, Mads 48
Normann Copenhagen 50, 165
Nørrebro 155
Nørrebro Bryghus 158
Nørrebro & Østerbro 150–165
Nørreport & Around 102
Norse Store 86
North Central Copenhagen 98–117
North of Copenhagen 168
North of Strøget 80
Nouvel, Jean 227
Nué 52
Nyboder 105
Nyboders Mindestuer 228
Ny Carlsberg Glyptotek 11, 73, 75
Nyhavn 16, 108, 109
Nymphomaniac 190
Det Ny Teater 207
Nytorv 76

O

Oehlenschläger, Adam 219
Ofeliaplads 109
Øieblikket 97
Øksnehallen 141
Ølfestival (Beer Festival) 184
Oliver's Garage 224
Oliver's Garage 173
OMA 229
Only God Forgives 191
opening hours 50, 245
  museums 59
opera 204
Operaen 123, 206, 227
Ordrupgaard & Finn Juhl Hus 168, 173
Øresund Bridge 175, 221
Øresund Fixed Link 227
Ørstedsparken 102
Oscar Bar & Café 117, 197
Østerbro 161

P

Palads 73, 193
Palæ Bar 84
Panton, Verner 226
Panum Koret 204
Papirøen 43
Parken 161
Parkmuseerne 105
parks 58
Parterre 126
PatéPaté 142
Paustian 165
payment 52
Peacock Theatre 205
Pedalos 163
Peder Oxe 82
Pelle the Conqueror 190
Performing Arts 202–209
Perspex fountain 70
Peter Beier 86
pharmacies 243
photography 127
Picnic at Glyptoteket 74
Pisserenden 80
Plænen 205
plague (1711) 217
planning 220
police 245
Politihistorisk Museum 155
Pony in Vesterbro 126
pop 201
Portland Towers 229
postal services 245
Posthus Teatret 193
Post Office Pilestræde 245
Poulsen, Louis 159
price codes
  accommodation 232
  restaurants 38
Prik 52
public holidays 245
public transport 238
Pusher 191

Q

Queen Margrethe 221
Queen's Birthday 184

R

Rådhuset 74
Rådhuspladsen & Ny Carlsberg Glyptotek 73
radio 244
Radisson SAS Royal Hotel 224
Ragnarock 179
The Rain 192
Rasmussen, Anders Fogh 221
Rasmussen, Lars Løkke 221
Red Chapel 192
Reffen 16, 43, 143
Reformation 215
Refshaleøen 129
Rejsekort 239
Rejseplanen 239
Relæ 157, 158
religion 245
Resources A-Z 241–257
Restaurant 56° 131
Restaurant Ida Davidsen 116
Restaurant Kanalen 126
Restaurant L'Alsace 83
Restaurant Radio 149
Restaurant Rebel 117
restaurants
  Around Vesterport & Central Station 73
  The Canal District 123
  cheap 44
  Christiania 127
  Frederiksberg 148
  Frederiksstaden & Kastellet 116
  high-end 40
  Kongens Nytorv & Nyhavn 108
  mid-range 42
  Nørrebro 156
  Nørreport & Around 102
  North of Copenhagen 173
  North of Strøget 82
  Østerbro 164
  Refshaleøen 131
  Rosenborg Slot & Around 107
  Slotsholmen & the Waterfront 97
  South of Strøget 87
  Tivoli 69
  vegetarian/vegan 40
  Vesterbro 140

Restaurant Smör 97
Rhythmic Music Conservatory 246
Ribersborgs Kallbadhus 175
Rice Market 83
Rigsråd 214
Riz Raz 87
road travel 238
rock 201
Rohde, Johan 224
Rosenborg Slot 105
Rosenborg Slot & Around 104
Roskilde 178
Roskilde Festival 186
Round Sjælland Yacht Race 186
Royal Cast Collection 112
Royal Copenhagen 77, 79
Royal Copenhagen Outlet 53, 149
Royal Danish Academy of Music 145, 204
Royal Danish Ballet 209
The Royal Danish Horticultural Garden 146
Royal Danish Playhouse 109
Royal Danish Theatre, Old Stage 209
Royal Family 221
Ruby 88
Ruinerne under Christiansborg 89, 94
Rundetårn 14, 81, 82, 90
Rungstedlund 169
Rust 199
Rutschebanen 71

S

Sadolin, Ebbe 226
safety & security 246
St Alban's Church 114
Le Saint-Jacques 164
St Alban's Church 245
Sakrementskirken 246
sales 53
Sanchez 142
Sankt Annæ Kirke 246
Sankt Annæ Plads 112
Sankt Ansgar Kirke 114
Sankt Hans Aften 186
Sankt Nikolaj Kirke 77
sausage wagons 42
Scandic Front 236
Scandic Kødbyen 236
Scandinavia Standard 49
Scandlines 238
Schack Palace 112
School of Architecture 246
seasons 26
sea travel 238
Sebastopol Café 160
Second Society 48
Shakespeare at Kronborg 173, 186, 208
Shopping 46–53
shopping centres 52
shops & services
- The Canal District 127
- Christiania 129
- Frederiksberg 149
- Frederiksstaden & Kastellet 117
- Kongens Nytorv & Nyhavn 111
- Nørrebro 161
- Nørreport & Around 104
- North of Strøget 84
- Østerbro 165
- Rosenborg Slot & Around 107
- Strøget 78
- Tivoli 72
- Vesterbro 144

Sidewalk 143
Den Sidste Dråbe 157, 161
sightseeing 56
sights & museums 59
- The Canal District 122
- East of Copenhagen 174
- Frederiksberg 146
- Frederiksstaden & Kastellet 114
- Kongens Nytorv & Nyhavn 108
- Nørrebro 155
- Nørreport & Around 102
- North of Copenhagen 171
- North of Strøget 82
- Østerbro 163
- Rådhuspladsen & Ny Carlsberg Glyptotek 74
- Refshaleøen 130
- Rosenborg Slot & Around 105
- Slotsholmen & the Waterfront 91
- South of Copenhagen 176
- South of Strøget 87
- Strøget 77
- Vesterbro 139
- West of Copenhagen 179

Sigurdsgade 199
The Silo 229
simpleRAW 83
Sjællandsgade Bad 155
SKAT 247
skateboarding 143
Skovshoved 168
Skovshoved Petrol Station 224
Skuespilhuset (Royal Danish Playhouse) 109, 207, 227
Slotsholmen & the Waterfront 88
Slotskælderen Hos Gitte 88
Slottet Malmöhus 175
Sluseholmen 228, 229
Smed, Esbem 192
smoking 198, 246
Sneakers & Coffee 157
Social Security Act of 1976 220
Södergatan 175
Sofie Kælderen 126
Sögreni of Copenhagen 86
Soho/Noho 141
Sømods Bolcher 86
Søndermarken 146
Sonny 84
Søpavillionen 199
Søren K 97
Søstjernen 50, 165
Søstrene Grene 79
Soulland 149
Souls 165
South Central Copenhagen 64–97
South of Copenhagen 176
South of Strøget 87
Space 10 139, 141
Spinderiet 53
Spiseloppen 127
Stalks and Roots 49
The Standard 108
Statens Museum for Kunst (SMK) 91, 106, 115
Stauning, Thorvald 220
Sticks'n'Sushi 42, 103
Stig P 149
Stilleben No.22 104
Stine Goya 49
S-tog local train 239
Store Strandstræde 108
Strædet 87
Streetmachine 85
Street Machine 143
Strøget 76
Strömma 240
Studenterhuset 84
Stud!o at The Standard 111
study 246
Sult 107
Summerbird 51, 86
Sun King 215
Superflex 225
Superkilen 143, 155, 225, 227
supermarkets 53
Svanemøllestranden 163
Sweet Treat 127
swimming
- harbour 12, 124

Synagoge 82

T

Tapperiet Brus 160
tax 245
tax-free shopping 52
taxis 240
Teater Hund 208
Teatermuseet 89
telephones 246
television 244
temperatures 242
theatre 207
- children 208

Thirty Years War 216
Thorning-Schmidt, Helle 221
Thorvaldsen, Bertel 83, 218
Thorvaldsens Museum 83, 96
Thotts Palais 108
Tietgen Students' Residence 227
Tigermom 158
time 246
Time's Up Vintage 48, 86
tipping 246
Tisvildeleje 169
Tivoli 15, 68, 70, 91, 205
Tivoli Christmas Season 187
Tivoli Food Hall 72
Tivoli Halloween Season 187
Tivoli's Christmas Market 72
Tivolis Koncertsal 205
Tjili Pop 160
toilets 246
Tøjhusmuseet 91, 96
Tom Rossau Showroom 149
Top 20 10–19
Torstensson's War 216
Torvehallerne 102, 103, 104, 228
tourist information 62, 247
tours 62
trains 238
transport 59, 238
- Christianshavn, Holmen & Refshaleøen 122
- day trips 169
- East of Copenhagen 174
- Nørrebro & Østerbro 154
- North Central 102
- North of Copenhagen 171
- South Central 77
- South of Copenhagen 176
- Vesterbro & Frederiksberg 138
- West of Copenhagen 178

travel advice 241
Treaty of Roskilde 216
Trinitatis Kirke 82
Trio 73
Les Trois Cochons 142
Tú a Tú 48, 157, 161
Turning Tower 175
TV 188
Tycho Brahe Planetarium 139
Tycho Brahe Planetarium Omnimax 193

U

Udlændingestyrelsen 247
universities 246
University of Copenhagen 80, 246
Urban Explorer CPH Tours 62
Utzon, Jørn 224

V

Værnedamsvej 139
Valdemar 214
Valdemar II 214
Ved Stranden 10 88
Vega 199
venues
- classical music 204, 206
- dance 208
- opera 204, 206
- theatre 207

Vesterbro 139
Vesterbro & Frederiksberg 134–149
Vesterport & Central Station 72
Vester Vov Vov 193
Vibskov, Henrik 48
views 56
Vikingeskibsmuseet 179
Vikings 214
Vinstue 90 200
Vinterberg, Thomas 190
Vinterjazz 17
visas & immigration 247
Visit Copenhagen Tourist Information Bureau 247
VM Houses 225
Vocabulary 248
von Trier, Lars 190, 191
Vor Frelsers Kirke 122, 123
Vor Frue Kirke 82, 83

W

Wake Up Copenhagen Bernstoffsgade 236
walking 240
WarPigs 141
waterbuses 239
waterfront 33, 88
weather 242
websites 249
weekend itinerary 20
Wegner, Hans J 224
weights & measures 247
West of Copenhagen 178
Winding Refn, Nicolas 191
Wivel, Anne 192
Won Hundred 49
Wood Wood 87
Wood Wood MUSEUM 104
work 247
world music 200
World War I 220
World War II 220

Z

Zealand 169
Zirup 88
Zoo Bar 84
Zoologisk Have 145, 146
Zoologisk Museum 163

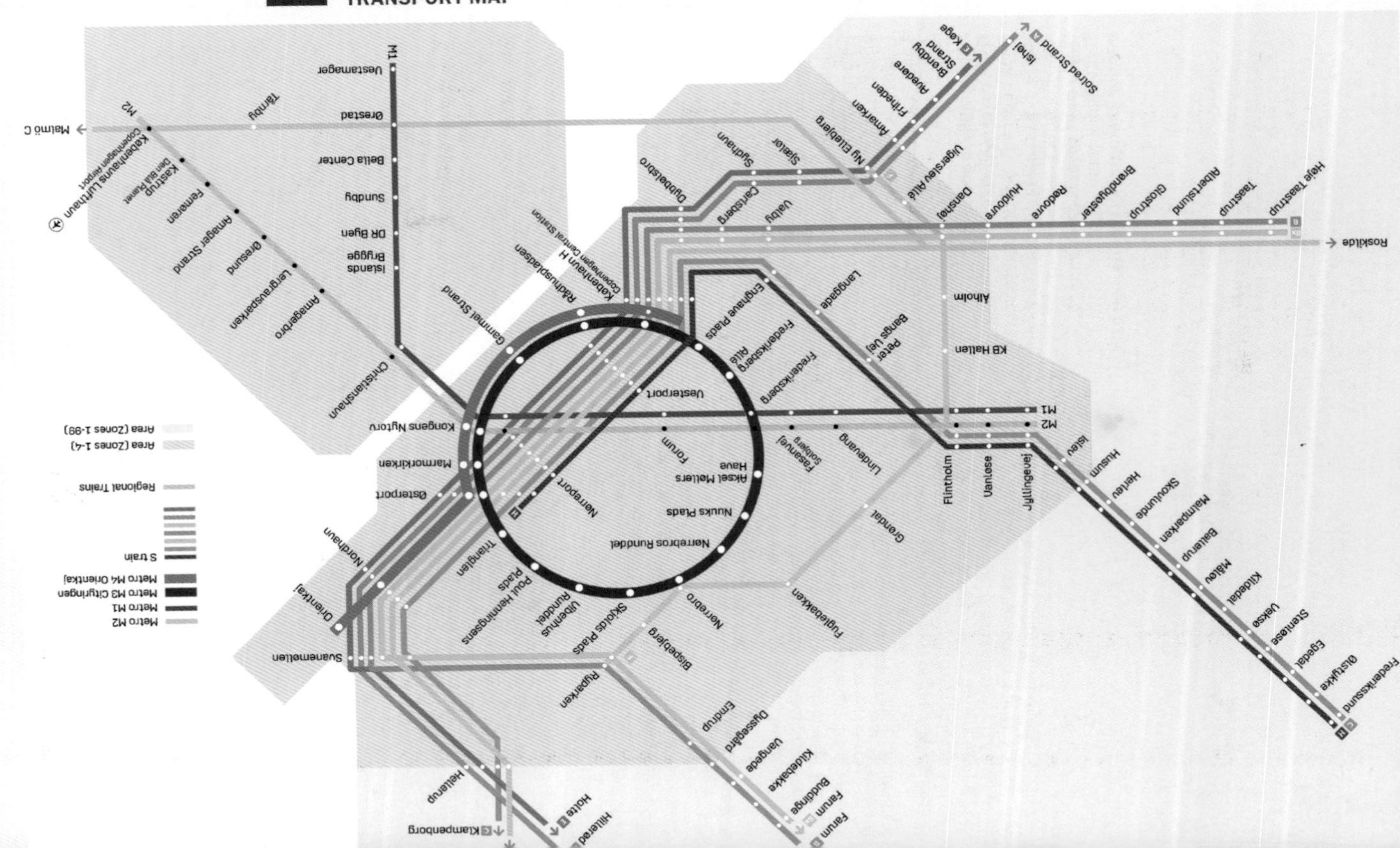
Metro M2
Metro M1
Metro M3 Cityringen
Metro M4 Orientkaj
S train
Regional Trains
Area (Zones 1-4)
Area (Zones 1-99)
Malmö C
Københavns Lufthavn
Copenhagen Airport
M2
Kastrup
Den Blå Planet
Femøren
Amager Strand
Øresund
Lergravsparken
Amagerbro
Tårnby
Christianshavn
Islands Brygge
DR Byen
Sundby
Bella Center
Ørestad
Vestamager
M1
Kongens Nytorv
Marmorkirken
Østerport
Nordhavn
Orientkaj
Svanemøllen
Hellerup
Klampenborg
Holte
Hillerød
Gammel Strand
Rådhuspladsen
København H
Copenhagen Central Station
Trianglen
Poul Henningsens Plads
Vibenshus Runddel
Skjolds Plads
Nørreport
Nørrebros Runddel
Nuuks Plads
Aksel Møllers Have
Forum
Vesterport
Ryparken
Bispebjerg
Nørrebro
Emdrup
Dyssegård
Vangede
Kildebakke
Buddinge
Farum
Fuglebakken
Grøndal
Enghave Plads
Frederiksberg Allé
Frederiksberg
Fasanvej
Solbjerg
Lindevang
Dybbølsbro
Carlsberg
Sydhavn
Valby
Sjælør
Ny Ellebjerg
Åmarken
Friheden
Avedøre
Brøndby Strand
Køge
Ishøj
Solrød Strand
Langgade
Peter Bangs Vej
Flintholm
Vanløse
Jyllingevej
M2
M1
KB Hallen
Ålholm
Danshøj
Vigerslev Allé
Hvidovre
Rødovre
Brøndbyøster
Glostrup
Albertslund
Taastrup
Høje Taastrup
Roskilde
Islev
Husum
Herlev
Skovlunde
Malmparken
Ballerup
Måløv
Kildedal
Veksø
Stenløse
Egedal
Ølstykke
Frederikssund

Credits

Crimson credits
Author Laura Hall
Editor Felicity Laughton
Listings editor Alicja Peszkowska
Cartography Gail Armstrong

Series Editor Sophie Blacksell Jones
Production/Editorial Manager Kate Michell
Production Designer Emilie Crabb
Print Manager Patrick Dawson
Design Mytton Williams

Chairman David Lester
Managing Director Andy Riddle

Advertising Media Sales House
Marketing Sophie Shepherd
Sales Lyndsey Mayhew

Author
This edition of *Time Out Copenhagen* was researched and updated by Laura Hall.

Acknowledgements
Laura would like to thank Alicja, Jim, Trœls, Claudia, Chris; everyone at Republikken and Cross-Border Communications; the team at Visit Copenhagen, and her family, Matt, Olivia and Ellie, for sharing their favourite places, hidden secrets and thoughts on the city, and helping with the research. The author and editor would also like to thank all contributors to previous editions of *Time Out Copenhagen*, whose work forms the basis of this guide.

Photography credits
Front cover MAISANT Ludovic/AWL Images
Back cover left: S-F/Shutterstock.com; centre: Kalamurzing/Shutterstock.com; right: CopenHot
Inside front cover Nigar Alizada/Shutterstock.com
Interior Photography credits, *see p250.*

Publishing information
Time Out Copenhagen City Guide 7th edition

July 2019

ISBN 978 1 780592 69 5
CIP DATA: A catalogue record for this book is available from the British Library

Published by Crimson Publishing
21d Charles Street, Bath, BA1 1HX (01225 584 950, www.crimsonpublishing.co.uk) on behalf of Time Out England.

Distributed by Grantham Book Services
Distributed in the US and Canada by Publishers Group West (1-510-809-3700)

Printed by Replika Press, India.